The President and the Members of the Commission of the European Communities to the President of the European Parliament

Sir,

We have the honour to present the General Report on the Activities of the Communities, which the Commission is required to publish by Article 18 of the Treaty establishing a Single Council and a Single Commission of the European Communities.

This report, for 1991, is the twenty-fifth since the merger of the executives.

In accordance with the procedure described in the Declaration on the system for fixing Community farm prices contained in the Accession Documents of 22 January 1972, the Commission has already sent Parliament the 1991 Report on the Agricultural Situation in the Community.

Under Article 122 of the Treaty establishing the European Economic Community, the Commission is also preparing a Report on Social Developments in the Community in 1991.

And, in accordance with an undertaking given to Parliament on 7 June 1971, the Commission is preparing its twenty-first annual Report on Competition Policy.

Please accept, Sir, the expression of our highest consideration.

Brussels, 11 February 1992

Jacques DELORS
President

Frans M.J.J. ANDRIESSEN
Vice-president

Henning CHRISTOPHERSEN
Vice-president

Manuel MARÍN
Vice-president

Filippo Maria PANDOLFI
Vice-president

Martin BANGEMANN
Vice-president

Leon BRITTAN
Vice-president

Carlo RIPA DI MEANA

António CARDOSO E CUNHA

Abel MATUTES

Peter M. SCHMIDHUBER

Christiane SCRIVENER

Bruce MILLAN

Jean DONDELINGER

Ray MAC SHARRY

Karel VAN MIERT

Vasso PAPANDREOU

The following currency abbreviations are being used in all language versions of the General Report and of the other reports published in conjunction with it.

ECU = European currency unit
BFR = Belgische frank/franc belge
DKR = Dansk krone
DM = Deutsche Mark
DR = Drachma
ESC = Escudo
FF = Franc français
HFL = Nederlandse gulden (Hollandse florijn)
IRL = Irish pound (punt)
LFR = Franc luxembourgeois
LIT = Lira italiana
PTA = Peseta
UKL = Pound sterling
USD = United States dollar

Summary

Contents

The Community in 1991

'The Community has too many international responsibilities to allow itself the luxury of failing to clear the hurdle that so many convinced Europeans want it to clear'
(Commission Declaration on the Intergovernmental Conferences on Political Union and Economic and Monetary Union, 27 November 1991)

In establishing what is to become an ever closer union among the peoples of Europe, the Heads of State or Government gave a new and powerful stimulus to the process of European integration at the Maastricht European Council on 9 and 10 December. The Community can now make great strides towards a balanced and coherent union. Its new impetus is a result of the confidence generated by the Single Act and the prospect of a unified internal market in 1993. It has two driving forces — the single currency and common defence. There is now an irreversible commitment to progressive and disciplined economic and monetary union which will allow the Community to exploit the potential of the internal market to the full and increase its influence so as to ensure greater monetary stability in the world at large. Economic and monetary union is based on the introduction of a single currency — at the latest by 1 January 1999 — to be managed by a single, fully independent central bank. It is one aspect of a closer union based on solidarity and cooperation which also incorporates the concept of European citizenship, the establishment of a cohesion fund, an increase in Community powers in a number of fields and the strengthening of democratic legitimacy. Another great step forward is the inclusion of provisions on a common foreign and security policy in the Treaty on European union covering all areas of foreign and security policy and establishing systematic cooperation between the Member States in the pursuit of their policies in the form of joint action. The union will now be able to affirm its political identity in the face of historic challenges and give Europe a real political role in the new world order.

The Community is already seen by outsiders as an important political force. Without waiting for the outcome of the intergovernmental conferences, it stuck to the task of honouring its commitments to its partners in the world while trying to respond to the many requests for help prompted by the turbulent political events, adapting its approach to suit each specific situation.

The Commission sent the Council an opinion on Austria's membership application and Sweden also applied to join the Community. At the end of the year — subject to a final decision on Court jurisdiction — the Community and the EFTA countries completed their preparations for the establishment of the European Economic Area which will not only offer these countries the advantages of the internal market but mark the beginning of a partnership whereby they apply Community legislation while the Community retains its full decision-making powers.

The Community negotiated and signed 'Europe Agreements' with Poland, Czechoslovakia and Hungary as a way of giving them a clear political signal and anchoring them firmly in a democratic and pluralist Europe. These agreements amount to far more than ordinary association agreements; they establish special links reflecting geographical proximity, shared values and growing interdependence. The Community mounted an operation to support the balance of payments of the countries of Central and Eastern Europe and the Soviet Union through medium-term loans. It also made sustained efforts to help restructure and rehabilitate the economy of the Soviet Union, in particular by implementing the first technical assistance programmes and granting a credit guarantee for ECU 1 250 million, credit of ECU 500 million and a food aid programme worth a total of ECU 450 million. Finally, the Community officially recognized the independence of the Baltic States and quickly took steps to bring them within the Phare programme and open negotiations for the conclusion of trade and cooperation agreements. Similar measures were taken for Albania.

The conflict in the Gulf showed the vital importance of Europe's Mediterranean 'flank'. The Community pursued its aid efforts for the countries most directly affected by the crisis, granting humanitarian aid to the Kurds and other refugees from the region and financial aid to Israel and the Occupied Territories. As part of the redirected Mediterranean policy proposed in June 1990 — under which aid to the region is increased threefold — the Commission negotiated fourth financial protocols with the Maghreb and Mashreq countries and Israel which will strengthen considerably their links with the Community.

The Community and the Member States responded to the worsening political and institutional crisis in Yugoslavia by taking restrictive measures. But to offset the negative effects on the republics which had cooperated in the quest for a peaceful solution at the Hague Conference, positive measures were adopted with regard to Bosnia-Hercegovina, Croatia, Macedonia and Slovenia.

The Community continued to forge closer links with the other industrialized nations: in the wake of the Transatlantic Declarations with the United States and Canada, a joint declaration was adopted with the aim of stepping up cooperation and dialogue with Japan.

The Fourth Lomé Convention, which came into effect on 1 September, aims to create an area of political stability and balanced economic development among the ACP countries. The Commission continued its work at operational level and, after intensive dialogue, was able to finalize its guidelines for aid and adopt indicative programmes with nearly all the countries concerned, while continuing to press for greater democracy, which is an essential condition for the success of development efforts.

In response to requests from the countries of Latin America and Asia for closer ties, the Community has been actively preparing the ground for the implementation of the guidelines for cooperation with them during the 1990s. The proposal for a Regulation, on which the Council gave a favourable opinion, reflects the Community's resolve to give greater, coordinated support to these countries in various forms, while stressing new priorities like the environment, the human dimension of development, the promotion of human rights and economic cooperation.

While shouldering its international responsibilities, the Community continued to take the necessary steps to complete the single frontier-free area. Decisive progress was made, particularly in fields where the greatest delays had built up, and the Council reached decisions or common positions on almost 85 % of the White Paper programme.

Much constructive work was done on the indirect taxation front; a Directive was adopted on the transitional arrangements for VAT and political agreement was reached on the approximation of VAT rates and certain excise duties and on duty-free allowances.

The Community reaffirmed the strategic importance of the common transport policy for the establishment of the single market in which the mobility of goods and persons is vital. Substantial progress was made in this field: the Commission adopted proposals for a third package of measures for implementing the single market in air transport and proposals on the final arrangements for allowing non-resident road hauliers to transport goods within a Member State, while the Council adopted a Directive on the development of Community rail links. The Council also finalized its work on opening up the market in inland waterway transport and the carriage of passengers by road.

The process of completing the internal market gathered pace in the agricultural and plant health fields with the adoption of the directive on the marketing of plant health products and the regulation to encourage biological farming techniques. A large number of harmonization measures were also taken on animal health.

The Commission opted for an open-market approach, combined with support for industrial modernization on the basis of its paper on industrial policy in an open and competitive environment and accordingly adopted four communications on electronics and data-processing, biotechnology, maritime industries and textiles and clothing.

The Community demonstrated how far ahead its researchers were when they were the first in the world to generate a substantial quantity of energy in a prototype fusion reactor — JET — operating under the Community thermonuclear fusion research programme.

With a view to placing European agriculture on a more competitive footing while respecting the social and economic equilibrium of rural areas, the Commission made proposals to the Council for a general debate on the future of the common agricultural policy and put forward a series of guidelines for action to reform the policy. The Commission is aware of the environmental impact of policies generally and added a substantial environmental component in its proposals for CAP reform, along the lines of what has been done for other policies.

The concern for swift, effective action to achieve a generally higher level of environmental protection was behind the Council's decisions adopting or recording agreement on major proposals such as those on the Community eco-label, imports and exports of dangerous substances, the protection of natural and semi-natural habitats and LIFE — the financial instrument to enhance the effectiveness of Community environmental facilities. Proposals were made for measures to cut CO_2 emissions and improve energy efficiency. Environmental protection was one of the major aims pursued by the European Energy Charter, signed at The Hague on 17 December. This Community initiative lays down the principles and procedures for cooperation involving not only the whole of Europe but also the USA, Japan, Canada and Australia, so as to develop a common awareness of energy supply and environmental questions among all the Charter's signatories.

The year 1992 has come to be regarded as a milestone in the life of the Community, and both the institutions and the Member States are facing the challenge of setting up a frontier-free area by 31 December where goods, persons, sevices and capital can move freely as demanded by the Treaty; the removal of border controls and the establishment of the final components of the internal market are matters of priority concern. Substantial progress is needed in vital areas, including the social dimension, if the internal market is to function properly from 1 January 1993. The single market creates the need to go further, to strengthen many of the links in the chain so as to make it an ever more powerful element of economic and social reality and of the lives of Europe's citizens. That is the project of competition, cooperation and solidarity towards which the achievements of 1991 drive us on with still greater confidence.

Chapter I

Towards European union

1. The Intergovernmental Conferences on Economic and Monetary Union and on Political Union, launched following the Rome European Council of 14 and 15 December 1990,[1] continued to work in parallel throughout the year. As a rule, there was a ministerial-level meeting once a month, ministers' representatives meeting once a week. Member States were asked to submit contributions throughout the process. Interinstitutional meetings between the Council, the Commission and Parliament underpinned these conferences which ended, at the Maastricht European Council of 9 and 10 December,[2] with an agreement by the Heads of State or Government on the draft Treaty on European union. Final legal editing and harmonization of the texts must be completed before the Treaty can be signed early in February.

---

[1]   Twenty-fourth General Report, point 4.
[2]   Bull. EC 12-1991.

Section 1

Economic and monetary union

2.   The work of the Intergovernmental Conference was based on the report submitted in 1989 by the Committee chaired by Mr Delors,[1] the Commission's communication on economic and monetary union, a preliminary draft treaty presented by the Commission to revise the Treaty establishing the European Community,[2] and the draft statute of the European System of Central Banks and of the European Central Bank, presented by the Committee of Governors of the Central Banks.

3.   Five ministerial meetings were held in the first half of the year. All the articles of the new Treaty, including aspects involving both political union and economic and monetary union, were given a first reading and the Presidency drew up a consolidated document laying down the guidelines for economic and monetary union and defining the structure of the European System of Central Banks.

4.   An informal meeting of Ministers for Economic and Financial Affairs took place in Luxembourg on 10 and 11 May.[3] Discussions centred on three aspects of the transitional period: the need for programmes to promote greater convergence, the institutional arrangements for Stage II and the move to Stage III.

5.   Two interinstitutional conferences were devoted to economic and monetary union in the first six months of the year. At the conference held in Brussels on 8 April participants reviewed progress to date, expressed their desire for greater democratic legitimacy and voiced their concerns about economic convergence and economic and social cohesion.[4] At the 11 June conference Parliament pointed out that it had been excluded from the Presidency's draft Treaty and criticized the lack of any reference to cohesion.[5] On 14 June Parliament adopted a resolution reiterating the measures to be subject to the co-decision procedure and confirming its understanding of the definition and content of economic and monetary union.[6]

---

[1]   Twenty-third General Report, point 137.
[2]   Supplement 2/91 — Bull. EC.
[3]   Bull. EC 5-1991, point 1.1.1.
[4]   Bull. EC 4-1991, point 1.1.2.
[5]   Bull. EC 6-1991, point 1.1.3.
[6]   OJ C 183, 15.7.1991; Bull. EC 6-1991, point 1.1.4.

6.   The Luxembourg European Council on 28 and 29 June confirmed that negotiations should continue on the basis of the Presidency's draft Treaty, noted that there were broad areas of agreement on the basic components of economic and monetary union, and welcomed the fact that several Governments intended to introduce multiannual programmes designed to secure sustainable progress on economic convergence.[1] On 10 July Parliament adopted a resolution regretting that a number of crucial questions had been postponed to the Maastricht European Council and urging that the Treaty be finalized in line with the conclusions of the Rome I European Council.[2]

7.   In a communication adopted on 3 July the Commission suggested that the Council invite the Member States to notify the Community of the medium-term strategies they intend to pursue to achieve or maintain economic convergence, by October at the latest, for approval by the end of the year.[3] The Council took up this suggestion on 8 July, in the context of the six-monthly multilateral surveillance exercise, asking Member States, where necessary, to develop medium-term adjustment programmes and to forward them to the Community within the time-limits proposed by the Commission.[3]

8.   At the interinstitutional conference held on 9 September Parliament stressed the need to avoid a 'two-speed' Europe and the importance of economic convergence and economic and social cohesion.[4]

9.   At an informal meeting of Ministers for Economic and Financial Affairs in Apeldoorn on 21 and 22 September agreement was reached on a number of outstanding points such as the beginning of Stage II, and the establishment of a European Monetary Institute, set for 1 January 1994, the basic principles underlying the procedure for transition to Stage III — within three years of the beginning of Stage II — and the possibility of derogations at that stage.[5]

10.   The 7 October ministerial meeting focused mainly on objective convergence criteria for determining transition to the final stage of economic and monetary union.[6] On 28 October Mr Kok, President of the Council, formally proposed a full draft treaty on economic and monetary union, accompanied by protocols on the statute of the European System of Central Banks and of the European Central Bank and the statute of the European Monetary Institute.

---

[1]   Bull. EC 6-1991, point I.12.
[2]   OJ C 240, 16.9.1991; Bull. EC 7/8-1991, point 1.1.1.
[3]   Bull. EC 7/8-1991, point 1.1.2.
[4]   Bull. EC 9-1991, point 1.1.1.
[5]   Bull. EC 9-1991, point 1.1.3.
[6]   Bull. EC 10-1991, point 1.1.1.

11.   In a resolution adopted on 24 October Parliament expressed satisfaction that the informal meeting in Apeldoorn had agreed that there could be no question of a two-speed economic and monetary union.[1]

12.   At the interinstitutional conference in Brussels on 12 November Parliament highlighted the major points of disagreement with the Council, in particular Parliament's role, economic and monetary cohesion and the need for a coherent institutional structure for the future Community.[2]

13.   Following an informal meeting of Ministers for Economic and Financial Affairs in Scheveningen on 1 December,[3] the 11th ministerial meeting on 2 and 3 December reached agreement on a draft text which was submitted to the European Council.[3] The main problems which still required a decision by the Maastricht European Council were the procedure for transition to Stage III, the reservations expressed by two Member States concerning the absence of a general opting-out clause, and a decision on the future headquarters of the European Monetary Institute and the European Central Bank. In addition, final agreement had to be reached on a number of problems which also affected political union, in particular the institutions and economic and social cohesion.

14.   At the Maastricht European Council on 9 and 10 December the Heads of State or Government reached agreement on the draft Treaty on European union based on texts relating to political union and on the draft Treaty on economic and monetary union.[3]

15.   The main feature of economic union as defined in Maastricht is the gradual introduction of a single currency administered by a single independent central bank.

16.   Before Stage II begins on 1 January 1994 Member States must, where necessary, adopt multiannual convergence programmes and the Council must assess progress made towards convergence. Member States must also ensure that, with certain exceptions, capital movements are completely liberalized in accordance with the new provisions of the Treaty.

17.   In Stage II, during which a European Monetary Institute will be established to coordinate monetary policies and prepare for Stage III by the end of 1996, Member States must endeavour to avoid excessive deficits and initiate steps leading to independence for their central banks.

---

[1]   OJ C 305, 25.11.1991; Bull. EC 10-1991, point 1.1.2.
[2]   Bull. EC 11-1991, point 1.1.3.
[3]   Bull. EC 12-1991.

18.   In preparation for the move to Stage III, the Commission and the European Monetary Institute will report to the Council on national legislation linked to the achievement of economic and monetary union and progress towards a high degree of convergence assessed by reference to four specific criteria (inflation, financial situation, membership of the exchange-rate mechanism and interest rates) and a number of other factors. In the light of these reports and Parliament's opinion, the Council — in this case the Heads of State or Government — will decide not later than 31 December 1996, on the basis of the recommendations of the Ministers for Economic and Financial Affairs, whether a majority of the Member States fulfil the necessary conditions for the adoption of a single currency and whether it is appropriate for the Community to move to Stage III. If so, it will set the date for the beginning of Stage III. If no date for this has been set by the end of 1997, Stage III will start on 1 January 1999 and will be confined to those Member States which fulfil the necessary conditions. The other Member States will benefit from a derogation which may be abrogated by the Council once the necessary conditions are satisfied. The position of the United Kingdom is covered by a separate protocol.

19.   As soon as the date for the beginning of Stage III is set, the European System of Central Banks and the European Central Bank will be established in accordance with the Treaty. If there are Member States with a derogation, a General Council will be constituted, representing all national central banks. Exchange rates will be irrevocably fixed without changing the external value of the ecu and the European System of Central Banks and the European Central Bank will exercise their powers in full. This will be followed in short order by the introduction of the ecu as the sole currency.

20.   Ratification of the Treaty implies an irrevocable commitment by the Member States to move to Stage III if they satisfy the necessary conditions. However, the United Kingdom will be allowed to reserve its decision and Denmark will be granted a similar exemption if, after a referendum, it decides not to move to Stage III. Where exemptions have been granted, the Member States concerned will not be regarded as belonging to the majority of Member States meeting the necessary conditions.

21.   At institutional level, the Commission's exclusive right of initiative in the form of recommendations or proposals has been maintained, except in the case of monetary legislation and exchange-rate policy where it shares its right of initiative with the European Central Bank. Furthermore, in certain circumstances the Member States may ask the Commission to make recommendations or proposals. Parliament will be associated with the Council's legislative acts under the assent procedure, the cooperation procedure or the consultation procedure. It will be consulted or at least informed in the case of most executive acts.

Section 2

Political union

22.   In the context of the negotiations on political union, a substantial number of amendments to the EEC Treaty were presented by the Member States. Parliament duly delivered its opinion, notably in the Martin report. The Commission made several contributions to the Intergovernmental Conference. They dealt with union citizenship, common external policy, democratic legitimacy: hierarchy of norms, executive powers, legislative procedure (co-decision), the social dimension and the development of human resources, economic and social cohesion, research and technological development, energy, environment, trans-European networks, culture and protection of the heritage, health, compliance with Court of Justice judgments, the Economic and Social Committee, human resources, financial provisions, the general structure of the Treaty and the Consultative Committee of Regional and Local Authorities.[1]

23.   On 14 January Parliament adopted a resolution on the Rome II European Council in which it stressed the urgent need for a common foreign and security policy, called for the elimination of the democratic deficit in the Community and asked to be consulted on citizenship and the results of the intergovernmental conferences before they were wound up.[2]

24.   The first interinstitutional conference took place in Brussels on 5 March and focused on democratic legitimacy and the role of the European Parliament (co-decision procedure and appointment of the Commission).[3]

25.   On 15 April the Luxembourg Presidency presented its first draft Treaty, comprising two separate sections.[4] The first proposed amendments to the EEC Treaty, with particular reference to the notion of union citizenship, Community competence and Parliament's powers. The second dealt with the common foreign and security policy, home affairs and judicial cooperation.

---

[1]   Supplement 2/91 — Bull. EC.
[2]   OJ C 48, 25.2.1991; Bull. EC 1/2-1991, point 1.1.1.
[3]   Bull. EC 3-1991, point 1.1.3.
[4]   Bull. EC 4-1991, point 1.1.3.

26.   On 18 April Parliament adopted a resolution proposing a clear hierarchy for Community acts.[1] On the same day it adopted a resolution on the enhancement of democratic legitimacy, pinpointing different areas in which it should have powers of co-decision or assent.

27.   A further interinstitutional conference took place in Strasbourg on 15 May.[2] The structure of the new Treaty and the Commission's role in the legislative procedure were among the matters discussed.

28.   On 14 June Parliament adopted a resolution in which it called for a single legal and institutional structure.[3]

In the face of criticism of the three-pillar formula (Community, common foreign and security policy, and home affairs and judicial cooperation) and fears that the Community would break up, the Luxembourg Presidency presented a revised version of its draft Treaty to a ministerial meeting on 18 June. This reaffirmed the federal nature of the union and restored the Commission's role wherever it had been undermined.[4]

29.   The European Council met in Luxembourg on 28 and 29 June.[5] After confirming that the final decision on the text of the Treaty would be taken at the Maastricht European Council, it agreed that the draft Treaty presented by the Luxembourg Presidency would form the basis for the next stage of the negotiations. It stressed the importance of the following points: full maintenance and development of the *acquis communautaire*, subsidiarity, economic and social cohesion, the introduction of union citizenship and a common foreign and security policy extending to all matters relating to the security of the union. A decision on the defence identity of the union was postponed to the final stage of the negotiations. Agreement was also reached on the objectives underlying the German delegation's proposals on home affairs and judicial cooperation.

30.   On 10 July Parliament adopted a resolution on the Luxembourg European Council in which it repeated its demands and regretted that a number of crucial questions had been postponed to the Maastricht meeting.[6]

31.   On 24 September the Dutch Presidency, which had taken over from the Luxembourg Presidency, presented a draft treaty which abandoned the three-pillar structure in favour of a single structure, highlighted the federal nature of the union and sought

---

[1]   OJ C 129, 20.5.1991; Bull. EC 4-1991, point 1.1.4.
[2]   Bull. EC 5-1991, point 1.1.3.
[3]   OJ C 183, 15.7.1991; Bull. EC 6-1991, point 1.1.7.
[4]   Bull. EC 6-1991, point 1.1.5.
[5]   Bull. EC 6-1991, points I.2 to I.12.
[6]   Bull. EC 7/8-1991, point I.1.

to increase Parliament's powers in a number of areas. At their meeting in Brussels on 30 September the Foreign Ministers rejected this draft treaty virtually unanimously, most Member States preferring to use the Luxembourg Presidency's draft as a basis for negotiation. [1]

32.   A fourth Interinstitutional Conference was held in Brussels on 1 October. [2]

On 10 October Parliament adopted a further resolution on the Intergovernmental Conference in general and the common foreign and security policy in particular. It favoured qualified majority voting on foreign policy issues and called for a single Community structure to cover aspects of external policy. [3]

33.   The last interinstitutional conference before the Maastricht European Council was held in Brussels on 5 November. [4]

34.   On 8 November the Dutch Presidency presented a revised draft Treaty which was very close to the Luxembourg draft of 18 June and reinstated the three-pillar structure. The conference met in restricted session in Noordwijk on 12 and 13 November to examine the new text. A number of issues remained unresolved; they included the scope of powers of co-decision, qualified majority voting in areas of Community competence, economic and social cohesion and the implementation of common measures under the common foreign and security policy.

35.   On 21 November Parliament adopted a final resolution before the Maastricht European Council. It considered that the compromise reached was inadequate on a number of points such as a single, coherent structure, the co-decision and assent procedures in respect of amendment of the Treaty, the efficiency of decision-making within the Council, the Commission's political role, economic and social cohesion, and development of the social and environmental dimension in the Community. [5]

36.   The Maastricht European Council on 9 and 10 December reached agreement on the draft Treaty on European union. [6]

37.   While respecting the principle of subsidiarity, the draft Treaty establishes a union based on the European Communities, supplemented by policies and cooperation on foreign affairs, security, justice and home affairs. However, the federal nature of the union was not highlighted at Maastricht.

---

[1]   Bull. EC 9-1991, point 1.1.4.
[2]   Bull. EC 10-1991, point 1.1.4.
[3]   OJ C 305, 25.11.1991; Bull. EC 10-1991, point 1.1.6.
[4]   Bull. EC 11-1991, point 1.1.6.
[5]   OJ C 326, 16.12.1991.
[6]   Bull. EC 12-1991.

38.   The new Treaty introduces union citizenship, defining the rights and obligations of nationals of the Member States. These include freedom of movement, right of residence, the right to vote and to stand as a candidate at municipal and European elections, and shared diplomatic protection outside the union.

39.   Community powers in areas such as education and vocational training, trans-European networks, industry, health, culture, development cooperation and consumer protection were confirmed or extended.

40.   In the social sphere, the European Council noted that 11 Member States wished to continue along the path marked out by the Social Charter in 1989 and agreed to annex a protocol on social policy to the Treaty.

41.   Existing provisions on economic and social cohesion were strengthened; express provision was made for the creation of a cohesion fund and a protocol defining a number of important principles was annexed to the Treaty.

42.   On the institutional front, Parliament's legislative powers were extended in a number of areas thanks to the co-decision procedure provided for in Article 189b. The Commission's term of office was extended to five years in line with that of Parliament, which has been given a say in its appointment. The scope for qualified majority voting has been extended. The Court of Justice has been authorized to fine Member States for failing to implement a judgment. The Court of Auditors has become a Community institution and a consultative committee on the regions has been set up.

43.   The provisions on a common foreign and security policy cover all areas of foreign and security policy and will lead in time to the framing of a common defence policy. The European Council will be responsible for defining the principles and guidelines of a common foreign and security policy. The Council, acting unanimously, will implement this policy, although provision is also made for qualified majority voting.

44.   The provisions on justice and home affairs provide for cooperation between the Member States of the union on right of asylum and immigration. Visa policy, however, will be a matter for the Community.

Chapter II

The single market and the Community economic and social area

Section 1

Economic and monetary policy

Priority activities and objectives

45.   *Strengthening economic and monetary policy coordination within the existing insti-tutional framework constitutes one of the priorities of Stage I of EMU, which began on 1 July 1990.[1] In order to progress towards economic convergence, a number of Member States, acting in response to a request from the Council,[2] implemented convergence programmes together with specific plans and measures for bringing about medium-term improvements that are being monitored at Community level. The arrangements for Stage I have thus been supplemented and the multilateral surveillance process reinforced with a view to preparing for the move to Stage II, in which closer convergence should allow Member States to satisfy the criteria for deciding on the transition to Stage III. In April the Central Bank Governors finalized a draft statute for the European Central Bank, which will have the task of directing Community monetary policy in the final stage of EMU.*

46.   *The characteristics and content of Stage III and of the transitional stage were discussed throughout the year at the Intergovernmental Conference, which, on completing its work on 3 December, unveiled the draft Treaty that was presented to the Maastricht European Council.[3]*

---

[1]   Twenty-fourth General Report, points 26 and 32.
[2]   Point 7 of this Report.
[3]   Points 18 to 21 of this Report.

The economic situation

47.   The overall economic situation in the Community was characterized by a slowdown in activity in the first half of the year followed by a recovery in the second half. The slackening of growth, which had already begun in 1990,[1] was largely due to cyclical corrections in a number of Member States. It was exacerbated, however, by the deterioration in the international environment and the Gulf crisis, which led to a temporary fall in business and consumer confidence. Despite a gradual economic upturn in real terms in the second half of the year, the rate of growth in the Community for the year as a whole was only 1.3%, roughly half the rate recorded the previous year. The component of demand which showed the sharpest deceleration was investment, which contracted by 0.5% following a rise of 4.1% in 1990.

The growth in consumption also declined to 1.7% in 1991 compared with 3.0% the previous year. The less favourable international environment was reflected in the external demand for goods and services, the rate of growth of which fell to 5.7% from 6.0% in 1990.

Owing to the economic slowdown, the number of jobs created (up 0.5%) failed to compensate for the growth in the labour force, resulting in an increase in the unemployment rate from 8.4% in 1990 to 8.6%. The rate of inflation (private consumption deflator) remained high at 5% despite the fall-off in real growth. The main reason for this was the rapid rise in nominal unit wage costs (up 6.2%).

48.   Convergence improved slightly. While remaining pronounced, the disparity between inflation rates and rates of growth in nominal unit wage costs in Member States narrowed a little. No further progress was made towards budgetary consolidation but this was due only in part to the fiscal effects of slower growth and to German unification. The relaxation of fiscal efforts to contain public expenditure was also a contributory factor.

Economic and monetary union

Improved policy coordination in Stage I

49.   The main economic and monetary policy aims being pursued during Stage I of EMU are improved convergence towards lower inflation and a reduction in abnormally high budget deficits and excessive public debt.

---

[1]   Twenty-fourth General Report, point 27 *et seq.*

50.   In accordance with Decision 90/141/EEC,[1] the Council carried out, on 28 January[2] and 8 July,[3] the half-yearly multilateral surveillance exercises covering economic developments and policies in the Member States.

51.   The events in the Gulf and the unexpected depth of the recession in the United Kingdom led the Commission to revise the economic assessment underlying its 1990-91 Annual Economic Report.[4] In July the Council (economic and financial affairs) adopted the revised Annual Economic Report[5] in the light of the opinions of Parliament[6] and the Economic and Social Committee.[7]

52.   In the 1991-92 Annual Economic Report, which it adopted on 4 December,[8] the Commission highlighted in particular the need to make further progress towards convergence through completing the single market, pursuing economic and monetary union, securing greater cohesion and, if possible, finalizing the work of the Uruguay Round.

Thrust of economic policy in 1991 and 1992

53.   If the EMU deadlines are to be met without difficulty, the Community must face up to two major economic policy challenges: to restore a more rapid rate of growth conducive to a decline in unemployment, and to improve nominal convergence. The cyclical slowdown which the Community is currently experiencing calls for prudent monetary and fiscal policies to prevent any further deterioration in performances in terms of stability, to permit progress towards a sounder price and cost environment and to ensure a return to higher rates of growth. At the same time, renewed structural efforts are required to improve further the functioning of the Community economy. Considerable progress was made in this respect in the 1980s, and the prospects for a rapid return to rates of growth that will bring down unemployment are good.

54.   Progress towards the degree of nominal convergence necessary to move to the final stage of EMU was unsatisfactory and there were worrying setbacks in some cases. On the occasion of the second multilateral surveillance exercise in July and on the basis of a Commission communication, the Council called for multiannual convergence programmes to be implemented with determination by the Member States concerned and

---

[1]   OJ L 78, 24.3.1990; Twenty-fourth General Report, point 32.
[2]   Bull. EC 1/2-1991, point 1.1.5.
[3]   Bull. EC 7/8-1991, point 1.1.2.
[4]   OJ C 190, 22.7.1991; Bull. EC 5-1991, point 1.2.1; initial proposal: OJ C 53, 28.2.1991; Twenty-fourth General Report, point 34.
[5]   OJ L 252, 7.9.1991; Bull. EC 7/8-1991, point 1.2.1.
[6]   OJ C 183, 15.7.1991; Bull. EC 6-1991, point 1.2.1.
[7]   OJ C 269, 14.10.1991; Bull. EC 7/8-1991, point 1.2.1.
[8]   Bull. EC 12-1991.

for those programmes to be monitored at Community level under the multilateral surveillance procedures.[1]

Medium-term economic development in the Community

55.   Despite short-term problems, the prospects for a medium-term resumption of growth and for an expansion in productive potential seem to be favourable. While the return on investment failed to maintain the record level achieved in 1989, it remained at a promising level, albeit not one that was compatible with full employment. Markets in the Community became a great deal more flexible during the second half of the 1980s, and the international environment should also improve with the end of the recession in North America. All of these factors, together with the lasting stimuli provided by such major Community projects as completion of the single market, progress towards EMU, the catching-up process in the less favoured countries and regions, the strategic promise of the future European Economic Area (EEA), the potential enlargement of the Community and the opening-up of the countries of Central and Eastern Europe, make for a satisfactory medium-term outlook.

Operation and strengthening of the EMS

56.   The European Monetary System (EMS) consolidated its position as a zone of monetary stability despite marked fluctuations in the exchange rates of third currencies. All the Member States of the Community, except for Greece and Portugal, currently participate in the exchange-rate mechanism (ERM) of the EMS. The Spanish peseta and the pound sterling are permitted to move within the wide fluctuation margin of 6% either side of their ecu central rates, while the other currencies remain within the narrow band of 2.25% either side of their central rates. The bilateral parity grid and hence the ecu central rates remained unchanged.

57.   In preparation for full participation in the ERM, the Portuguese monetary authorities began to use a reference basket of five ERM currencies (German mark, French franc, Italian lira, Spanish peseta and sterling) to assess movements in the escudo. Previously, a basket of 13 currencies, including several non-Community currencies, had been used.

---

[1]   Point 7 of this Report.

Wider use of the ecu

58.   At its meeting in Luxembourg, [1] the European Council confirmed the ecu's future role as the single currency of economic and monetary union. However, the nature of the ecu during the transitional phase continued to be the subject of discussion within the framework of the Intergovernmental Conference and also among market operators. The Commission called, in this connection, for the currency amounts defining the ecu to be fixed definitively in order to dispel any uncertainty as to its definition during the transitional phase leading to the single currency and to safeguard the continuity of ecu markets which have already shown considerable quantitative and qualitative growth, while at the same time enabling the ecu to reinforce itself naturally in the event of any realignments in EMS central rates.

59.   The level of activity on the ecu bond market was again remarkable, up by almost 30% on the previous year. The rapid growth on all ecu markets prompted the Commission to organize, for operators and public or monetary authorities, a conference in Luxembourg in September on the theme 'Monetary and financial instruments in ecus: statistical aspects', at which all the available statistical information was presented.

60.   Against this background of rapid growth in the ecu-denominated bond market, the Commission explored with market operators the possibility of defining and regularly publishing reference rates showing ecu interest-rate levels for various maturities.

61.   In order for markets to expand further and for all economic agents to have the opportunity to familiarize themselves with the use of the future single currency, the Commission arranged for a detailed analysis to be made in all Member States of any rules and regulations that might impede use of the ecu. The findings will be presented in 1992 and are expected to give rise to practical measures for removing any obstacles to use of the ecu.

62.   It also began to examine to what extent pilot schemes for using the ecu could be encouraged or extended in fields where its use seemed especially easy and appropriate, e.g. tourism.

63.   In April the Commission adopted a proposal on the use of the ecu for paying Community staff. Following the failure to secure Parliament's agreement, the practicalities of a new proposal are being looked into.

---

[1]   Bull. EC 6-1991, point I.2 *et seq.*

64.   The Commission also welcomed the decisions of the Swedish authorities on 17 May[1] and the Finnish authorities on 7 June[2] to link their currencies to the ecu on the basis of fluctuation margins of 1.5% and 3% respectively.

These decisions are likely to extend the zone of monetary stability created by the EMS.

The Community and international monetary and financial matters

65.   The annual meeting of the International Monetary Fund was held in Bangkok on 13 October. The Community was represented by Mr Kok, President of the Council, and by Mr Christophersen, Commission Vice-President. The international monetary and financial issues tackled included in particular the nature and extent of aid for the Soviet Union and the responses of the international financial community to developments in Eastern Europe.

66.   At its 36th meeting, held in Washington in April, the Interim Committee of the International Monetary Fund (IMF) advocated a medium-term world strategy for dealing with the new problems posed by the reforms and reconstruction processes under way in Central and Eastern Europe and in the developing countries. The strategy is based on an increase in global saving (to be achieved particularly through further budgetary consolidation measures), on structural reform and trade liberalization policies designed to improve the allocation of resources and on monetary and fiscal policies aimed at reducing real interest rates and boosting economic activity under stable price conditions. At its 37th meeting in Bangkok, held immediately prior to the IMF's annual meeting, the Interim Committee examined the new prospects for reform which had emerged in the Soviet Union and the progress of the reforms undertaken in Central and Eastern Europe. As for economic policy recommendations, it emphasized the need for an increase in global saving and for structural reforms.

67.   At their annual summit meeting,[3] the Heads of State or Government of the seven leading industrialized democracies (G7) and the representatives of the Community reaffirmed the need to continue the process of coordinating economic policies within the framework of the medium-term strategy formulated at previous summits and announced a series of measures for assisting the reform process in the Soviet Union.

---

[1]   Bull. EC 5-1991, point 1.2.2.
[2]   Bull. EC 6-1991, point 1.2.3.
[3]   Point 853 of this Report.

Community initiatives and financial activities

Development of financing techniques

Venture capital

68. In December the Commission reviewed and extended two Community instruments, Eurotech Capital,[1] the pilot scheme for financing technological innovation through capital injections for small and medium-sized firms, and the Seed Capital project, the aim of which is to provide seed capital for new firms. There are also plans for reorganizing the Venture Consort pilot programme for setting up transnational venture capital consortia with a view to providing eligible firms with a Community contribution on top of that provided by the consortium.

Support for setting up joint ventures in the countries of Central and Eastern Europe

69. On 30 January the Commission adopted a decision to fund a programme — Joint Venture Phare programme (JOPP)[2] — the aim of which is to encourage, in the various countries benefiting from the Phare programme and in the small and medium-sized business sector, the setting-up and development of joint ventures comprising at least one Community partner and one local partner. As in the case of the ECIP programme (EC International Investment Partners),[3] which pursues similar objectives in various Asian, Latin American and Mediterranean countries,[4] the JOPP programme consists of a number of sections covering the various phases of setting up and developing a joint venture.

Community borrowing and lending

Borrowing and lending activity

70. On 9 October the Commission adopted the 11th report on the Community's borrowing and lending activities, covering 1990.[5] According to the report, borrowing in 1990 totalled ECU 13.6 billion (up 10.5% on 1989). Almost all the Community loans

---

[1]   Twenty-second General Report, point 167.
[2]   Bull. EC 1/2-1991, point 1.3.13.
[3]   Point 954 of this Report.
[4]   Twenty-second General Report, point 1000.
[5]   Bull. EC 10-1991, point 1.5.10.

were made by the EIB (ECU 12 174.2 million, or nine tenths of total Community lending) and by the ECSC (ECU 993.8 million).

71.   The Commission also adopted, in February, the 14th six-monthly report on the rate of utilization of NCI tranches.[1]

European Bank for Reconstruction and Development (EBRD)

72.   The EBRD, which was set up to finance economic development projects in Central and Eastern Europe,[2] was inaugurated on 14 April in the presence of many Heads of State or Government. With capital of ECU 10 billion, it will promote the development of the private sector, to which at least 60% of its committed funds must go. By the end of the year, when all of its capital had been paid in, just over 50% of its commitment capacity had been reached.

The Bank's strategy over the next few years will be to give priority to supporting privatization, developing infrastructures and rehabilitating the environment in the recipient countries.

Its first loan was granted in June for an energy project in Poland.

The Commission and the Bank cooperate within the framework of their mutual activities in the countries of Central and Eastern Europe. An agreement was reached to make available to the Bank in 1992 from the Community budget two allocations of not more than ECU 25 million and ECU 15 million for the Phare programme and technical assistance to the USSR respectively. This will allow the Bank to step up technical assistance in the recipient countries.

Medium-term financial assistance for the countries of Central and Eastern Europe and for other third countries

73.   Following the impetus given by the European Council at its meeting in Rome in December 1990,[3] the Commission, as the coordinating institution for the Group of 24 industrialized countries, presented to the Council a series of Community measures based on an individualized approach and taking the form of medium-term financing over and above that provided by international financial institutions. Limited in time, this financial assistance is conditional and subject to an IMF agreement being concluded with the recipient countries.

---

[1]   Bull. EC 1/2-1991, point 1.2.3.
[2]   Twenty-fourth General Report, point 54.
[3]   Twenty-fourth General Report, point 52.

74. The Council adopted four decisions granting financial assistance of ECU 375 million to Czechoslovakia,[1] ECU 290 million to Bulgaria,[2] ECU 375 million to Romania[3] and ECU 180 million to Hungary.[4] In the case of Hungary, the amount granted was in addition to the ECU 870 million provided last year.[5] All of these measures, which were designed to support the adjustment and reform programmes implemented by the recipient countries, were matched by an equivalent financial contribution from the other member countries of the Group of 24. The amount of medium-term assistance committed by the Group of 24 to the countries of Central and Eastern Europe thus totalled some ECU 2.4 billion in 1991, around 50% of which was borne by the Community. The Commission paid out, in respect of the first of the two tranches agreed for each loan, ECU 185 million to Czechoslovakia, ECU 150 million to Bulgaria, ECU 190 million to Romania and ECU 100 million to Hungary. If the ECU 260 million representing the second tranche of the loan granted to Hungary in 1990 is included, the funds mobilized by the Commission for medium-term financial assistance for the countries of Central and Eastern Europe amounted to ECU 885 million in 1991.

75. In May the Council extended[6] to Czechoslovakia, Bulgaria and Romania its Decision 90/62/EEC granting a Community guarantee to the European Investment Bank against losses under loans for projects in Hungary and Poland.[7]

76. In April the Commission extended[8] to Romania the draft decision[9] that would enable ECSC loans to be made in Czechoslovakia, Bulgaria and Yugoslavia. The ECSC Consultative Committee gave its endorsement on 7 June.[10]

77. In the context of Community aid for those Middle Eastern and Mediterranean countries adversely affected by the Gulf conflict, the Council decided on 22 July to grant a medium-term loan of ECU 160 million to Israel.[11] This loan was made available to Israel in a single tranche and was accompanied by an interest-rate subsidy totalling ECU 27.5 million charged to the general budget of the European Communities.

---

[1]   OJ L 56, 2.3.1991; Bull. EC 1/2-1991, point 1.3.21; Commission proposal: OJ C 37, 13.2.1991.
[2]   OJ L 174, 3.7.1991; Bull. EC 6-1991, point 1.3.15; Commission proposal: OJ C 96, 12.4.1991.
[3]   OJ L 208, 30.7.1991; Bull. EC 7/8-1991, point 1.3.18; Commission proposal: OJ C 121, 7.5.1991; Bull. EC 5-1991, point 1.3.13.
[4]   OJ L 174, 3.7.1991; Bull. EC 6-1991, point 1.3.16; Commission proposal: OJ C 97, 13.4.1991; Bull. EC 3-1991, point 1.3.12.
[5]   OJ L 58, 7.3.1991; Twenty-fourth General Report, point 50.
[6]   Bull. EC 5-1991, point 1.3.7.
[7]   Twenty-fourth General Report, point 49.
[8]   Bull. EC 4-1991, point 1.3.7.
[9]   Twenty-fourth General Report, point 51.
[10] Bull. EC 6-1991, point 1.3.12.
[11] OJ L 227, 15.8.1991; Bull. EC 7/8-1991, point 1.3.19; Commission proposal: OJ C 68, 16.3.1991; Bull. EC 1/2-1991, point 1.3.23.

In response to the wish expressed by the European Council at its meeting in Luxembourg,[1] the Council decided on 23 September to grant a medium-term loan of ECU 400 million to Algeria[2] to help it carry through the political and economic reforms under way and to bolster its balance-of-payments position. An initial tranche of ECU 250 million was paid by the Commission to the Algerian authorities in November.

78.   In December the Council decided to grant to the USSR and its constituent republics a medium-term loan of ECU 1 250 million in order to enable agricultural and food products and medical supplies to be imported from the Community and from the countries of Central and Eastern Europe.[3] The loan will be made available in 1992 in three instalments.

---

[1]   Bull. EC 6-1991, point I.29.
[2]   OJ L 272, 28.9.1991; Bull. EC 9-1991, point 1.3.26; Commission proposal: OJ C 192, 23.7.1991; Bull. EC 7/8-1991, point 1.3.23.
[3]   OJ L 362, 31.12.1991; Bull. EC 12-1991; Commission proposal: OJ C 320, 11.12.1991; Bull. EC 11-1991, point 1.3.3.

Section 2

Completing the internal market

Priority activities and objectives

79.   *The Community institutions pursued the task of implementing the Commission's White Paper on completing the internal market[1] by 1 January 1993, with a steady rate of progress being maintained essentially thanks to Parliament, which succeeded in issuing opinions within the deadlines set and thus in making up for the delays which had built up in 1990. A total of 228 measures have already been adopted, representing almost 85 % of the programme set out. In addition, the European Council called on the Council to take the requisite decisions by the end of 1991 in view of the time needed for the transposition and implementation of Community legislation in the Member States.[2]*

Among the important decisions taken this year, special reference must be made to those relating to the removal of controls at frontiers, in particular: the abolition of the single administrative document in intra-Community trade from 1 January 1993 and the changes in Community transit arrangements; the new transitional VAT regime and the abolition of baggage checks at airports for persons travelling within the Community; the rules on weapons controls; the new arrangements for collecting statistics on intra-Community trade; and the abolition of veterinary and plant-health checks.

In addition, the Council completed its work programme on technical regulations by adopting the last remaining directives on the recognition of authorizations for pharmaceutical products and by introducing Community type-approval for passenger vehicles.

However, as indicated in the Commission's sixth annual report concerning the implementation of the White Paper [3] and in its communication on the implementation of measures for completing the internal market[4] a number of matters which are not strictly linked to the abolition of controls at frontiers but which are nevertheless very important to the activity of firms in an integrated market are still outstanding. They include the creation of a Community trade mark and, in the area of company law, the proposal for a European Company, which progressed a good deal closer to a decision during the year.

---

[1]   Nineteenth General Report, points 162 to 166.
[2]   Bull. EC 6-1991, point I.13.
[3]   Bull. EC 6-1991, point 1.2.8.
[4]   Bull. EC 12-1991.

The Ministers responsible had an opportunity to review progress to date and to introduce greater coherence into the treatment of the different priorities within the Council at their meetings in Vianden on 8 and 9 March and in Amsterdam on 13 and 14 September. At the latter meeting, they dealt in particular with questions relating to the abolition of physical controls at frontiers and the many formalities still remaining in intra-Community trade. Accordingly, they instructed the national officials responsible for coordination work on the internal market within the Member States to monitor, in conjunction with the Commission, the process of eliminating controls at frontiers on the basis of a comprehensive list of all operations currently carried out at customs posts.

In a communication dated 18 December,[1] the Commission identified the difficulties associated with the elimination of frontier controls on individuals and goods and established the priorities for ensuring the removal of all controls by the end of 1992.

In tandem with the work of the Council, the Commission pursued its task of managing the single market. Proposals were put forward to make Community type-approval for motor vehicles and motor cycles compulsory, to extend to new products the rules relating to the new approach to technical harmonization and to bring public services within the scope of the transparency rules introduced for public service contracts awarded by administrations. A number of directives, particularly in the agri-foodstuffs and chemical sectors, require implementing measures most of which have been either adopted by the Commission or proposed to the Council.

For two years, monitoring transposition of legislation adopted among other things under the programme contained in the White Paper has been a constant matter of concern for the Commission, guaranteeing as it does the credibility of the objective and generating confidence between Member States. With the exception of Italy, there has been a steady improvement in the rate of transposition by Member States in the last two years. Although 39 legal instruments entered into force in 1991, the rate of transposition rose to 77.2.

The Commission must also ensure that the implementation of legislation follows the principle of subsidiarity, whereby considerable responsibility lies with the Member States. Accordingly, it has laid emphasis on the organization of exchanges of information between administrations to ensure that the internal market is managed jointly and that confidence in the operation of each of the administrative systems is reinforced. Such exchanges of information take place essentially through the electronic data-transmission networks set up between national administrations[2] and through the exchanges arranged between such administrations under the Matthaeus programme,[3] which has been extended to all areas of the single market.

---

[1]   Bull. EC 12-1991.
[2]   Point 336 of this Report.
[3]   Point 92 of this Report.

BUSINESS ENVIRONMENT

Removal of physical frontiers

Checks on goods

Movement of goods within the Community

Simplification of checks and formalities in trade

Single administrative document

80.   On 21 March the Council adopted Regulation (EEC) No 717/91[1] eliminating use of the single administrative document in trade in Community goods within the Community from 1 January 1993.

Simplification of transit procedures

81.   On 21 March the Council adopted Regulation (EEC) No 719/91,[2] on the use in the Community of TIR and ATA carnets as transit documents, which is designed to adapt the rules of application of the TIR and ATA Conventions to reflect the fact that from 1 January 1992 the Community will be considered to form a single territory. Regulation (EEC) No 1593/91,[3] adopted by the Commission on 12 June, lays down arrangements for implementing the provisions of Regulation (EEC) No 719/91 relating to infringements or irregularities committed in connection with operations carried out under cover of a TIR or ATA carnet.

Other simplifications

82.   On 21 March the Council adopted Regulation (EEC) No 718/91[4] amending Regulation (EEC) No 3/84 introducing arrangements for movement with the Community of

---

[1]   OJ L 78, 26.3.1991; Bull. EC 3-1991, point 1.2.12; Commission proposal: OJ C 214, 29.8.1990; Twenty-fourth General Report, point 63.
[2]   OJ L 78, 26.3.1991; Bull. EC 3-1991, point 1.2.20; Commission proposal: OJ C 142, 12.6.1990; Twenty-fourth General Report, point 65.
[3]   OJ L 148, 13.6.1991; Bull. EC 6-1991, point 1.2.15.
[4]   OJ L 78, 26.3.1991; Bull. EC 3-1991, point 1.2.14; Commission proposal: OJ C 212, 25.8.1990; Twenty-fourth General Report, point 66.

goods sent from one Member State for temporary use in one or more Member States, to extend its scope pending its repeal, in principle on 1 January 1993.[1]

83.   On 20 June the Council adopted Directive 91/342/EEC[2] amending Directive 83/643/EEC[3] on the facilitation of physical inspections and administrative formalities in respect of the carriage of goods between Member States, with a view to introducing further simplifications for the period prior to completion of the internal market.

84.   On 19 December the Council adopted a Regulation concerning the elimination of controls and formalities applicable to the cabin and checked baggage of passengers taking an intra-Community flight and the baggage of passengers making an intra-Community sea crossing, to ensure that such passengers enjoy the freedom of movement conferred by Article 8a of the Treaty.[4]

85.   On 11 December, in order to take account of the abolition of internal frontiers as of 1 January 1993, the Council adopted Regulation (EEC) No 3648/91[5] repealing Council Regulation (EEC) No 3690/86[6] concerning the abolition within the framework of the TIR Convention of customs formalities on exit from a Member State at a frontier between two Member States and Regulation (EEC) No 4283/88[7] on the abolition of certain exit formalities at internal Community frontiers — introduction of common border posts.

Coordinated development of computerized administrative procedures

86.   Certain customs procedures need to be adapted and modernized. This involves setting up procedures and systems for centralized electronic data transmission. To this end the Commission has continued its work programme covering the computerized management of Community customs legislation, particularly with regard to tariff quotas (already operational for some Member States), Community transit arrangements (a pilot project is in preparation), the second generation integrated Community tariff and binding tariff information issued by Member States (a databank has been operational since the end of 1991). Computerized anti-fraud networks are also being modernized.

---

[1]   OJ L 2, 4.1.1984; Seventeenth General Report, point 221.
[2]   OJ L 187, 13.7.1991; Bull. EC 6-1991, point 1.2.9; Commission proposal: OJ C 204, 15.8.1990; Twenty-fourth General Report, point 66.
[3]   OJ L 359, 22.12.1983.
[4]   OJ L 374, 31.12.1991; Bull. EC 12-1991; Commission proposal: OJ C 212, 25.8.1990; Twenty-fourth General Report, point 66.
[5]   OJ L 348, 17.12.1991; Bull. EC 12-1991; Commission proposal: OJ C 143, 1.6.1991; Bull. EC 5-1991, point 1.2.4.
[6]   OJ L 341, 4.12.1986; Twentieth General Report, point 185.
[7]   OJ L 382, 31.12.1988; Twenty-second General Report, point 200.

With regard to taxation, a feasibility study is under way with a view to the introduction from 1993 of an electronic data transfer system on control of intra-Community flows.[1]

Mutual assistance, administrative cooperation and fraud control

87. The Commission pursued its efforts to increase the effectiveness of fraud control by concluding mutual assistance agreements with non-member countries such as Andorra,[2] with the EFTA countries (by establishing the European Economic Area)[3] and with Poland, Hungary and Czechoslovakia (in the framework of the Europe agreements).[4] In the same context, it further perfected and extended the Scent network (System for a customs enforcement network)[1] linking the various anti-fraud departments in the Community, and Community fact-finding missions were sent to non-member countries.

88. Work was also carried out to establish by 1992 a computerized customs system (SID) to step up the fight against drug trafficking at the Community's external frontiers. The Commission also took part in the work of the G7 countries on trade in precursors (drugs) and as a result proposed that Council Regulation (EEC) No 3677/90[5] be amended.[6]

89. On 27 February[7] and 15 May[8] respectively the Economic and Social Committee and Parliament issued their opinions on the proposal[9] to amend Council Directive 76/308/EEC on mutual assistance for the recovery of claims in respect of import duties and VAT.[10] In the light of their comments the Commission amended its proposal on 19 July.[11]

90. In November, the Council agreed to a proposal for a Regulation on administrative cooperation in the field of indirect taxation.[12]

91. Following adoption by the Council of Regulation (EEC) No 1911/91 on the application of Community law to the Canary Islands,[13] on 14 November the Commission

---

[1] Twenty-fourth General Report, point 69.
[2] OJ L 250, 7.9.1991; Bull. EC 7/8-1991, point 1.2.14.
[3] Point 846 of this Report.
[4] Point 823 of this Report.
[5] OJ L 357, 20.12.1990; Twenty-fourth General Report, point 167.
[6] Point 210 of this Report.
[7] OJ C 69, 18.3.1991; Bull. EC 1/2-1991, point 1.2.37.
[8] OJ C 158, 17.6.1991; Bull. EC 5-1991, point 1.2.18.
[9] OJ C 306, 6.12.1990; Twenty-fourth General Report, point 71.
[10] OJ L 73, 19.3.1976; Tenth General Report, point 78.
[11] Bull. EC 7/8-1991, point 1.2.32.
[12] Point 195 of this Report.
[13] Point 526 of this Report.

adopted Regulation (EEC) No 3399/91[1] amending Regulation (EEC) No 137/79[2] on the institution of a special method of administrative cooperation for applying intra-Community treatment to the fishery catches of vessels of Member States, and a Regulation[3] amending Regulation (EEC) No 408/86[4] on the free movement of goods between the Community, Spain and Portugal during the transitional period.

Training: the Matthaeus programme

92.   On 20 June the Council adopted Decision 91/341/EEC[5] on a programme of Community action on the subject of the vocational training of customs officials (Matthaeus programme), the aim of which is to prepare officials for the implications of the single market with a view to ensuring that customs legislation is uniformly applied at the Community's external frontiers, this being vital for the efficient functioning of the frontier-free internal market. A series of training schemes are planned to establish close, ongoing cooperation among national customs administrations at all levels. A Decision adopted by the Commission on 13 December[3] lays down arrangements for implementing Council Decision 91/341/EEC.

Customs union: the external dimension

Harmonization of customs rules on trade with non-member countries

Common Customs Tariff, Combined Nomenclature and Taric

93.   On 1 January the system of binding tariff information provided for by Council Regulation (EEC) No 1715/90[6] came into force. A computerized system for the electronic transfer of data is in preparation.

94.   On the basis of Regulation (EEC) No 2658/87,[7] the Commission adopted the Combined Nomenclature (CN) applicable in 1992[8] and a number of regulations intended to ensure uniform application of the CN.

---

[1]   OJ L 320, 22.11.1991.
[2]   OJ L 20, 27.1.1979.
[3]   Bull. EC 12-1991.
[4]   OJ L 46, 25.2.1986; Twentieth General Report, point 187.
[5]   OJ L 187, 13.7.1991; Bull. EC 6-1991, point 1.2.14; Commission proposal: OJ C 13, 19.1.1991; Twenty-fourth General Report, point 73.
[6]   OJ L 160, 26.6.1990; Twenty-fourth General Report, point 74.
[7]   OJ L 256, 7.9.1987; Twenty-first General Report, point 157.
[8]   OJ L 259, 16.9.1991; Bull. EC 7/8-1991, point 1.2.11.

95.   The new edition of Taric, the integrated Community tariff, which was published in June, incorporates all Community measures applicable to trade with non-member countries, product by product. Taric now incorporates certain export restrictions, the nomenclature of refunds and the list of endangered species of wild flora and fauna (Cites).

96.   On the basis of Council directives, the Commission conducted negotiations for an agreement between the Community, the Government of Denmark and the local government of the Faeroes, which was initialled in June. It will ensure that uniform rates are applied by the Member States to goods originating in the Faeroes from 1 January 1992. On 19 August[1] the Commission presented a proposal for the conclusion of the Agreement and on 2 December the Council adopted a Decision to that effect.[2]

97.   On 26 June the Council adopted Regulation (EEC) No 1911/91 on the application of Community law to the Canary Islands in the customs territory of the Community.[3]

Economic tariff matters

98.   In 1991, 250 tariff quotas or ceilings, whether required under agreements or introduced unilaterally, were opened by way of derogation from the normal application of customs duties, in order to secure the Community supply situation for certain products on favourable terms. During the same period CCT duties were temporarily suspended on about 1 700 products or groups of products, mainly chemicals and electronic goods.

99.   On 3 December, as part of the Community's development policy, the Council adopted Regulations extending the application of Regulations Nos 3831/90, 3832/90, 3833/90 and 3835/90[4] applying generalized tariff preferences (GSP) in respect of products imported from the countries concerned.[5]

Concomitantly, on 16 December[5] the Council amended Regulation No 3833/90, designed to extend to the Central American countries GSP concessions already granted to the Andean Pact countries.

---

[1]   Bull. EC 7/8-1991, point 1.3.88.
[2]   OJ L 371, 31.12.1991; Bull. EC 12-1991.
[3]   Point 526 of this Report.
[4]   OJ C 370, 31.12.1990; Twenty-fourth General Report, point 795.
[5]   Point 997 of this Report.

Customs procedures with economic impact

100.   On 25 July, in order to ensure uniform application of the arrangements for the temporary importation of means of transport from 1 January 1993, the Commission adopted Regulation (EEC) No 2249/91[1] laying down provisions for the implementation of Regulation (EEC) No 1855/89.[2]

101.   Since the establishment of the single market entails adapting the procedures applying to the ATA carnet, on 31 July the Commission adopted Regulation (EEC) No 2365/91[3] laying down the conditions for use of the ATA carnet for the temporary importation of goods into the customs territory of the Community or their temporary exportation from that territory.

102.   Regulation (EEC) No 3677/86[4] was replaced by Commission Regulation (EEC) No 2228/91[5] laying down certain provisions for the implementation of inward processing relief arrangements.

In an effort to simplify the formalities to be completed in inward processing operations or processing under customs control carried out in a customs warehouse, a free zone or a free warehouse, on 13 June the Commission adopted Regulation (EEC) No 1656/91[6] laying down special provisions applicable to certain types of these operations, and on 14 November it adopted Regulation (EEC) No 3339/91 laying down rates of compensatory interest applicable to customs debts incurred in relation to compensating products or goods in the unaltered state.[7]

103.   The Commission also amended[8] Regulations (EEC) Nos 2561/90 and 2562/90[9] laying down provisions for the implementation of customs warehousing arrangements and those for free zones and free warehouses, in order to comply with the United Nations standard formats.

104.   On 21 March the Council adopted Regulation (EEC) No 720/91[10] amending Regulation (EEC) No 2763/83[11] on arrangements permitting goods to be processed

---

[1]   OJ L 204, 27.7.1991; Bull. EC 7/8-1991, point 1.2.15.
[2]   OJ L 186, 30.6.1989; Twenty-third General Report, point 164.
[3]   OJ L 216, 3.8.1991; Bull. EC 7/8-1991, point 1.2.13.
[4]   OJ L 351, 12.12.1986; Twentieth General Report, point 174.
[5]   OJ L 210, 31.7.1991.
[6]   OJ L 151, 15.6.1991; Bull. EC 6-1991, point 1.2.12.
[7]   OJ L 316, 16.11.1991.
[8]   OJ L 228, 17.8.1991; Bull. EC 7/8-1991, point 1.2.8.
[9]   OJ L 246, 10.9.1990; Twenty-fourth General Report, point 85.
[10]   OJ L 78, 26.3.1991; Bull. EC 3-1991, point 1.2.15; Commission proposal: Twenty-fourth General Report, point 84.
[11]   OJ L 272, 5.10.1983; Seventeenth General Report, point 211.

under customs control before being put into free circulation. A Commission Regulation of 18 December[1] amended the list of goods which may benefit from the arrangements, as annexed to Council Regulation (EEC) No 2763/83.[2]

Origin of goods

105. On 25 February, in order to further the harmonization of origin rules at Community level, the Council adopted Regulation (EEC) No 456/91[3] including petroleum products in the scope of Regulation (EEC) No 802/68 on the common definition of the concept of the origin of goods.[4]

106. Under Protocol 1 to the Lomé Convention, the ACP-EEC Customs Cooperation Committee adopted four decisions on derogations from the origin rules for Lesotho[5] and Fiji[6] (certain garments) while Senegal[7] and Fiji[7] were granted derogations for their canned tuna under the automatic derogations procedure.

107. In December the Joint Committees under the Agreements with the EFTA countries adopted Decision No 3/91 introducing a derogation from the origin rules of those Agreements for taco shells.

108. On 25 November the Council adopted Regulation (EEC) No 3451/91 establishing provisions for the implementation of the Joint Declaration attached to Decision No 1/89 of the EEC-Malta Association Council.[8]

General legislation

109. Following Parliament's opinion of 20 February[9] on the Commission proposal for a Regulation establishing a Community customs code,[10] the Commission sent an amended proposal to the Council.[11] The aim of the proposal is to consolidate the corpus of customs rules in a single text.

---

[1]   Bull. EC 12-1991.
[2]   OJ L 272, 5.10.1983; Seventeenth General Report, point 211.
[3]   OJ L 54, 28.2.1991; Bull. EC 1/2-1991, point 1.2.16.
[4]   OJ L 148, 28.6.1968.
[5]   OJ L 73, 20.3.1991.
[6]   OJ L 134, 29.5.1991.
[7]   OJ L 187, 13.7.1991.
[8]   OJ L 327, 29.11.1991; Bull. EC 11-1991, point 1.2.7.
[9]   OJ C 72, 18.3.1991; Bull. EC 1/2-1991, point 1.2.15.
[10] OJ C 128, 23.5.1990; Twenty-fourth General Report, point 91.
[11] OJ C 97, 13.4.1991; Bull. EC 3-1991, point 1.2.13.

110.   On 15 February the Commission adopted a report on the operation of the system set up under Regulation (EEC) No 3842/86 laying down measures for prohibition of the release of counterfeit goods for free circulation.[1]

111.   On 30 July the Commission decided to set up an Advisory Committee on Customs and Indirect Taxation[2] in order to step up the dialogue between the parties involved. It will be made up of representatives of Community-level or international professional or consumer bodies affected by customs and tax matters.

Duty relief

112.   On 7 November the Council adopted Regulation (EEC) No 3357/91[3] amending Regulation (EEC) No 918/83 setting up a Community system of reliefs from customs duty;[4] this would simplify the procedure for the release for free circulation of goods of a value not exceeding ECU 22 and reform the administrative procedure for granting relief for imports of certain scientific instruments or apparatus (known as 'Unesco' reliefs).

Monitoring the implementation of Community customs law[5]

113.   Although virtually all Community customs law is governed by regulations which, because they are directly applicable in the Member States, should not give rise to practical or legal disputes, the Commission has found that the Member States unilaterally adopt national rules which are sometimes in breach of Community legislation. It is therefore still necessary to monitor compliance with Community customs law; this involves both an examination of the implementing provisions taken by the Member States and on-the-spot checks of customs administration procedures. The checks carried out have revealed failures to comply with legislation which have led the Commission to initiate infringement proceedings in all areas of customs law, ranging from procedures with economic impact, tariff classification, customs debt and customs value to exercise of the right of representation for the drawing-up of customs declarations.

---

[1]   OJ L 357, 18.12.1986; Twentieth General Report, point 178.
[2]   OJ L 241, 30.8.1991; Bull. EC 7/8-1991, point 1.2.10.
[3]   OJ L 318, 20.11.1991; Bull. EC 11-1991, point 1.2.5; Commission proposal: Bull. EC 1/2-1991, point 1.2.13.
[4]   OJ L 105, 23.4.1983; Seventeenth General Report, point 217.
[5]   For more detailed information see the ninth annual report to Parliament on Commission monitoring of the application of Community law (to be published in 1992).

Harmonization of animal health and plant health rules

114.　On 18 December, the Commission approved the setting up of an animal health and plant health office responsible for organizing and implementing inspection, monitoring and supervisory measures. [1]

Legislation on plant health, seeds and other propagating material and feedingstuffs

115.　On 25 October and 4 November the Commission amended its three proposals for Regulations [2] on the marketing of various plants, seeds and other propagating material. [3] On 19 December the Council adopted the proposal for a Regulation on the marketing of ornamental plant propagating material and ornamental plants. [4]

116.　On 15 July the Council adopted Directive 91/414/EEC concerning the placing of plant protection products on the market, [5] legislation of primary importance for completion of the internal market in this area. Its strict requirements on human safety and protection of the environment are designed to assure consumers and public opinion of the quality of food production and to eliminate the present distortions in competition between farmers, by guaranteeing availability throughout the Community of products offering the same degree of security and effectiveness. The Council also adopted on 6 and 19 December two Directives [6] amending Directive 77/93/EEC on protective measures against the introduction into the Member States of organisms harmful to plants or plant products. [7] In addition, on 24 June it adopted Regulation (EEC) No 2092/91, designed to encourage organic farming, [8] which sets minimum production and inspection requirements for agricultural products and foodstuffs placed on the market.

117.　The Commission's plant health inspection team has commenced its work. A system of notification between Member States and technical seminars will also be instituted.

---

[1]　Bull. EC 12-1991.
[2]　OJ C 296, 15.11.1991; Bull. EC 10-1991, points 1.2.127 and 1.2.128; OJ C 307, 27.11.1991.
[3]　OJ C 46, 27.2.1990; OJ C 52, 3.3.1990; OJ C 54, 6.3.1990; Twenty-fourth General Report, point 104.
[4]　Bull. EC 12-1991; Commission proposals: OJ C 82, 3.3.1990; Twenty-fourth General Report, point 104; OJ C 307, 27.11.1991.
[5]　OJ L 230, 19.8.1991; Bull. EC 7/8-1991, point 1.2.203; Commission proposals: OJ C 212, 9.9.1976; Tenth General Report, point 317; OJ C 89, 10.4.1989; Twenty-third General Report, point 183; OJ C 93, 11.4.1991; Bull. EC 3-1991, point 1.2.113.
[6]　OJ L 363, 31.12.1991; Bull. EC 12-1991; Commission proposals: OJ C 29, 8.2.1990; Twenty-fourth General Report, point 104; OJ C 186, 18.7.1991; Bull. EC 6-1991, point 1.2.155; OJ C 205, 6.8.1991; Bull. EC 7/8-1991, point 1.2.204; Twenty-fourth General Report, point 104.
[7]　OJ L 26, 31.1.1977.
[8]　OJ L 198, 22.7.1991; Bull. EC 6-1991, point 1.2.153; Commission proposals: OJ C 4, 9.1.1990; Twenty-third General Report, point 183; OJ C 101, 18.4.1991; Bull. EC 3-1991, point 1.2.110.

Veterinary and animal husbandry legislation

118.   Completion of the internal market has demanded accelerated harmonization of legislation in 1991. The most important decisions have been on the veterinary side, covering import inspection and rules applying to internal Community trade.

119.   As far as epizootic diseases are concerned, the Commission adopted proposals on prevention of outbreaks of disease and poisoning through contamination of foodstuffs [1] and on harmonization of control measures against Newcastle disease [2] and avian influenza. [3] Within the framework of Council Decision 90/424/EEC on expenditure in the veterinary field [4] numerous decisions were taken to grant assistance for programmes to eradicate brucellosis, leucosis, tuberculosis, ovine brucellosis, rabies, Newcastle disease, bovine pleuropneumonia and horse sickness. On 19 July it adopted a report [5] on the situation as regards classical swine fever, accompanied by four proposals for stepping up action against this disease, drawn up in the light of experience acquired and the improved health status of the Community's pig herds.

The Commission also adopted provisions on trade in bovine animals and swine, [6] following the Council's decision to stop vaccination against foot-and-mouth disease. [7]

The Commission also had to take measures against a new pig disease [8] and against the risk of cholera being introduced from South America. [9]

120.   On 4 March the Council extended the scope of Decision 90/424/EEC on expenditure in the veterinary field [4] to include contagious bovine pleuropneumonia, [10] and on 26 June amended Directive 64/432/EEC [11] to update its provisions on diagnosis of bovine brucellosis and enzootic bovine leucosis. [12]

121.   A great deal of veterinary inspection was carried out with the aim of completing by the end of the year the survey in the Member States commenced in 1990 on the

---

[1]   OJ C 253, 27.9.1991; Bull. EC 9-1991, point 1.2.81.
[2]   OJ C 146, 5.6.1991; Bull. EC 4-1991, point 1.2.93.
[3]   OJ C 231, 5.9.1991; Bull. EC 7/8-1991, point 1.2.189.
[4]   OJ C 224, 18.8.1990; Twenty-fourth General Report,point 96.
[5]   OJ C 226, 31.8.1991; Bull. EC 7/8-1991, point 1.2.176.
[6]   OJ L 86, 6.4.1991; Bull. EC 3-1991, point 1.2.100.
[7]   OJ L 224, 18.8.1990; Twenty-fourth General Report, point 98.
[8]   OJ L 106, 26.4.1991; Bull. EC 4-1991, point 1.2.92; OJ L 183, 9.7.1991; Bull. EC 7/8-1991, point 1.2.179.
[9]   OJ L 73, 20.3.1991; Bull. EC 3-1991, point 1.2.99; OJ L 209, 31.7.1991; Bull. EC 7/8-1991, point 1.2.202.
[10]   OJ L 66, 13.3.1991; Bull. EC 3-1991, point 1.2.102; Commission proposal: Bull. EC 12-1990, point 1.3.220.
[11]   OJ 121, 29.7.1964.
[12]   OJ L 268, 24.9.1991; Bull. EC 6-1991, point 1.2.134; Commission proposal: OJ C 300, 29.11 1990; Bull. EC 11-1990, point 1.3.150.

application of the legislation relating to residues and banning the use of growth hormones, as well as carrying out by the end of 1992 an inspection of all approved establishments in the Community.

122. On 15 July the Council adopted a Directive on principles for the organization of veterinary checks on animals from third countries[1] and amending Directives 89/662/EEC[2] and 90/425/EEC.[3]

123. Close monitoring of the health situation called for many inspection visits and also visits to establishments in third countries approved for export of fresh meat to the Community. A list of countries from which Member States may import meat products was adopted.[4]

Findings from a number of visits to the United States led the Commission to prohibit imports of American fresh meat and, following bilateral consultations on the terms for resumption of the trade, a new list of establishments authorized to export such meat to the Community was drawn up. Consultations are continuing on the terms acceptable for an increased flow of imports.

124. Turning to public health, on 4 February[5] the Council amended Decision 90/218/EEC on administration of bovine somatotropin,[6] and later in the year adopted directives on production and marketing of fresh meat,[7] on conditions for granting temporary limited derogations from specific Community health rules on production and marketing of fresh meat,[8] and on production and marketing of live bivalve molluscs[9] and fishery products.[10]

---

[1] OJ L 268, 24.9.1991; Bull. EC 7/8-1991, point 1.2.175; Commission proposal: OJ C 89, 6.4.1991; Bull. EC 3-1991, point 1.2.98.
[2] OJ L 395, 30.12.1989.
[3] OJ L 224, 18.8.1990.
[4] OJ L 195, 18.7.1991.
[5] OJ L 37, 9.2.1991; Bull. EC 1/2-1991, point 1.2.150; Commission proposal: OJ C 2, 4.1.1991; Bull. EC 12-1990, point 1.3.221.
[6] OJ L 116, 8.5.1990; Twenty-fourth General Report, point 100.
[7] OJ L 268, 24.9.1991; Bull. EC 7/8-1991, point 1.2.193; Commission proposal: OJ C 84, 2.4.1990; Bull. EC 1/2-1990, point 1.1.100.
[8] OJ L 268, 24.9.1991; Bull. EC 7/8-1991, point 1.2.194; Commission proposal: OJ C 84, 2.4.1990; Bull. EC 1/2-1990, point 1.1.230.
[9] OJ L 268, 24.9.1991; Bull. EC 7/8-1991, point 1.2.201; Commission proposal: OJ C 84, 2.4.1990; Twenty-fourth General Report, point 100.
[10] OJ L 268, 24.9.1991; Bull. EC 7/8-1991, point 1.2.200; Commission proposal: OJ C 84, 2.4.1990; Twenty-fourth General Report, point 100.

125. The Council also adopted health rules applying to fresh poultrymeat,[1] rabbit meat,[2] aquaculture products,[3] and sheep and goats.[4]

Application of Article 115

126. In line with the approach defined in 1987,[5] the Commission continued in 1991 to apply Article 115 of the Treaty using very strict criteria. The result is a substantial fall in the number of authorizations for application of intra-Community surveillance measures, which have dropped from 1 300 in 1987 to 185 in 1991. Authorizations for protective measures fell from 112 in 1990 to 48 for 1991. The triggering threshold for such measures has risen considerably, so permitting a volume of imports into free circulation not previously attained for the product concerned. The main products affected by these measures are textiles, cars, motorcycles and electronic goods (car radios and colour televisions). In collaboration with the Member States the Commission has examined the circumstances in the industries producing certain sensitive products with a view to drawing up industrial policy measures enabling the undertakings in question to cope with the new conditions of competition resulting from completion of the single market. For bananas, the only agricultural product at present the subject of action under Article 115, Community arrangements are being drawn up that will replace the Member States' present measures and import arrangements and meet the Community's obligations under GATT and the Lomé Convention.

Checks on individuals

127. Commission proposals and Council decisions that directly affect individuals (tax-free allowances, easing of intra-Community controls) are dealt with in the second part of this Section ('A people's Europe').[6]

---

[1] OJ L 268, 24.9.1991; Bull. EC 6-1991, point 1.2.139; Commission proposal: OJ C 327, 30.12.1989; Bull. EC 10-1989, point 2.1.166.
[2] OJ L 268, 24.9.1991; Commission proposal: OJ C 327, 30.12.1989; Bull. EC 10-1989, point 2.1.162.
[3] OJ L 46, 19.2.1991; Bull. EC 1/2-1991, point 1.2.142; Commission proposal: OJ C 84, 2.4.1990; Bull. EC 1/2-1990, point 1.2.150.
[4] OJ L 46, 19.2.1991; Bull. EC 1/2-1991, points 1.2.143 and 1.2.144; Commission proposals: OJ C 48, 27.2.1989; Twenty-second General Report, point 208.
[5] Twenty-first General Report, point 196.
[6] Point 205 *et seq.* of this Report.

Removal of technical and legal frontiers

Free movement of goods

Removal of non-tariff barriers [1]

128.   The Commission stepped up its efforts[2] to remove non-tariff barriers to trade between Member States, in particular under Articles 30, 34 and 36 of the EEC Treaty, whose implementation by the Member States it monitors. In all, around 1 500 cases were examined. Faced with a growing number of complaints, the Commission made a great effort, during the infringement proceedings, to find general solutions based on the principle of mutual recognition, so as to make individual solutions more widely applicable. Similarly, it continued the practice of holding meetings with Member States at which all complaints and infringements concerning a particular Member State are examined, thus making it possible in many cases to reach pragmatic solutions consistent with Community law. Parliament endorsed the principle of such meetings in its resolution of 22 February on the seventh annual report on the monitoring of the application of Community law.[3] The Commission also persisted in its efforts to disseminate information, especially in the form of press releases on particularly significant cases. On 15 October it adopted a communication clarifying the scope of Articles 30 and 36 of the EEC Treaty as regards the names under which foodstuffs are sold,[4] since there are no exhaustive Community rules on the matter. It explained in what circumstances a recipient Member State may, in accordance with the decisions of the Court of Justice, tax an imported product in cases where the product does not display the characteristics which consumers may legitimately expect or is sold under a name different from that under which it is marketed in the Member State of manufacture.

Prevention of further barriers

129.   Directive 83/189/EEC,[5] which was amended by Directive 88/182/EEC[6] and lays down a procedure for the provision of information in the field of technical standards and regulations, continues to be a particularly valuable means of removing new technical barriers to intra-Community trade. The number of draft technical regulations notified

---

[1]   Further information is contained in the ninth annual report to Parliament on Commission monitoring of the application of Community law (1991) (to be published in 1992).
[2]   Twenty-fourth General Report, point 107.
[3]   OJ C 72, 18.3.1991; Bull. EC 1/2-1991, point 1.7.4.
[4]   OJ C 270, 15.10.1991.
[5]   OJ L 109, 26.4.1983; Seventeenth General Report, point 150.
[6]   OJ L 81, 26.3.1988; Twenty-second General Report, point 179.

pursuant to the Directive went up by 12.7%, from 386 in 1990 to 435 in 1991. Since the information procedure came into force, the Commission has received a total of 1 766 notifications. During the year, it issued in 165 cases a detailed opinion concerning the breaches of Community law to which the draft regulations might give rise. For their part, the Member States took such decisions in 127 cases.

130.   Under the agreement between the Community and the EFTA countries establishing a system for exchanging information on draft technical regulations,[1] which came into force on 1 November 1990, the Commission received 5 notifications in the last two months of 1990 and 120 in 1991. Altogether, 35 observations were addressed to the EFTA countries on behalf of the Community.

Harmonization of laws

131.   As part of the efforts to bring Member States' laws more closely into line, special attention was paid to certain sectors.

132.   As regards pharmaceuticals, the Commission adopted four measures supplementing the technical harmonization already achieved: Directives 91/356/EEC and 91/412/EEC laying down the principles and guidelines for good manufacturing practice for medicinal products for human use[2] and veterinary medicinal products[3] respectively, Directive 91/507/EEC[4] updating Council Directive 75/318/EEC on the approximation of laws relating to the testing of medicinal products[5] and a Decision approving a framework contract for cooperation with the Council of Europe on the standardization of biological substances.[6]

133.   After Parliament had delivered its opinion at first reading,[7] the Commission, on 18 July, amended[8] its proposals for Council directives on the legal status for the supply of medicinal products,[9] on their labelling for human use and on package leaflets,[9] on their wholesale distribution[9] and on their advertising.[10] On 22 July the Council reached political agreement[11] on common positions which were formally adopted on 21 Octo-

---

[1]   OJ L 291, 23.10.1990; Twenty-fourth General Report, point 108.
[2]   OJ L 193, 17.7.1991; Bull. EC 6-1991, point 1.2.22.
[3]   OJ L 228, 17.8.1991; Bull. EC 7/8-1991, point 1.2.25.
[4]   OJ L 270, 26.9.1991; Bull. EC 7/8-1991, point 1.2.24.
[5]   OJ L 147, 9.6.1975.
[6]   Bull. EC 7/8-1991, point 1.2.26.
[7]   OJ C 183, 15.7.1991; Bull. EC 6-1991, points 1.2.25 to 1.2.28.
[8]   OJ C 207, 8.8.1991; Bull. EC 7/8-1991, points 1.2.3 to 1.2.6.
[9]   OJ C 58, 8.3.1990; Twenty-fourth General Report, point 112.
[10]   OJ C 163, 4.7.1990; Twenty-fourth General Report, point 112.
[11]   Bull. EC 7/8-1991, points 1.2.3 to 1.2.6.

ber.[1] On 12 June[2] and 4 July[3] respectively Parliament and the Economic and Social Committee gave their opinions on a set of measures[4] comprising a proposal for a Regulation and three proposals for Directives on the future system for the free movement of medicinal products for human and veterinary use, including the establishment of a European Agency for the Evaluation of Medicinal Products. On 31 October the Commission amended these proposals.[5] Parliament also gave its opinion at first reading[6] on two proposals for Directives[7] widening the scope of Community pharmaceutical legislation to include homeopathic medicinal products for human use and for animal treatment, and on 5 August the Commission amended these proposals too.[8] On 19 December the Council adopted a common position on the proposal regarding homeopathic medicinal products for human use. It also authorized the Commission to negotiate an agreement with Israel on good laboratory practice.[9]

134.   With regard to foodstuffs, the Commission endeavoured to continue and intensify harmonization, either by adopting directives itself, such as Directive 91/71/EEC relating to flavourings,[10] Directive 91/72/EEC relating to the designation of flavourings in the list of ingredients on the labels of foodstuffs[10] or Directive 91/321/EEC on infant formulae and follow-on formulae,[11] or by transmitting to the Council new proposals for Directives on infant formulae and follow-on formulae intended for export to third countries[12] and on strengthening assistance and cooperation in the scientific examination of questions relating to food;[13] the Economic and Social Committee delivered its opinion on this last proposal on 30 October.[14]

The Commission also adopted two proposals on colouring matters,[15] as well as a proposal for the amendment of Directive 88/344/EEC[16] on extraction solvents.[17]

135.   On 22 April the Council adopted Directive 91/238/EEC[18] amending Directive 89/396/EEC on the indications or marks identifying the lot to which a foodstuff

---

[1]   Bull. EC 10-1991, points 1.2.12 to 1.2.15.
[2]   OJ C 183, 15.7.1991; Bull. EC 6-1991, point 1.2.23.
[3]   OJ C 269, 14.10.1991; Bull. EC 7/8-1991, point 1.2.23
[4]   OJ C 330, 31.12.1990; Twenty-fourth General Report, point 112.
[5]   OJ C 310, 30.11.1991; Bull. EC 10-1991, point 1.2.16.
[6]   OJ C 183, 15.7.1991; Bull. EC 6-1991, points 1.2.24 and 1.2.29.
[7]   OJ C 108, 1.5.1990; Twenty-fourth General Report, point 112.
[8]   OJ C 244, 19.9.1991.
[9]   Bull. EC 12-1991.
[10]   OJ L 42, 15.2.1991; Bull. EC 1/2-1991, point 1.2.27.
[11]   OJ L 175, 4.7.1991; Bull. EC 5-1991, point 1.2.12.
[12]   Bull. EC 11-1991, point 1.2.11.
[13]   OJ C 108, 23.4.1991; Bull. EC 3-1991, point 1.2.8.
[14]   OJ C 14, 20.1.1992; Bull. EC 10-1991, point 1.2.8.
[15]   OJ C 12, 18.1.1992; Bull. EC 12-1991.
[16]   OJ L 157, 24.6.1988; Twenty-second General Report, point 218; proposal for amendment: Bull 12-1991.
[17]   OJ C 11, 17.1.1992; Bull. EC 12-1991.
[18]   OJ L 107, 27.4.1991; Bull. EC 4-1991, point 1.2.6; Commission proposal: OJ C 267, 23.10.1990; Twenty-fourth General Report, point 111.

belongs[1] and abolishing the lot-marking obligation in respect of individual packs of ice-cream. On 25 July the Commission proposed[2] to extend by one year the period of application of Directive 89/396/EEC, so as to take into account the technical difficulties encountered by manufacturers when purchasing marking equipment. Parliament endorsed the proposal on 23 October.[3] The Council adopted a common position on 19 December.[4]

136.   Further to the opinions of the Economic and Social Committee[5] and Parliament,[6] the Commission amended[7] its proposal for a Directive on sweeteners for use in foodstuffs;[8] the Council agreed a common position on 7 November,[9] which it formally adopted on 19 December.[4]

137.   Technical harmonization, already well advanced as regards motor vehicles, continued. In June and July the Commission adopted a package of proposals for Directives on exhaust systems,[10] wheeled agricultural or forestry tractors,[11] the masses and dimensions of certain categories of motor vehicle,[12] speed-limitation devices,[13] the external projections on certain vehicles,[14] and type-approval of two- or three-wheel motor vehicles.[15] The Economic and Social Committee delivered its opinion on the proposal on type-approval of two- and three-wheel vehicles in October,[16] its opinion on the proposal on speed-limitation devices in November, [17] and its opinions on the proposals on exhaust systems, masses and dimensions, and external projections in December,[18] when Parliament delivered opinions on speed-limitation devices and type-approval of two- and three-wheel vehicles.[18] The Council adopted common positions on those last two proposals on 19 December.[18]

The Commission adopted a proposal for a Directive on a single Community type-approval system for vehicles.[19] This last proposal, which is based on total harmonization,

1   OJ L 186, 30.6.1989; Twenty-third General Report, point 195.
2   OJ C 219, 22.8.1991; Bull. EC 7/8-1991, point 1.2.27.
3   OJ C 305, 25.11.1991; Bull. EC 10-1991, point 1.2.11.
4   Bull. EC 12-1991.
5   OJ C 120, 6.5.1991; Bull. EC 3-1991, point 1.2.26.
6   OJ C 129, 20.5.1991; Bull. EC 4-1991, point 1.2.7.
7   OJ C 175, 6.7.1991; Bull. EC 6-1991, point 1.2.30.
8   OJ C 242, 27.9.1990; Twenty-fourth General Report, point 111.
9   Bull. EC 11-1991, point 1.2.4.
10   OJ C 193, 24.7.1991; Bull. EC 6-1991, point 1.2.19.
11   OJ C 193, 24.7.1991; Bull. EC 6-1991, point 1.2.18.
12   OJ C 230, 4.9.1991; Bull. EC 7/8-1991, point 1.2.19.
13   OJ C 229, 4.9.1991; Bull. EC 7/8-1991, point 1.2.20.
14   OJ C 230, 4.9.1991; Bull. EC 7/8-1991, point 1.2.21.
15   OJ C 110, 25.4.1991; Bull. EC 3-1991, point 1.2.7.
16   OJ C 14, 20.1.1992; Bull. EC 10-1991, point 1.2.17.
17   Bull. EC 11-1991, point 1.2.16.
18   OJ C 13, 20.1.1992; Bull. EC 12-1991.
19   OJ C 301, 21.11.1991; Bull. EC 7/8-1991, point 1.2.2.

constitutes a key element in the freedom of movement for this sector: as from 1 January 1993, it will be possible for a vehicle which has undergone the full type-approval process in one Member State to be registered throughout the Community; provision has been made for a transitional period during which manufacturers will still be able to opt for a national type-approval procedure that, provided it is completed successfully before 1 January 1996, will remain valid until 31 December 1997.

The Commission also adopted Directive 91/422/EEC[1] adapting to technical progress Council Directive 71/320/EEC on the approximation of laws relating to braking devices.[2] On 8 February it amended[3] its proposals for Directives on glazing,[4] the masses and dimensions of motor vehicles of category M1,[5] and pneumatic tyres for motor vehicles;[6] Parliament delivered a second opinion on the tyres proposal (first reading) on 13 December,[7] and the Council agreed the common positions on all three proposals on 19 December.[7] On 27 March the Council adopted Directive 91/226/EEC relating to the spray-suppression devices of certain categories of motor vehicles and their trailers.[8]

On 6 and 10 December the Commission adopted two Directives[9] adapting Council Directive 74/297/EEC on the interior fittings of motor vehicles[10] and Council Directive 76/756/EEC on lighting and light-signalling devices on motor vehicles and their trailers.[11]

138.   As regards chemicals, considerable progress was made on harmonization. The Council adopted Directives relating to restrictions on the marketing and use of polychlorinated biphenyls,[12] cadmium[13] and certain substitutes for polychlorinated biphenyls (PCBs).[14] For its part, the Commission adopted three Directives adapting to technical progress Council Directive 88/379/EEC on the classification, packaging and labelling of

---

[1]   OJ L 233, 22.8.1991; Bull. EC 7/8-1991, point 1.2.22.
[2]   OJ L 202, 6.9.1971.
[3]   OJ C 95, 12.4.1990; Twenty-fourth General Report, point 110.
[4]   OJ C 51, 27.2.1991; Bull. EC 1/2-1991, point 1.2.24.
[5]   OJ C 51, 27.2.1991; Bull. EC 1/2-1991, point 1.2.25.
[6]   OJ C 51, 27.2.1991; Bull. EC 1/2-1991, point 1.2.26.
[7]   Bull. EC 12-1991.
[8]   OJ L 103, 23.4.1991; Bull. EC 3-1991, point 1.2.23; Commission proposal: OJ C 263, 16.10.1989; Twenty-third General Report, point 194; OJ C 203, 14.8.1990; Twenty-fourth General Report, point 110.
[9]   OJ L 366, 31.12.1991; Bull. EC 12-1991.
[10] OJ L 165, 20.6.1974; Eighth General Report, point 112.
[11] OJ L 262, 27.9.1976; Tenth General Report, point 121.
[12] OJ L 85, 9.4.1991; Bull. EC 3-1991, point 1.2.25; Commission proposal: OJ C 117, 4.5.1988; Twenty-second General Report, point 219.
[13] OJ L 186, 12.7.1991; Bull. EC 6-1991, point 1.2.20; Commission proposals: OJ C 8, 13.1.1990; Twenty-fourth General Report, point 113.
[14] OJ L 186, 12.7.1991; Bull. EC 6-1991, point 1.2.21; Commission proposals: OJ C 24, 1.2.1990; Twenty-third General Report, point 196; Twenty-fourth General Report, point 113.

dangerous substances,[1] Council Directive 90/35/EEC on child-resistant fastenings,[2] and Council Directive 76/769/EEC as regards asbestos.[3]

139.   On 9 September, the Commission adopted a proposal for a Directive[4] providing for a legislative consolidation of Directive 76/769/EEC on the marketing and use of certain dangerous substances and preparations,[5] on which the Economic and Social Committee delivered its opinion on 27 November,[6] as well as a proposal amending Directive 76/769/EEC for the 12th time,[7] which the Economic and Social Committee endorsed on 29 May.[8]

140.   On 5 December the Commission adopted a proposal for a Directive on fertilizers,[4] which would consolidate Directives 76/116/EEC,[9] 80/876/EEC,[10] 87/94/EEC[11] and 77/535/EEC.[12]

Implementation of the new approach to technical harmonization and standards

Technical harmonization

141.   Under the new approach to harmonization, as defined by the Council in its Resolution of 7 May 1985,[13] the Commission approved two proposals for Directives, one concerning medical devices[14] and the other amending Council Directive 89/336/EEC on electromagnetic compatibility, in order to allow industry to adapt to the new system and to give the European Committee for Electrotechnical Standardization (Cenelec) further time in which to complete the standardization work undertaken.[15] The Economic and Social Committee delivered an opinion on the electromagnetic compatibility proposal on 25 September.[16] Parliament delivered its opinion on that proposal on 13 December, and the Council adopted a common position on 19 Decem-

---

[1]   OJ L 76, 22.3.1991; Bull. EC 3-1991, point 1.2.24.
[2]   OJ L 238, 22.7.1991; Bull. EC 7/8-1991, point 1.2.18.
[3]   OJ L 363, 31.12.1991; Bull. EC 12-1991.
[4]   Bull. EC 12-1991.
[5]   OJ L 262, 27.9.1976.
[6]   Bull. EC 11-1991, point 1.2.14.
[7]   OJ C 46, 22.2.1991; Bull. EC 1/2-1991, point 1.2.23.
[8]   OJ C 191, 22.7.1991; Bull. EC 5-1991, point 1.2.11.
[9]   OJ L 24, 30.1.1976.
[10]   OJ L 250, 23.9.1980; Fourteenth General Report, point 125.
[11]   OJ L 342, 4.12.1987; Twenty-first General Report, point 203.
[12]   OJ L 213, 22.8.1977.
[13]   OJ C 136, 4.6.1985; Nineteenth General Report, point 210.
[14]   OJ C 237, 12.9.1991; Bull. EC 7/8-1991, point 1.2.7.
[15]   OJ C 162, 21.6.1991; Bull. EC 5-1991, point 1.2.8.
[16]   OJ C 339, 31.12.1991; Bull. EC 9-1991, point 1.2.6.

ber.[1] The Commission also entrusted the European Committee for Standardization (CEN) with standardization work with a view to preparing harmonization for upholstered furniture.

142. On 21 June, the Council adopted Directive 91/368/EEC amending Directive 89/392/EEC on machinery[2] in order to extend its scope to cover mobile machinery and lifting appliances.

143. On 13 December, the Commission adopted a proposal for a Directive on appliances and protection systems for use in a potentially explosive atmosphere.[1]

144. On 17 May it adopted a communication concerning the transitional measures applicable in Germany in the context of the harmonization of technical rules for certain products.[3]

145. On 7 June it adopted a proposal for a Directive on the approximation of the laws of the Member States relating to units of measurement,[4] which aims to consolidate Directive 80/181/EEC[5] and its successive amendments; the Economic and Social Committee delivered its opinion on this proposal on 25 September.[6]

Standardization

146. On 28 January the Commission began consultations on the content of the Green Paper on the development of European standardization.[7] It has received almost 250 reactions from industry and other interested parties, standardization agencies and governments. These discussions encouraged debate and change in the European standardization bodies, CEN (European Committee for Standardization), Cenelec (European Committee for Electrotechnical Standardization) and ETSI (European Telecommunications Standards Institute), which took active steps to improve efficiency. The European Community also held high-level discussions with international bodies such as ISO (International Organization for Standardization) and IEC (International Electrotechnical Commission) and with the United States Government.

---

[1] Bull. EC 12-1991.
[2] OJ L 198, 22.7.1991; Bull. EC 6-1991, point 1.2.17; original Directive: OJ L 183, 29.6.1989; Twenty-fourth General Report, point 199; Commission proposals: OJ C 37, 17.2.1990; Twenty-third General Report, point 199; OJ C 268, 24.10.1990; Twenty-fourth General Report, point 114; Bull. EC 5-1991, point 1.2.9.
[3] Bull. EC 5-1991, point 1.2.6.
[4] OJ C 185, 17.7.1991; Bull. EC 6-1991, point 1.2.16.
[5] OJ L 39, 15.2.1980.
[6] OJ C 339, 31.12.1991; Bull. EC 9-1991, point 1.2.7.
[7] OJ C 20, 28.1.1991; Twenty-fourth General Report, point 117.

147. In a resolution of 11 July,[1] Parliament expressed its support for the approach developed in the Green Paper on standardization and for any measure likely to promote an increase in the efficiency of procedures, coordination and structures, the participation of industry, information for interested parties and the development of relations with third countries. The Economic and Social Committee also approved the Green Paper, underlining, in its opinion of 20 March, the importance of participation by trade unions and consumer organizations.[2]

148. On 13 December, following up the points set out in its Green Paper, the Commission presented a communication on standardization in the European economy.[3]

Recognition of tests and certificates

149. Further to its communication of 24 July 1989 concerning a global approach to certification and testing,[4] the Commission adopted on 17 May a proposal for a Regulation concerning the affixing and use of the CE mark of conformity on industrial products,[5] on which the Economic and Social Committee delivered its opinion on 30 October;[6] the two main aims of the proposal are to harmonize the rules on marking laid down in the 10 Directives[7] which have been adopted under the new approach and will, therefore, be amended and to fix harmonized bases for future Community legislation in the technical field. The Commission is thus proposing to give material effect to the presumption of conformity with the Community laws laying down conformity assessment procedures and enacted under the new approach. The CE mark will have to be affixed by the manufacturer or his authorized agent established in the Community or, failing this, by the person responsible for placing the product on the Community market.

150. On 10 October Parliament delivered its second opinion[8] at first reading on certain budgetary aspects of the proposal for a Council Regulation on the Community trade mark.[9]

---

1   OJ C 240, 16.9.1991; Bull. EC 7/8-1991, point 1.2.17.
2   OJ C 120, 6.5.1991; Bull. EC 3-1991, point 1.2.22.
3   Bull. EC 12-1991.
4   OJ C 267, 19.10.1989; Twenty-third General Report, point 201.
5   OJ C 160, 20.6.1991; Bull. EC 5-1991, point 1.2.7.
6   OJ C 14, 20.1.1992; Bull. EC 10-1991, point 1.2.9.
7   OJ L 220, 8.8.1987; Twenty-first General Report, point 205; OJ L 187, 16.7.1988; Twenty-second General Report, point 603; OJ L 40, 11.2.1989; Twenty-second General Report, point 221; OJ L 139, 23.5.1989; Twenty-third General Report, point 199; OJ L 183, 29.6.1989; Twenty-third General Report, point 199; OJ L 399, 30.12.1989; Twenty-third General Report, point 199; OJ L 189, 20.7.1990; Twenty-fourth General Report, point 114; OJ L 196, 26.7.1990; Twenty-fourth General Report, point 114; OJ L 128, 23.5.1991; Bull. EC 4-1991, point 1.2.49.
8   OJ C 280, 28.10.1991; Bull. EC 10-1991, point 1.2.8.
9   OJ C 351, 31.12.1980.

151.   On 19 December the Council adopted a Decision deferring from 28 December 1991 to 31 December 1992 the date by which the laws of the Member States must comply with Council Directive 89/104/EEC to approximate the laws of the Member States relating to trade marks.[1]

Government procurement

152.   In the field of government procurement, the Commission completed the legislative programme set out in the White Paper on the internal market[2] by adopting on 25 September a proposal for a Directive relating to the coordination of procedures for the award of public service contracts in the water, energy, transport and telecommunications sectors[3] (the 'excluded' sectors) and amending accordingly Directive 90/531/EEC[4] on public works and supply contracts in those sectors, so as to include service contracts.

153.   Work progressed as planned in the other areas of government procurement. On 16 September the Council adopted a common position[5] on the proposal for a Directive relating to remedies in the 'excluded' sectors,[6] which had been amended by the Commission in June[7] following the opinion delivered by Parliament in March (first reading).[8]

154.   On 30 August the Commission amended[9] its proposal for a Directive relating to the award of public service contracts[10] to take account of the opinions delivered in May by the Economic and Social Committee[11] and Parliament.[12] The amended proposal was agreed by the Council on 19 December.[13]

155.   On 24 October the Commission adopted Recommendation 91/561/EEC on the standardization of notices of public contracts, which seeks to structure the information to be supplied under the various headings.[14]

[1]   Decision: OJ L 6, 11.11.1992; Bull. EC 12-1991; Commission proposal: Bull. EC 11-1991, point 1.2.17.
[2]   Nineteenth General Report, points 161 to 166.
[3]   OJ C 337, 31.12.1991; Bull. EC 9-1991, point 1.2.2.
[4]   OJ L 297, 29.10.1990; Twenty-fourth General Report, point 121.
[5]   Bull. EC 9-1991, point 1.2.9.
[6]   OJ C 216, 31.8.1990; Twenty-fourth General Report, point 122.
[7]   OJ C 179, 10.7.1991; Bull. EC 6-1991, point 1.2.31.
[8]   OJ C 106, 22.4.1991; Bull. EC 3-1991, point 1.2.27.
[9]   OJ C 250, 15.9.1991; Bull. EC 7/8-1991, point 1.2.29.
[10]   OJ C 23, 31.1.1991; Twenty-fourth General Report, point 123.
[11]   OJ C 191, 22.7.1991; Bull. EC 5-1991, point 1.2.13.
[12]   OJ C 158, 17.6.1991; Bull. EC 5-1991, point 1.2.13.
[13]   Bull. EC 12-1991.
[14]   OJ L 305, 6.11.1991; Bull. EC 10-1991, point 1.2.18.

156.   The Commission also stepped up its monitoring of the application of the rules on public contracts and continued its examination of the texts transposing the Directives on supplies (Directive 88/295/EEC),[1] works (Directive 89/440/EEC)[2] and remedies (Directive 89/665/EEC).[3] Moreover, it intensified its training measures and information campaigns for the parties involved in this sector.[4]

157.   At international level, the Commission also took part in GATT talks on the extension of the GATT agreement on public procurement to works and service contracts and to regional and local entities and entities operating in the 'excluded' sectors. The existing Community rules on public procurement were incorporated into the Agreement on the European Economic Area.[5]

Free movement of workers and of members of the professions

158.   The details of the Commission proposals and Council decisions directly affecting individuals (removal of restrictions, mutual recognition of diplomas, access to economic activity, special rights of individuals and passport) are given in the second part of this section, 'A people's Europe'.

Common market in services

Financial services

Banks and other financial institutions

159.   On 10 June the Council adopted Directive 91/308/EEC on prevention of the use of the financial system for the purpose of money laundering;[6] this was in line with the hopes expressed by the European Council at its meetings in Dublin[7] and Rome.[8] The Directive was accompanied by a statement committing Member States to enact, by 31 December 1992 at the latest, criminal legislation determining the penalties to be applied for infringement of the provisions of the Directive.

---

[1]   OJ L 127, 20.5.1988; Twenty-second General Report, point 178.
[2]   OJ L 210, 21.7.1989; Twenty-third General Report, point 203.
[3]   OJ L 395, 30.12.1989; Twenty-third General Report, point 203.
[4]   See ninth annual report to Parliament on Commission monitoring of the application of Community law (1991) (to be published in 1992).
[5]   Point 846 of this Report.
[6]   OJ L 166, 28.6.1991; Bull. EC 6-1991, point 1.2.6; Commission proposal: OJ C 106, 28.4.1990; Twenty-fourth General Report, point 128; OJ C 324, 24.12.1990; Twenty-fourth General Report, point 128; Bull. EC 5-1991, point 1.2.15.
[7]   Bull. EC 6-1990, point I.1.
[8]   Bull. EC 12-1990, point I.1.

160. Continuing the action undertaken on the basis of the second banking Directive (89/646/EEC),[1] the Commission adopted on 20 March a proposal for a Directive on monitoring and controlling large exposures of credit institutions,[2] which contains stricter standards than those set out in the 1986 recommendation on large exposures[3] and is designed to reinforce the solidity and stability of the Community banking system. A transitional provision authorizes the competent authorities to grant the institutions concerned a maximum period of five years in which to adjust to the limits laid down. The Economic and Social Committee delivered an opinion on this proposal on 25 September.[4]

161. The Commission adopted on 6 June a proposal for a Directive[5] amending Directive 89/299/EEC on the own funds of credit institutions[6] with a view to terminating the provisional arrangement under which the Council alone was empowered to make technical adjustments and permitting Danish mortgage credit institutions transformed into public limited companies to continue, for a transitional period, to count the joint and several commitments of their borrowers as own funds. The Economic and Social Committee and Parliament delivered their opinions on 25 September[7] and 11 December[8] respectively; the Council adopted a common position on 16 December.[8] In view of the special nature of the Fund for General Banking Risks (FGBR), the Council on 3 December adopted Directive 91/633/EEC,[9] which definitively included it in the items constituting original own funds defined in Directive 89/299/EEC.[6]

162. On 25 January the Commission amended[10] its proposal for a Regulation on guarantees issued by credit institutions and insurance companies.[11]

163. On 16 December the Council adopted a common position on the Directive[12] relating to the supervision of credit institutions on a consolidated basis and replacing Directive 83/350/EEC,[13] on which Parliament had delivered an opinion (first reading)

---

[1] OJ L 386, 30.12.1989; Twenty-third General Report, point 210.
[2] OJ C 123, 9.5.1991; Bull. EC 3-1991, point 1.2.6.
[3] OJ L 33, 4.2.1987; Twentieth General Report, point 224.
[4] OJ C 339, 31.12.1991; Bull. EC 9-1991, point 1.2.11.
[5] OJ C 172, 3.7.1991; Bull. EC 6-1991, point 1.2.33.
[6] OJ L 124, 5.5.1989; Twenty-third General Report, point 211.
[7] OJ C 339, 31.12.1991; Bull. EC 9-1991, point 1.2.12.
[8] OJ C 13, 20.1.1992; Bull. EC 12-1991.
[9] OJ L 339, 11.12.1991; Bull. EC 12-1991; Commission proposal: OJ C 239, 14.9.1991; Bull. EC 7/8-1991, point 1.2.31.
[10] OJ C 53, 28.2.1989; Bull. EC 1/2-1991, point 1.2.30.
[11] OJ C 51, 28.1.1991; Twenty-third General Report, point 213.
[12] Bull. EC 12-1991; Commission proposals: OJ C 315, 14.2.1990; Twenty-fourth General Report, point 127; OJ C 332, 21.12.1991; Bull. EC 12-1991.
[13] OJ L 386, 30.12.1989; Twenty-third General Report, point 211.

on 20 November,[1] with the Economic and Social Committee having delivered its opinion on 27 February.[2]

164.   On 5 July the Banking Advisory Committee elected as its chairman Jean-Louis Butsch, Director-General at the Banque de France and Secretary-General of the Commission Bancaire in France.

Payment systems

165.   Following the adoption on 26 September 1990 of the discussion paper 'Making payments in the internal market',[3] the Commission received the reactions of interested parties, including those of the Economic and Social Committee.[4] It also defined the next stages of the programme it had embarked on to facilitate, speed up and reduce the cost of money transfers in the Community and decided to set up two working parties to assist it in its work. The first consists of representatives of banks and central banks. The second, the purpose of which is to provide a link between financial institutions and users, comprises representatives of small and medium-sized businesses, the distributive trades and consumers. Both working parties met several times in the course of the year.

Insurance

166.   On 22 February the Commission adopted a report concerning the operations referred to in Directive 79/267/EEC and undertaken by composite and specialized companies.[5] In the report, which covers the last 10 years, it suggests, among other things, that the current restrictions on composite companies regarding freedom of establishment and freedom to provide services should be abolished.

167.   On 25 February the Commission put forward a proposal for a third Council Directive[6] on the coordination of laws, regulations and administrative provisions relating to the taking-up and pursuit of the business of direct life assurance and amending accordingly Directives 79/267/EEC[7] and 90/619/EEC.[8] The aim of the proposal is to complete the internal market in this sector and to apply the principle of mutual

---

[1]   OJ C 326, 16.12.1991; Bull. EC 11-1991, point 1.2.20.
[2]   OJ C 102, 18.4.1991; Bull. EC 1/2-1991, point 1.2.32.
[3]   Twenty-fourth General Report, point 129.
[4]   OJ C 120, 6.5.1991; Bull. EC 3-1991, point 1.2.29.
[5]   Bull. EC 1/2-1991, point 1.2.33.
[6]   OJ C 99, 16.4.1991; Bull. EC 1/2-1991, point 1.2.6.
[7]   OJ L 63, 13.3.1979.
[8]   OJ L 330, 29.11.1990; Twenty-fourth General Report, point 133.

recognition of authorizations and prudential systems by the Member States; the Economic and Social Committee delivered its opinion on 30 October.[1]

168.   On 30 May the Commission adopted Decision 91/323/EEC[2] relating to the application of Council Directive 72/166/EEC on the approximation of the laws of the Member States relating to insurance against civil liability in respect of the use of motor vehicles and to the enforcement of the obligation to insure against such liability.[3] This Decision, to which is annexed the Multilateral Guarantee Agreement between insurers' bureaux signed in Madrid on 15 March, requires Member States to refrain from making any checks on insurance against civil liability in respect of vehicles which are normally based in a Member State or in certain third countries.

169.   On 20 June the Council adopted Decision 91/370/EEC on the conclusion of the Agreement between the Community and the Swiss Confederation concerning direct insurance other than life assurance.[4] This Decision was supplemented on the same date by Directive 91/371/EEC on the implementation of that Agreement and by Regulation (EEC) No 2155/91 laying down particular provisions for the application of Articles 37, 39 and 40 of the Agreement. The exchange of instruments of ratification may take place only when the Commission has established that Directive 91/371/EEC has been implemented by the Member States.

170.   On 19 December the Council adopted a Directive setting up an Insurance Committee.[5]

171.   On 19 December it also adopted a Directive on the annual accounts and consolidated accounts of insurance companies.[6]

172.   On the same day, with a view to adopting a common position, the Council agreed[7] on the proposal for a third Council Directive on the coordination of laws, regulations and administrative provisions relating to direct insurance other than life assurance and amending Directives 73/239/EEC[8] and 88/357/EEC.[9] The common position takes account of the Economic and Social Committee's opinion[10] of 28 February.

---

[1]   OJ C 14, 20.1.1992; Bull. EC 10-1991, point 1.2.20.
[2]   OJ L 177, 5.7.1991; Bull. EC 5-1991, point 1.2.14.
[3]   OJ L 103, 2.5.1972; Directive as last amended by Council Directive 90/232/EEC of 14.5.1990: OJ L 129, 19.5.1990; Twenty-fourth General Report, point 134.
[4]   OJ L 205, 27.7.1991; Bull. EC 6-1991, point 1.2.34; Commission proposal: OJ C 53, 5.3.1990; Twenty-third General Report, point 216.
[5]   OJ L 374, 31.12.1991; Bull. EC 12-1991; Commission proposal: OJ C 230, 15.9.1990; Twenty-fourth General Report, point 136.
[6]   Bull. EC 12-1991; Commission proposal: Twentieth General Report, point 233.
[7]   OJ L 374, 31.12.1991; Bull. EC 12-1991.
[8]   OJ L 228, 16.8.1973.
[9]   OJ L 172, 4.7.1988; Twenty-second General Report, point 238.
[10] OJ C 99, 16.4.1991; Bull. EC 1/2-1991, point 1.2.36.

173.   On 16 October the Commission adopted a proposal for a Council Directive relating to the freedom of management and investment of funds held by institutions for retirement provision. The proposal is intended to facilitate the free movement of capital and freedom to provide services in connection with the financial management of these institutions. [1]

174.   On 18 December the Commission adopted a Recommendation concerning insurance brokers in the internal market. [2]

Stock exchanges and transferable securities

175.   On 30 January and 20 November the Economic and Social Committee [3] and Parliament (first reading) [4] gave their opinions on the proposal for a Directive on the capital adequacy of investment firms. [5]

176.   On 23 September Sir Leon Brittan and Mr Richard C. Breeden, Chairman of the US Securities and Exchange Commission, signed a joint statement on cooperation on securities. [6]

Creation of a financial area

Liberalization of capital movements and removal of exchange controls

177.   Following the complete liberalization of capital movements in eight Member States from 1 July 1990, [7] progress this year concerned the four Member States (Ireland, Greece, Spain and Portugal) authorized under Directive 88/361/EEC to maintain certain restrictions temporarily in force. [8]

An important advance in this regard was the removal by Greece as from 6 May of all the restrictions on investment in real estate and operations in securities covered by a derogation [9] under Decision 85/594/EEC authorizing certain protective measures. [10]

---

[1]   OJ C 312, 3.12.1991; Bull. EC 10-1991, point 1.2.4.
[2]   Bull. EC 12-1991.
[3]   OJ C 69, 18.3.1991; Bull. EC 1/2-1991, point 1.2.31.
[4]   OJ C 326, 16.12.1991; Bull. EC 11-1991, point 1.2.19.
[5]   OJ C 152, 21.6.1990; Twenty-fourth General Report, point 138.
[6]   Bull. EC 9-1991, point 1.3.32.
[7]   Twenty-fourth General Report, point 140.
[8]   OJ L 178, 8.7.1988; Twenty-second General Report, point 180.
[9]   OJ L 357, 20.12.1990; Bull. EC 12-1990, point 1.3.2.
[10]   OJ L 393, 31.12.1985; Nineteenth General Report, point 148.

With the repeal of this derogation,[1] the provisions of Directive 88/361/EEC now apply to all capital movements. The restrictions imposed in Ireland, Spain and Portugal were also further relaxed. It is noteworthy that the measures taken to speed up the process of removing restrictions on capital movements did not give rise to any major disturbances in the foreign exchange markets or to pronounced strains within the EMS.

178. Following the positive developments with regard to exchange controls, the Commission concentrated on identifying indirect obstacles to capital movements, which impede the effective financial integration of the Community. Such obstacles may take the form of tax incentives to promote the use of domestic financial instruments, prior notification requirements or restrictions on the investment policy of institutional investors. A number of such barriers have been identified by the Commission, which has set in train measures to eliminate them.

Balance-of-payments support mechanism

179. Following the request from Greece for financial assistance to support its balance of payments and its economic programme of adjustments and reforms, the Council, by a decision of 4 March[2] under Regulation (EEC) No 1969/88,[3] granted a loan of ECU 2.2 billion in three instalments.

A propitious legal and tax environment for businesses

Company law

180. On 6 May the Commission amended its proposal for a Council Regulation on the Statute for a European Company[4] to take account of the views expressed by Parliament[5] and the Economic and Social Committee.[6] The amendments clarify or improve a number of points in the proposal.[7] On the same date the Commission also amended its proposal for a Directive complementing the Statute for a European Company with regard to the involvement of employees[4] to take account of the views of Parliament[8] and the

---

[1] OJ L 143, 7.6.1991; Bull. EC 6-1991, point 1.2.2.
[2] Point 1271 of this Report.
[3] OJ L 178, 8.7.1988; Twenty-second General Report, point 256.
[4] OJ C 263, 16.10.1989; Twenty-third General Report, point 232.
[5] OJ C 48, 25.2.1991; Bull. EC 1/2-1991, point 1.2.69.
[6] OJ C 124, 21.5.1990; Twenty-fourth General Report, point 145.
[7] OJ C 176, 8.7.1991; Bull. EC 5-1991, point 1.2.46.
[8] OJ C 48, 25.2.1991; Bull. EC 1/2-1991, point 1.2.70.

Economic and Social Committee. [1] The amendments related in particular to the procedures for adopting the model of participation, for appointing candidates to the supervisory board and for electing the representatives of the employees within the European Company. [2]

181. On 28 February the Economic and Social Committee delivered an additional opinion[3] on the proposal for a 13th Directive on company law, concerning takeover and other general bids. [4]

Following the opinions delivered by the Economic and Social Committee on 3 July[5] and by Parliament (first reading) on 10 July,[6] the Commission adopted on 20 November a third amendment[7] to the proposal for a fifth Council Directive based on Article 54 of the EEC Treaty concerning the structure of public limited companies and the powers and obligations of their organs. [8] This third version, which forms part of the package of measures for removing obstacles to takeover bids, was presented by the Commission[9] along with a proposal for an amendment[10] to Council Directive 77/91/EEC on the formation of public limited companies and the maintenance and alteration of their capital. [11] In view of the opinions on the proposed amendment delivered by the Economic and Social Committee on 3 July[12] and by Parliament (first reading) on 10 July,[13] the Commission amended its original proposal on 20 October. [14]

Economic and commercial law

182. Further progress was made towards concluding a convention on insolvency procedures based on the principles of limited universality and plurality, with a view to securing mutual recognition of judicial decisions and establishing certain rules on conflict and uniform laws.

---

[1] OJ C 124, 21.5.1990; Twenty-fourth General Report, point 145.
[2] OJ C 138, 29.5.1991; Bull. EC 5-1991, point 1.2.47.
[3] OJ C 69, 18.3.1991; Bull. EC 1/2-1991, point 1.2.71.
[4] OJ C 64, 14.3.1989; Twenty-second General Report, point 261; Supplement 3/89 — Bull. EC.
[5] OJ C 269, 14.10.1991; Bull. EC 7/8-1991, point 1.2.78.
[6] OJ C 240, 16.9.1991; Bull. EC 7/8-1991, point 1.2.78.
[7] OJ C 321, 12.12.1991; Bull. EC 11-1991, point 1.2.36.
[8] OJ C 131, 13.12.1972; Supplement 10/72 — Bull. EC.
[9] OJ C 7, 11.1.1991; Twenty-fourth General Report, point 144.
[10] OJ C 8, 12.1.1991; Twenty-fourth General Report, point 144.
[11] OJ L 26, 31.1.1977; Tenth General Report, point 139.
[12] OJ C 269, 14.10.1991; Bull. EC 7/8-1991, point 1.2.77.
[13] OJ C 240, 16.9.1991; Bull. EC 7/8-1991, point 1.2.77.
[14] OJ C 317, 7.12.1991.

Intellectual and industrial property

Industrial design

183.   A consultative document entitled 'Green paper on the legal protection of industrial design' was published in July. It is intended as a basis for wide-ranging consultations
with interested parties in preparation for the drafting of Community legislation.

Pharmaceutical patents

184.   The proposal for a Council Regulation concerning the creation of a supplementary
protection certificate for medicinal products[1] was endorsed by the Economic and Social
Committee on 30 January.[2] The Council adopted its common position on 19 December.[3]

Copyright and neighbouring rights

185.   In conclusions adopted on 7 June, the Ministers responsible for cultural affairs,
meeting within the Council, expressed their support for the Commission's overall
approach to the harmonization of copyright and neighbouring rights and for its determination to seek a high level of protection for authors, artists and producers.[4]

186.   On 17 July the Commission approved a proposal for a Directive on the coordination of certain rules concerning copyright and neighbouring rights applicable to
satellite broadcasting and cable retransmission;[5] the aim of the proposal is essentially
to promote the establishment of a single European broadcasting area by laying down
common rules on copyright.

187.   On 14 May the Council adopted the Directive on the legal protection of computer
programs.[6]

---

[1]   OJ C 114, 8.5.1990; Twenty-fourth General Report, point 151.
[2]   OJ C 69, 18.3.1991; Bull. EC 1/2-1991, point 1.2.72.
[3]   Bull. EC 12-1991.
[4]   Bull. EC 6-1991, point 1.2.62.
[5]   OJ C 250, 1.10.1991; Bull. EC 7/8-1991, point 1.2.76.
[6]   OJ L 122, 17.5.1991; Bull. EC 5-1991, point 1.2.45; Commission proposals: OJ C 91, 12.4.1989;
      Twenty-second General Report, point 332; OJ C 320, 20.12.1990; Twenty-fourth General Report,
      point 149.

188.   On 3 July the Economic and Social Committee delivered an opinion[1] on the proposal for a Directive on rental right, lending right, and on certain rights related to copyright[2] and an opinion[3] on the proposal for a Council Decision concerning the accession of the Member States to the Berne Convention for the Protection of Literary and Artistic Works and to the International Convention for the Protection of Performers, Producers of Phonograms and Broadcasting Organizations (Rome Convention).[2] On 20 November Parliament endorsed the proposal relating to the Berne and Rome Conventions.[4]

189.   On 23 September the Council adopted a decision on the Community's participation in preparatory work and in a future diplomatic conference on the settlement of intellectual property disputes between States[5] and a decision on Community participation in the Committee of Government Experts responsible for examining the possibility of a protocol to the Berne Convention for the Protection of Literary and Artistic Works.[6]

190.   On 29 October the Council authorized the Commission to negotiate an agreement on the subject of intellectual property with the Republic of Korea.[7]

Legal protection of topographies of semiconductor products

191.   In a Decision adopted on 12 December,[8] the Commission amended its Decision 90/451/EEC in accordance with Council Decision 90/511/EEC[9] determining the countries to the companies or other legal persons of which legal protection of topographies of semiconductor products is extended; the amendment adds Finland to the list.

---

[1]   OJ C 269, 14.10.1991; Bull. EC 7/8-1991, point 1.2.80.
[2]   OJ C 53, 28.2.1991; Twenty-fourth General Report, point 150.
[3]   OJ C 269, 14.10.1991; Bull. EC 7/8-1991, point 1.2.79.
[4]   OJ C 326, 16.12.1991; Bull. EC 11-1991, point 1.2.35.
[5]   Bull. EC 9-1991, point 1.2.32.
[6]   Bull. EC 9-1991, point 1.2.33.
[7]   Bull. EC 10-1991, point 1.2.38.
[8]   OJ L 9, 15.1.1992; Bull. EC 12-1991.
[9]   OJ L 285, 17.10.1990; Twenty-fourth General Report, point 148.

Company taxation

192. As a follow-up to the communication of 18 April 1990,[1] a high-level committee was set up to consider company taxation after completion of the single market; it held its inaugural meeting in Brussels on 21 January.[2]

The committee's objective is to present, within one year, a report on the impact of taxation on company decision-making and on the risks of distortion of competition or of relocation which may result from the coexistence of different tax policies in a single market.

193. On 20 March the Economic and Social Committee delivered its opinion[3] on the proposal for a Directive on a common system of taxation applicable to interest and royalty payments made between parent companies and subsidiaries in different Member States,[4] as well as an opinion[5] on the proposal for a Council Directive concerning arrangements for the taking into account by enterprises of the losses of their permanent establishments and subsidiaries situated in other Member States.[4]

Removal of tax frontiers

Indirect taxation

Value-added tax (VAT)

194. Following up the conclusions adopted on 18 March,[6] the Council on 24 June arrived at a comprehensive agreement on VAT rates applicable within the Community from 1 January 1993.[7] The agreement provides for a standard VAT rate not lower than 15% and for the possibility of applying one or two reduced rates not lower than 5% and retaining for a transitional period existing extra-low rates and zero-rating.

---

[1] Twenty-fourth General Report, point 154.
[2] Bull. EC 1/2-1991, point 1.2.73.
[3] OJ C 120, 6.5.1991; Bull. EC 3-1991, point 1.2.53.
[4] OJ C 53, 28.2.1991; Twenty-fourth General Report, point 154.
[5] OJ C 120, 6.5.1991; Bull. EC 3-1991, point 1.2.54.
[6] Bull. EC 3-1991, point 1.2.4.
[7] Bull. EC 6-1991, point 1.2.5.

195.   On 16 December the Council adopted a Directive[1] supplementing the common system of VAT and amending Directive 77/388/EEC[2] in preparation for the common system of VAT to be applied in the Community as from 1 January 1993. Following Parliament's first reading,[3] the Commission amended on 7 May its amended proposal[4] for a Regulation concerning administrative cooperation in the field of indirect taxation.[5] On 11 November the Council informally approved the administrative cooperation proposal.[6] The adoption of the Directive supplementing the common system of VAT means that VAT controls at internal Community frontiers will disappear on 1 January 1993, with a transitional mechanism to apply in principle until 31 December 1996. The new scheme dispenses with customs procedures and encourages the free movement of individuals by removing the ceilings on travellers' allowances. Likewise on 11 November the Council agreed to authorize the continuation of duty-free sales, on certain conditions, until 30 June 1999.[6] The agreement reached on administrative cooperation establishes a framework for the controls which Member States will need to apply in order to ensure that the transitional VAT arrangements function properly. The key component of the new scheme is the regular exchange of information between Member States' administrations, with a computerized network allowing fast and efficient transmission of data.

196.   Parliament delivered on 12 June an opinion[7] on the proposal for a Council Directive on the approximation of VAT rates under the common system[8] and on 19 April an opinion (first reading)[9] on the proposal for a Council Directive determining the scope of Article 14(1)(d) of Directive 77/388/EEC as regards exemption from value-added tax on the final importation of certain goods.[10] The Economic and Social Committee gave its opinion on this proposal on 24 April.[11]

197.   On 14 March the Commission adopted a proposal for a Council Decision authorizing the Federal Republic of Germany to exempt from VAT the supply of services in respect of the management of credit and credit guarantees by a person or a body other

---

[1]   Bull. EC 12-1991; Commission proposal: OJ C 252, 22.9.1987; OJ C 237, 12.9.1990; Twenty-fourth General Report, point 156; OJ C 131, 22.5.1991; Bull. EC 5-1991, point 1.2.16.
[2]   OJ L 145, 13.6.1977; Eleventh General Report, point 219.
[3]   OJ C 324, 24.12.1990; Twenty-fourth General Report, point 156.
[4]   OJ C 131, 22.5.1991; Bull. EC 5-1991, point 1.2.17.
[5]   OJ C 187, 27.7.1990; Twenty-fourth General Report, point 156.
[6]   Bull. EC 11-1991, point 1.2.1.
[7]   OJ C 183, 15.7.1991; Bull. EC 6-1991, point 1.2.36.
[8]   OJ C 250, 18.9.1987; Twenty-first General Report, point 153.
[9]   OJ C 129, 20.5.1991; Bull. EC 4-1991, point 1.2.11.
[10]   OJ C 23, 31.1.1991; Twenty-fourth General Report, point 158.
[11]   OJ C 159, 17.6.1991; Bull. EC 4-1991, point 1.2.11.

than the one which granted the credits[1] and, as a result, derogating from Article 2(1) of Council Directive 77/388/EEC.[2]

198.   In response to the need for administrative cooperation as spelt out in the Commission proposal and on the basis of experience with the Matthaeus programme, a pilot project involving the exchange of national VAT officials, known as Interfisc, was launched in October.

Excise duties and other indirect taxes

199.   As requested by the European Council at its meeting in Rome last December, the Commission adopted on 19 February a proposal for a Directive concerning harmonization in the road transport sector and fixing certain rates and target rates of excise duty on mineral oils.[3] The proposal is designed mainly to supplement and amend the 1989 proposal[4] on the approximation of rates of excise duty on mineral oils, notably as regards petrol (ECU 495 per 1 000 litres of leaded petrol and ECU 445 per 1 000 litres of unleaded petrol) and diesel fuel (ECU 245 to ECU 270 per 1 000 litres). The proposal was endorsed by the Economic and Social Committee on 24 April.[5]

200.   On 30 January the Economic and Social Committee delivered its opinion[6] on the package of proposals adopted by the Commission in September 1990[7] and supplementing the first package of measures proposed in 1989.[8] The proposals concern the structures of excise duties on mineral oils, alcoholic beverages and manufactured tobacco. The Committee also gave its views on the proposal concerning the general arrangements for products subject to excise duty and on the holding and movement of such products.[9]

201.   On 12 and 13 June Parliament delivered its opinions[10] on the proposal for a Directive on the general arrangements for products subject to excise duty and on the holding and movement of such products[7] and on the proposals concerning the approximation of the rates[11] and the harmonization of the structures[7] of excise duty on mineral

---

[1]   Bull. EC 3-1991, point 1.2.30.
[2]   OJ L 145, 13.6.1977; Eleventh General Report, point 219.
[3]   OJ C 66, 14.3.1991; Bull. EC 1/2-1991, point 1.2.5.
[4]   OJ C 16, 23.1.1990; Twenty-third General Report, point 247.
[5]   OJ C 159, 17.6.91; Bull. EC 4-1991, point 1.2.14.
[6]   OJ C 69, 18.3.1991; Bull. EC 1/2-1991; points 1.2.39 to 1.2.41.
[7]   OJ C 322, 21.12.1990; Twenty-fourth General Report, point 159.
[8]   OJ C 12, 18.1.1990, OJ C 16, 23.1.1990; Twenty-third General Report, point 247.
[9]   OJ C 69, 18.3.1991; Bull. EC 1/2-1991, point 1.2.38.
[10] OJ C 183, 15.7.1991; Bull. EC 6-1991, points 1.2.37 to 1.2.39.
[11] OJ C 262, 1.10.1987; Twenty-fourth General Report, point 153.

oils. In accordance with the guidelines adopted previously,[1] the Council on 24 June reached an agreement in principle based on the Commission proposals on the fixing of a number of minimum rates for mineral oils, cigarettes and certain alcoholic beverages, with the target rates proposed by the Commission continuing to act as benchmark values.[2] On 16 December the Council likewise informally agreed to the Commission proposal on the holding and movement of products subject to excise duties.[3]

Monitoring the application of Community provisions in the field of indirect taxation

202.   The Commission continued its monitoring of the application of Community provisions. Its departments carried out within an *ad hoc* working group a new systematic examination of the conformity of measures adopted by Member States with a view to implementing tax directives, and in particular the sixth VAT Directive.[4] The smooth cooperation between Member States made it generally possible to bring to an end any infringements without having to initiate proceedings under Article 169 of the EEC Treaty.

As regards the application of Article 95 of the EEC Treaty, an important decision was taken by the Court in the matter of the excise duty on beer. The Court found that a system of flat-rate taxation on importation was contrary to the principle of transparency.

Trans-European networks

203.   The integration of national markets through the internal market programme will not be fully effective economically and socially unless firms and individuals have access to trans-European networks in the areas of transport, telecommunications, energy and training so that they are able to make optimum use of the various legal instruments on which operation of the single market is based. This was the thrust of the Commission's communication of December 1990,[5] which served as a basis for the Commission's working programme in 1991; the Economic and Social Committee delivered an own-initiative opinion on the communication on 30 October.[6]

204.   On 2 October the Commission adopted a communication identifying the priority objectives regarding the establishment of electronic data-transmission networks linking

---

[1]   Twenty-fourth General Report, point 160.
[2]   OJ C 12, 18.1.1990; OJ C 16, 23.1.1990; Twenty-third General Report, point 247.
[3]   OJ C 322, 21.12.1990; Twenty-fourth General Report, point 159.
[4]   OJ L 145, 13.6.1977; Eleventh General Report, point 219.
[5]   Twenty-fourth General Report, point 60.
[6]   OJ C 14, 20.1.1992; Bull. EC 10-1991, point 1.2.21.

administrations in order to ensure the proper functioning of the internal market, particularly with regard to customs, indirect taxation, statistics, veterinary and plant-health controls, and border controls.[1] This programme will make use of the various budgetary resources available and will involve coordination of the decisions to be made by national administrations. Supporting measures have already been taken to enable the least developed Member States to acquire the equipment necessary for the operation of such networks.

A PEOPLE'S EUROPE

External frontier controls

205.   On 9 October the Commission adopted two communications, one on the right of asylum[2] and the other on immigration.[3] Given the persistence of large-scale migratory movements, demographic pressure in the southern countries and the emergence of the Central and East European countries as potential sources of emigration, the Commission is proposing an immigration strategy based on action at three levels, namely the inclusion of migration in the Community's external policy, the control of migratory movements and the integration of legal immigrants in the host country.

206.   The Maastricht European Council[4] had considered a report from the ministers responsible for immigration which took account of the Commission's two communications. On the basis of the conclusions reached at Maastricht, the Council on 16 December asked the ministers responsible to implement the programme set out in that report.

207.   Immigration policy was also the subject of an own-initiative opinion delivered by the Economic and Social Committee on 28 November.[5]

---

[1]   Bull. EC 10-1991, point 1.2.3.
[2]   Point 218 of this Report.
[3]   Bull. EC 10-1991, point 1.2.2.
[4]   Point 1128 of this Report.
[5]   Bull. EC 11-1991, point 1.2.10.

Removal of intra-Community physical frontiers

Legislation on weapons

208.   On 18 June the Council adopted Directive 91/477/EEC on control of the acquisition and possession of weapons,[1] in preparation for the forthcoming abolition of
intra-Community frontiers on 1 January 1993.

Possession of narcotic drugs

209.   On 24 April the Economic and Social Committee delivered its opinion on the
proposal for a Directive on the manufacture and the placing on the market of certain
substances used in the illicit manufacture of narcotic drugs and psychotropic substances.[2]

210.   In response to the recommendations of the Chemical Action Force, set up by the
participants at the Western Economic Summit held in Houston in 1990,[3] and with
particular reference to the monitoring of exports, the Commission on 22 November
proposed an amendment[4] to Council Regulation (EEC) No 3677/90 on the illicit
manufacture of narcotic drugs and psychotropic substances.[5]

211.   On 27 November the Commission sent the Council a proposal for a Regulation
on the establishment of a European Drugs Monitoring Centre and a European Information Network on Drugs and Drug Addiction (Reitox).[6] The European Council
meeting in Luxembourg in June lent its support to this initiative,[7] which is designed to
tackle five main areas of concern, namely a reduction in the demand for drugs, national
and Community strategies and policies, international cooperation and the geopolitics of
supply, drug trafficking, and the drug economy. The European Council had asked the
ECCD to coordinate the operation. Meeting in The Hague in September, the ECCD
decided that the Centre should be based on a Community legal act.

212.   On 11 November the Council and the Ministers for Health adopted a resolution
calling on the Commission to draw up a systematic inventory of policies, measures and

---

[1]   OJ L 256,   13.9.1991; Bull. EC 6-1991,   point 1.2.7; Commission proposals: OJ C 235,   1.9.1987;
     Twenty-first General Report, point 261; OJ C 299, 28.11.1989; Twenty-third General Report, point 253;
     OJ C 265, 20.10.1990; Twenty-fourth General Report, point 164.
[2]   OJ C 159, 17.6.1991; Bull. EC 4-1991, point 1.2.5.
[3]   Twenty-fourth General Report, point 691.
[4]   Bull. EC 11-1991, point 1.2.15.
[5]   OJ L 357, 20.12.1990; Twenty-fourth General Report, point 167.
[6]   Bull. EC 11-1991, point 1.2.196.
[7]   Bull. EC 6-1991, point I.18.

public health projects in the Member States aimed at the treatment and rehabilitation of drug addicts who are the subject of penal measures. [1]

Free movement of persons

213.   The Coordinators Group dealing with the free movement of persons, which was set up following the decision of the European Council in Rhodes in December 1988, continued its work and in June submitted to the European Council in Luxembourg a report which took stock of progress in implementing the programme set out in the 'Palma document'. A further progress report was laid before the Maastricht European Council expressing strong disappointment at the fact that the difficulty which existed between Spain and the United Kingdom and was holding up the signing of the agreement on the crossing of external frontiers had still not been resolved. The agreement included provision for many of the measures called for in the Palma document. The Coordinators also noted that most of the other measures still outstanding fell into the category described by the Palma document as desirable rather than essential, so that failure to take them would not place obstacles in the way of the achievement of free movement of persons.

214.   On 21 November Parliament adopted a resolution on the free movement of professional footballers. [2]

Right of entry and of residence

215.   The Directive on the right of residence for students, [3] adopted last year together with the Directives on the right of residence for retired persons and for other Community nationals, was the subject of proceedings for annulment brought by Parliament with the Commission as intervener. At issue is the procedure under which the Directive was adopted, and more specifically the legal basis finally chosen by the Council (Article 235 of the EEC Treaty).

---

[1]   OJ C 304, 23.11.1991; Bull. EC 11-1991, point 1.2.201.
[2]   OJ C 326, 16.12.1991; Bull. EC 11-1991, point 1.2.8.
[3]   OJ L 180, 13.7.1990; Twenty-fourth General Report, point 168.

Right of establishment

Recognition of diplomas

216.   On the basis of the Commission's amended proposal,[1] the Council continued its work on the adoption of a second general system for the recognition of professional education and training, and on 19 December it reached agreement in principle on a common position.[2] Like Directive 89/48/EEC,[3] which it supplements, the proposal sets out to facilitate the exercise of the regulated professions; it shares the earlier Directive's general features and extends the recognition system to include professional and vocational education and training involving less than three years of higher education or not involving such higher education. The Commission adopted a proposal for a Council Directive to facilitate the free movement of doctors and the mutual recognition of their diplomas, certificates and other evidence of formal qualifications.[2]

217.   The Commission published a notice on the equivalence of vocational training qualifications between Member States in the textile industry.[2]

Special rights

Right of asylum and status of refugees

218.   On 9 October the Commission adopted a communication on the right of asylum in which it set out the general problems encountered, notably within the framework of the Geneva Convention, and emphasized the need for a common approach on the matter.[4] On 16 December the Council examined this question as part of the follow-up to the European Council meeting in Maastricht.[5]

Right of petition

219.   In accordance with Parliament's rules of procedure and the Interinstitutional Agreement signed in 1989,[6] the Commission sent 324 communications concerning petitions to Parliament; this reflects the intensive use made of the right of petition by

---

[1]   OJ C 217, 1.9.1990; Twenty-fourth General Report, point 170.
[2]   Bull. EC 12-1991.
[3]   OJ L 19, 24.1.1989; Twenty-second General Report, point 289.
[4]   Bull. EC 10-1991, point 1.2.2.2.
[5]   Point 206 of this Report.
[6]   OJ C 217, 1.9.1990; Twenty-fourth General Report, point 912.

Community citizens. As in previous years, the subjects most frequently raised included social security, the environment, taxation, the right of residence, recognition of qualifications, and free movement of persons and goods.

Right to vote in local elections

220.   In its contribution to the Intergovernmental Conference on Political Union of 30 March, [1] the Commission gave its backing to the inclusion in the Treaty of provisions on European citizenship, including the right to vote in local elections. Giving European citizens the right to vote in municipal elections in the local authority district in which they are resident is one of the Commission's prime objectives.

Recognition of driving licences

221.   On 29 July the Council adopted Directive 91/439/EEC on driving licences, [2] which, from 1 July 1996, will supersede Directive 80/1263/EEC. [3] The new Directive provides that the holder of a driving licence issued by a Member State will no longer be required, on transferring his residence to another Member State, to exchange his licence for one issued by the host Member State. It also provides for greater harmonization of the conditions governing the issue of licences. A new Community model driving licence has also been established.

Taxation

Tax-paid allowances

222.   On 27 March the Council adopted Directive 91/191/EEC [4] amending Directive 69/169/EEC [5] and providing for an increase in value limits on intra-Community travellers' allowances. Derogations are granted for Denmark and Ireland, allowing them to impose quantitative limits on duty-free imports of tobacco and alcoholic beverages

---

[1]   Supplement 2/91 — Bull EC.
[2]   OJ L 237, 24.8.1991; Bull. EC 7/8-1991, point 1.2.287; Commission proposals: OJ C 48, 27.2.1989; Twenty-second General Report, point 291; OJ C 29, 5.2.1991; Bull. EC 1/2-1991, point 1.2.242.
[3]   OJ L 375, 31.12.1980; Fourteenth General Report, point 421.
[4]   OJ L 94, 16.4.1991; Bull. EC 3-1991, point 1.2.5; Commission proposals: OJ C 245, 26.9.1989; Twenty-third General Report, point 264; OJ C 70, 20.3.1990; Twenty-fourth General Report, point 173.
[5]   OJ L 135, 4.6.1969.

purchased during journeys of very short duration. On 19 December the Council adopted a Directive extending these exemptions until the end of 1992. [1]

Health

223.   On 4 June the Council and the Ministers for Health meeting within the Council adopted an action plan as part of the 1991-93 'Europe against AIDS' programme to be conducted as a cooperative endeavour by the Member States and the relevant international organizations. [2]

224.   On 4 June the Council and Health Ministers also adopted a declaration on action to combat the use of drugs in sport, underlining the importance of the 1992 Olympic Games to be held in Spain and France. [3] Subsequently the Commission adopted a communication providing information for the public and for sporting circles and proposing that the Council adopt a code of conduct on this issue. [4]

225.   A major step was taken this year in the fight against cancer, when on 15 May the Commission amended for the second time its proposal for a Directive designed to ban all forms of direct and indirect tobacco advertising. [5] In the same month the Economic and Social Committee [6] and Parliament [7] delivered their opinions on the proposal regarding the labelling of tobacco products. [8] The Commission amended the proposal in September [9] and the Council agreed on a common position in November. [10]

226.   In a communication it published on 30 September the Commission gave a highly encouraging account of the activities undertaken from 1986 to 1990 [11] under the Community action programme on toxicology for health protection. [12]

---

[1]   OJ L 373, 31.12.1991; Bull. EC 12-1991; Commission proposal: OJ C 333, 24.12.1991; Bull. EC 11-1991, point 1.2.3.
[2]   OJ L 175, 4.7.1991; Bull. EC 6-1991, point 1.2.215; Commission proposals: OJ C 13, 19.1.1991; Bull. EC 12-1990, point 1.3.300; OJ C 160, 20.6.1991; Bull. EC 5-1991, point 1.2.167.
[3]   OJ C 170, 29.6.1991; Bull. EC 6-1991, point 1.2.218.
[4]   Bull. EC 11-1991, point 1.2.200.
[5]   OJ C 167, 27.6.1991; Bull. EC 5-1991, point 1.2.165.
[6]   OJ C 191, 29.7.1991; Bull. EC 5-1991, point 1.2.166.
[7]   OJ C 240, 16.9.1991; Bull. EC 7/8-1991, point 1.2.288.
[8]   OJ C 29, 5.2.1991; Twenty-fourth General Report, point 177.
[9]   OJ C 260, 5.10.1991; Bull. EC 9-1991, point 1.2.129.
[10]   Bull. EC 11-1991, point 1.2.195.
[11]   Bull. EC 9-1991, point 1.2.128.
[12]   OJ C 184, 23.7.1986; Twentieth General Report, point 503.

227.   On 4 June the Council and Health Ministers adopted conclusions on action to be taken on texts adopted since 1989 in the field of public health.[1] On 11 November they also adopted two resolutions, one on health and the environment and the other concerning fundamental health-policy choices, in which it called on the Commission to prepare a report as a preliminary for more detailed discussions.[2]

Audiovisual policy

228.   In a communication adopted on 20 February, taking stock of a year's work on audiovisual policy,[3] the Commission reaffirmed its intention of continuing to focus its activities on the three aspects set out in its communication of 21 February 1990, i.e. rulemaking, promotion of the programme industry and the development of new technologies.[4]

229.   On the legislative side, the Commission adopted two proposals for Directives which are related to the general problem of intellectual property, but affect the audiovisual sector. One was on the coordination of certain rules concerning copyright and neighbouring rights applicable in satellite broadcasting and cable retransmission[5] and the other on rental right, lending right and certain rights related to copyright.[5] In the same area, the Council adopted two Decisions on 23 September, one on the Community's participation in a diplomatic conference on the settlement of disputes between States in the field of intellectual property and its participation in preparatory work for the conclusion of a protocol to the Berne Convention.[6]

230.   The Commission continued implementing the Media programme,[7] including the inauguration of the Media Business School in Madrid;[8] it developed proven distribution and production mechanisms such as the European Film Distribution Office and the European Script Fund (to support creative independent production talent) and launched new large-scale operations such as Greco (a group to promote independent productions).

231.   Lastly, on the technological side, the Commission made two moves. On 9 July it adopted a proposal for a Directive on the adoption of standards for the satellite

---

[1]   OJ C 170, 29.6.1991; Bull. EC 6-1991, point 1.2.217.
[2]   OJ C 304, 23.11.1991; Bull. EC 11-1991, points 1.2.198 and 1.2.199.
[3]   Bull. EC 1/2-1991, point 1.2.249.
[4]   Twenty-fourth General Report, point 178.
[5]   Point 186 of this Report.
[6]   Point 188 of this Report.
[7]   OJ C 127, 23.5.1990; Twenty-fourth General Report, point 179.
[8]   Bull. EC 4-1991, point 1.2.145.

broadcasting of television signals.[1] After Parliament and the Economic and Social Committee had delivered their opinions, the Commission amended its proposal on 6 December and the Council adopted a common position on 18 December. On 24 July it approved a communication on encouraging audiovisual production in the context of the strategy for high-definition television.[2]

Culture

232.   In 1991 the Commission proceeded with a number of activities launched in previous years relating to books and reading, training and Europe's architectural heritage. It also developed and rationalized its work on promoting European culture. On 7 June and 14 November the Ministers for Cultural Affairs adopted a number of resolutions and conclusions on the Theatre,[3] the training of arts administrators,[4] the new rules affecting Community artists visiting the United States[5] and copyright and neighbouring rights.[6] Resolutions were also adopted on 14 November on arrangements concerning archives and on cultural networks.[7]

In a resolution adopted on 25 October Parliament offered its support to the policy of the Ministers for Cultural Affairs and encouraged the promotion of the Theatre and music.[8]

233.   Following up its 1989 communication on books and reading,[9] the Commission issued a first set of statistics on book publishing in Europe capable of being developed and added to in future years. The pilot project in support of the translation of contemporary literature entered its second full year; 39 projects were selected in a first round and a further 37 in a second. The European literature and translation prizes were entrusted to the Irish Arts Council and presented on 26 November at a ceremony in Dublin, this year's European City of Culture. A network of five European colleges of literary translation met in Procida, Italy, in September. A total of ECU 146 000 was divided between them for bursaries.

234.   In response to the Ministers' adoption in November 1990 of conclusions endorsing its communication on vocational training in the arts, the Commission appointed a

---

[1]   Point 374 of this Report.
[2]   Bull. EC 7/8-1991, point 1.2.291.
[3]   OJ C 188, 19.7.1991; Bull. EC 6-1991, point 1.2.224; Bull. EC 11-1991, point 1.2.208.
[4]   OJ C 188, 19.7.1991; Bull. EC 6-1991, point 1.2.222.
[5]   OJ C 188, 19.7.1991; Bull. EC 6-1991, point 1.2.223.
[6]   Point 185 of this Report.
[7]   Bull. EC 11-1991, points 1.2.207 and 1.2.208.
[8]   OJ C 305, 25.11.1991; Bull. EC 10-1991, point 1.2.199.
[9]   Twenty-third General Report, point 708.

training coordinator to implement the proposals concerning conservation/restoration and translation.[1] The Commission continued its support for a number of initiatives in the training field, notably for the European certificate of cultural administration and through the European Community Youth and Baroque Orchestras.

235.   Continuing its support for the Community's architectural heritage, the Commission made its selection on 24 July of innovative conservation pilot projects on this year's theme of 'Testimonies to production activities in industry, agriculture, crafts, etc.'[2] Of the 433 applications received, 37 projects were chosen, receiving aid totalling ECU 2.6 million. Four sites of exceptional historical importance received aid from the Community budget: the Acropolis, Mount Athos, Lisbon and Coimbra. In addition, 108 grants were made to six institutions of European repute specializing in conservation techniques.

236.   On 14 November the Ministers for Cultural Affairs meeting within the Council appealed to the parties involved in the fighting in Yugoslavia to take the necessary steps to ensure the preservation of Dubrovnik and Split, both of which appear on the world cultural heritage list.[3]

237.   For the first time the Commission published a list of grants made to activities in support of the arts and of the European heritage. Under the 'Platform Europe' programme the Commission awarded grants totalling ECU 1 557 420 to 92 projects in a wide variety of artistic activities. The results were published in the Commission's new arts *Newsletter*, which was mailed to opinion leaders and arts professionals all over the Community in 1991.

238.   The Commission continued its support for setting up a European Committee for Business, the Arts and Culture, based in London. It took part in a wide range of international conferences and symposia, including several organized by the Council of Europe for the new democracies of Central and Eastern Europe. The Commission extended its cooperation with other pan-European institutions and, at bilateral level, was negotiating new cultural agreements with Hungary, Czechoslovakia, Poland and a number of Latin American countries.

239.   On 9 September Parliament adopted a resolution on cultural relations between the Community and Central and Eastern Europe.[4]

---

[1]   Twenty-fourth General Report, point 181.
[2]   Bull. EC 7/8-1991, point 1.2.297.
[3]   Bull. EC 11-1991, point 1.3.25.
[4]   OJ C 267, 14.10.1990; Bull. EC 9-1991, point 1.2.136.

Protection of personal data

240.   The Commission's communication of 18 July 1990 on the protection of individuals in relation to the processing of personal data in the Community and information security [1] received a broadly favourable opinion from the Economic and Social Committee. [2]

Protection of personal data is one of the main concerns in the context of the organization of immigration, customs and police controls at the Community's external frontiers. The European Council instructed the *ad hoc* Group on Immigration to prepare a convention on data protection, to be ready by 30 June 1992. [3] It is therefore vital to maintain consistency between the Community approach and the line which will be followed in the intergovernmental context. Furthermore, as 31 December 1992 looms large on the horizon and given the impetus being imparted to telecommunications technologies, the crossfrontier flow of data is becoming a fact of daily life in many areas, in particular international transfers of funds, medical data and marketing files, cooperation between tax and social authorities, and so on. This makes it essential that a Community instrument ensuring a comparable level of protection throughout the Community be adopted in the very near future.

---

[1]   OJ C 277, 5.11.1990; Twenty-fourth General Report, point 186.
[2]   OJ C 159, 17.6.1991; Bull. EC 4-1991, point 1.2.140.
[3]   Bull. EC 6-1991, point I.17.

Section 3

Competition [1]

Priority activities and objectives

241. Since the inception of the common market, competition policy has been used to promote economic integration, stimulate growth and improve the well-being of consumers by improving productivity and inducing innovation. This is becoming increasingly important as the internal market nears completion in 1992 since the advantage of the single market cannot be fully achieved unless competition is fully effective. In setting its priorities, therefore, the Commission is focusing particularly on developing competition and opening up markets in sectors where there has been least progress in integration.

The first year of implementation of the Merger Control Regulation demonstrated that the Regulation has a crucial role to play in restructuring industry to meet the challenge of the single market. The procedures established for dealing with notifications, together with the practice of pursuing informal contacts at the pre-notification stage, enable the Commission to make effective use of its new powers in this area. While the Commission was able to clear the great majority (90%) of notified mergers within the one-month deadline, the need to maintain effective competition, which is one of the Regulation's basic criteria, prompted it to intervene in three mergers, imposing specific conditions in authorizing them, and to prohibit one merger.

In its efforts to open up and integrate markets in which competition was eliminated or greatly restricted as a result of national measures, the Commission received the backing of the Court of Justice, which, in an important judgment,[2] upheld the Commission's power, through directives, to define the requirements incumbent on Member States, under Article 90(1) of the EEC Treaty, with regard to undertakings to which they have granted special or exclusive rights, requirements which may include the outright abolition of certain exclusive rights.

With regard to State aid, the Commission adopted on 24 July a communication on the practical implementation of equality of treatment between public and private undertak-

---

[1] For further details, see the *Twenty-first Report on Competition Policy* (1991), to be published by the Office for Official Publications of the European Communities in 1992, in conjunction with this General Report.
[2] Judgment of 19.3.1991, Case C-202/88 (Competition in the markets for telecommunications terminals).

ings;[1] *in particular, it proposed to the Member States a system of annual reports that would ensure transparency in financial transfers between public authorities and publicly owned companies, in accordance with the provisions of Directive 80/723/EEC on transparency.*[2] *In Cases C-303/88* Italy v Commission[3] *and C-305/89* Italy v Commission,[4] *the Court of Justice reaffirmed the validity of the 'investor in a market economy' principle used by the Commission in determining whether aid is involved. The judgments in these two cases also confirm the Commission's powers to recover aid that has been granted illegally and that is incompatible with the common market.*

General rules applying to businesses

Agreements and abuses of dominant positions

242.   On 31 May, so as to give the Community greater scope for action in harmonizing and opening up insurance markets, the Council adopted Regulation (EEC) No 1534/91, which empowers the Commission to lay down the conditions under which certain categories of cooperation agreement between insurance companies may be exempted under Article 85(3) of the EEC Treaty.[5]

243.   In the telecommunications sector, the current policy of removing rules and regulations which impede free competition within the common market means that firms need information on how the competition rules are applied on these markets. In order to meet this requirement, the Commission adopted on 26 July guidelines on the application of EEC competition rules in the telecommunications sector,[6] pursuant to its communication of 9 February 1988[7] on implementation of the Green Paper on telecommunications,[8] which provides for an overall examination in 1992 of the subsequent stages of liberalization in this sector.

244.   The policy of liberalizing air transport was continued and on 14 May the Council adopted a Regulation enabling the Commission to take urgent interim measures against

---

[1]   Bull. EC 7/8-1991, point 1.2.75.
[2]   OJ L 195, 29.7.1980; Fourteenth General Report, point 195; OJ L 229, 28.8.1985; Nineteenth General Report, point 404.
[3]   OJ C 105, 20.4.1991.
[4]   OJ C 101, 18.4.1991.
[5]   OJ L 143, 7.6.1991; Bull. EC 5-1991; point 1.2.20; Commission proposal: OJ C 16, 23.1.1990; Twenty-third General Report, point 378.
[6]   OJ C 233, 6.9.1991; Bull. EC 7/8-1991, point 1.2.35.
[7]   Twenty-second General Report, point 403.
[8]   Twenty-first General Report, point 353.

anti-competitive practices in this sector, notably as regards fares.[1] On 17 July the Commission adopted two proposals for Council Regulations formally extending the Commission's powers to enforce competition rules to include domestic air transport.[2]

245.   On 4 December the Commission decided to publish a notice clarifying the scope for European consumers to use the services of intermediaries so as to purchase their motor vehicle in the country where prices are lowest.[3]

246.   Aware of growing worldwide market interpenetration and interdependence, the Commission is increasingly using its influence to extend application of the principles of competition policy among its trading partners. It has also been endeavouring to develop cooperation with the competition authorities in other parts of the world, one result of which has been the signing of a cooperation agreement with the United States antitrust authorities.[4] The competition rules provided for in the Agreement on a European Economic Area are designed to establish a system ensuring that competition between the contracting parties is not distorted. To that end, the rules which make up the body of Community legislation will apply throughout the Area, whether they are competition rules applying to enterprises or rules on State aid, State monopolies of a commercial nature, public enterprises or holders of special or exclusive rights.

The system will allow EFTA to set up an independent structure with equivalent powers and similar functions to those of the Commission in the competition field. The Agreement thus paves the way for competition on equal terms, thereby helping to foster integration in the Area and benefiting the 360 million consumers concerned.

However, following the opinion of the Court of Justice dated 14 December, it will be necessary to review the system of legal controls originally proposed.

Application of the competition rules: specific cases

Agreements and abuses of dominant positions

247.   In applying the competition rules, the Commission has been careful to focus its efforts on those cases which best allow it to help promote the single market and to maintain all that has already been achieved and has refrained from taking action in other

---

[1]   OJ L 122, 17.5.1991; Bull. EC 5-1991, point 1.2.21; Commission proposal: OJ C 155, 26.6.1990; Twenty-fourth General Report, point 190; OJ C 101, 18.4.1991; Bull. EC 3-1991, point 1.2.31.
[2]   OJ C 225, 30.8.1991; Bull. EC 7/8-1991, points 1.2.33 and 1.2.34.
[3]   Bull. EC 12-1991.
[4]   Bull. EC 9-1991, point 1.2.14.

cases where it felt that the national authorities or courts were able to deal with the matter. It adopted 17 decisions applying Articles 85 and 86 of the EEC Treaty, including four decisions formally rejecting complaints.

In the ECSC sphere, three cases were initiated under Article 47 during the year covered by the report.

Some 100 cases were also initiated under Articles 65 and 66 of the ECSC Treaty; in 31 of these, a decision was taken under Article 66 and in one a decision was taken under Article 65. In addition, 47 transactions were exempted from prior Commission authorization, and 20 cases were settled by comfort letter.

Decision No 25/67/ECSC was amended to bring it more into line with practical requirements under the ECSC Treaty.

The main cases during the reference period included the closure of the Ravenscraig steel works (Scotland), the setting-up of Consol[1] (coal), the merger of Ensidesa and Altos Hornos de Vizcaya (Spain), and the agreement between Ilva and Falck (Italy).

As at 31 December there were 2 287 cases pending, of which 1 732 were applications for negative clearance or notifications for exemptions (282 received in 1991), 328 complaints (83 received in 1991) and 227 cases in which the Commission had started proceedings on its own initiative (23 of them in 1991).

On 24 July, in line with its policy of underpinning the development of the single market, the Commission imposed a record fine on Tetra Pak for having abused its dominant position, in breach of Article 86 of the EEC Treaty, in an attempt to partition markets and eliminate competition in packaging machinery and cartons for liquid and semi-liquid food products.[2] The Commission also imposed fines for infringement of Article 85 of the EEC Treaty in two cases involving export restrictions aimed at partitioning the common market, one relating to cognac (Martell Piper/DMP)[3] and the other to photocopiers (Toshiba).[4]

In several cases, the Commission took action to get agreements amended or obtain undertakings in order to put an end to restrictions of competition and promote the opening-up of markets. The cases in question included agreements between electricity-generating companies in the Netherlands that infringed Article 85(1)[5] and the agreements between the members of the satellite television channel Eurosport.[6]

---

[1]   Bull. EC 10-1991, point 1.2.29.
[2]   Bull. EC 7/8-1991, point 1.2.39.
[3]   OJ L 185, 17.7.1991; Bull. EC 5-1991, point 1.2.23.
[4]   OJ L 287, 17.10.1991; Bull. EC 6-1991, point 1.2.41.
[5]   OJ L 28, 2.2.1991; Bull. EC 1/2-1991, point 1.2.47.
[6]   OJ L 63, 9.3.1991; Bull. EC 1/2-1991, point 1.2.45.

On 11 January the Commission adopted a Decision pursuant to Article 15(6) of Regulation No 17/62[1] finding that agreements providing for the exclusive distribution of cosmetic products (Vichy) through pharmacies infringed Article 85.[2]

On 4 December the Commission adopted a Decision under Article 85 finding that the boycott of the motor-vehicle intermediary ECO System by the Peugeot group was incompatible with the common market since it impeded parallel imports of motor vehicles within the common market (ECO System/Peugeot).

After obtaining undertakings from the parties or amendments to the agreements they had concluded, the Commission authorized agreements in the air transport sector relating to cooperation between computerized reservation systems (Amadeus/Sabre)[3] and to the rules of the International Air Transport Association (IATA) concerning its collective systems of agencies.[4] The Amadeus/Sabre agreement having been abandoned for business reasons, the Commission is examining whether Community legislative provisions on computerized reservation systems[5] need to be amended.

Following the removal of a number of anti-competitive clauses in the relevant contracts, the Commission adopted a Decision authorizing a network of selective distribution agreements in the cosmetics and luxury perfumery sector (Yves Saint-Laurent Parfums).[6]

Merger control

248. The Commission received 63 notifications in 1991 under the Merger Control Regulation.[7] The confidential talks which frequently take place prior to notification and during which firms may be dispensed from the need to provide information that is not essential to the notification have helped to facilitate the efficient implementation of the Regulation and to ensure that the strict deadlines which it imposes on the Commission are met.

Following examination of the mergers notified, and applying the 'dominant position' criterion laid down in Article 2 of the Regulation, the Commission was able in the great majority of cases (i.e. 50 cases out of a total of 61) to conclude, during the initial stage of the procedure, that the mergers in question were compatible with the common market. In five cases the Regulation was found not to be applicable either because the mergers notified were cooperative in nature or because control was not acquired.

---

[1]   OJ 13, 21.2.1962.
[2]   OJ L 75, 21.3.1991.
[3]   Bull. EC 7/8-1991, point 1.2.36.
[4]   OJ L 258, 16.9.1991; Bull. EC 7/8-1991, point 1.2.37.
[5]   OJ L 10, 15.1.1991; Bull. EC 12-1990, point 1.3.45.
[6]   OJ L 12, 18.1.1992; Bull. EC 12-1991.
[7]   OJ L 395, 30.12.1989; OJ L 257, 21.9.1990; Twenty-third General Report, point 376; Supplement 2/90 — Bull. EC.

In six cases, the Commission decided to initiate the detailed investigation procedure because of 'serious doubts' as to their compatibility with the common market; in one of these cases (Tetra Pak/Alfa-Laval),[1] the Commission concluded that its doubts were not confirmed, and it adopted a final decision finding the merger compatible with the common market; in three other cases (Alcatel/Telettra,[2] CEAC/Magneti Marelli[3] and Varta/Bosch),[4] the mergers were authorized only subject to the imposition of conditions ensuring the severing of certain structural links which the parties had with other firms. However, in a fifth case (Aérospatiale-Alenia/De Havilland),[5] it concluded that the dominant position on the regional aircraft market which would have resulted from the acquisition of the Canadian manufacturer by the Franco-Italian consortium was incompatible with the common market. In the sixth case (Accor/Wagons Lits), a detailed investigation is under way.

The rules of competition applied to forms of State intervention

State aid

249.   With scarcely one year to go to the completion of the single market, the control of State aid is one of the Community's policy priorities: there must be strict control of measures that might significantly reduce the benefits to the Community of dismantling physical, technical and tax barriers.

250.   The Commission accordingly pursued[6] its systematic review, based on Article 93(1) of the EEC Treaty, of all the aid schemes operating in the Member States; the development of the common market towards greater integration requires changes in, or indeed the abolition of, a number of aid schemes. This exercise applies mainly to general investment aid schemes, which have harmful effects on competition and on trade between Member States and which do not pursue any objective in the Community interest. In particular, given the objective of ensuring greater economic and social cohesion, the Commission generally takes a stricter stand on aid granted in the richest regions than it does on aid granted in the poorer, peripheral regions.

---

[1]   Bull. EC 7/8-1991, point 1.2.44.
[2]   OJ L 122, 17.5.1991; Bull. EC 4-1991, point 1.2.16.
[3]   OJ L 222, 10.8.1991; Bull. EC 5-1991, point 1.2.26.
[4]   Bull. EC 7/8-1991, point 1.2.49.
[5]   OJ L 334, 5.12.1991; Bull. EC 10-1991, point 1.2.24.
[6]   Twenty-fourth General Report, point 202.

General schemes

251.   On 31 July the Commission decided to approve aid required to facilitate a major privatization programme presented by the Greek Government; it based its decision on Article 92(3)(b) of the EEC Treaty, under which aid to remedy a serious disturbance in the economy of a Member State may be considered to be compatible with the common market.

252.   As regards the privatization process on the territory of the former German Democratic Republic, the decision taken will enable the Commission to check — without impeding the operation of the Treuhandanstalt — that the latter's activities are not having the effect of distorting competition to an extent contrary to the Community interest. In particular, the Commission takes the view that no aid element is involved where a firm is sold to the highest bidder or to the only bidder, following a public call for bids; where these conditions are not met, major privatizations or privatizations involving sensitive sectors must be notified. An accelerated prior examination procedure will be established.

Industry schemes

253.   The Commission continued to seek a reduction in aid granted on an industry-wide basis; such schemes have a significant impact in the most prosperous regions and thus run the risk of negating the effects of regional aid and the efforts of the Community's structural Funds.

It renewed[1] the Community framework on State aid to the motor vehicle industry[2] and undertook to review it again by the end of 1992. A large number of planned aid measures were notified to the Commission or came to its attention as many manufacturers decided to establish new production capacity in the Community.

In the synthetic fibres industry the tendency for the rate of capacity utilization to improve has been reversed over the last two years; the Commission extended for a further year the code limiting aid to the industry, which was to have expired on 19 July 1991.[3] Thus, the Commission will continue to take an unfavourable view of aid measures which would help to create fresh overcapacity, and to give sympathetic consideration to measures designed to cut overcapacity by restructuring the industry or facilitating a switch to other activities.

---

[1]   OJ C 81, 26.3.1991.
[2]   OJ C 123, 18.5.1990; Twenty-third General Report, point 386.
[3]   OJ C 173, 8.7.1989; Twenty-third General Report, point 386.

254.   Since Commission Decision No 322/89/ECSC, which lays down the code govern-ing aid to the steel industry, [1] was due to expire on 31 December 1991, the Commission, acting under Article 95 of the ECSC Treaty, adopted the new steel aid code[2] on 27 November, after consulting the ECSC Consultative Committee and with the assent of the Council, which endorsed the code unanimously on 18 November. The new code extends the previous one for five years, subject to a number of amendments.

The main amendments relate to the rules on aid for research and development, which have now been aligned on those laid down in the Community framework for State aid for research and development,[3] and to the scope for regional aid. Because of their derogatory nature, the rules on regional aid have been extended for only three years, up to 31 December 1994. During this period, the regional aid rules will apply to Portuguese SMEs under the same conditions as for Greece. Lastly, aid granted to firms in the former German Democratic Republic will have to be accompanied by a reduction in production capacity in that territory.

255.   Acting under Council Directive 90/684/EEC on aid to shipbuilding (the seventh shipbuilding Directive),[4] the Commission decided on 18 December to reduce the 1992 ceiling for permitted production aid for shipbuilding from 13 to 9%.[5] In the case of the building of small ships and conversion activities, the maximum is reduced from 9 to 4.5%.

Regional schemes

256.   Competition policy can work in parallel with other Community measures to make a valuable contribution to the strengthening of economic and social cohesion. The Commission continues to base its decisions in respect of regional aid measures on the principles that such aid should be geographically concentrated and that its level should be differentiated according to the gravity of the situation. It took decisions on a large number of individual regional aid measures in the various Member States, and in particular on changes to the regional aid scheme operating in Germany.

The Commission studied possible mechanisms for improving the linkage between competition policy as it affects regional aid, on the one hand, and the activities of the structural Funds, on the other, while at the same time reinforcing the joint pursuit of the Community interest.

---

[1]   OJ L 38, 10.2.1989; Twenty-third General Report, point 387.
[2]   OJ L 362, 31.12.1991; Bull. EC 11-1991, point 1.2.26.
[3]   OJ C 83, 11.4.1986.
[4]   OJ L 380, 31.12.1990; Twenty-fourth General Report, point 205.
[5]   OJ C 10, 16.1.1992; Bull EC 12-1991.

The Commission is currently studying the effects of aid towards highly capital-intensive investment on trade within the Community.

State monopolies

257.   As preparations proceeded for the single market in energy, to be achieved in 1992, the Commission found itself confronted with import and export monopolies for gas and electricity which it considered were liable to restrict trade within the Community. It initiated infringement proceedings against a number of Member States.[1]

Public enterprises and enterprises with special or exclusive rights

258.   Acting under Commission Directive 80/723/EEC on the transparency of financial relations between Member States and public undertakings,[2] as amended by Directive 85/413/EEC,[3] the Commission decided to introduce a new reporting system designed to identify when aid is present in financial flows between public authorities and publicly owned companies.[4] In the case of public companies in the manufacturing sector with an annual turnover exceeding ECU 250 million, Member States will be required to submit annual reports to the Commission.

The Commission did not take any position on the question of public ownership and has always scrupulously ensured neutrality in its dealings with companies with different forms of ownership. It recognizes that public enterprises are sometimes expected to play a public service role alongside or in addition to their basic commercial activities; this may lead to distortion of competition in certain circumstances.

The Commission's communication deals only with the identification of State aid, which will then have to be considered under the same rules as apply to private companies.

259.   Following Commission action under Article 90 of the EEC Treaty, Belgium and Denmark put an end to State measures which infringed the Treaty. Belgian rules had previously required certain categories of central government civil servants to use the services of the national airline, Sabena; and in Denmark express mail had been included among the services reserved to the Danish postal service.

---

[1]   Bull. EC 3-1991, point 1.2.48.
[2]   OJ L 195, 29.7.1980; Fourteenth General Report, point 195.
[3]   OJ L 229, 28.8.1985; Nineteenth General Report, point 404.
[4]   OJ C 273, 18.10.1991; Bull. EC 7/8-1991, point 1.2.75.

International aspects

260.   The Europe agreements[1] concluded with Hungary, Poland and Czechoslovakia include provisions relating to competition which refer specifically to the rules of the Treaty. The Association Council will have up to three years after the entry into force of the agreements to decide on the procedures for applying those rules.

---

[1]   Point 823 of this Report.

Section 4

Industrial strategy and services

Priority activities and objectives

261.   This year the Commission focused its efforts on implementing its communication on industrial policy in an open and competitive environment, on which the Council stated its position in November 1990;[1] in particular it adopted four communications on electronics and information technologies,[2] biotechnology,[3] maritime industries[4] and textiles and clothing.[5] These communications reflect the Community's industrial policy by rejecting interventionist measures in favour of an open market approach and the promotion of positive adjustment. The best way of preparing the ground for positive adjustment is to implement a Community reference framework and use the various general instruments of industrial policy in a coordinated fashion.

In view of the worsening of the economic situation on account of the recession in the USA and the UK, the Gulf War, and a slight downturn in investment in the Community, some industries have been forced to continue with the restructuring needed to establish a single market and take account of technological change.

These developments were brought out in Panorama of EC industry 1991/92, *published in October, which the Commission produced with the help of the professional associations which represent industry at Community level. This reference work describes in detail structural and economic changes in the 180 main industrial and service sectors in the Community.*

Two general topics were also highlighted by recent work in the sphere of industrial policy: (i) competition on world markets and how to ensure the competitive operation of those markets and (ii) the self-financing of investments by businesses. On 11 July Parliament adopted a resolution on industrial policy[6] in which it supports the Commission's efforts to stimulate high-technology industries and emphasizes the need to implement coherent strategies.

---

[1]   Twenty-fourth General Report, point 212.
[2]   Point 278 of this Report.
[3]   Point 276 of this Report.
[4]   Point 270 of this Report.
[5]   Point 275 of this Report.
[6]   OJ C 240, 16.9.1991; Bull. EC 7/8-1991, point 1.2.82.

The Commission also continued to implement its communication[1] on industrial cooperation with the countries of Central and Eastern Europe under the Phare programme[2] and in cooperation with the Group of 24 and international financial institutions. Similar activities are also provided for under the Regulation on technical assistance for the Soviet Union.[3]

Steel

262.   For the second consecutive year crude steel production in the Community (excluding production in the five new German *Länder*, which is estimated at around 4 million tonnes) fell, totalling 132 million tonnes compared with 136 million tonnes in 1990. This reduction, which was mainly caused by the continued economic downturn in the Community, worsened for a while because of the events in the Gulf. The resulting downward trend in production was arrested towards the middle of the year. However, it was also accompanied by a further disturbing reduction in steel prices in the first half of the year and, except for a slight increase in export prices, there was no subsequent price recovery.

263.   In accordance with the guidelines set out in its communication on the future of the ECSC Treaty,[1] the Commission decided that the forward programmes for steel[4] should in future cover a six-month period and should also include an annual forecast. Exceptionally, however, in view of the uncertainty prevailing at the beginning of the year, programmes were published for the first and second quarters. Apart from giving quantitative crude steel forecasts, the programmes continued to analyse the individual product markets. The content of the programmes was also enhanced, in particular as a result of better coverage of the EFTA markets, in advance of the exchange of information which will take place in the context of the European Economic Area.[5]

264.   As regards the ECSC Treaty, which expires in 2002, the Commission thought it appropriate, acting under Article 97, to initiate a debate about its future[1] and, on 13 March, adopted a communication in which it set out its preferred option, namely to allow the Treaty to run its course while gradually incorporating the coal and steel sectors

---

[1]   Twenty-fourth General Report, point 212.
[2]   Point 818 of this Report.
[3]   Point 820 of this Report.
[4]   Bull. EC 1/2-1991, point 1.2.76; Bull. EC 3-1991, point 1.2.56; Bull. EC 5-1991, point 1.2.49; Bull. EC 6-1991, point 1.2.65.
[5]   Point 846 of this Report.

into the future Treaty. This option received broad support from the Council[1] in its conclusions of 29 April. The ECSC Consultative Committee also endorsed this option.[2]

To assess the financial consequences, the Commission and the European Parliament are examining, in a spirit of cooperation, the best solution to the economic and financial problems. Looking ahead to the expiry of the ECSC Treaty, the Council asked the Commission on 18 November to submit an analysis of the impact of the various financing options on the amount of the levy and on the level of reserves.

265. Cooperation on steel with the countries of Central and Eastern Europe continued,[3] in particular under the Phare programme.[4]

Transport

Motor industry

266. The Commission continued its endeavours along the lines set out in its communication on a single motor-vehicle market.[5] It concluded an informal arrangement with Japan,[6] agreed in conjunction with Parliament, the Member States and interested parties, with a view to achieving the complete liberalization of the Community market by 31 December 1999 subject to a transitional period designed to improve the industry's competitive position.

267. The Commission continued its activities (in particular concerning technical harmonization, approximation of indirect taxation, management of State intervention, coordination of research and technological development, promotion of training and retraining schemes) aimed at gradually putting in place a set of incentives designed to enable the European motor industry as a whole to cope with the gradual disappearance of the protection from Japanese competition which it enjoys in certain Member States. In accordance with its work programme and in the light of the European Parliament resolution of 13 June,[7] the Commission also endeavoured to promote social dialogue in the sector. Recognizing the increasingly international nature of the factors that determine competitiveness, after its in-depth study of the European component manu-

---

[1]   Bull. EC 4-1991, point 1.2.41.
[2]   Bull. EC 6-1991, point 1.2.64.
[3]   For the external elements of the steel plan, please refer to 'Individual sectors' in Section 10 'Commercial policy' in Chapter III of this Report.
[4]   Points 817 to 819 of this Report.
[5]   Twenty-third General Report, point 277.
[6]   Point 1060 of this Report.
[7]   OJ C 183, 15.7.1991; Bull. EC 6-1991, point 1.2.66.

facturing industry,[1] the Commission this year launched a study to look at ways of promoting efficient distribution networks which provide the best possible service to the consumer.

268.   The Commission strove to place these endeavours within a framework of continuous consultation with Community industries in the context of the slowing down of the economy and the differentiation of markets. The increase in new passenger car registrations in the European Community had continued in 1989 for the fifth consecutive year,[2] bringing the total increase since 1984 to over 32%. After such a marked improvement, the prospects for 1990-91 had to be very moderate, especially as the market was already showing signs of sagging.

1991 turned out to be a year of marked contrasts, with poor performances in the United Kingdom, France and Spain being more than offset by spectacular growth in demand in reunified Germany. Including the new German *Länder*, sales in the European Community of new passenger cars and light goods vehicles amounted to an estimated 13.9 million units in 1991, a slight increase compared with 1990 (13.73 million units), but not enough to prevent a worsening in the financial position of most manufacturers.

Railway equipment

269.   The Commission drafted a report on technical and economic conditions (including technical compatibility) governing the feasibility and competitiveness of a European combined road-rail transport network.

Shipbuilding

270.   On 18 September, in view of the increasing importance of the Community's maritime dimension, the Commission adopted a communication[3] on new challenges for maritime industries the aim of which is to find the Community's answer to current and future challenges. The approach pursued is a general and horizontal one and covers such varied aspects as shipowners' activities, shipbuilding, ships' equipment and services. The Commission proposes the creation of a discussion forum made up of representatives of all the parties concerned — maritime industries, research institutes, national administrations and the Community itself. The purpose of this forum is not only to organize

---

[1]   Twenty-fourth General Report, point 220.
[2]   Twentieth General Report, point 337; Twenty-first General Report, point 281; Twenty-second General Report, point 309; Twenty-third General Report, point 276; Twenty-fourth General Report, point 218.
[3]   Bull. EC 9-1991, point 1.2.31.

a broad exchange of views but also to prepare a report identifying the priority areas and the types of action to be taken in order to improve the competitiveness of the Community's maritime industries.

271.   In line with the 1978 Council resolution on the reconstruction of the shipbuilding industry[1] the Commission adopted, on 8 November, a report on the state of the industry in the Community in 1990.[2] This shows that, despite the Gulf crisis, the trend was fairly positive, especially in terms of the level of new orders which was particularly favourable in the first half of the year. On 22 November Parliament also adopted a resolution on this subject.[3]

272.   Throughout the year the Commission took part in formal negotiations within the OECD concerning a multilateral agreement on the removal of obstacles to normal competition[4] and in December it set the maximum level of aid authorized for shipbuilding for 1992.[5]

273.   Contacts were maintained with industry representatives and government experts with a view to assessing the industry's research and development and technical harmonization requirements (ships' equipment).

Textiles and clothing

274.   On 5 April the Commission adopted its annual report on the situation in the textile and clothing industry[6] in which it highlights in particular the considerable structural disparities between Community regions.

275.   On 23 October it adopted a communication on improving the competitiveness of the Community's textile and clothing industry[7] which follows the approach set out in the communication on industrial policy in an open and competitive environment[8] and in which it proposes to focus its commercial policy efforts on the opening up of non-Community markets and the promotion of Community exports, action to combat dumping and subsidies and fraudulent declarations of origin, and protection of designs and models. To create a more favourable environment for businesses in this industry,

---

[1]   OJ C 229, 27.9.1978; Twelfth General Report, point 126.
[2]   Bull. EC 11-1991, point 1.2.38.
[3]   OJ C 326, 16.12.1991; Bull. EC 11-1991, point 1.2.39.
[4]   Point 1048 of this Report.
[5]   Point 255 of this Report.
[6]   Bull. EC 4-1991, point 1.2.40.
[7]   Bull. EC 10-1991, point 1.2.35.
[8]   Twenty-fourth General Report, point 212.

the Commission advocates improving the quality of services to businesses, and in particular better information, better training, more research, and help for reconversion and diversification. Also on 23 October the Commission adopted a communication concerning the Community Retex scheme which is designed to diversify economic activities and modernize viable businesses in areas which are heavily dependent on the textile industry.[1] On 22 October Parliament adopted a resolution on the restructuring of the textile and clothing industry.[2]

Biotechnology

276.   In a communication[3] which it adopted on 17 April the Commission examined the prospects for a competitive biotechnology industry in the Community and advanced a number of conclusions and recommendations which were favourably received by the Council[4] on 28 November. The Commission suggested setting up a transparent regulatory framework involving an integrated risk-assessment procedure and a single notification procedure for new biotechnological products, more adequate patent protection, and the setting up of an appropriate consultative structure at Community level to consider the ethical problems liable to arise.

The Commission also prepared a biotechnology standardization mandate for the European Committee for Standardization and, on 11 July, held the first meeting of the Round Table on biotechnology with representatives of the industry and other interested parties.

277.   The highlights of the year as regards international cooperation were the discussions which took place within the framework of the OECD and the EEC-US High-Technology Working Party.

Electronics and information technology

278.   On 26 March the Commission adopted a communication[5] designed to apply to the European electronics and information technology industries the Community's new industrial policy approach. After noting that the Community industry is under-

---

[1]   Bull. EC 10-1991, point 1.2.36.
[2]   OJ C 305, 25.11.1991; Bull. EC 10-1991, point 1.2.37.
[3]   Bull. EC 4-1991, point 1.2.35.
[4]   Bull. EC 11-1991, point 1.2.45.
[5]   Bull. EC 3-1991, point 1.2.50.

represented in sectors such as semiconductors, peripherals and consumer electronics, the Commission proposed action relating to demand, technology, training, external relations and the business environment in order to facilitate the necessary adjustment decisions.

The communication was favourably received by the Council,[1] which on 29 April adopted conclusions in which it asked the Commission to propose specific initiatives and measures to apply the guidelines laid down. The Economic and Social Committee adopted an own-initiative opinion on this subject in November.[2]

Services

279.   The proposal for a Decision establishing a multiannual programme for the development of statistics on services,[3] which is currently before the Council, was endorsed by Parliament.[4] The Commission exploited for the first time the data gathered so far by Eurostat, which indicate a disturbing reduction in trade between Member States. While the contribution of services to value-added within the Member States continues to increase, their share in intra-Community trade has fallen by 12% in real terms over the last 10 years or so.

280.   With a view to reversing this trend, the Commission, in the light of recent case-law, upholds the view that Article 59 *et seq.* should be so interpreted as to ensure that services benefit from the same degree of liberalization and interpenetration as that already achieved in relation to the free movement of goods.

In July the Commission published a first study of one of the sectors involving services, namely gambling and gaming;[5] this was followed up in December by an 'audit' of the operators concerned.

---

[1]   Bull. EC 4-1991, point 1.2.36.
[2]   Bull. EC 11-1991, point 1.2.34.
[3]   Twenty-fourth General Report, point 225.
[4]   Point 1235 of this Report.
[5]   *Gambling in the single market — A study of the current legal and market situation,* Luxembourg 1991.

Aerospace

Aeronautical industry

281.   The Commission set about the tasks announced in its communication of 23 July 1990 on a competitive European aeronautical industry[1] by examining the factors influencing the competitive position of engine, equipment and aircraft manufacturers in the three sectors concerned, namely business jets, which have been badly affected by the fluctuations and weakness of the dollar, regional aircraft, where there is overcapacity, and helicopters, where the need for rationalization is compounded by the problem of finding alternatives to military activities. This examination should enable it to assess the situation on these markets in order to initiate a general debate with the Member States and the industry.

Space industry

282.   The Commission, in close conjunction with the space industry, operators and users, started work on a communication on the European space industry, the aim of which, in line with the communication on industrial policy,[2] is to identify the problems faced by the industry and the role the Commission could play to ensure its harmonious development.

Other activities

283.   In order to implement the guidelines laid down by the Council[3] and to take account of the resolution on the footwear industry adopted by the European Parliament in February,[4] the Commission, in conjunction with the Member States and the circles concerned, endeavoured, with the mostly general means available, to make its contribution to the achievement of the positive adjustment required for the integration of this sector in the single market. The launching of new programmes during the year, in particular concerning cooperative research and training, is likely to result in the stepping up of the efforts concerned.

---

[1]   Twenty-fourth General Report, point 226.
[2]   Twenty-fourth General Report, point 212.
[3]   Twenty-fourth General Report, point 227.
[4]   OJ C 72, 18.3.1991; Bull. EC 1/2-1991, point 1.2.78.

284.   To implement the Council resolution of July 1989 on the development of the Community mining industry,[1] the Commission, in conjunction with the Member States and the industry, continued to examine matters relating to access to and dissemination of geological and mining data, vocational training, taxation and social welfare schemes, and external aspects of mining policy.

Specific development programme for Portuguese industry (Pedip)

285.   All the operational programmes approved under the Pedip programme[2] are now being implemented. As, in view of the time-limits laid down, no further applications could be accepted under the programme for the restructuring of the wool industry, activity during the year concerned only the management of subsidies already decided upon before 31 December 1990.

Coordination between Pedip and the other operational programmes under the Community support framework for Portugal was ensured, and the Monitoring Committee held regular quarterly meetings. The Commission also helped to assess the impact of Pedip on the structure of Portuguese industry and changes in business behaviour, taking into account the innovative features of and the scope for applying methods used in other structural measures, and the information needed for the final report which the Commission is to submit to the Council and the European Parliament before the end of 1993 under Regulation (EEC) No 2053/88.[3] The Portuguese authorities submitted on schedule the third annual report on the implementation of the various operational programmes, from which it emerged that the programme is proceeding normally. Utilization of the financial resources from the additional budget heading proceeded according to plan; commitment appropriations totalling ECU 119.8 million and payment appropriations totalling ECU 114.4 million entered in the 1990 budget were fully utilized. Consequently, for the fourth consecutive year since Pedip was launched, all the budget appropriations were used.

---

[1]   OJ C 207, 12.8.1989; Twenty-third General Report, point 286.
[2]   OJ L 185, 15.7.1988; Twenty-second General Report, point 536.
[3]   OJ L 185, 15.7.1988.

Section 5

Enterprise policy

Priority activities and objectives

286.   In the run-up to the completion of the internal market, the need to take account of the requirements of enterprises remains a priority task. Against this background, the Council decision revising the programme for the improvement of the business environment and the promotion of the development of enterprises, and in particular small and medium-sized enterprises (SMEs), was adopted on 18 June.[1] It provided for the expansion of measures to remove administrative, financial and legal constraints and to formulate rules facilitating economic activity in general, including the creation and transfer of businesses, the opening-up of public procurement and administrative simplification. It also sought to improve the effectiveness of information for enterprises on national and Community policies, rules and activities which concerned them. In addition, it underlined the importance of encouraging cooperation and partnership between businesses from different regions of the Community and from different economic sectors, and of opening up external markets. It provided in particular for the release of an additional ECU 25 million for the action programme for SMEs.

In April the Council adopted a resolution[2] on the action programme for SMEs, including craft industry enterprises. Reaffirming its determination to make substantial progress in the area of policies to promote SMEs, it outlined a number of priorities: vocational skills and training, easing of administrative burdens, information and consultation, and cooperation between firms.

Promotion of enterprises and the business environment

287.   In line with the Council's request,[3] the system for assessing the impact of Community legislation on businesses,[4] which now covers specific legislative proposals, was further refined by improving the procedures for consulting SME organizations.

---

[1]   OJ L 175, 4.7.1991; Bull. EC 6-1991, point 1.2.63.
[2]   Bull. EC 4-1991, point 1.2.39.
[3]   OJ L 141, 2.6.1990; Twenty-fourth General Report, point 233.
[4]   Twenty-third General Report, point 292.

288. Extensive research was carried out on the legal and practical situation in the different Member States with regard to the settlement of debts between firms. Possible Community action to ensure transparency of payment conditions was examined with representatives of the Member States and of business.

289. Two guides for SMEs were produced, one on the rules of competition and the other on the financial and fiscal aspects of the single market.

Supply of business services — Improving the adaptability of firms to the internal market

Improving the flow of information

290. Following rapid expansion last year,[1] the Euro-Info-Centre (EIC) network entered a phase of consolidation. There are now 210 centres, of which seven are located in the five new German *Länder*. To improve the quality of the network, the Committee composed of representatives of the Member States adopted recommendations on criteria for measuring the quality of EIC services, and a major publicity campaign was launched to inform SMEs about the services offered by the EIC network. The number of enquiries from small firms continued to grow, reaching some 200 000. In September, the second annual conference of Euro-Info-Centres was held in Berlin,[2] a symbolic location in view of the opening of the centres in the new German *Länder*. Other centres will be opening shortly in Warsaw, Prague and Vienna.

Fostering cooperation

291. As part of the development of the policy to foster cooperation between enterprises, the confidential Business Cooperation Network (BC-Net) was expanded; it now has some 600 members, both public and private, throughout the Community, including in the five new German *Länder*, and in March it was extended to the EFTA countries and to Poland. The annual conference, held in Paris in July, highlighted the important role played by BC-Net in the Community and internationally.

292. The coverage of the Business Cooperation Centre (BCC) was extended. Now covering 45 countries in all five continents, it is an effective vehicle for promoting business contacts of a non-confidential nature.

---

[1]   Twenty-fourth General Report, point 235.
[2]   Bull. EC 9-1991, point 1.2.35.

293.   As a result of its continuing success, the 'Europartenariat' operation[1] is now a twice-yearly event. On the first occasion, it was held in Oporto, Portugal, on 17 and 18 June. Over 1 000 enterprises took part, establishing some 5 000 contacts. On the second occasion, in Leipzig on 2 and 3 December, it was more specifically aimed at firms in the five new German *Länder*, and generated great interest. About 1 500 enterprises from 30 or so countries took part, and almost 7 000 contacts were established.

294.   The 'Interprise' programme, which is focused on market niches or on markets which are complementary from an economic or sectoral viewpoint, was very successful in promoting contacts and cooperation between enterprises in the regions concerned.

295.   With regard to subcontracting, an overall strategy based on better knowledge of the market and on improvements in its functioning is currently being developed. In addition, the possibility of linking databases and exchanging information on subcontracting is being examined with a view to establishing a dedicated network.

Preparing small businesses for 1992

296.   Following the assessment made of the programmes of experimental training schemes (1989/90),[2] which sought to help small businesses prepare for the single market in 1992, it was agreed to extend the schemes to a greater number of SMEs. A two-pronged strategy was devised involving, on the one hand, the establishment of a network of trainers specializing in the preparation of SMEs for the single market and, on the other, the creation of a reference centre to facilitate the exchange of information in the network.

297.   In January, a pilot scheme entitled 'Euromanagement' was launched with a view to conducting audits among SMEs. It will assess the resources of European enterprises which develop or apply new technologies, the aim being to foster the conclusion of transnational cooperation agreements linked to the Community research and technological development programmes or to the exploitation of the results of these programmes.

298.   Consultations were also held with representatives of the craft sector and small businesses on matters linked to the definition of standards and to quality-certification procedures with a view to developing an action plan to assist these enterprises. Pilot programmes were launched to increase and make more effective the participation of SMEs in public procurement. Following the unification of Germany, a programme has been specially tailored to small businesses in the new *Länder*, including seminars and

---

[1]   Twenty-first General Report, point 293.
[2]   Twenty-second General Report, point 340.

conferences on questions relating to the European Community and the single market. The objective is to facilitate their integration into the Community and thus to boost the region's economic development.

Seed capital

299.   Under a Community pilot scheme launched in 1988,[1] 24 European Seed Capital Funds have been established in order to promote the creation of enterprises in the Community. In December the Commission decided to set up another such Fund in the new German *Länder*. The Funds form a European network whose main objective is the transfer of experience at European level.

Other measures to assist small businesses

300.   On 5 September the Commission adopted a communication on the role of mutual guarantee systems in the Community,[2] which highlights the general problems encountered by SMEs in obtaining sufficient funding at reasonable cost and the role of mutual guarantee schemes (MGSs) in alleviating this problem. At the end of November the first conference of MGSs in the Community took place in Madrid, supported by the Commission in collaboration with the Spanish association of mutual guarantee schemes (Cesgar); the conference adopted a declaration on the establishment of a European association.

The cooperative, mutual and non-profit sector

301.   Further to its communication of December 1989[3] which was endorsed by the Economic and Social Committee[4] and by Parliament,[5] the Commission adopted in December three proposals for Council Regulations for new European-level forms of organization, the European cooperative society (SCE),[6] the European mutual society (CME)[6] and the European association (EA);[6] these proposals are intended to facilitate the transnational activities of enterprises in this sector and are accompanied by proposals for Directives supplementing them with regard to the involvement of employees.[7]

---

[1]   Twenty-second General Report, point 339.
[2]   Bull. EC 9-1991, point 1.2.34.
[3]   Twenty-third General Report, point 300.
[4]   OJ C 332, 31.12.1990; Twenty-fourth General Report, point 243.
[5]   OJ C 48, 25.2.1991; Bull. EC 1/2-1991, point 1.2.75.
[6]   The abbreviations are based on Latin forms of words.
[7]   Bull. EC 12-1991.

302.   The Commission also developed, in close collaboration with the representative organizations, a three-year programme based initially on measures to improve the legal and statistical information available on enterprises in this sector.

The distributive trades

303.   In response to a Council resolution of 14 November 1989,[1] the Commission adopted on 6 March a communication entitled 'Towards a single market in distribution',[2] which highlighted the key role that the distributive trades will assume in establishing the new distribution channels which will be needed if the single market is to be a success. In this context, the Commission launched 'COMM 2000', a programme of pilot projects to promote modern commercial methods through the application of new commercial technology.[3]

Tourism

304.   In accordance with the Council Decision designating 1990 'European Tourism Year',[4] the Commission adopted in March a report[5] which takes stock of the situation. The general success of the initiative was highlighted by the Ministers responsible for tourism in the Community and the EFTA countries at their meeting in April.

305.   At the request of Parliament,[6] the Council and the Economic and Social Committee,[7] the Commission adopted on 26 March a proposal for a Council Decision concerning a Community action plan to assist tourism.[8] This plan follows two main lines of action: firstly, strengthening of the horizontal approach to tourism by improving the competitiveness of the tourist industry in the Community and coordinating Community and national policies and, secondly, support for specific measures to assist tourism designed in particular to develop rural, cultural and social tourism. Parliament adopted two further resolutions on this matter in June[9] and December.[10]

---

[1]   OJ C 297, 25.11.1989; Twenty-third General Report, point 301.
[2]   Bull. EC 3-1991, point 1.2.51.
[3]   OJ C 209, 10.8.1991.
[4]   Twenty-third General Report, point 302.
[5]   Bull. EC 3-1991, point 1.2.57.
[6]   OJ C 19, 28.1.1991; Twenty-fourth General Report, point 245.
[7]   OJ C 332, 31.12.1990; Twenty-fourth General Report, point 245.
[8]   Bull. EC 3-1991, point 1.2.52.
[9]   OJ C 183, 15.7.1991; Bull. EC 6-1991, point 1.2.67.
[10]   OJ C 13, 20.1.1992; Bull. EC 12-1991.

Section 6

Research and technology

Priority activities and objectives

306.   The main features of 1991 in the research and technological development field were the success achieved by researchers, particularly the JET team, and the launching of virtually all of the 15 specific programmes under the new framework programme (1990 to 1994). [1] In the course of the cooperation procedure certain differences emerged between the Council, the European Parliament and the Commission concerning the conditions for implementing these new programmes. An interinstitutional compromise signed on 17 April ironed out these differences and removed the obstacles to the formal adoption of the programmes.

On 7 June the Council adopted the new research programmes in the fields of communication technologies, [2] telematic systems, [3] marine science and technology, [4] the environment, [5] and life sciences and technologies for developing countries. [6] On 8 July it adopted the new research programme in the field of information technology. [7]

On 9 September the Council likewise formally adopted the new research and technological development programmes in the fields of industrial and materials technologies, [8] agriculture and agro-industry, including fisheries, [9] biomedicine and health, [10] and non-nuclear energy. [11]

On 28 November the Council formally adopted the new research and technological development programme in the field of nuclear fission safety [12] and on 19 December the

---

[1]   OJ L 117, 8.5.1990; Twenty-fourth General Report, point 247.
[2]   Point 377 of this Report.
[3]   Point 379 of this Report.
[4]   Point 322 of this Report.
[5]   Point 319 of this Report.
[6]   Point 334 of this Report.
[7]   Point 367 of this Report.
[8]   Point 313 of this Report.
[9]   Point 329 of this Report.
[10]   Point 332 of this Report.
[11]   Point 336 of this Report.
[12]   Point 342 of this Report.

new research and training programme in the field of controlled thermonuclear fusion. [1]
*Also on 28 November, the Council adopted common positions on two of the last three
programmes awaiting adoption, namely the research programme in the field of biotechnology* [2] *and the human capital and mobility programme,* [3] *designed to encourage the mobility
of research scientists.*

*A number of calls for research proposals were published for all of the programmes
adopted. The first wave of projects selected from proposals submitted before the end of
the year in response to calls for proposals for the programmes adopted in June and
September will become fully operational from the beginning of 1992.*

*Other noteworthy features of 1991 include the presentation by the Commission of its
proposals for the activities of the Joint Research Centre for the period 1992-94,* [4] *the
development of international scientific cooperation based on the Council's conclusions of
20 November 1990,* [5] *the end of the negotiations on the second stage of the ITER
quadripartite thermonuclear fusion project,* [6] *the expansion of trade with the United
States,* [7] *the development of cooperation with the EFTA countries* [8] *and the launching of
the first cooperative projects with the countries of Central and Eastern Europe.* [9]

Community R&TD policy

Framework programme 1990 to 1994

307. The main feature of 1991 was the adoption of almost all the specific programmes
under the framework programme. [10]

Joint Research Centre

308. During the year the eight institutes of the JRC saw an increase in their operational
and budgetary independence and consolidated their role in the Centre's four areas of

---

[1]   Point 346 of this Report.
[2]   Point 325 of this Report.
[3]   Point 351 of this Report.
[4]   Point 309 of this Report.
[5]   Twenty-fourth General Report, point 250.
[6]   Point 347 of this Report.
[7]   Point 361 of this Report.
[8]   Point 359 of this Report.
[9]   Point 357 of this Report.
[10]   Point 306 of this Report.

activity: specific research programmes under the framework programme, support for Commission departments, exploratory research and work under contract for outside bodies. The demand for work in support of Commission departments in the field of science and technology was particularly heavy, up 28 % on 1990. The main sectors concerned were agriculture, the environment and energy. A large number of multi-annual agreements were signed between the JRC and the Commission, designed to ensure continuity and long-term participation. The amount of work carried out under contract for outside third parties, as well as the number of contracts involved, also continued to increase, with the value of orders placed with the JRC for the period 1989-91 rising to over ECU 40 million. Advanced materials and actinides research were the sectors mainly concerned.

309.   On 22 July the Commission adopted a communication setting out its proposals for the activities to be undertaken by the JRC during the period 1992-94.[1] These proposals are based on an in-depth analysis of the JRC's current achievements and take into account the status of work in progress, as reported in the JRC annual reports for 1988, 1989 and 1990, and the guidance from the programme evaluation carried out by a high-level panel of independent experts. The proposals also form part of the strategic long-term programme up to 2000, which was drafted at the beginning of 1990. The Commission proposes that the four categories of JRC activity be maintained. As regards the specific research programmes, the JRC is expected to continue to contribute to the objectives of the third framework programme (1990 to 1994) in the fields of industrial technologies and materials, measurement and testing, the environment, nuclear fission safety, controlled thermonuclear fusion, and human capital and mobility. Under the heading of scientific and technical support for the Commission there are plans to reinforce the customer/contractor relationship through multiannual contracts. The new activities planned for the period 1992-94 include the operation of a centre for the validation of alternative testing methods, in particular to replace tests on animals in toxicology. As far as contract work for third parties is concerned, the emphasis will be on making better use of the JRC's know-how through original and creative marketing techniques in partnership with national bodies. The Commission's communication contains three proposals covering activities which require a Council decision: specific programmes based on the EEC Treaty, specific programmes based on the Euratom Treaty and a supplementary programme for Euratom on the operation of the HFR reactor under the heading of work for third parties. In order to situate these proposals within the general context, the communication also contains a proposal for a resolution on the activities to be undertaken by the Joint Research Centre during the period

---

[1]   OJ C 234, 7.9.1991; Bull. EC 7/8-1991, point 1.2.89.

1992-94. Parliament[1] and the Economic and Social Committee[2] gave their opinions on these proposals in December.

Information technologies and telecommunications

310.   Information on research and technological development activities in the field of information technologies and telecommunications is to be found in Section 7 'Telecommunications, information industries and innovation' of Chapter II of this Report.

Industrial technologies and materials

311.   The Commission continued to implement the programme of research and technological development in the field of industrial technologies and materials (1989-92) (Brite/Euram).[3] On completion of the contract negotiations, a start was made on the 146 projects, totalling ECU 180 million, selected following a second call for proposals which closed on 14 September 1990.[4] Thirty-two further projects, totalling ECU 40 million, were selected from a second evaluation of 101 projects which had been deemed satisfactory but in need of improvement in the first evaluation. On 25 February the Commission published a communication on the evaluation report by a group of independent experts on 28 aeronautics projects under the Brite/Euram programme.[4] On 16 and 17 April the first Brite/Euram aeronautics days, attended by 600 representatives from industry, universities and the public sector, provided an opportunity to review the results of the first pilot stage of the programme and to identify priorities for the future.

312.   The Commission also continued to implement the programme of research and technological development in the field of raw materials and recycling (1990-92).[5] Once the contract negotiations had been concluded, work began on a large number of the 69 projects selected,[6] totalling ECU 23 million.

---

[1]   OJ C 13, 20.1.1992; Bull. EC 12-1991.
[2]   Bull. EC 12-1991.
[3]   OJ L 98, 11.4.1989; Twenty-third General Report, point 323.
[4]   Twenty-fourth General Report, point 258.
[5]   OJ L 359, 8.12.1989; Twenty-third General Report, point 324.
[6]   Twenty-fourth General Report, point 259.

313. On 9 September the Council formally adopted the new research and technological development programme in the field of industrial technologies and materials (1990 to 1994).[1] This programme, which has a budget of ECU 670 million, covers three areas: materials and raw materials, design and manufacturing, and aeronautics. One of the aims of the new programme, which is larger than any previous programme in this area, is to provide a framework for cooperative research projects (Craft projects) in which groups of SMEs which do not have their own research facilities can appoint an outside research association to do work for them. A call for proposals[2] was published on 24 December.

314. In December the Council adopted a common position[3] on the proposal for a specific programme in the field of measurement and testing[4] on which Parliament had delivered an opinion[5] (first reading) in November.

315. The JRC's Institute for Advanced Materials continued its studies on the behaviour of new materials. It developed new measuring capabilities with a view to future industrial contract research. Progress was also made in component testing, in particular in the measurement of the growth of defects in both the inner and outer surfaces of tubular structures under thermal fatigue conditions. In addition, the strength of chrome-manganese stainless steel alloys was successfully increased by a factor of two. The E-Marc consortium,[6] which brings together a number of major European materials research organizations within a European Economic Interest Grouping, began operation.

Measurement and testing

316. The Commission continued to implement the programme of research in the field of applied metrology and chemical analysis (1988-92).[7] In the chemical analysis field 30 new projects were started, designed primarily to resolve problems in implementing the Directives on agricultural products, foodstuffs and the environment. In the metrology field 18 new projects were started on subjects which included the development of standard systems of measurement for verifying integrated circuits and slightly rough surfaces.

317. The JRC's Central Bureau for Nuclear Measurements continued its work in the field of nuclear measurements and standards. The shift in emphasis from nuclear to

---

[1] OJ L 269, 25.9.1991; Bull. EC 9-1991, point 1.2.39.
[2] OJ C 323, 24.12.1991.
[3] Bull. EC 12-1991.
[4] OJ C 174, 16.7.1990; Twenty-fourth General Report, point 263.
[5] OJ C 326, 16.12.1991; Bull. EC 11-1991, point 1.2.48.
[6] Twenty-fourth General Report, point 261.
[7] OJ L 206, 30.7.1988; Twenty-second General Report, point 371.

non-nuclear fields and from fundamental research to applications continued. In the nuclear field the programme of inter-laboratory measurements of low-enriched uranium, initiated by the Esarda, was completed. In the non-nuclear field, the Bureau continued its activities in support of the Community Bureau of Reference programme, preparing several new reference materials. Contract work for outside clients included the study of cadmium traces in plastics and analysis of uranium dioxide powder. The JRC's Institute for Safety Technology also constructed a reaction wall to study structure behaviour and prepared a concerted-action programme, to be implemented by 20 European laboratories.

Environment

318.   The Commission continued to implement the programmes of research (1989-92)[1] on the environment (STEP) and on climatology and natural hazards (Epoch). The 144 projects selected from the two main calls for proposals, plus the 12 projects resulting from a special call for proposals,[2] became fully operational. From 20 to 24 May, in association with the European Science Foundation and the Italian National Council for Research (CNR), the Commission held the first European symposium on terrestrial ecosystems, in Florence.

319.   On 7 June the Council formally adopted the new research and technological development programme in the field of the environment (1990 to 1994).[3] This programme is divided into four parts covering the Community's participation in global change programmes, technologies and engineering for the environment, research on economic and social aspects of environmental issues and technological and natural hazards. The programme is open to participation by all European countries, with the part on global change being open to non-European countries as well. The Commission received 62 proposals in response to a first call for proposals published on 16 July;[4] 49 of these were selected for funding.

320.   In the context of its research on atmospheric pollution, the JRC's Institute for the Environment continued its work on modelling and its experimental activities. On

---

[1]   OJ L 359, 8.12.1989; Twenty-third General Report, point 319.
[2]   Twenty-fourth General Report, point 265.
[3]   OJ L 192, 16.7.1991; Bull. EC 6-1991, point 1.2.68; Commission proposal: OJ C 174, 16.7.1990, OJ C 327, 29.12.1990; Twenty-fourth General Report, point 266.
[4]   OJ C 184, 16.7.1991.

the subject of soil and water pollution by waste, a stochastic model was used to study the problem of pollutant migration in soils. The Institute also carried out a first set of experiments as part of the European project on microphytic toxins in the Mediterranean. In the field of industrial hazards, the Institute for Systems Engineering developed expert systems to improve man/machine interaction for process control operators in accident situations. The Institute for Safety Technology continued to develop techniques to study pressure variation mechanisms in chemical reactors and models to predict gas cloud dispersion. The Institute for Remote Sensing Applications continued its work on land use mapping and completed the installation of the European microwave signature laboratory. [1]

Marine science and technology

321.   The Commission continued to implement the programme of research in the field of marine science and technology (1989-92) (MAST). [2] Four new research projects were selected, bringing the total to 46 (21 on marine science, 10 on coastal zone engineering and 15 on marine technology). Two calls for proposals for horizontal support measures were published (a feasibility study of an abyssal laboratory, [3] in March, and an oceanographic data base, [4] in July.

322.   On 7 June the Council formally adopted the new research and technological development programme in the field of marine science and technology (1990 to 1994). [5] This programme, which has a total budget of ECU 104 million, is divided into five parts: marine science, coastal zone science and engineering, marine technology, support measures and large-scale targeted projects. Two calls for proposals were published in June [6] and October [7] respectively. In response to the first of these the Commission received 119 proposals, of which 22 were selected for funding.

---

[1]   Twenty-fourth General Report, point 267.
[2]   OJ L 200, 13.7.1989; Twenty-third General Report, point 345.
[3]   OJ C 68, 16.3.1991.
[4]   OJ C 198, 21.7.1991.
[5]   OJ L 192, 16.7.1991; Bull. EC 6-1991, point 1.2.69; Commission proposal: OJ C 174, 16.7.1990, OJ C 321, 21.12.1990; Twenty-fourth General Report, point 269.
[6]   OJ C 169, 28.6.1991.
[7]   OJ C 284, 31.10.1991.

Life sciences and technologies

Biotechnology

323.   The Commission continued to implement the programme of research and technological development in the field of biotechnology (1989-92) (Bridge). [1] The 61 projects [2]
selected following the first call for proposals got under way after completion of the
contract negotiations. Fourteen projects were selected following the separate call for
proposals on risk assessment. [2] The number of 'T' projects (large-scale targeted projects
involving between 20 and 30 different laboratories) rose to seven. Thirteen summer
schools on issues related to modern biology were held in Greece, Spain and Portugal.

324.   Coordination in the field of biotechnology continued with a further meeting of
the EC/US task force on biotechnology research, the launching in both printed and
electronic form of a European biotechnology information service, the setting up within
the Commission of a biotechnology coordination committee and the preparation of a
Commission communication on promoting environmental awareness in the Community's biotechnology industry. [3]

325.   On 28 November the Council adopted a common position [4] on the new research
and technological development programme in the field of biotechnology (1990 to 1994). [5]
This programme is divided into three parts — molecular approaches, cellular and
organism approaches, and ecology and population biology — and emphasizes the ethical
and social aspects of biotechnology research. On 9 October Parliament delivered an
opinion [6] (first reading) on the programme, which led the Commission to amend its
proposal. [7]

Agricultural and agro-industrial research

326.   The Commission continued to implement the programme of research and technological development in the field of agro-industry (1989-93) [8] (Eclair). On completion of
the contract negotiations, a start was made on all of the projects selected in 1990. [9] Fifty

---

[1]   OJ L 360, 9.12.1989; Twenty-third General Report, point 331.
[2]   Twenty-fourth General Report, point 271.
[3]   Point 276 of this Report.
[4]   Bull. EC 11-1991, point 1.2.45.
[5]   OJ C 174, 16.7.1990; Twenty-fourth General Report, point 273.
[6]   OJ C 280, 28.10.1991; Bull. EC 10-1991, point 1.2.43.
[7]   OJ C 289, 7.11.1991; Bull. EC 10-1991, point 1.2.43.
[8]   OJ L 60, 3.3.1989; Twenty-third General Report, point 333.
[9]   Twenty-fourth General Report, point 274.

mobility grants were also awarded and three studies, one of which was on the subject of bioplastics, were launched.

327.   The Commission also continued to implement the research and technological development programme in the field of food science and technology (1989-93) (Flair). [1] Twenty-four mobility grants were awarded and three studies, one of which concerned the irradiation of foodstuffs, were launched.

328.   The implementation of the Community programme of research in the field of competitiveness of agriculture and management of agricultural resources (1989-93) [2] continued. Seventy-nine research projects, totalling over ECU 50 million, were selected and launched. Work relating to the training and mobility of research scientists and the development of the Agrep and Euragris networks also continued.

329.   On 9 September the Council formally adopted the new research and technological development programme in the field of agriculture and agro-industry, including fisheries (1991 to 1994). [3] This programme, which has a total budget of ECU 333 million, covers four areas: primary production in agriculture, forestry, aquaculture and fishing; inputs to agriculture, forestry, aquaculture and fishing; processing of biological raw materials from agriculture, forestry, aquaculture and fishing, and end use and products. A first call for proposals under this programme was published in October. [4]

Biomedicine and health

330.   The fourth Community coordination programme in the field of medical and health research (1987-91) [5] continued in 1991, during which time Turkey joined the programme. [6] Several concerted-action projects were extended to include new participants, and teams from as many as 17 different countries are now involved in some of these projects.

331.   The Commission also continued to implement the programme of research in the field of human genome analysis (1990-92). [7] The 17 research projects selected following

[1]   OJ L 200, 13.7.1989; Twenty-third General Report, point 334.
[2]   OJ L 58, 7.3.1990; Twenty-fourth General Report, point 276.
[3]   OJ L 265, 21.9.1991; Bull. EC 9-1991, point 1.2.37; Commission proposal: OJ C 174, 16.7.1990; Twenty-fourth General Report, point 275; OJ C 77, 22.3.1991; Bull. EC 3-1991, point 1.2.59; Bull. EC 7/8-1991, point 1.2.85.
[4]   OJ C 264, 10.10.1991.
[5]   OJ L 334, 24.11.1987; Twenty-first General Report, point 314.
[6]   Bull. EC 10-1991, point 1.2.50.
[7]   OJ L 146, 26.7.1990; Twenty-fourth General Report, point 279.

the call for proposals published in 1990[1] got under way after completion of the contract negotiations. Twenty training grants were also awarded. On 14 August a call for proposals for studies on the ethical, social and legal aspects of research in the field of human genome analysis was published.[2]

332.   On 9 September the Council formally adopted the new research and technological development programme in the field of biomedicine and health (1990 to 1994).[3] This programme, which has a total budget of ECU 133 million, covers four areas: development of coordinated research on prevention, care and health systems, major health problems and diseases with great socio-economic impact, human genome analysis and research in biomedical ethics.

Life sciences and technologies for developing countries

333.   The programme of research and technological development in the field of science and technology for development (1987-91)[4] was completed in 1991. A further amount of ECU 5 million was added to the original programme budget on a proposal by Parliament. This additional funding was used to finance five quality projects not selected from the last call for proposals owing to lack of funds and a number of workshops on ways of incorporating environmental aspects in future projects.

334.   On 7 June the Council adopted the new programme of research and technological development in the field of science and technology for development (1990 to 1994).[5] This programme, which has a total budget of ECU 111 million, covers the areas of tropical agriculture (improving food plant production, developing livestock farming and fisheries using systems suited to local conditions, restoring the environment, developing agricultural activities of high economic value) and medicine, health and nutrition (new methods for diagnosing and treating bacterial, parasitical and viral diseases, organization of health care systems in the developing countries and improving the nutritional condition of the population). The Commission received 243 proposals in response to a first invitation to tender[6] published on 18 July; 59 of these were selected for funding.

---

[1]   Twenty-fourth General Report, point 279.
[2]   OJ C 212, 14.8.1991.
[3]   OJ L 267, 24.9.1991; Bull. EC 9-1991, point 1.2.38; Commission proposal: OJ C 174, 16.7.1990, OJ C 11, 17.1.1991; Twenty-fourth General Report, point 280; Bull. EC 7/8-1991, point 1.2.86.
[4]   OJ L 355, 17.12.1987; Twenty-first General Report, point 345.
[5]   OJ L 196, 19.7.1991; Bull. EC 6-1991, point 1.2.70; Commission proposal: OJ C 174, 16.7.1990, OJ C 15, 23.1.1991; Twenty-fourth General Report, point 282.
[6]   OJ C 186, 18.7.1991.

Energy

Non-nuclear energy

335.   The Commission continued to implement the programme of research and technological development in the field of non-nuclear energies (1989-92) (Joule).[1] A number
of major international conferences were held, including a conference on biomass, in
April, in Athens, a conference on solar photovoltaic conversion, in April, in Lisbon,
and a conference on fuel cells, in July, in Athens.

336.   On 9 September the Council formally adopted the new research and technological
development programme in the field of non-nuclear energy (1990 to 1994).[2] The aim
of this programme, which has a budget of ECU 157 million, is to develop new, economically viable energy options which have little or no impact on the environment (especially
on climate). It covers four areas: analysis of strategies and modelling, use of fossil fuels,
with a minimum of emissions, renewable energy sources and rational energy utilization
and management. A first call for proposals under this programme was published on
13 September.[3]

Nuclear fission safety

337.   The Commission continued to implement the programme of research and technological development in the field of radiation protection (1990-91).[4] The Commission
participated in the IAEA evaluation of the consequences of the Chernobyl accident and
completed the tasks entrusted to it. It took part in a number of projects carried out at
the Chernobyl Centre for International Research (CHECIR) and established arrangements for collaboration between Soviet and European teams in the field of radioecology,
decontamination and emergency situation management. In collaboration with the World
Health Organization studies of the effects of the Chernobyl accident on public health
were also initiated.

338.   The JRC's Institute for Safety Technology continued its activities in the field of
reactor safety, in particular work on the FARO experimental installation and the Phebus
experiment, the latter carried out in collaboration with the CEA.

---

[1]   OJ L 98, 11.4.1989; Twenty-third General Report, point 343.
[2]   OJ L 257, 14.9.1991; Bull. EC 9-1991, point 1.2.36; Commission proposal: OJ C 174, 16.7.1990;
       Twenty-fourth General Report, point 284, OJ C 76, 21.3.1991; Bull. EC 3-1991, point 1.2.60, Bull.
       EC 7/8-1991, point 1.2.87.
[3]   OJ C 287, 13.9.1991.
[4]   OJ L 200, 13.7.1989; Twenty-third General Report, point 316.

339.   The Commission continued to implement the research programme on the management and storage of radioactive waste (1990-94). [1] Ninety research projects, totalling ECU 33 million, were initiated following the call for proposals published in 1990. [2] The Commission also published a third report on the waste management situation in the Community. The JRC's Institute for Safety Technology completed the construction of the Petra pilot plant to study alternative waste treatments.

340.   The Commission continued to implement the research and training programme on remote handling in hazardous or disordered nuclear environments (1989-93) (Teleman). [3] A second call for proposals for the design of demonstration machines was published in October. [4] The implementation of the programme of research (1989-93) [5] on the decommissioning of nuclear installations also continued, with the development of large-scale pilot operations in reactors and various plants involved in the fuel cycle.

341.   The JRC's Institute for Transuranium Elements continued its studies of the physical properties of fuels at extremely high temperatures. Research on the thermal expansion of uranium dioxide above its melting temperature produced initial results. The Institute also extended its work to include characterization of nuclear waste for the purposes of temporary or final storage. With regard to the inspection of fissile materials, the Institute for Systems Engineering completed the development of a technique employing ultrasonic seals to identify containers used for the transport and storage of fissile materials. It also developed a computer system for the optical surveillance of nuclear material and a laser measurement system for the surveillance of storage sites.

342.   On 28 November the Council adopted a new research and technological development programme in the field of nuclear fission safety. [6] The programme, which has a budget of ECU 36 million, covers the two areas of radiation protection and reactor safety. It will be implemented through shared-cost projects (in the case of radiation protection) and intensive concerted-action projects (in the case of reactor safety). A first call for proposals under this programme was published on 13 December. [7]

---

[1]   OJ L 395, 30.12.1989; Twenty-third General Report, point 340.
[2]   Twenty-fourth General Report, point 288.
[3]   OJ L 226, 3.8.1989; Twenty-third General Report, point 341.
[4]   OJ C 255, 1.10.1991.
[5]   OJ L 98, 11.4.1989; Twenty-third General Report, point 342.
[6]   OJ L 336, 7.12.1991; Bull. EC 11-1991, point 1.2.47; Commission proposal: OJ C 247, 2.10.1990; Twenty-fourth General Report, point 292.
[7]   OJ C 322, 13.12.1991.

Controlled thermonuclear fusion

343.   Activities continued under the programme of research and training in the field of controlled thermonuclear fusion (1988-92),[1] focusing on research into magnetic confinement. The three additional heating systems of the JET (Joint European Torus) were brought up to full power. In November the first-ever preliminary experiments with tritium were carried out in the JET producing 2 megawatts of fusion power. The construction and placing in service of medium-sized devices continued in the associated laboratories.

344.   The NET (Next European Torus) team at Garching continued its activities in connection with the preliminary international thermonuclear experimental reactor project (ITER).[2] Its contribution to the evaluation of the project included a recommendation to increase the technical and physical margins of the future installation.

345.   The JRC's Institute for Systems Engineering continued work on the design of components for the future NET/ITER machine and the development of remote handling techniques. The Institute for Advanced Materials carried out new studies on the effects of irradiation and thermal fatigue on materials. The Institute for Safety Technology continued the construction of the tritium-handling laboratory, Ethel.

346.   On 19 December the Council formally adopted the new research and technological training programme in the field of controlled thermonuclear fusion (1990 to 1994).[3] The programme, which has a total budget of ECU 416 million, covers four areas: 'next step' design, long-term technical development, JET and the support programme.

347.   On the basis of directives for negotiations issued by the Council,[4] a Commission delegation reached an *ad referendum* agreement with the delegations of Japan, the United States and the Soviet Union on the implementation of the detailed study of the ITER project. A protocol covering the first period was adopted. The detailed study would be carried out at Garching (Germany), Naka (Japan) and San Diego (United States) by a joint international team. The official headquarters of the ITER Council would be in Moscow.

---

[1]   OJ L 222, 12.8.1988; Twenty-second General Report, point 380.
[2]   Point 347 of this Report.
[3]   OJ L 375, 31.12.1991; Bull. EC 12-1991; Commission proposal: OJ C 261, 16.10.1990; Twenty-fourth General Report, point 295.
[4]   Twenty-fourth General Report, point 295.

Human capital and mobility

348.   Under the programme to stimulate the international cooperation and interchange needed by European research scientists (1988-92)[1] (Science), 632 proposals relating to twinning or research operations were submitted for evaluation; 97 of these were selected for Commission funding totalling ECU 7.3 million. During the year 429 applications were received for research bursaries and 103 for research grants, of which 92 and 42 respectively were approved. In addition, 4 applications for subsidies were received for high-level training courses, of which 1 was approved.

349.   The Commission continued to implement the Community stimulation plan for economic science (SPES) (1989-92).[2] At Parliament's request, the amount allocated to the programme was increased by ECU 5.9 million. One hundred and forty-five research, network and funding proposals were submitted, of which 84 were approved.

350.   The implementation of the Community plan of support to facilitate access to large-scale scientific facilities (1988-92)[3] also continued. Five new facilities were chosen. In the light of the recommendations of seven panels of experts[4] and the conclusions of the Round Table meeting on synchrotron facilities in Europe, several pilot projects designed to increase the number of users of this type of facility were launched. During the year the Commission received 1 300 applications for bursaries or grants for research at pre-doctoral, doctoral or post-doctoral level in all the fields covered by the various specific programmes. Five hundred of these were approved, totalling ECU 22.3 million.

351.   On 28 November the Council adopted a common position[5] on the new research and technological development programme in the field of human capital and mobility (1990 to 1994). This programme has a total budget of ECU 493 million and covers four types of activity: training bursaries (mainly for young, post-doctoral research scientists), support measures for scientific cooperation networks, support measures for access to large-scale scientific facilities and European scientific conferences. Parliament delivered an opinion (first reading) on the programme in May[6] and the Commission produced an amended proposal in June.[7]

---

1   OJ L 206, 30.7.1988; Twenty-second General Report, point 195.
2   OJ L 44, 16.2.1989; Twenty-third General Report, point 148.
3   OJ L 98, 11.4.1989; Twenty-third General Report, point 350.
4   Twenty-fourth General Report, point 298.
5   Bull. EC 11-1991, point 1.2.46.
6   OJ C 158, 17.6.1991; Bull. EC 5-1991, point 1.2.60.
7   OJ C 188, 19.7.1991; Bull. EC 6-1991, point 1.2.71.

Dissemination and utilization of R&TD results from Community programmes

352.   Information on activities relating to the dissemination and utilization of R&TD results is to be found in Section 7 'Telecommunications, information industries and innovation' of Chapter II of this Report.

Measures in support of the framework programme

Support for science and technology

353.   Work continued under the programme on strategic analysis, forecasting and evaluation in matters of research and technology (1989-92) (Monitor). [1] A first two-yearly report (1989-90) was published. It deals with the social and economic implications of technological change and the main problems confronting political decision-makers. The monograph section is on telecommunications. In April the second 'Europrospective' conference was held, providing an opportunity for exchange of experience between European forecasting specialists on both methodologies and research results. The initial results of forecasting studies on economic and social cohesion, the 'globalization' of the economy and technology, and technological assessments of anthropocentric production systems and health technology were also published. Under the SAST programme the findings of studies on the scope for scientific and technological collaboration between the Community and newly-industrializing countries (summary reports and country analyses) and on the interaction between research and standardization were published. Under the Spear programme a number of studies were initiated dealing with the impact of the framework programme on industry. The three expert networks set up to study the economic impact of research, training in assessment and research impact indicators [2] continued their work, and a fourth network on the assessment of scientific infrastructure programmes in less-favoured areas was set up.

354.   A number of programmes, including those on large-scale facilities, science and technology for development, human genome analysis and SPES, were also submitted for evaluation by panels of independent experts. The evaluation report on the aeronautics section of the Brite/Euram programme was published. Assessments of the

---

[1]   OJ L 200, 13.7.1989; Twenty-third General Report, point 351.
[2]   Twenty-fourth General Report, point 300.

applied metrology, chemical analysis, Brite/Euram and Joule programmes were also initiated.

The JRC's Institute for Technology Forecasting published studies on the competitiveness of Europe's space industry, power supplies for high-speed train networks and the Japanese technological response to global environmental problems. A study on technological and economic forecasting in the environment industry was also initiated. A documentation and information system was also developed in support of the S/T observation and assessment activities.

Support for Community policies

355.   Activities in the space sector continued. In October a panel of independent experts published a report aimed at helping the Commission to define in more detail the Community's future role in the space sector. Following the generally favourable response to the Commission's Green Paper on satellite telecommunications,[1] a start was made on preparing the implementing regulations for the proposed new system. In the field of earth observation, three studies on the subjects of soil infrastructure requirements, Europe's technical capability in interpreting satellite data and conditions for the development of applications markets were completed. Several earth observation projects involving the Joint Research Centre and the European Space Agency were developed. The Commission also continued to cooperate closely with the ESA, carrying out a joint study on industrial aspects of Europe's space effort and ways of protecting industrial property rights in respect of satellite data and of promoting a European commercial launch service capability.

356.   The eight institutes of the JRC continued to provide scientific and technical support for the Commission.[2]

International scientific and technical cooperation

357.   Scientific and technical cooperation with the countries of Central and Eastern Europe and the Soviet Union was gradually implemented in line with the Council's conclusions of 20 November 1990. The economic and trade cooperation agreements concluded, or due to be concluded with these countries, including Albania and the Baltic States, provided a legal basis for scientific and technical cooperation. Subcommittees on science and technology were set up, in collaboration with Hungary and the USSR

---

[1]   Twenty-fourth General Report, point 312.
[2]   Point 308 of this Report.

in particular. A number of meetings and workshops were organized on information services (in Luxembourg in January), plant biotechnology (in Budapest in March), cancer (in Budapest in April), the environment of the Black Sea (in Varna in September), interaction between the environment and health (in Moscow in October) and bioelectronics (in Brussels in November). The opening up, in some fields, of the third framework programme to bodies and firms in Eastern Europe was an important step forward. The environment, non-nuclear energies, biomedical research and nuclear safety are now concerned. Measures to provide scientific and technological assistance under the Phare programme got under way, in Czechoslovakia and Hungary in particular, as did measures to promote the exchange of experience and know-how between scientists and industrialists in the field of economics and management (ACE). Scientific cooperation with the Soviet Union developed mainly in the fields of nuclear safety (Community participation at the Tchernobyl research centre) and research on fusion energy (cooperation within the framework of the ITER project). In these two fields specific cooperation agreements were also negotiated.

358.   European scientific and technical cooperation (COST) continued with the entry into force of memorandums of understanding in respect of the following projects: COST 230 (Stereoscopic television), 238 (Prediction and retrospective ionospheric modelling over Europe), 317 (Socio-economic effects of the Channel Tunnel), 509 (Corrosion and protection of metals in contact with concrete), 614 (Impacts of high CO_2 levels, climate change and air pollutants on tree physiology) and 814 (Crop development for the cool and wet regions of Europe). Two projects were launched in the social sciences field, on the following topics: Europe's integration and the labour force, and ageing and technology. On 21 November, at the Ministerial Conference held to mark the 20th anniversary of COST, the number of member countries was increased from 19 to 23 with the accession of Iceland, Poland, Hungary and Czechoslovakia. A resolution was adopted which referred to the possibility of future geographical enlargement. The Conference was followed by a scientific forum which provided an opportunity for an initial exchange of views between scientists from both the former and the new member countries of COST.

359.   Alongside the ongoing negotiations between the Community and the EFTA countries for the conclusion of a Treaty on the establishment of a European Economic Area, which culminated in a political agreement in October,[1] bilateral cooperation with these countries in the field of science and technology continued. The following agreements relating to the participation of EFTA countries in programmes under the second framework programme came into force in 1991: the agreement with Austria on medical research,[2] the agreements with Finland, Sweden and Switzerland on applied metrology

---

[1]   Point 846 of this Report.
[2]   OJ L 74, 20.3.1990; Twenty-first General Report, point 253.

and chemical analysis,[1] the agreements with Austria and Finland on economic science (SPES)[2] and the agreement with Iceland on the Science programme. The Commission also approved an administrative arrangement with Sweden on the management and storage of radioactive waste on 12 September. On 25 November the Council adopted a common position[3] on the Commission's proposal concerning the association of Austria, Finland and Norway with the programme of research in the field of the environment (STEP),[4] on which Parliament[5] and the Economic and Social Committee[6] had delivered favourable opinions. On the same date it also adopted a common position[7] on the proposal[8] concerning the association of Sweden and Iceland with the STEP (environment) and Epoch (climatology) programmes on which Parliament[9] and the Economic and Social Committee[10] had delivered favourable opinions. On 31 July the Commission also submitted two proposals[11] for Community-COST multilateral agreements on the participation of certain EFTA and COST countries in the Bridge biotechnology programme and the Flair programme of research in food science and technology. Parliament[12] and the Economic and Social Committee[13] gave their opinions on these proposals in November and the Council adopted a common position[14] in December.

360.   The Commission continued to contribute to the management and funding of Eureka projects, and there was a marked increase in the number of projects involving the Commission directly. In order to further improve coordination between Community research and technological development programmes and Eureka projects, the Commission joined all Eureka strategic projects and 'umbrella' projects, which combine a number of measures on a common theme. The JRC took part in three new projects: Euroenviron-Tracy (study of heavy metals in trace quantities) Euroenviron mobile analytical laboratory (in situ sample analysis), and Cefir (ceramic fibres). The Commission contributed to the evaluation of Eureka activities in 1990 and 1991. The evaluation report resulting from this exercise recommends, in particular, that the interaction between Eureka activities and Community programmes be actively encouraged and developed.

---

[1]   OJ L 61, 7.3.1991; Bull. EC 1/2-1991, point 1.2.86.
[2]   OJ L 61, 7.3.1991; Bull. EC 1/2-1991, point 1.2.85.
[3]   Bull. EC 11-1991, point 1.2.43.
[4]   OJ C 179, 10.7.1991; Bull. EC 5-1991, point 1.2.50.
[5]   OJ C 305, 25.11.1991; Bull. EC 10-1991, point 1.2.41.
[6]   OJ C 14, 20.1.1992; Bull. EC 10-1991, point 1.2.41.
[7]   Bull. EC 11-1991, point 1.2.44.
[8]   OJ C 163, 22.6.1991; Bull. EC 5-1991, point 1.2.51.
[9]   OJ C 305, 25.11.1991; Bull. EC 10-1991, point 1.2.42.
[10]   OJ C 14, 20.1.1992; Bull. EC 10-1991, point 1.2.42.
[11]   OJ C 224, 29.8.1991; Bull. EC 7/8-1991, points 1.2.93 and 1.2.94.
[12]   OJ C 326, 16.12.1991; Bull. EC 11-1991, points 1.2.50 and 1.2.51.
[13]   Bull. EC 11-1991, points 1.2.50 and 1.2.51.
[14]   Bull. EC 12-1991.

361.   International cooperation with the industrialized countries outside Europe was strengthened and extended. The joint EC/US scientific and technological cooperation committee set up in 1990[1] held its first meeting in February in Washington and its second in November in Brussels.[2] Within this framework the Community and the United States launched a joint study of the external cost of the fuel cycle. The biotechnology research task force set up in 1990[1] held its second meeting in Brussels in July. In October the United States and the Community held informal talks in Brussels on international collaboration in mega-projects. The Commission also had discussions with the Japanese science administration on the application of research to environmental issues, and areas for cooperation were identified. The Commission also played a very active role in negotiations on the Japanese proposal for international cooperation on intelligent manufacturing systems. On 17 May the Commission and the New Zealand Government signed an administrative arrangement on scientific and technological cooperation.

362.   Scientific cooperation with countries in Latin America, Asia and the Mediterranean was strengthened and extended, and the geographical area covered was further expanded. Agreements which included a scientific and technical cooperation component came into force with Chile, Mexico, Uruguay and Paraguay. Scientific cooperation with China, interrupted following the events of 1989, was gradually resumed. In November the Centre for Biotechnology Research, established in Beijing in cooperation with the Community, was inaugurated and began its activities.[3] Cooperation with Israel, suspended in 1990 at the request of the European Parliament, was also gradually resumed. Contacts were also established with other Mediterranean countries, including Tunisia, with the aim of setting up cooperative projects. During the year, 80 joint research projects, five workshops and 180 research fellowships were funded, the overall budget for these activities amounting to ECU 27.5 million.

Other activities

363.   Acting under Article 55 of the ECSC Treaty and in accordance with the medium-term guidelines for steel research (1991-95),[4] the Commission selected 142 steel research projects totalling   ECU 45.1 million   and   12   demonstration   projects   totalling ECU 13.5 million. In addition, seven projects were placed on a reserve list. Bodies from the five new German *Länder* are involved in 13 of the projects. Twenty-two of the projects are specifically concerned with environmental problems. The Commission also

---

[1]   Twenty-fourth General Report, point 255.
[2]   Point 854 of this Report.
[3]   Point 924 of this Report.
[4]   OJ C 252, 6.10.1990; Twenty-fourth General Report, point 304.

decided to earmark ECU 2 million for a programme of coordinated-action projects to adapt production techniques to environmental requirements.

Under Article 55 of the ECSC Treaty the Commission decided to grant financial aid totalling ECU 18 million to 82 research projects concerning health, medicine, safety and hygiene in mines and the technical battle against pollution in and around steelworks (ECSC social research).

364. Under the first joint research programme on safety in ECSC industries,[1] the Commission granted financial aid of ECU 224 400.

365. A call for proposals was published under the Euret research programme,[2] as a result of which nine projects were selected and four concerted-action projects initiated.

---

[1]   OJ C 325, 29.12.1989; Twenty-third General Report, point 430.
[2]   Point 729 of this Report.

Section 7

Telecommunications, information industries and innovation

Priority activities and objectives

366.   On 26 March, further to its communication of November 1990 on industrial policy in an open and competitive environment,[1] the Commission adopted a communication entitled 'The European electronics and information technology industry: state of play, issues at stake and proposals for action' in which it identifies five courses of action relating to demand, technology, training, external relations and the business environment in order to facilitate adjustment decisions by businesses and enhance user satisfaction. Following on from this communication, the Council of Ministers (industry) adopted, on 18 November, a resolution on electronics, information and communication technologies which emphasizes the importance of these 'enabling' industries and the need to create a favourable environment for improving their competitiveness.[2]

The communication, which provoked much discussion, particularly on how to ensure the industry's long-term future, is now the basis for implementing the third framework programme (1990 to 1994),[3] under which three specific programmes on information and communications technology are now being carried out:

(i)   the specific programme on information technologies is geared towards the new generations of technologies:[4] microelectronics, information processing systems and software, advanced office and home technology systems and peripherals, computer-integrated manufacturing and engineering, and basic research. It also includes a new multidisciplinary initiative in the field of open microprocessor systems, plus five specific large-scale projects: integrated circuit design and manufacture (in collaboration with Jessi), transfer of software development methods to users, high-performance computing and high-resolution display technology based on liquid crystals;

(ii)   the specific programme on communications technology[5] aims to develop and introduce integrated broadband communications (IBC);

---

[1]   Twenty-fourth General Report, point 212.
[2]   Bull. EC 11-1991, point 1.2.33.
[3]   Twenty-fourth General Report, point 247.
[4]   Point 367 of this Report.
[5]   Point 377 of this Report.

(iii) the specific programme on telematics systems in areas of general interest[1] has the priority task of supporting the establishment of trans-European networks in seven main areas: government departments closely involved in the implementation of the internal market, transport services, health care, flexible and distance learning, libraries, linguistic research and engineering and rural areas.

Various activities were undertaken in the field of telecommunications: a common strategy for developing networks and services, particularly through the implementation of open network provision,[2] implementing the single market in telecommunications terminal equipment[2] and introducing the Telematique programme,[2] which follows on from the STAR programme. Furthermore, at the Council's request, the Commission continued to implement Community policy by preparing a communication on telecommunications equipment which follows on from the communication on the European electronics and information technology industry.

Most measures in this field have a bearing on the Community's external relations policy, particularly with regard to the countries of Central and Eastern Europe.

In addition, a proposal for a Directive on the adoption of standards for satellite broadcasting of television signals was proposed.[2] The Commission closely monitored the activities of the European economic interest grouping Vision 1250 (HDTV promotion and production) and chaired its Committee of Sponsors.[3] It also coordinated preparations for the high-definition transmission of the Albertville and Barcelona Olympic Games and the Seville World Fair, and took part in the work of the International Radio Consultative Committee on an international HDTV production standard.

Work was stepped up on activities undertaken under the Value programme for the dissemination and utilization of scientific and technological research results and the Sprint programme for innovation and technology transfer.[4] The Economic and Social Committee and the European Parliament gave their opinions on the proposal for a Council Decision on the dissemination and utilization of knowledge from specific Community research and technological programmes[5] which was adopted by the Commission at the end of 1990. The encouraging results of the first stage of the Impact programme (1989 to 1990) prompted the Council to adopt a new programme (1991 to 1995) designed to extend the period and scope of the activities involved in the establishment of an information services market.[6]

---

[1]   Point 379 of this Report.
[2]   Point 374 of this Report.
[3]   Twenty-fourth General Report, point 312.
[4]   Points 396 to 398 of this Report.
[5]   Twenty-fourth General Report, point 326.
[6]   Point 399 of this Report.

Much work was done on standardization in the different areas of information technology and telecommunications and the international aspects of standardization occupied a significant proportion of the Commission's attention.

Information technology — Esprit

367. On 8 July the Council adopted a specific R&TD programme in the field of information technologies (1990 to 1994),[1] which, while launching a new phase of Esprit,[2] is also part of the third R&TD framework programme.[3]

368. Esprit's new phase is the basis for the technology initiative identified in the Commission's communication on the European electronics and information technology industry.[4] Among the five proposed lines of action, the communication calls for a second generation of R&TD, ranging from basic research to industrial projects with clear potential for commercialization.

369. The new phase of Esprit represents an important aspect of the Community's new approach to IT and electronics: more tightly focused and integrated; more concerned with feedback between users and suppliers, in order to link technology push with market pull; looking upstream to strengthen training in advanced topics and techniques; and directing more effort towards technology transfer. The first general call for proposals[5] was launched on 27 July and two special calls were issued in August.

The general call for proposals was closed on 14 October. Some 1 300 proposals were received, representing R&D activities amounting to ECU 7.6 billion. This call for proposals was approximately five times oversubscribed. Following the evaluation of the proposals, a start was made on contract negotiations, so as to enable the R&D activities to begin in early 1992.

370. The Esprit 1991 conference and forum were held in November, concurrently with an exhibition presenting the results of over 100 Esprit projects, covering both prototypes and products already on the market. 182 new results were recorded under the Esprit programme, bringing the total to nearly 500.

371. An additional special project was started to promote SME usage of ASIC (application-specific integrated circuit) technology, and special regional schemes were

---

[1]   OJ L 218, 6.8.1991; Bull. EC 7/8-1991, point 1.2.96; Commission proposal: OJ C 174, 16.7.1990, OJ C 30, 6.2.1991; Twenty-fourth General Report, point 311.
[2]   OJ L 118, 6.5.1988; Twenty-second General Report, point 405.
[3]   OJ L 117, 8.5.1990; Twenty-fourth General Report, point 247.
[4]   Bull. EC 3-1991, point 1.2.50; Bull. EC 4-1991, point 1.2.36; Supplement 3/91 — Bull. EC.
[5]   OJ C 198, 27.7.1991.

launched in Greece, Portugal and Spain, in particular to accelerate the take-up of microelectronics technology.

372. On the international front, substantial progress was made in drawing up commonly acceptable terms of reference for a study covering the feasibility of cooperative research into advanced computer-integrated manufacturing systems. The discussions involved the Community, EFTA, the USA, Japan, Canada and Australia.

Telecommunications

373. The Commission continued to implement Community policy, the guidelines for which were set out in the 1987 Green Paper on the development of the common market for telecommunications services and equipment[1] and, specifically as regards satellite communications, in a second Green Paper, which was favourably received by the Council in 1990[2] and by the Economic and Social Committee in April.[3]

374. The other activities in this field were carried out within the framework of the lines of action set out by the Commission in its communication of June 1986:[4]

(i)   The framing of a common strategy for the development of networks and services: the Commission drew up the third progress report on the introduction of the integrated services digital network (ISDN) in the European Community.[5] It started work on implementation of open network provision (ONP) in the Member States, with the help of the Committee set up for this purpose under framework Directive 90/387/EEC;[6] on 12 February it adopted a proposal for a Directive on the application of open network provision to leased lines,[7] on which the Economic and Social Committee gave its opinion in July;[8] Parliament also delivered an opinion on first reading in October[9] and the Council adopted a common position on 18 December.[10] On 7 June and 13 December the Commission also adopted proposals for, respectively, a recommendation on the harmonized provision of a minimum set of packet-switched data services[11] and a recommendation on a minimum set of ISDN

---

[1]   Twenty-first General Report, point 353.
[2]   Twenty-fourth General Report, point 312.
[3]   OJ C 159, 17.6.1991; Bull. EC 4-1991, point 1.2.48.
[4]   Twentieth General Report, point 401.
[5]   Bull. EC 11-1991, point 1.2.62.
[6]   OJ L 192, 24.7.1990; Twenty-fourth General Report, point 312.
[7]   OJ C 58, 7.3.1991; Bull. EC 1/2-1991, point 1.2.92.
[8]   OJ C 269, 14.10.1991; Bull. EC 7/8-1991, point 1.2.99.
[9]   OJ C 305, 25.11.1991; Bull. EC 10-1991, point 1.2.52.
[10] Bull. EC 12-1991.
[11] Bull. EC 6-1991, point 1.2.80.

services. [1] The Community also continued with its efforts to develop mobile communications. On 3 June, the Council adopted Directive 91/287/EEC[2] and Recommendation 91/288/EEC[3] on the frequency bands to be designated for the coordinated introduction of digital European cordless telecommunications (DECT) in the Community. On 12 June the Commission adopted a proposal for a Directive on digital short-range radio (DSRR). [4]

The idea of a standard international access code for public telephone networks was endorsed by the adoption of a Council Decision on the harmonization of the international telephone access code in the Community. [5]

In June Parliament adopted a resolution[6] on the proposal for a Council Decision[7] on the introduction of a standard Europe-wide emergency call number. The proposal was based on Article 100a of the Treaty and Parliament questioned the need for the change of legal basis (Article 235) proposed by the Council.

Turning to satellite television, on 26 June the Commission sent the Council a proposal for a Directive on the adoption of the MAC family of standards as the sole European standards for HDTV;[8] opinions on this proposal were delivered by the Economic and Social Committee[9] and by Parliament[10] (first reading) in November, which led the Commission to adopt an amended proposal with respect to which the Council agreed on a common position on 18 December. [11]

(ii) Creation of a single market in telecommunications equipment: on 29 April the Council adopted the Directive on the approximation of the laws of the Member States concerning telecommunications terminal equipment,[12] including mutual recognition of conformity, and on 4 November it agreed on a resolution setting out a plan of action for the gradual introduction of a competitive market in satellite

---

[1]   Bull. EC 12-1991.
[2]   OJ L 144, 8.6.1991; Bull. EC 6-1991, point 1.2.78; Commission proposal: OJ C 187, 27.7.1990; Twenty-fourth General Report, point 312; Bull. EC 5-1991, point 1.2.66.
[3]   OJ L 144, 8.6.1991; Bull. EC 6-1991, point 1.2.77; Commission proposal: OJ C 187, 27.7.1990; OJ C 9, 15.1.1991; Twenty-fourth General Report, point 312.
[4]   OJ C 189, 20.7.1991; Bull. EC 6-1991, point 1.2.79.
[5]   Bull. EC 12-1991, Commission proposal: OJ C 157, 15.6.1991; Bull. EC 5-1991, point 1.2.63.
[6]   OJ C 183, 15.7.1991; Bull. EC 6-1991, point 1.2.81.
[7]   OJ C 269, 21.10.1989; Twenty-third General Report, point 360.
[8]   OJ C 194, 25.7.1991; Bull. EC 6-1991, point 1.2.73.
[9]   Bull. EC 11-1991, point 1.2.60.
[10]   OJ C 326, 16.12.1991; Bull. EC 11-1991, point 1.2.60.
[11]   OJ C 332, 21.12.1991; Bull. EC 12-1991.
[12]   OJ L 128, 23.5.1991; Bull. EC 4-1991, point 1.2.49; Commission proposal: OJ C 211, 17.8.1989; Twenty-third General Report, point 360; OJ C 187, 27.7.1990; Twenty-fourth General Report, point 312; Bull. EC 1/2-1991, point 1.2.93.

communications,[1] which it formally adopted in December.[2] On 22 October Parliament adopted a resolution on European space policy;[3]

(iii) Implementation of a Community programme to promote the development of certain less favoured areas in the Community (STAR):[4] as the STAR programme came to an end during the year, a two-year programme, called Telematique, was set up to replace it;[5]

(iv) Achievement of a social consensus on the measures taken to establish a European telecommunications area: the joint committee which the Commission decided to set up in 1989[6] continued its work;

(v) Setting-up of Community-level coordination in the postal sector: the Commission continued to study the situation in this sector with a view to submitting a Green Paper to the Council.

Communications technologies

375.   Following the two calls for proposals for the RACE[7] programme published in July 1987 and July 1988,[8] a total of 93 transnational research and development projects have been launched. Most of these projects are to be continued into 1992. As a result of these cooperative efforts over 1 000 reports and technical specifications have been produced so far. Common functional specifications have been published for 44 different aspects of IBC systems and over 330 contributions have been made to the work of standardization bodies. Opto-electronics technologies that will make possible widespread use of optical fibres have been developed and 21 patents have been registered.

376.   A strategic study was carried out of the situation as regards the development of advanced communications in Europe. It confirmed that the establishment of such communications is essential for the competitiveness of European business in the 1990s.

377.   In June the Council approved the extension of Community R&D efforts on integrated broadband communications as a continuation of ongoing RACE activities by adopting a specific programme on communications technology[9] as part of the third

---

[1]   Bull. EC 11-1991, point 1.2.55.
[2]   Bull. EC 12-1991.
[3]   OJ C 305, 25.11.1991; Bull. EC 10-1991, point 1.2.51.
[4]   OJ L 305, 31.10.1986; Twentieth General Report, point 519.
[5]   Point 506 of this Report.
[6]   Twenty-third General Report, point 360; Twenty-fourth General Report, point 312.
[7]   Research and development on advanced communications technologies in Europe — OJ L 16, 21.1.1988; Twenty-first General Report, point 354.
[8]   Twenty-second General Report, point 404, Twenty-third General Report, point 361.
[9]   OJ L 192, 16.7.1991; Bull. EC 6-1991, point 1.2.74.

framework programme for research and technological development 1990 to 1994. The budget for these activities is ECU 486 million for the duration of the third framework programme.

378. Following this Council Decision a call for proposals was published in the Official Journal on 12 June.[1] Nearly 200 project proposals have been submitted.

Telematic services of general interest

379. In June, to promote understanding of how new information and communications technologies can best help to meet the key economic and social needs of the 1990s, the Council adopted Decision 91/353/EEC on a new specific programme of research and technological development in the field of telematic systems in areas of general interest.[2] In June calls for proposals were published[3] in the seven areas covered by the programme: the establishment of trans-European networks between government departments and the areas of transport, health care, flexible and distance learning, telematic systems for rural areas, linguistic research and engineering and libraries.

Government departments

380. The work concerning government departments will be an essential complement to the legislative and regulatory measures needed for completion of the single market. They will be required to give a trans-European dimension to their activities and significantly improve their information exchange capabilities. As the key areas for applications of telematics appear to be customs services and social services, a call for proposals[4] was published in August and 40 proposals were received.

Transport

381. The proposed projects on telematic systems for transport management will build on the R&D under the Drive programme,[5] but will also cover intermodal transport. The Drive programme focused on telematics for road transport and ended this year. As a result of the call for proposals[4] published in August, 150 proposals were received.

---

[1] OJ C 154, 12.6.1991.
[2] OJ L 192, 16.7.1991; Bull. EC 6-1991, point 1.2.75.
[3] OJ C 157, 15.6.1991.
[4] OJ C 218, 21.8.1991.
[5] OJ L 206, 30.7.1988; Twenty-second General Report, point 406.

Health care

382.   In the health care sector, work continued on the opportunities identified by the AIM exploratory action[1] for collaborative R&D related to telematics. The objective is to stimulate the development of harmonized applications of telematics in health care and the development of a European health care information infrastructure, taking into account the needs of users and technological opportunities. The R&D will concentrate on interoperability of national systems, the establishment of standards, user acceptability, data integrity and confidentiality. As a result of the call for proposals[2] published in August, 193 proposals were received.

Distance learning

383.   In the area of flexible and distance learning, the Delta exploratory action[3] has successfully identified opportunities to share experience and resources in the development of learning systems. Follow-up work concentrated on providing opportunities for interoperability between national systems, and on defining standards, architecture and functional specifications.

384.   The aim is to establish trans-European flexible and distance learning services based on telematic systems. These will make a major contribution to solving the problems posed by Europe's growing training needs in terms of flexibility, accessibility and support. Support was given for pilot projects to verify the technology, to test concepts and to demonstrate interoperability. As a result of the call for proposals, 110 proposals were received.

Rural areas

385.   The introduction of telematic systems in rural areas will be a gradual process, because of the cost and the lifetime of the systems installed. The objectives of the R&D are to create the conditions for small businesses to provide more diverse employment opportunities in rural areas; to establish the infrastructure for provision of improved commercial, social, educational and health services to dispersed and isolated populations; to raise the level of awareness about telematics in rural areas; to make equipment and services easier to use by rural communities; to prepare the ground for

---

[1]   OJ L 314, 22.11.1988; Twenty-second General Report, point 406, Twenty-fourth General Report, point 319.
[2]   OJ C 218, 21.8.1991.
[3]   OJ L 206, 30.7.1988; Twenty-second General Report, point 406, Twenty-fourth General Report, point 320.

the harmonized planning and introduction of telematics infrastructures in rural areas, and to ensure that telematics does not contribute to further centralization of business and administrative activities and a loss of the cultural and economic diversity in rural areas. As a result of the call for proposals, 150 proposals were received.

Linguistic research and engineering

386.   Work continued on the implementation of the specific programme concerning the follow-up of Eurotra[1] after the Advisory Committee had approved the work programme in February. Six shared-cost projects concerning linguistic research of general interest were selected following a call for proposals[2] published in March.

387.   Following the adoption of the linguistic research and engineering programme, as part of the specific programme on 'telematics systems of general interest', the work programme was approved by the Telematics Management Committee and the first call for proposals was published in August.[3] Ninety proposals were received. Projects will be selected in January 1992.

388.   The Commission continued to develop and implement the Systran machine translation system as part of the fifth action plan for the improvement of information transfer between languages. Thirteen language pairs are now accessible to all departments in Brussels and Luxembourg, resulting in 6 000 requests from officials from numerous departments in 1991.

389.   Work also began on a new programme relating to the use of computer technology for the processing of Community languages.

Libraries

390.   The 'libraries' section of the specific programme in the field of telematic systems of general interest is aimed at encouraging the development of computerized catalogues, interconnecting library systems, stimulating new electronic services in libraries and the availability of telematic products and services relevant to libraries. Work concentrated this year on the launching of this new programme. A first call for proposals[4] was published in July and closed in December. Eighty-five proposals were received and the evaluation process was set in train with a view to starting the work in 1992.

---

[1]   OJ L 358, 21.12.1990; Twenty-fourth General Report, point 322.
[2]   OJ C 59, 8.3.1991.
[3]   OJ C 218, 21.8.1991.
[4]   OJ C 184, 16.7.1991; OJ S 132, 16.7.1991.

Computerized telecommunication of data, information and administrative documents

Tedis

391.   In July the Council gave the go-ahead for the second phase[1] of the Tedis programme[2] which is to run for three years. It was allocated a budget of ECU 25 million, including ECU 4 million for 1991 and ECU 6 million for 1992. The action programme discussed with the Member States immediately resulted in a call for tenders[3] covering all the programme topics, but giving priority to telecommunications and the interconnection of services and networks for EDI. Many reports, case studies and documents on specific aspects of EDI were finalized, as was the report on the 12 pilot projects[4] in the first phase.

Insis

392.   On the basis of the results of the strategy study[5] on the revision of the Insis programme[6] which was completed during the year, the Commission undertook preparatory work with a view to implementing the main recommendations of the study, namely revision of the Insis programme to speed up the use of applications based on current technology and to place it in a much wider context, which would also include the Caddia programme. While this revision work was proceeding, the current Insis programme activities continued during the year taking account of the changes suggested by the strategic study.

Caddia

393.   Caddia[7] activities proceeded in accordance with the work programme in the three areas of customs, agriculture and statistics. Feasibility studies were also conducted in five Member States on the implementation of computer systems for data interchange

---

[1]   OJ L 208, 30.7.1991; Bull. EC 7/8-1991, point 1.2.97; Commission proposal: OJ C 311, 12.12.1990; Twenty-fourth General Report, point 314.
[2]   Trade electronic data interchange systems.
[3]   OJ C 217, 20.8.1991; OJ S 156, 20.8.1991.
[4]   Twenty-fourth General Report, point 314.
[5]   Twenty-fourth General Report, point 315.
[6]   Interinstitutional system of integrated services — OJ L 368, 28.12.1982; Twentieth General Report, point 406.
[7]   Cooperation on automation of data and documentation on imports/exports and agriculture — OJ L 145, 5.6.1987; Twenty-first General Report, point 357.

between the Commission and the Member States, and similar studies will be undertaken in the other Member States. The strategy study on the objectives of the Caddia programme[1] was completed and the results discussed with representatives of the Member States. The study's recommendations seek to extend the Caddia programme so as to include other sectors of activity and to place it in a wider context which would include the Insis programme and future applications of computerized telecommunications in the implementation of the single market.

Standardization

394.   A particular feature of 1991 was the considerable scope of the new areas covered and particularly computer-integrated manufacturing, the exchange of medical data, electromagnetic compatibility and the exchange of messages between libraries. Standardization in telecommunications was geared essentially towards completing basic infrastructure such as the integrated services digital network, mobile communications, high-definition television, telematics services, satellite communications, terminal equipment and access to networks. Because of the scale of these activities, there was an exponential increase in the standardization work given by the Commission to the European standardization organizations and to the European Telecommunications Standards Institute. In accordance with the recommendations of the Green Paper on standardization,[2] new methods and procedures were set up to speed things up and improve efficiency, particularly as regards cooperation between the European standardization organizations, applying the harmonized standards in the Member States and increasing the involvement in the pre-standardization process of private bodies representing industry and consumers. The conformance testing service programme[3] continued with the launching of the fourth phase[4] in the setting up of conformance testing services in the various fields of telecommunications (ISDN, DECT, satellites, etc.). A number of mutual recognition agreements on certification in the field of information technologies were concluded by certification bodies and accredited laboratories in specific areas. In addition, standardization was encouraged in public contracts. This meant that suitable information media should be made available to those responsible for awarding public contracts in the Member States.

395.   At international level, cooperation between the European standardization organizations and international bodies was intensified during the year, under the agreements

[1]   Twenty-third General Report, point 363.
[2]   OJ C 20, 28.1.1991; Twenty-fourth General Report, point 117.
[3]   Twenty-third General Report, point 367, Twenty-fourth General Report, point 324.
[4]   OJ C 125, 15.5.1991.

concluded in 1989, through exchanges of information between the Commission and EFTA, particularly on technical regulations, and ongoing discussions with American, Asian and Central European countries.

Dissemination and utilization of the results of Community and national research and technological development programmes

396. Work on the dissemination and utilization of knowledge derived from the specific research and technological development programmes, which took off in 1990 after the adoption of the Value programme,[1] continued during the year. The Cordis electronic information service[2] launched experimentally in November 1990 now has eight data-bases covering programmes, the Commission's 'COM' documents, publications, programme-based research projects, partners, R&TD news, the results obtained and a base containing all the Community acronyms. The number of users of this service is increasing rapidly, having reached around 2 000. Other dissemination activities continued, as far as publications are concerned. A call for proposals concerning dissemination[3] published on 20 March was extremely successful since 170 proposals were received. In addition to the conventional procedures for protecting the results of research obtained by the Joint Research Centre and managing the Community's intellectual property, a new experimental scheme was launched which is designed to help contractors involved in Community biotechnology programmes who wish to protect their findings. The call for proposals published in 1990[4] concerning the exploitation of results was republished,[5] and an announcement of opportunities to promote Community R&TD exploitation projects was also published. Another important achievement of 1991 was a joint project with the Brite programme which has already made it possible to evaluate the exploitation potential of 75 projects and which will enable the results of 160 new projects to be evaluated between autumn 1991 and spring 1992. Work continued on the pilot schemes to set up relay centres in Greece and Portugal to promote Community R&TD.

397. In September the Economic and Social Committee gave its opinion[6] on the proposal for a Council Decision on the dissemination and utilization of knowledge from specific Community research and technological development programmes.[7] The European Parliament gave its opinion (first reading) on the proposal in December.[8]

---

1   OJ L 200, 13.7.1989; Twenty-third General Report, point 369.
2   OJ C 202, 3.8.1988; Twenty-fourth General Report, point 325.
3   OJ C 74, 20.3.1991.
4   OJ C 134, 1.6.1990; Twenty-fourth General Report, point 325.
5   OJ C 148, 7.6.1991.
6   OJ C 339, 31.12.1991; Bull. EC 9-1991, point 1.2.41.
7   OJ C 53, 28.2.1991; Twenty-fourth General Report, point 326.
8   Bull. EC 12-1991.

Promotion of innovation and technology transfer

398.   The strategic programme for innovation and technology transfer (Sprint)[1] provides a unique framework in which Community activities in the fields of technology transfer, the application of innovatory techniques and the understanding of the concept of innovation can help to complement other national or Community policies. Work continued in 1991 in three different areas:

(i)   Facilitating the transfer of new technologies to firms: a call for proposals[2] published in May brought in more than 100 applications to set up new networks of research and technology organizations which are intended to give smaller firms better access to new technologies. A pilot scheme (known as 'technology performance financing') to promote the uptake of new innovatory technology by traditional industries was set up with the participation of major financial institutions, following a call for proposals[3] published in March. Some 30 large-scale technology transfer projects received following a call for proposals were subjected to rigorous review, especially in view of budgetary restrictions. As a result, only half of these projects will progress to the definition phase.

(ii)   Strengthening innovation and technology transfer support service infrastructure: the support to networks of innovation support services such as technology transfer intermediaries and research organizations was continued. A second call for proposals[4] to collect applications from potential science park promoters or developers wishing to gain access to foreign expertise within the science park consultancy scheme[5] was published in July. Various support measures were undertaken to facilitate the formation of the networks and improve their operational efficiency, taking account of the disparate level of development and services in the different parts of the Community. As regards management techniques which encourage innovation, support was given to a series of activities in areas such as quality analysis. In addition, work began on organizing the third edition of the European Community design prize.

(iii)   Improving the awareness and understanding of innovation and exchanging experience on national and Community innovation policies: exploratory studies and preliminary projects were launched this year as part of the European innovation observatory.

---

[1]   Strategic programme for innovation and technology transfer — OJ L 112, 25.4.1989; Twenty-third General Report, point 370.
[2]   OJ C 122, 8.5.1991.
[3]   OJ C 65, 13.3.1991.
[4]   OJ C 198; 27.7.1991.
[5]   OJ C 186, 27.7.1990; Twenty-fourth General Report, point 327.

Finally, a panel of high-level experts was formed to help with the Sprint mid-term review, with the aim of assessing the results achieved so far and proposing possible modifications to the programme.

Development of an information services market

399.   The aim of the Commission's work in the context of the plan of action for the establishment of an information services market (Impact)[1] is to reduce legal and economic uncertainty in the market, to promote the use of electronic information services and to encourage European cooperation between market operators on pilot and demonstration projects. On 12 December the Council adopted a Decision on the continuation and extension of the Impact programme (Impact II).[2] A report on the most important events and developments in the information services market was prepared by the European information market observatory[3] for approval by the Commission and for communication to Parliament and the Council. The Commission also reinforced the support and guidance services offered by its ECHO server so as to facilitate users' access to electronic information services.

400.   The 14 pilot and demonstration projects set up in 1990[4] continued, and four new projects were launched in the fields of road transport, tourism and patents.

401.   National relay centres have been set up in less developed regions to improve liaison with the Commission with regard to development of the information services market.

[1]   OJ L 288, 21.10.1988; Twenty-second General Report, point 415.
[2]   Bull. EC 12-1991; Commission proposal: OJ C 53, 28.2.1991; Bull. EC 1/2-1991, point 1.2.94.
[3]   Twenty-third General Report, point 372.
[4]   Twenty-fourth General Report, point 328.

Section 8

Coordination of structural policies

Priority activities and objectives

402.   Continuing its implementation of the reform of the structural Funds,[1] the Com-mission decided on 24 April[2] to extend until the end of 1993 the validity of the lists of areas eligible under Objective 2[3] and on 11 June to allocate the remaining ECU 2 798 million among the Member States.[4] It adopted the corresponding Community support frameworks (CSFs) in December.[5] Pursuant to Regulation (EEC) No 3575/90 extending the activities of the structural Funds to the territory of the former German Democratic Republic,[6] the Commission also adopted in March a Community support framework for the five new Länder and eastern Berlin[7] together with Community support frameworks for the fisheries sector.[8] More generally, in an endeavour to enhance transparency, the Commission assigned the job of evaluation to independent experts with a view to identify-ing, for all objectives of the reform, the socioeconomic impact of structural assistance and to analyse the mechanisms for implementing Community measures through the new instrument for assistance constituted by the Community support framework (CSF).

The Commission also sought to obtain from each of the Member States the qualitative and/or quantitative information which it requires to assess whether the Member States have in fact met the additionality requirements.

The Commission also formally adopted the Prisma,[9] Telematique[9] and Leader[10] Com-munity initiatives. Subsequent to their adoption, there are now 12 initiatives in place under Regulation (EEC) No 4253/88.[11]

---

[1]   OJ L 185, 15.7.1988; OJ L 374, 31.12.1988; Twenty-second General Report, points 533 and 534; Bull. EC 4-1991, point 1.2.78.
[2]   Bull. EC 4-1991, point 1.2.78.
[3]   OJ L 113, 26.4.1989, Twenty-third General Report, point 483.
[4]   Bull. EC 6-1991, point 1.2.127.
[5]   Bull. EC 12-1991.
[6]   OJ L 353, 17.12.1990; Twenty-fourth General Report, point 24.
[7]   Point 408 of this Report.
[8]   Point 614 of this Report.
[9]   Point 506 of this Report.
[10]   Point 543 of this Report.
[11]   OJ L 374, 31.12.1988; Twenty-second General Report, point 534.

Pursuant to the above Regulation, the second annual report on the implementation of the reform of the structural Funds in 1990, which includes an assessment of the impact of other Community policies in this area, was approved by the Commission on 23 October[1] and adopted on 4 December.[2] The first annual report, for 1989, was presented to the social partners in March and Parliament gave its opinion on it in July,[3] as the Economic and Social Committee had done in April.[4]

403.   The draft Treaty on European union agreed by the Heads of State or Government at the European Council held in Maastricht on 9 and 10 December includes a section on economic and social cohesion, and provides in particular for the creation of a cohesion Fund.

Implementation of the reform of the structural Funds

404.   The Commission continued to implement the reform of the Funds by approving virtually all the operational programmes submitted to it for Objective 5b,[5] as well as some residual operational programmes for other Objectives, and beginning its appraisal of the programmes submitted under the first Community initiatives adopted the previous year[6] and the Community support frameworks for the fisheries sector.[7]

405.   With the exception of those concerned with Objective 5b, most of the monitoring committees provided for in Regulation (EEC) No 4253/88,[8] which form an essential part of the reform and in particular of the partnership arrangements, have been established. Their rules of procedure have either received or are awaiting final approval.

406.   In order to improve the procedures for approving structural assistance and its financing, the Commission adopted and implemented two series of measures, one to improve the mechanisms and procedures for implementing structural assistance and the other to improve budgetary implementation of the structural Funds.

407.   In keeping with the amendment to Article 130 of the Treaty proposed by the Intergovernmental Conference on Political Union, the Commission continued its work to facilitate the EIB's involvement in programmes part-financed by the Funds.

---

[1]   Bull. EC 10-1991, point 1.2.69.
[2]   Bull. EC 12-1991.
[3]   OJ C 240, 16.9.1991; Bull. EC 7/8-1991, point 1.2.126.
[4]   OJ C 159, 17.6.1991; Bull. EC 4-1991, point 1.2.63.
[5]   Point 539 of this Report.
[6]   Twenty-fourth General Report, point 332.
[7]   Point 614 of this Report.
[8]   OJ L 374, 31.12.1988; Twenty-second General Report, point 534.

Community support framework for structural assistance in the new German *Länder*

408. On 13 March the Commission formally approved the Community support framework providing structural assistance to the new *Länder* and eastern Berlin over the period 1991-93,[1] which had been drawn up in close cooperation with the German authorities.

In the absence of sufficiently reliable statistics, it was impossible at that stage to classify the regions and areas in terms of the regional and rural Objectives of the reform of the structural Funds. Otherwise, all the provisions and procedures of the reform apply to the new *Länder* and to eastern Berlin.

Of the ECU 3 billion made available to the structural Funds from the general budget, the ERDF received ECU 1 500 million, the ESF ECU 900 million and the EAGGF Guidance Section ECU 600 million. Over the same period additional assistance will be provided by EIB loans totalling ECU 1 500 million and ECSC loans totalling ECU 1 100 million.

---

[1] OJ L 114, 7.5.1991; Bull. EC 3-1991, point 1.2.77.

Section 9

Employment and social policy

Priority activities and objectives

409.   In the context of work on implementing the Single Act[1] and completing the internal market, the emphasis was placed on developing the kind of accompanying measures in the social sphere without which neither the large economic area nor the single market would be complete. There was continuing active input, then, in pursuance of the Commission's action programme relating to the implementation of the Community Charter of the Fundamental Social Rights of Workers, the object of which is to improve the employment and working conditions for people throughout the Community.

The Council adopted a Directive with a view to promoting the safety and health of workers with a fixed-duration employment relationship or a temporary employment relationship, which was on the list of most urgent measures proposed by the Commission. It also adopted two common positions on the protection of pregnant women and women who have recently given birth and on safety and health requirements at temporary or mobile work sites. At its meeting in Luxembourg in June, the European Council requested that the discussions in the Council on the Commission's action programme should be intensified so that the necessary decisions could be adopted, having regard to the specific situation and practices of each Member State. At the end of the European Council held in Maastricht on 9 and 10 December, a protocol annexed to the future Treaty was adopted, whereby it was agreed to authorize 11 Member States to use the institutions, procedures and mechanisms of the European Community for the purposes of adopting and applying, in their cases, the decisions required for the further implementation of the Social Charter. This agreement, which provides for qualified majority voting in some of the areas covered, is in addition to the Treaty provisions and existing Community legislation, which are binding on the Community's 12 Member States.

The Commission, meanwhile, transmitted to the Council all the proposals needed for its programme to be fully implemented, more particularly in the following fields: conditions of employment and collective redundancies, subcontracting, fair pay, industrial relations, participation and consultation of workers in companies and living and working conditions

---

[1]   Twentieth General Report, points 1 to 4; Supplement 2/86 — Bull. EC.

of certain disadvantaged social groups. On 4 December[1] it adopted a report listing the initiatives it had undertaken and stressing the basic principles underpinning its action, those of subsidiarity, the diversity of national systems and maintaining the competitiveness of undertakings.

The Commission also continued the work it started in 1987[2] under its action programme in the field of health and safety at work, and adopted a communication on the convergence of social protection objectives and policies.

It also sought to develop social dialogue at multi-sector level by setting up new working parties, following up joint opinions at national and sectoral levels, and initiating work in new sectors.

410.   On 12 September, Parliament adopted a resolution on the completion of the single market and the social dimension, in which it called on the Council to adopt the appropriate directives.[3] The Economic and Social Committee called for more account to be taken of the social dimension in Community policies.[4]

Employment

Dialogue with management and labour

411.   The political-level steering group set up in 1989[5] under the social dialogue initiated on the basis of the conclusions reached at the Val Duchesse meeting on 12 November 1985[6] continued to meet in 1991.

In January[7] it took note of the adoption by the working party on the 'prospects for a European labour market' of a joint opinion on new technologies, work organization and adaptability of the labour market, in which the two sides stressed the need for a fresh approach to adaptability and flexibility in firms with a view to strengthening competitiveness and profitability and thus promoting employment, better working conditions and a higher quality of life.

In September the partners to the social dialogue adopted a joint opinion on the practicalities of access to vocational training, emphasizing the vital importance of

---

[1]   Bull. EC 12-1991.
[2]   Twenty-first General Report, point 445.
[3]   OJ C 267, 14.10.1991; Bull. EC 9-1991, point 1.2.56.
[4]   OJ C 191, 22.7.1991; Bull. EC 5-1991, point 1.2.77.
[5]   Twenty-third General Report, point 395.
[6]   Nineteenth General Report, point 74.
[7]   Bull. EC 1/2-1991, point 1.2.113.

training for business competitiveness. On 31 October the *ad hoc* management and labour working party on the social dialogue agreed to transmit to the Presidency of the European Council and the Commission its agreement on the proposals for the wording of Articles 118(4), 118a and 118b of the new Treaty on political union under discussion. This agreement covers the consultation of management and labour at the drafting stage for Commission proposals and the possibility, where appropriate, of their reaching agreements on which general validity may be conferred by Council decision on a proposal from the Commission.

Employment and the labour market

412.   The third annual report on employment in Europe (1991), adopted by the Commission on 17 July,[1] highlights the challenges facing the Community in the 1990s and points to the fact that, after five years (1980-85) of job creation on a substantial scale, there is likely to be a significant slowdown in job growth as a result of low production growth. In other words, the growth in jobs will fall short of the growth in the active population, the result being that the rate of unemployment increased from 8.4% in 1990 to 8.6% in 1991. In this context, and with a view to stimulating job growth, the Annual Economic Report (1990-91)[2] advocates a structural reform of the labour markets, placing the emphasis more on providing vocational retraining than on paying unemployment benefit.

413.   In June the Council finally adopted the Directive, under Commission proposals on atypical work, on the improvement in the safety and health at work of workers with a fixed-duration employment relationship or a temporary employment relationship, the aim being to give such workers the same level of protection as other workers in the same undertaking.[3]

414.   The Standing Committee on Employment met on two occasions: in May[4] it considered a Commission working document on the 'situation and prospects for employment in the Community' and endorsed the growth and employment strategy proposed by the Commission; in November[5] it turned its attention to the position of women in society and on the labour market and recommended an active policy on training and the encouragement of employment for women, particularly in the context of the third equal opportunities programme.[6]

---

[1]   Bull. EC 7/8-1991, point 1.2.131.
[2]   Point 51 of this Report.
[3]   OJ L 206, 29.7.1991; Bull. EC 6-1991, point 1.2.102; Commission proposal: OJ C 224, 8.9.1990; Twenty-fourth General Report, point 337; OJ C 305, 15.2.1990; Twenty-fourth General Report, point 337.
[4]   Bull. EC 5-1991, point 1.2.78.
[5]   Bull. EC 11-1991, point 1.2.87.
[6]   Point 442 of this Report.

415. On 4 July the Economic and Social Committee adopted an own-initiative opinion in respect of the annual employment report (1990), in which it called for a guaranteed right for all workers to initial and continuing training and the implementation of measures for worker retraining. [1] Meanwhile Parliament, on 14 June, adopted a resolution on unemployment in the new German *Länder* [2] and, on 10 October, two resolutions on the restructuring of the Colgate-Palmolive group and the closing of a Seagate factory. [3]

Freedom of movement for workers and migration policy

416. In view of the stabilization of migration from Spain and Portugal to the other Member States and the substantial improvement in the employment situation in Spain and Portugal since they became members of the Community, the Council decided in June to bring the end of the transitional period laid down in the Acts of Accession forward to 31 December 1991, and to make the derogating measures in respect of the free movement of workers applying in Luxembourg inapplicable from 31 December 1992. [4]

417. On 5 September the Commission put to the Council a proposal [5] to amend Regulation (EEC) No 1612/68 [6] as regards, in particular, the operating methods of the European system for the international clearance of vacancies and applications for employment, Sedoc.

418. On 24 April [7] and 26 September [8] respectively, the Economic and Social Committee adopted an opinion and an additional opinion on the status of migrant workers from third countries.

419. The Commission continued its work on the possible creation of European citizens' advice bureaux, whose main functions would be to inform firms and workers about employment and training and to facilitate consultation between institutional, economic and social partners on both sides of a border.

---

[1]   OJ C 269, 14.10.1991; Bull. EC 7/8-1991, point 1.2.132.
[2]   OJ C 183, 15.7.1991; Bull. EC 6-1991, point 1.2.109.
[3]   OJ C 280, 28.10.1991; Bull. EC 10-1991, points 1.2.73 and 1.2.74.
[4]   OJ L 206, 29.7.1991; Bull. EC 6-1991, point 1.2.112; Commission proposal: Bull. EC 4-1991, point 1.2.67.
[5]   OJ C 254, 28.9.1991; Bull. EC 9-1991, point 1.2.57.
[6]   OJ L 257, 19.10.1968.
[7]   OJ C 159, 17.6.1991; Bull. EC 4-1991, point 1.2.73.
[8]   OJ C 339, 31.12.1991; Bull. EC 9-1991, point 1.2.63.

European Social Fund and structural operations

European Social Fund

420.   To supplement the arrangements set up by the reform of the structural Funds, the Commission adopted the Community support framework (CSF) for the five new *Länder* of the Federal Republic of Germany and the eastern part of Berlin, the ESF contribution being set at ECU 900 million. [1]

421.   On 3 May the Commission adopted a report on European Social Fund operations in 1989, on the basis of Article 25 of Regulation (EEC) No 4253/88, indicating that 75 % of the ECU 3 580 million in aid approved for this period went on measures on behalf of young people under 25, while 50 % of the aid approved went to less favoured regions. [2]

422.   In 1991 ECU 4 799 million was available in commitment appropriations. [3] These appropriations were committed as and when operational programmes and global subsidies were adopted by the Commission.

423.   The amounts committed are set out in Table 1.

TABLE 1

Appropriations committed

(million ECU)

Objective 1: Regions whose development is lagging behind	2 247.4
Objective 2: Regions affected by industrial decline	341
Objectives 3 and 4: Long-term unemployment and occupational integration of young people	1 537.2
Objective 5b: Development of rural areas	91.5
Eastern regions of Germany	270
Community initiatives	299.5
Total	4 786.6

424.   Payment appropriations available for 1991 came to ECU 4 215 million, of which ECU 4 186 million was spent.

---

[1]   Point 408 of this Report.
[2]   Bull. EC 5-1991, point 1.2.80.
[3]   Full data on the Social Fund will be given in the annual report for 1991.

425.   In the course of 1991, the Commission adopted a large number of operational programmes associated with the implementation of the Community support frameworks, including those to benefit the new *Länder* and eastern Berlin,[1] to the sum of ECU 900 million for the European Social Fund.

The sums granted in respect of programmes under Objectives 3 and 4 (but excluding Objective 1 regions) are as follows: Belgium (ECU 134.8 million), Denmark (ECU 0.5 million), Spain (ECU 62.61 million), France (ECU 5.9 million), Italy (ECU 128 million), Luxembourg (ECU 4.7 million), and the United Kingdom (ECU 10.1 million).

426.   The Commission also carried out a series of *ex ante* assessment studies of the main CSFs associated with Objectives 3 and 4, and of several operational programmes.[2]

427.   As regards Community initiatives, approval was given for three programmes involving ECU 104.11 million (NOW), of which ECU 94.27 million for the ESF, ECU 262.29 million (Euroform), of which ECU 253.8 million for the ESF, and ECU 148.78 million (Horizon), of which 129.21 million for the ESF. This makes a grand total of ECU 534.68 million, not including a sum of ECU 19.5 million in technical assistance for these initiatives.[3]

428.   On 22 February, the European Parliament adopted a resolution on the operation of the European Social Fund, in which it reiterated its call for a fair distribution of Social Fund resources between men and women, in order to combat women's unemployment effectively.[4] In a resolution adopted on 12 July, it stressed that the structural Funds should give equal weight to the development of human resources and the financing of structures,[5] while in a resolution of 24 October it emphasized the need to improve financial control and cash flows as part of the draft review of the rules governing the ESF.[6] On 12 September it also adopted a resolution on the Horizon initiative.[7]

Measures for ECSC workers

429.   In 1991 ECU 166 million was granted in redeployment aid, pursuant to Article 56(2)(b) and (1)(c) of the ECSC Treaty, to 71 560 ECSC workers. The average grant per worker, which still stood at ECU 2 320 in 1990 (transitional period), was ECU 2 184. The object of the aid was to supplement income in the event of unemployment or early retirement or to help with resettlement. This year saw the first decisions

---

[1]   Point 408 of this Report.
[2]   Point 402 of this Report.
[3]   Point 506 of this Report.
[4]   OJ C 72, 18.3.1991; Bull. EC 1/2-1991, point 1.2.116.
[5]   OJ C 240, 16.9.1991; Bull. EC 7/8-1991, point 1.2.130.
[6]   OJ C 305, 25.11.1991; Bull. EC 10-1991, point 1.2.77.
[7]   OJ C 267, 14.10.1991; Bull. EC 9-1991, point 1.2.60.

to grant aid for ECSC redeployment in the five new German *Länder*. In addition to the conventional aid programmes, aid was given in 1991 under the Community's Rechar scheme,[1] to which the ECSC contributes ECU 36 million, and in respect of the social measures for the steel industry (ECU 20 million).

430.   In December the Commission adopted a progress report on ECSC redeployment aid in 1990, which also describes the results achieved since the new bilateral agreements with the Member States entered into force.[2]

A breakdown of the total sum granted in aid by country and sector is given in Table 2.

TABLE 2

Redeployment aid — Appropriations committed in 1991

Member State	Steel industry and iron ore mining				Coal industry			
	Conventional aid		Social measures		Conventional aid		Rechar	
	Workers	Amount (ECU)	Workers	Amount (ECU)	Workers	Amount (ECU)	Workers	Amount (ECU)
Belgium	360	1 080 000			550	1 650 000	1 440	3 162 330
Denmark								
Germany	20 874	36 920 611	13 576	12 760 478	15 193	26 731 428	3 580	14 320 000
Greece	43	86 000						
Spain	1 580	4 451 638	360	391 737	1 119	3 357 000	369	1 544 000
France					3 506	22 609 061[1]	3 984	9 071 385
Ireland								
Italy	13 855	41 678 654	5 061	5 507 173				
Luxembourg	1 162	3 486 000	569	584 704				
Netherlands	933							
Portugal	3 092	3 791 636	193	210 015	70	210 000	40	100 310
United Kingdom	1 675	4 641 596	637	545 893	7 548	15 385 325	17 791	7 495 233
Total	43 574	96 136 135	20 396	20 000 000	27 986	69 942 814	27 204	35 693 258

[1] Increase in appropriation or number of workers in relation to the existing programmes.

431.   The appropriations of ECU 48 million for the implementation of the 1991 tranche of the 11th ECSC subsidized housing scheme,[3] on which a progress report was issued on 12 December,[2] were increased by ECU 4 million to provide housing in the five new German *Länder*.

---

[1]   Point 509 of this Report.
[2]   Bull. EC 12-1991.
[3]   Twenty-second General Report, point 490.

Aid for disaster victims

432.   In the course of the year the Commission granted emergency assistance in six cases totalling ECU 3.15 million to the families of disaster victims.

Social security and living and working conditions

Social security and other schemes

433.   On 7 May and 26 June respectively, the Commission adopted two important proposals for recommendations under the Social Charter: the first, which seeks to further the integration of the least advantaged sections of the population, calls on the Member States to recognize the individual general right to a guarantee of sufficient benefits and resources for all those residing in the territory of the Member State who do not have access to resources equal to or higher than a specified amount;[1] the second concerns the convergence of social protection objectives and policies, and is designed to ensure that differences in social protection systems between Member States do not hamper the free movement of persons and to avoid any diminution of social protection as a result of attempts to take advantage of the most generous national systems.[2] The Commission is thus proposing a convergence strategy based on the definition of common objectives to be implemented by the Member States within the framework of their national systems. The Economic and Social Committee delivered an opinion on the first proposal on 30 October[3] and on the second on 28 November.[4]

434.   In its final report submitted in February[5] to the Council and the European Parliament on the second European poverty programme 1986-89,[6] the Commission presented a general stocktaking of innovatory measures in action-research projects focusing on priority themes such as the long-term unemployed, the elderly, migrants and refugees, and suggested approaches for appropriate anti-poverty policies to be implemented at all levels of the Community.

435.   On 17 October the Commission adopted Decision 91/544/EEC establishing a Liaison Group on the Elderly.[7]

---

[1]   OJ C 163, 22.6.1991; Bull. EC 5-1991, point 1.2.75.
[2]   OJ C 194, 25.7.1991; Bull. EC 6-1991, point 1.2.101.
[3]   OJ C 14, 20.1.1992; Bull. EC 10-1991, point 1.2.80.
[4]   Bull. EC 11-1991, point 1.2.89.
[5]   Bull. EC 1/2-1991, point 1.2.120.
[6]   OJ L 2, 3.1.1985.
[7]   OJ L 296, 16.10.1991; Bull. EC 10-1991, point 1.2.89.

436.   On 31 October the Economic and Social Committee adopted an own-initiative opinion on single-parent families.[1]

437.   During the 1990/91 academic year the Executive Committee of the Paul Finet Foundation considered 509 applications and awarded 509 scholarships representing a total amount of BFR 11 833 581.

Social security for migrant workers

438.   On 25 June the Council adopted a Regulation[2] amending Regulations 1408/71[3] and 574/72[4] on the application of social security schemes to employed persons, to self-employed persons and to members of their families moving within the Community, to take account of judgments given by the Court of Justice. On 12 July the Commission proposed a new amendment to these same Regulations to reflect changes made in the Member States in the wake of German unification.[5] Parliament and the Economic and Social Committee delivered favourable opinions on this proposal on 11 October[6] and 19 December[7] respectively. The Commission proposed a further amendment to the same Regulations on 13 December to extend entitlement under them to all persons insured under social security schemes, particularly students and others not engaged in an occupational activity.[7]

439.   In December the Council endorsed[7] a proposal for a Regulation to simplify and accelerate payment and calculation of pensions for workers who have worked in several Member States,[8] and a proposal for a Regulation on mixed-type non-contributory benefits, i.e. benefits which fall within the category of both social security and social assistance.[9]

440.   On 17 July the Commission also adopted a communication with a view to stimulating debate in the Community;[10] it examines supplementary pension schemes in workers' social protection systems and their effect on the freedom of movement of workers.

---

[1]   OJ C 14, 20.1.1992; Bull. EC 10-1991, point 1.2.90.
[2]   OJ L 206, 29.7.1991; Bull. EC 6-1991, point 1.2.111; Commission proposal: OJ C 221, 5.9.1990; Twenty-fourth General Report, point 354.
[3]   OJ L 149, 5.7.1971.
[4]   OJ L 74, 27.3.1972.
[5]   OJ C 219, 22.8.1991; Bull. EC 7/8-1991, point 1.2.134.
[6]   OJ C 305, 25.11.1991; Bull. EC 10-1991, point 1.2.76.
[7]   Bull. EC 12-1991.
[8]   OJ C 206, 11.8.1989; Twenty-third General Report, point 414.
[9]   OJ C 240, 21.9.1985; Nineteenth General Report, point 435.
[10]   Bull. EC 7/8-1991, point 1.2.138.

441.   The Court of Justice delivered 11 judgments on cases referred by national courts concerning the interpretation or validity of regulations, while 19 cases are still before the Court.

Equal opportunities for men and women

442.   On 21 May the Council adopted a resolution[1] on the third medium-term Community action programme on equal opportunities,[2] on which Parliament had given an opinion in January,[3] calling on the Member States to take steps to increase the number of women in employment, to upgrade their contribution to economic, social and public life, and to make it easier for men and women to reconcile their family and occupational responsibilities.

443.   With the same aim in mind, the Commission adopted, on 3 July, a proposal for a Council recommendation on child care, designed to take account of the increasing number of women and mothers in the economic process;[4] Parliament[5] and the Economic and Social Committee[6] delivered opinions in November and the Council gave its political agreement in December.[7] In a resolution adopted on 13 December Parliament addressed the broad issue of childhood in the European Community.[8]

444.   On the same date, it also approved[9] — before formally adopting in November[10] — a recommendation accompanied by a code of practice calling on the Member States to take measures to promote the prevention of all forms of sexual harassment, on which Parliament adopted an opinion on 22 October.[11] On 19 December the Council adopted a statement to accompany the recommendation.[7]

445.   Parliament adopted several resolutions on the single market of 1992 and its consequences for women in the Community,[12] on child care,[13] on a European prize for

---

[1]   OJ C 142, 31.5.1991; Bull. EC 5-1991, point 1.2.76.
[2]   OJ C 142, 31.5.1991; Twenty-fourth General Report, point 356.
[3]   OJ C 48, 25.2.1991; Bull. EC 1/2-1991, point 1.2.121.
[4]   OJ C 242, 7.9.1991; Bull. EC 7/8-1991, point 1.2.129.
[5]   OJ C 326, 16.12.1991; Bull. EC 11-1991, point 1.2.96.
[6]   Bull. EC 11-1991, point 1.2.96.
[7]   Bull. EC 12-1991.
[8]   OJ C 13, 20.1.1992; Bull. EC 12-1991.
[9]   Bull. EC 7/8-1991, point 1.2.28.
[10]   Bull. EC 11-1991, point 1.2.95.
[11]   OJ C 305, 25.11.1991; Bull. EC 10-1991, point 1.2.87.
[12]   OJ C 48, 25.2.1991; Bull. EC 1/2-1991, point 1.2.121.
[13]   OJ C 129, 20.5.1991; Bull. EC 4-1991, point 1.2.72.

women,[1] and on the judgment of the Court of Justice[2] on equal treatment for men and women.[3]

446.   On 3 January the Commission amended[4] its proposal concerning the safety and health protection of pregnant women and women who have recently given birth, and in May Parliament adopted a resolution on the legal basis (Article 118a), calling on the Council to adopt a common position without delay. The Council gave its agreement to the common position on 6 November[5] and then formally adopted it on 19 December.[6]

447.   The Community NOW initiative to promote equal opportunities for women in employment and vocational training[7] was officially launched on 31 January at a seminar organized in Brussels by the Commission. This initiative is one of a series of programmes financed by the European Social Fund but set up in response to requests by the Member States.

Social integration of the disabled

448.   On 6 February the Commission adopted a proposal for a Council Directive on minimum requirements to improve the mobility and the safe transport to work of workers with reduced mobility.[8] This proposal provides for the gradual adaptation and redesign of means of transport to take account of the specific situation of the users. In its opinion on the proposal, the Economic and Social Committee called for the safety concept to apply to both private and public forms of transport.[9] Parliament delivered its opinion on 20 November,[10] which led the Commission to amend its proposal.[11] In December the Council called on the Commission to draw up an action programme to make public transport more accessible to persons with reduced mobility.[12]

449.   On 2 October the Commission also made a proposal to the Council to continue and extend activities under Helios I by carrying out a third programme (Helios II, 1992-96) costing an estimated ECU 47.3 million.[13]

---

[1]   OJ C 158, 17.6.1991; Bull. EC 5-1991, point 1.2.87.
[2]   OJ C 289, 17.11.1989.
[3]   OJ C 280, 28.10.1991; Bull. EC 10-1991, point 1.2.88.
[4]   OJ C 250, 1.2.1991; Bull. EC 1/2-1991, point 1.2.117.
[5]   Bull. EC 11-1991, point 1.2.90.
[6]   Bull. EC 12-1991.
[7]   Twenty-fourth General Report, point 342.
[8]   OJ C 68, 16.3.1991; Bull. EC 1/2-1991, point 1.2.112.
[9]   OJ C 191, 22.7.1991; Bull. EC 5-1991, point 1.2.88.
[10]   OJ C 326, 16.12.1991; Bull. EC 11-1991, point 1.2.94.
[11]   OJ C 15, 21.1.1992; Bull. EC 12-1991.
[12]   OJ C 18, 24.1.1992; Bull. EC 12-1991.
[13]   OJ C 293, 12.11.1991; Bull. EC 10-1991, point 1.2.71.

Labour law, industrial relations and living and working conditions

450.   On 14 October the Council adopted Directive 91/533/EEC relating to the drawing up of a written declaration regarding an employment relationship,[1] which stipulates that an employer shall notify an employee of the essential aspects of the contract or employment relationship by written declaration not later than two months after the commencement of employment.

451.   On 21 March the Economic and Social Committee also endorsed[2] the proposal for a Council Directive on the establishment of a European Works Council in Community-scale undertakings or groups of undertakings for the purposes of informing and consulting employees,[3] on which Parliament also gave its opinion in July,[4] as a result of which the Commission amended its proposal on 16 September.[5]

452.   Under its action programme relating to the implementation of the Community Charter of the Fundamental Social Rights of Workers, on 19 June the Commission adopted a proposal for a Council Directive,[6] on which the Economic and Social Committee gave an opinion in December,[7] concerning the posting of workers in the framework of the provision of services, which seeks to coordinate the laws of the Member States with a view to ensuring adequate protection for workers posted by their undertaking to a Member State other than the country whose legislation governs their employment relationship.

453.   On 9 July the Commission adopted a proposal for a Council recommendation concerning the promotion of employee participation in profits and enterprise results (including equity participation), with special reference to profit-sharing, employee share ownership and stock option schemes.[8]

454.   The Commission also adopted, on 18 September, a proposal for a Council Directive concerning the approximation of Member States' legislation on collective redundancies.[9] Its object is to amend Directive 75/129/EEC[10] and provide protection for workers by strengthening legal requirements covering decisions taken at transnational level by undertakings or groups of undertakings.

---

[1]   OJ L 288, 18.10.1991; Bull. EC 10-1991, point 1.2.72.; Commission proposal: OJ C 24, 31.1.1991; Twenty-fourth General Report, point 362; OJ C 222, 27.8.1991; Bull. EC 7/8-1991, point 1.2.135.
[2]   OJ C 120, 6.5.1991; Bull. EC 3-1991, point 1.2.79.
[3]   OJ C 39, 15.2.1991; Twenty-fourth General Report, point 363.
[4]   OJ C 240, 16.9.1991; Bull. EC 7/8-1991, point 1.2.143.
[5]   OJ C 336, 31.12.1991; Bull. EC 9-1991, point 1.2.62.
[6]   OJ C 225, 30.8.1991; Bull. EC 6-1991, point 1.2.103.
[7]   Bull. EC 12-1991.
[8]   OJ C 245, 20.9.1991; Bull. EC 7/8-1991, point 1.2.127.
[9]   OJ C 310, 30.11.1991; Bull. EC 9-1991, point 1.2.55.
[10] OJ L 48, 22.2.1975; Nineteenth General Report, point 222.

455.   In an opinion adopted on 11 December the Commission proposed guidelines for measures to enhance transparency in wages and salaries on the labour market and ensure respect for the right to fair pay by strict application of existing national legislation.[1]

European Foundation for the Improvement of Living and Working Conditions

456.   In the course of 1991 the Foundation implemented its programme entitled '1992 and beyond — New opportunities for action to improve living and working conditions in Europe'.

Activities for 1991 can be classified into six fields: the development of working relations and participation, restructuring working life, promoting health and safety, protecting the environment for workers and the general public, improving living standards and the quality of life for all and assessing the technologies of the future. In all these fields the Foundation carried out research or investigations or held round table discussions.

Health and safety

Health and safety at work

457.   The Council declared 1992 to be the 'European Year of Safety, Hygiene and Health at Work' and, on 29 July, adopted a public awareness action programme to run in the Community from 1 March 1992.[2] Parliament had already given its views on this proposal in May,[3] and it was then amended by the Commission in June.[4]

458.   After Parliament had given its opinion,[5] the Council, on 25 June, adopted a Directive[6] amending Directive 83/477/EEC on the protection of workers from the risks related to exposure to asbestos at work.[7]

459.   On 25 June the Council also agreed a common position[8] — before formal adoption on 1 October — on the proposal for a Directive on the minimum health and

---

[1]   Bull. EC 12-1991.
[2]   OJ L 214, 2.8.1991; Bull. EC 7/8-1991, point 1.2.141; Commission proposal: OJ C 293, 23.11.1991; Twenty-fourth General Report, point 372; OJ C 175, 6.7.1991; Bull. EC 6-1991, point 1.2.114.
[3]   OJ C 158, 17.6.1991; Bull. EC 5-1991, point 1.2.83.
[4]   OJ C 175, 6.7.1991; Bull. EC 6-1991, point 1.2.114.
[5]   OJ C 129, 20.5.1991; Bull. EC 4-1991, point 1.2.69.
[6]   OJ L 206, 29.7.1991; Bull. EC 6-1991, point 1.2.116; Commission proposal: OJ C 161, 30.6.1990; Twenty-fourth General Report, point 370.
[7]   OJ L 263, 24.9.1983; Seventeenth General Report, point 340.
[8]   Bull. EC 6-1991, point 1.2.115; Bull. EC 10-1991, point 1.2.83.

safety requirements for improved medical treatment on board vessels,[1] as amended by the Commission[2] following the opinion of Parliament.[3] Parliament delivered an opinion on second reading on 20 November,[4] and the Commission adopted a re-examined proposal on 20 December.[5]

460.   On 26 September the Commission formally adopted a proposal, which it had approved on 24 April, for a Council Regulation establishing a European Agency for Safety and Health at Work, the aim being to supply the Community and the Member States with useful technical, scientific and economic information in the field.[6]

461.   On 30 April the Commission adopted a Directive[7] adapting to technical progress the Directive on the approximation of the laws of the Member States concerning electrical equipment for use in potentially explosive atmospheres in mines susceptible to firedamp.[8] The proposal for a Directive on the implementation of minimum safety and health requirements at temporary or mobile work sites[9] (eighth individual Directive within the meaning of framework Directive 89/391/EEC) was the subject of an amended proposal from the Commission on 9 April,[10] following the opinions of the European Parliament[11] and of the Economic and Social Committee[12] and was formally adopted by the Council on 19 December.[5]

462.   In July Parliament gave its opinion[13] on first reading on the proposal for a Council Directive concerning the minimum requirements for the provision of safety and/or health signs at work,[14] which was amended by the Commission on 9 October[15] and was the subject of Council agreement on a common position in December;[5] Parliament[16] and the Economic and Social Committee[17] also gave their views on the proposal for a Council Directive for improving the safety and health protection of workers in the extractive

---

[1]   OJ C 183, 29.7.1991; Twenty-fourth General Report, point 371.
[2]   OJ C 74, 20.3.1991; Bull. EC 1/2-1991, point 1.2.118.
[3]   OJ C 48, 25.2.1991; Bull. EC 1/2-1991, point 1.2.118.
[4]   OJ C 326, 16.12.1991; Bull. EC 11-1991, point 1.2.91.
[5]   Bull. EC 12-1991.
[6]   OJ C 271, 16.10.1991; Bull. EC 4-1991, point 1.2.64.
[7]   OJ L 134, 29.5.1991; Bull. EC 4-1991, point 1.2.71.
[8]   OJ L 59, 2.3.1982; Sixteenth General Report, point 328.
[9]   OJ C 213, 28.8.1990; Twenty-fourth General Report, point 371.
[10]   OJ C 112, 27.4.1991; Bull. EC 4-1991, point 1.2.70.
[11]   OJ C 72, 18.3.1991; Bull. EC 1/2-1991, point 1.2.119.
[12]   OJ C 120, 6.5.1991; Bull. EC 3-1991, point 1.2.80.
[13]   OJ C 240, 16.9.1991; Bull. EC 7/8-1991, point 1.2.139.
[14]   OJ C 53, 28.2.1991.
[15]   OJ C 279, 26.10.1991; Bull. EC 10-1991, point 1.2.81.
[16]   OJ C 280, 28.10.1991; Bull. EC 10-1991, point 1.2.85.
[17]   OJ C 191, 22.7.1991; Bull. EC 5-1991, point 1.2.86.

industries[1] (individual directive within the meaning of Directive 89/391/EEC), where-upon the Commission amended its proposal.[2]

463.   The proposal for a Council Directive concerning certain aspects of the organi-zation of working time[3] was amended by the Commission in April[4] to reflect Parlia-ment's opinion on first reading.[5]

464.   Under framework Directive 89/391/EEC,[6] the Commission on 27 November adopted a proposal for a Directive concerning minimum health and safety requirements on board fishing vessels.[7]

465.   As regards protection for workers against hazards associated with exposure to chemical agents, the Commission adopted a Directive laying down a first list of occu-pational exposure limit values for 27 chemical, physical or biological agents.[8] It adopted a communication on the ratification procedure for the ILO Convention concerning safety in the use of chemicals at work[9] and, on 25 September, a communication to the Council on an ILO report on the prevention of industrial disasters. The Advisory Committee on Safety, Hygiene and Health Protection at Work[10] held four plenary meetings during the year and adopted seven opinions on the Green Paper on European standardization and on proposals for Directives on health and safety on board fishing vessels, protective devices and systems intended for use in explosive atmospheres, pressure vessels, health and safety in respect of transport activities and places of work on board means of transport, hazards associated with exposure to biological agents at work and protection for young people at work.

Health and safety (ECSC)

466.   The Safety and Health Commission for the Mining and Other Extractive Industries held three plenary meetings at which it considered a draft proposal on the health and safety of workers in the extractive industries prospecting and mining mineral raw materials in mines and quarries and several other draft proposals for Directives, including the draft proposal for a Council Directive on the approximation of Member States' legislation on protective devices and systems intended for use in potentially explosive atmospheres.

---

[1]   OJ C 32, 7.2.1991.
[2]   Bull. EC 12-1991.
[3]   OJ C 254, 9.10.1990; Twenty-fourth General Report, point 371.
[4]   OJ C 124, 14.5.1991; Bull. EC 4-1991, point 1.2.65.
[5]   OJ C 72, 18.3.1991; Bull. EC 1/2-1991, point 1.2.115.
[6]   OJ L 183, 29.6.1989; Twenty-third General Report, point 427.
[7]   OJ C 337, 31.12.1991; Bull. EC 11-1991, point 1.2.92.
[8]   OJ L 177, 5.7.1991; Bull. EC 5-1991, point 1.2.85.
[9]   Bull. EC 6-1991, point 1.2.117.
[10]   OJ L 185, 9.7.1974.

Section 10

Human resources, education, training and youth

Priority activities and objectives

467.   Following the work done in previous years to get a series of vocational training action programmes up and running — strengthened this year by the extension and development of the Petra programme and the launching of the Force programme — the Commission looked to the future and sought to initiate a wide-ranging debate on future policy options in this field.

In three basic memorandums, dealing with higher education,[1] vocational training[2] and open distance learning,[3] the Commission pinpointed the major problems which the Community will have to tackle and the broad lines of its future action in these areas.

The Community also confirmed its international standing in matters of education and training, witness the success of the Tempus programme and contacts made with a view to furthering transatlantic cooperation.

However, the highlight of the year as regards education was the agreement reached at the Maastricht European Council on the Treaty on European union, which now includes a chapter on education, vocational training and youth.

The future of the teaching profession generated much discussion in Member States' education ministries and elsewhere.

A similar response was evoked by the formulation and development of a Community youth policy.

Cooperation in education

468.   On 25 November the Council and Ministers for Education adopted conclusions concerning a pilot action for multilateral school partnerships covering the school years 1992/93 and 1993/94, intended to strengthen the European dimension in education.[4]

---

[1]   Point 474 of this Report.
[2]   Point 470 of this Report.
[3]   Point 473 of this Report.
[4]   OJ C 321, 12.12.1991; Bull. EC 11-1991, point 1.2.85.

469.   They also adopted a resolution on education research and statistics in the Community.[1]

Vocational training

470.   On 11 December the Commission adopted a memorandum on Community policy guidelines on vocational training in the 1990s.[2] The main purpose is to generate discussion on all matters affecting training other than compulsory schooling; the memorandum sets out the new challenges which will have to be faced in the coming years and which are adding to the importance of vocational training policies. It describes what has been achieved in the past in terms of a common vocational training policy based on principles laid down by the Council in 1963,[3] with special reference to the Community action programmes implemented since 1985. Finally, it proposes guidelines for future action in the Community in this field.

Initial training

471.   On 22 July the Council adopted a Decision[4] amending Decision 87/569/EEC concerning an action programme for the vocational training of young people and their preparation for adult and working life.[5]

This Decision concerns the second stage of the Petra programme, scheduled to run for three years from 1 January 1992. The estimated cost is ECU 177.4 million, with ECU 29 million earmarked for 1992. The programme aims to support and supplement, through measures at Community level, the policies and activities of the Member States geared to ensuring that all young people in the Community who so wish receive one or, if possible, two or more years' initial vocational training in addition to their full-time compulsory education. It is also designed to encourage Community-wide cooperation on vocational guidance and to give young people the opportunity to benefit from periods of training or work experience in other Member States.

---

[1]   OJ C 321, 12.12.1991; Bull. EC 11-1991, point 1.2.84.
[2]   Bull. EC 12-1991.
[3]   OJ 63, 20.4.1963; Sixth General Report, point 183.
[4]   OJ L 214, 2.8.1991; Bull. EC 7/8-1991, point 1.2.144. Commission proposal: OJ C 322, 21.12.1990; Twenty-fourth General Report, point 380; OJ C 181, 12.7.1991; Bull. EC 6-1991, point 1.2.105.
[5]   OJ L 346, 10.12.1987; Twenty-first General Report, point 395.

472.   In April the Economic and Social Committee adopted an own-initiative opinion on training, safety and protection of the environment.[1]

Training for technological change

473.   On 12 November the Commission adopted a memorandum on open distance learning,[2] following on from a report it had approved on 24 May on open and distance higher education. In its memorandum, the Commission underlined the need to facilitate access to vocational training at all levels and to improve the quality of training by the use of open learning techniques and multimedia resources. It also pinpointed a number of strategic elements, including in-house training, and the specific needs of workers and small and medium-sized businesses.

Higher education

474.   On 5 November the Commission adopted a memorandum on higher education in the Community in which it examined the contribution that higher education can make to help the Community to meet the challenges facing it in the 1990s and after the turn of the century, stressing the need to formulate new policies and identify the main avenues of change.[3]

475.   On 28 October the Council adopted decisions formally concluding bilateral agreements between the European Economic Community and the EFTA countries to establish cooperation on education and training under the Erasmus programme.[4] The agreements are designed to enable these countries, which have been involved in the Comett programme since 1 January 1990,[5] to participate in the Erasmus programme too from the 1992/93 academic year.

476.   On 22 May the Commission adopted the annual report of the Erasmus programme for the 1990/91 academic year and announced that the selection procedure for 1991/92 would enable about 1 200 higher-education establishments to take part in an inter-university cooperation programme and Erasmus funds to be made available to some 59 000 students throughout the Community.

---

[1]   OJ C 159, 17.6.1991; Bull. EC 4-1991, point 1.2.76.
[2]   Bull. EC 11-1991, point 1.2.83.
[3]   Bull. EC 11-1991, point 1.2.82.
[4]   OJ L 332, 3.12.1991; Bull. EC 10-1991, point 1.2.91.
[5]   OJ L 156, 21.6.1990; Twenty-fourth General Report, point 382; Commission proposal: Bull. EC 4-1991, point 1.2.74.

477.   On 7 June the Commission adopted the final report on the first phase of the Comett programme. During the three operational years of Comett I, more than 1 300 projects were initiated, involving more than 6 000 firms, 1 500 universities and 1 000 other organizations. The total funding provided was ECU 52.5 million.

478.   On 25 November the Council and Ministers for Education adopted conclusions on cooperation for the reinforcement of mobility in higher education.[1] The Commission was invited to make proposals for intensifying the use of academic credit transfer systems and educational modules by higher education institutions in Member States, for encouraging convergence of the start of the academic year and for developing a computerized database for student information purposes.

479.   Also on 25 November the Council and Ministers for Education adopted conclusions asking the Commission to undertake a comparative study of methods used in the Member States for quality assessment in higher education.[2] This might lead to pilot projects aimed at cooperation in this area and possible instruments for strengthening cooperation.

480.   In January Parliament adopted a resolution on the European dimension at university level, with particular reference to teacher and student mobility.[3]

481.   And on 10 and 12 September it passed resolutions on the establishment of a European Law Academy[4] and on academic freedom at universities in Germany's new Länder.[5]

Continuing training

482.   In conjunction with the two sides of industry, the Commission started implementing the action programme for the development of continuing vocational training in the Community (the Force programme).[6]

---

[1]   OJ C 321, 12.12.1991; Bull. EC 11-1991, point 1.2.81.
[2]   OJ C 321, 12.12.1991; Bull. EC 11-1991, point 1.2.80.
[3]   OJ C 48, 25.2.1991; Bull. EC 1/2-1991, point 1.2.122.
[4]   OJ C 267, 14.10.1991; Bull. EC 9-1991, point 1.2.65.
[5]   OJ C 267, 14.10.1991; Bull. EC 9-1991, point 1.2.66.
[6]   OJ L 156, 21.6.1990; Twenty-fourth General Report, point 386.

Language learning

483.   On 13 December the Commission adopted the annual report on the Lingua action programme to promote foreign language teaching and learning in the Community.[1]

European Centre for the Development of Vocational Training

484.   As part of its 1989-92 action programme and in accordance with Community decisions, the European Centre for the Development of Vocational Training continued its activities in research and development, documentation and information. In giving effect to freedom of movement and furthering the objectives of economic and social cohesion in the Community, considerable resources were brought to bear on increasing comparability of vocational training qualifications and defining occupational profiles. The Centre looked into the matter of regional disparities and put in hand a series of studies on training in firms, methods of preparing training programmes and measures to encourage workers to take part in training schemes. At the same time, studies were completed on the mobility of human and financial resources and on vocational guidance structures. Substantial investment was also made in the training of trainers and the requirements of small businesses. Publication of a series of monographs describing vocational training systems in the Member States was started; it should be finished in 1992.

Exchanges of experience and experts at Community level helped considerably to spread information on a large number of vocational training issues. Dialogue on research priorities continued in the Forum of Research Institutes, in which representatives of the EFTA countries also took part. All these activities enabled the Centre to contribute to the development of cooperation between the two sides of industry as a means of establishing a European social dialogue.

Youth

Community initiatives to assist young people

485.   On 29 July the Council adopted a Decision[2] establishing the second phase of the 'Youth for Europe' action programme, designed to promote youth exchange and

[1]   Bull. EC 12-1991.
[2]   OJ L 217, 6.8.1991; Bull. EC 7/8-1991, point 1.2.146; Commission proposal: OJ C 308, 8.12.1990; Twenty-fourth General Report, point 388; OJ C 175, 6.7.1991; Bull. EC 6-1991, point 1.2.106.

mobility projects.[1] The amount estimated to be needed for Community financing of this second phase (from 1 January 1992 to 31 December 1994) is ECU 25 million, providing for direct support for project-centred youth exchanges and mobility, assistance for transnational projects enabling young people to participate in voluntary service activities in the educational, social, cultural or environmental protection fields, and the continuation of Community aid to promote short study visits, further training and pilot projects for youth workers.

486.   In response to the Commission's memorandum on young people in the European Community,[2] the Council and the Ministers meeting within the Council adopted on 26 June a resolution on priority actions to be implemented by the Member States, aimed at intensifying cooperation between structures responsible for youth work, informing young people, stimulating the initiative and creativity of young people and cooperating in the training of youth workers, particularly with regard to the European dimension.[3] They invited the Commission to support these actions, with due respect for the principle of subsidiarity.

487.   Ministers also took note of a communication adopted by the Commission on 3 June entitled 'Keeping young Europeans informed'.[4]

488.   On 14 June Parliament adopted a resolution on Community policies and their impact on youth, calling for increased funding for programmes targeted at young people (Erasmus, Lingua, Petra, Comett, Youth for Europe) and for the development of information programmes geared to young people.[5]

489.   On 4 October the Commission adopted the activity report for 1990 on the Youth for Europe programme.

Youth Forum of the European Communities

490.   The Commission helped support the activities of the Youth Forum, which in 1991 concentrated on work leading up to the formulation of a proper Community youth policy. The Forum also gave consideration to its own internal organization.

---

[1]   OJ L 158, 25.6.1988; Twenty-second General Report, point 468.
[2]   Twenty-fourth General Report, point 388.
[3]   Bull. EC 6-1991, point 1.2.104.
[4]   Point 1215 of this Report.
[5]   OJ C 183, 15.7.1991; Bull. EC 6-1991, point 1.2.108.

Training assistance for the countries of Central and Eastern Europe

Higher education

491. On 11 December the Commission adopted a proposal for a Council Decision extending by one year the validity of Council Decision 90/233/EEC establishing the Tempus programme.[1] This trans-European mobility scheme, part of the Phare programme, is designed to provide training assistance for eligible countries in Central and Eastern Europe. The purpose of the extension is to give the Community authorities the opportunity to examine a new proposal on the future of the programme, to be drawn up shortly in the light of the impending assessment of results to date, while ensuring continuity of implementation.

European University Institute

492. The Commission contributed ECU 3 035 000 to the academic and research activities of the European University Institute in Florence,[2] more particularly the research library and the European library (Eurolib programme), information technology, research projects, the European Policy Unit and the Jean Monnet chair, Jean Monnet scholarships, the European Culture Research Centre and the European Law Academy.

493. In the 1991/92 academic year the Institute had slightly more than 300 researchers and 40 full-time teachers, in accordance with the objectives set in the 1980s. With help from the Tempus programme and other contributions, it had some 15 researchers from Central Europe and the USSR. In conjunction with the College of Europe and the Maastricht Institute, it was operating a special one-year programme for 20 researchers from the countries of Central and Eastern Europe, again with Tempus support.

494. An appraisal group set up by the High Council made recommendations to the Institute at its meeting on 19 and 20 December on developments over the next 10 years.[3]

495. On 26 October Mr R. F. M. Lubbers, Prime Minister of the Netherlands and current President of the European Council, gave the annual Jean Monnet lecture on 'Our Europe'.

---

[1] OJ C 11, 17.1.1992; Bull. EC 12-1991.
[2] The activities of the European University Institute are described in a brochure which can be obtained from the Institute at Badia Fiesolana, 5 via dei Roccettini, San Domenico di Fiesole, I-50016 Florence.
[3] This report may be obtained from the Institute.

Section 11

Regional policies

Priority activities and objectives

496.   The Community's policy this year has continued to strive towards the goal of greater economic and social cohesion, to which the implementation of the reformed structural instruments represents a major contribution. In this connection, aid towards the process of structural adjustment was actively pursued, in particular with the adoption of a large number of operational programmes under the Community support frameworks (CSFs) and Community initiatives on the one hand and the extension of measures for Objective 2 areas on the other.

The Commission also set up the CSF for the new German Länder *and approved the corresponding operational programmes.*

On 16 October, the Commission adopted the report entitled 'Europe 2000: Outlook for the development of the Community's territory', designed to provide a reference framework for national planning policies and a valuable planning instrument at Community level for the formulation of structural policies and future development schemes.

Formulation and launching of regional policies

Formulation of regional policies

497.   On the basis of guidelines set out in a preliminary document presented to the ministers responsible for regional policy in November 1990,[1] the Commission adopted a report on 16 October entitled 'Europe 2000 — Outlook for the development of the Community's territory',[2] designed to help the authorities responsible for regional planning and land management in the Member States to pursue effective regional policies based on a comprehensive overview of the Community territory. The report

---

[1]   Twenty-fourth General Report, point 397.
[2]   Bull. EC 10-1991, point 1.2.92.

analyses the various factors which will affect the use of Community territory over the next 10 years, including the demographic and economic context, infrastructures, and the situation and future prospects of the various geographical regions. It also draws attention to the need for information exchange systems between the Member States and the importance of establishing a system of consultation which will allow a Community-wide debate on questions of regional development.

Meeting in The Hague on 18 and 19 November, the ministers with responsibility for regional policy and planning judged the report to be a useful first step in establishing a framework for the future development of the Community's territory. They asked for the work to be continued in a systematic way and stressed the value of cross-frontier collaboration as well as cooperation between cities and regions. They also called for the creation of a network linking planning research institutes in the Community. A spatial development committee would also be set up.

In an own-initiative opinion on 25 September,[1] the Economic and Social Committee approved the guidelines put forward in the report while stressing the need to promote the human capital of the regions.

498.   When adopting, at its meeting on 21 and 22 February, an opinion on a preliminary 'Europe 2000' document,[2] the Consultative Council of Local and Regional Authorities[3] recalled its interest in the Commission's work on regional planning.

499.   Following the Consultative Council's request for its role to be strengthened, the Commission proposed to the Intergovernmental Conference on Political Union the establishment under the new treaty of a committee of regional and local authorities comprising a greater number of members than the existing Consultative Council, which could be consulted on all proposals concerning Community regional policy.[4] The draft treaty agreed by the European Council at Maastricht[5] makes provision for the setting up of this committee.

500.   The Committee on the Development and Conversion of Regions[6] met in plenary session on 7 March, 15 April and 9 December, and discussed in particular the areas eligible under Objective 2 and the corresponding CSFs.

---

[1]   OJ C 339, 31.12.1991; Bull. EC 9-1991, point 1.2.70.
[2]   Bull. EC 1/2-1991, point 1.2.124.
[3]   OJ L 247, 6.9.1988; Twenty-second General Report, point 516.
[4]   Supplement 2/91 — Bull. EC.
[5]   Point 42 of this Report.
[6]   OJ L 374, 31.12.1988.

Guidelines

501. On 23 April, pursuant to Article 25 of the coordinating Regulation (EEC) No 4253/88,[1] the Commission adopted the report on the activities of the ERDF for 1989 from which it emerges that commitments undertaken reached 99 % of available appropriations, or ECU 4 710.42 million.[2]

Social and economic situation and development of the regions

502. The fourth periodic report on the social and economic situation and the development of the regions of the Community, adopted by the Commission in December 1990,[3] was the subject on 25 September of a favourable opinion by the Economic and Social Committee,[4] which proposed topics to be examined when preparing the next report to be adopted in 1993.

Regional development at Community level

503. A new programme of pilot projects called 'Regions and cities of Europe' (Recite), based on Regulation (EEC) No 4254/88,[1] was launched in July with a call to regional and local authorities in the Community to make proposals concerning cooperation networks for the realization of joint projects of an economic nature.[5] The existing programme of exchanges of experience launched in 1989 on the basis of Article 10 of the Regulation and designed to help regional and local authorities to establish initial contacts, exchange information and analyse ideas for joint schemes, was continued this year. A further series of pilot projects was also launched this year under the same Regulation with the aim of examining new ways of resolving certain problems in urban areas such as the siting of economic activities in residential areas, the pollution of the environment and the restructuring of historic town centres. Other towns and cities will be able to make use of the lessons drawn from these projects, thus helping to develop the urban aspect of future Community policies.

---

[1]   OJ L 374, 31.12.1988; Twenty-second General Report, point 534.
[2]   Bull. EC 4-1991, point 1.2.77.
[3]   Twenty-fourth General Report, point 402.
[4]   OJ C 339, 31.12.1991; Bull. EC 9-1991, point 1.2.69.
[5]   OJ C 198, 27.7.1991.

Implementation of the reform of the structural Funds in regard to regional objectives

Eligibility of regions and areas

504.   Pursuant to Regulation (EEC) No 2052/88[1] and after consulting the Committee on the Development and Conversion of Regions, the Commission decided on 30 April[2] to maintain unchanged up to the end of 1993 the list of declining industrial areas eligible under Objective 2.[3] This Decision is intended to provide the areas concerned with the necessary stability for implementing longer-term programmes.

Regional plans and Community support frameworks

505.   To support the restructuring of the economy of the new German *Länder* and their integration into the internal market, the Commission adopted on 13 March[4] a Community support framework for Berlin (east), Mecklenburg-Western Pomerania, Brandenburg, Saxony-Anhalt, Thuringia and Saxony.[5] The CSF provides for total spending of ECU 3 billion, including ECU 1.5 billion from the ERDF. The Commission adopted corresponding regional operational programmes on 26 March.

Community initiatives

506.   After consulting Parliament,[6], the Economic and Social Committee[7] and the Committee on the Development and Conversion of Regions, the Commission formally adopted on 25 January the guidelines[8] for operational programmes to be implemented within the framework of two Community initiatives: Telematique, which has a budget of ECU 200 million to promote the use of advanced telecommunications services in the least favoured regions of the Community (Objective 1 regions), and Prisma, which has a budget of ECU 100 million to assist firms in the least favoured regions to profit from the completion of the single market by improving certain services, in particular in the area of product quality and access for small and medium-sized businesses to public

---

[1]   OJ L 185, 15.7.1988; Twenty-second General Report, point 533.
[2]   Bull. EC 4-1991, point 1.2.78.
[3]   OJ L 113, 26.4.1989; Twenty-third General Report, point 462.
[4]   Point 408 of this Report.
[5]   OJ L 353, 17.12.1990; Twenty-fourth General Report, points 23 and 24.
[6]   OJ C 19, 28.1.1991; Twenty-fourth General Report, point 407.
[7]   OJ C 332, 31.12.1990; Twenty-fourth General Report, point 407.
[8]   OJ C 33, 8.2.1991; Bull. EC 1/2-1991, points 1.2.129 and 1.2.30.

contracting. The Commission also formally adopted the Leader initiative dealing with rural development, [1] and approved a new initiative, Retex, in December to help regions heavily dependent on the textiles and clothing sector. [2] Under the Envireg, Stride, Regis, Interreg and Regen initiatives adopted in 1990, the Member States have this year presented a series of operational programmes in line with guidelines laid down by the Commission.

Regional operational programmes (including integrated approaches and IMPs)

507. Since the majority of the integrated programmes presented under Objectives 1 and 2 were adopted in 1990, this year has been devoted essentially to approval of programmes under Objective 5b or relating to the implementation of the Community initiatives. In both cases the Commission has urged an integrated and multifund approach. [3]

508. In the case of the operational programmes, projects and global grants arising from the Community support frameworks for regions eligible under Objective 1, the Decisions adopted by the Commission this year related to Greece (ECU 215 million), Spain (ECU 1203 million), Italy (ECU 585 million), Portugal (ECU 48 million) and France (ECU 19 million).

Under Objective 2 the operational programmes, projects and global grants adopted related to the United Kingdom (ECU 8 million), France (ECU 2 million) and Spain (ECU 8 million).

Under Objective 5b the operational programmes, projects and global grants arising from the CSFs concerned France (ECU 13 million, Belgium (ECU 8 million), Italy (ECU 27 million), the United Kingdom (ECU 92 million) and Spain (ECU 28 million).

509. In the area of Community initiatives, numerous operational programmes were approved and are listed in Table 3.

510. In the field of integrated Mediterranean programmes (IMPs), a detailed analysis was carried out of the actual state of progress in the implementation of the French and Italian programmes as of 31 March 1991, and the Commission decided on 31 July to reallocate a reserve of ECU 253.23 million included under the special budget heading

---

[1]   Point 543 of this Report.
[2]   Bull. EC 12-1991.
[3]   The figures given in this section should be read in conjunction with the figures relating to the ESF (points 420 to 428 of this Report) and the EAGGF Guidance Section (points 575 and 576 of this Report).

TABLE 3

Commitments approved in 1991

(million ECU)

	Rechar	Envireg	Stride	Inter-reg [1]	Regis	Regen	Prisma	Telema-tique
Belgium	7.474	—	2.270	—	—	—	—	—
Denmark	—	—	1.840	—	—	—	—	—
Germany	15.945	—	4.025	2.742	—	—	—	—
Greece	—	16.347	9.358	37.203	—	48.000	—	—
Spain	7.078	38.016	43.433	105.098	19.417	—	4.555	7.138
France	8.599	5.309	18.149	—	8.174	—	—	—
Ireland	—	2.797	13.065	—	—	3.977	9.382	11.000
Italy	—	62.510	35.305	—	—	—	2.327	4.175
Luxembourg	—	—	—	—	—	—	—	—
Netherlands	—	—	0.870	—	—	—	—	—
Portugal	2.709	21.584	4.430	25.185	4.505	—	—	10.786
United Kingdom	—	2.188	—	—	—	—	—	—
Multi	—	—	—	76.593	—	—	—	—
Total	41.805	148.751	132.745	246.821	32.096	51.977	16.264	33.099

[1] 16 Interreg programmes were adopted in 1991, 8 of which concerned at least two countries.

for the IMPs by allocating an additional ECU 60 million to the French IMPs and ECU 193.23 million to the Italian programmes. This decision also means that all the IMP appropriations have now been allocated between the French and Italian regions.

Global grants

511. Over the last year, the instrument of global grants for assistance provided under CSFs has developed in a way which, despite its limitations (arising mainly from its innovative nature and the degree of administrative resistance which it has encountered), has nevertheless included model projects which demonstrate its considerable potential. These mainly involve the establishment in various regions of the Community (Italy, Spain, Portugal, Ireland) of local development strategies. In addition to these terri-torially-based global grants it is also possibile to grant 'technical' global grants, i.e. relating to a specific financing technique (e.g. interest subsidies) or a particular sector (tourism for example).

Technical assistance and studies

512.   Within the budget envelopes provided for in the CSFs and operational programmes under Objectives 1 and 2 to cover technical assistance, measures have been
financed to ensure effective monitoring of such schemes, which include developing and
operating a follow-up system with computer support involving preparatory and assessment studies, checks on compliance with other Community policies, and publicity for
development schemes part-financed under the CSFs and the programmes. The Commission has also financed on its own initiative, and in addition to the above, various
studies and technical assistance measures, particularly concerning the implementation
and assessment of regional schemes which it is part-financing. Under this heading the
Commission has undertaken a series of *ex ante* assessment studies of the largest-volume
CSFs under Objectives 1 and 2 on the one hand and of several operational programmes
on the other. [1]

TABLE 4

ERDF commitments in 1991 — Broken down by Objective

(million ECU)

	Objective 1	Objective 2	Objective 5b	Transitional measures (not linked to an Objective)	Innovative measures [1] (Art. 10)	Technical assistance [1] (Art. 7)	Total
Belgium	—	70.145	3.425	0.864	0.001	—	74.435
Denmark	—	13.701	3.264	5.879	3.278	—	26.122
Germany	—	149.512	56.361	40.279	0.002	0.005	246.159
Greece	925.089	—	—	—	5.477	0.020	930.586
Spain	1 373.054	246.388	41.639	25.789	4.603	2.175	1 693.648
France	63.075	195.880	65.291	8.506	1.952	0.194	334.898
Ireland	280.079	—	—	—	0.002	0.015	280.096
Italy	1 219.908	122.915	48.106	49.702	0.003	0.032	1 440.666
Luxembourg	—	2.024	0.487	—	—	—	2.511
Netherlands	—	21.336	4.185	1.950	0.002	—	27.473
Portugal	920.519	—	—	—	5.667	12.696	938.882
United Kingdom	79.382	418.603	87.467	—	5.357	—	590.809
Commission	11.424	2.926	50.544	11.699	43.060	5.910	125.563
Total	4 872.530	1 243.430	360.769	144.668	69.404	21.047	6 711.848

[1] Regulation (EEC) No 4254/88.

---

[1]   Point 402 of this Report.

TABLE 5

ERDF commitments in 1991 — Broken down by type of assistance

(million ECU)

	Community programmes and initiatives; non-quota measures	Operational programmes and national programmes of Community interest (NPCI) [2]	Innovative measures [1] (Articles 7 and 10)	Total
Belgium	10.722	63.712	0.001	74.435
Denmark	8.276	14.568	3.278	26.122
Germany	92.947	153.205	0.007	246.159
Greece	186.244	738.845	5.497	930.586
Spain	346.426	1 340.444	6.778	1 693.648
France	87.281	245.471	2.146	334.898
Ireland	62.084	217.994	0.018	280.096
Italy	291.318	1 149.314	0.034	1 440.666
Luxembourg	2.206	0.305	—	2.511
Netherlands	2.129	25.342	0.002	27.473
Portugal	163.194	757.325	18.363	938.882
United Kingdom	40.159	545.293	5.357	590.809
Commission	76 593	—	48.970	125.563
Total	1 369.579	5 251.818	90.451	6 711.848

[1] Regulation (EEC) No 4254/88.
[2] Including large projects and global grants.

Other operations

Conversion loans

513. New ECSC conversion loans granted by the Commission in 1991 totalled ECU 654.7 million, helping to create 45 089 jobs.[1] Of the ECU 101.1 million committed to finance interest-rate subsidies under the 1991 ECSC budget, 93.8% was used to increase the amounts allocated for previous loans.

---

[1]   OJ C 188, 28.7.1990.

TABLE 6

ECSC conversion loans

	1975-90		1991		1975-91	
	1	2	1	2	1	2
Belgium	254.3	15 729	35.5	2 664	289.8	18 393
Denmark	11.7	854	—	—	11.7	854
Germany	1 729.3	121.071	175.1	13 131	1 904.4	134 202
Greece	5.0	375	—	—	5.0	375
Spain	123.0	9 223	53.6	437	176.6	9 660
France	762.2	55 403	57.4	4 304	819.6	59 707
Ireland	4.4	420	—	—	4.4	420
Italy	783.2	52 303	78.4	5 882	861.6	58 185
Luxembourg	25.8	2 100	—	—	25.8	2 100
Netherlands	33.5	2 372	4.3	324	37.8	2 696
Portugal	20.0	1 500	—	—	20.0	1 500
United Kingdom	2 215.9	123 879	250.4	18 347	2 466.3	142 226
Saar/Lorraine/ Luxembourg cross-border operation	100.0	5 000	—	—	100.0	5 000
Community	6 068.3	390 229	654.7	45 089	6 723.0	435 318

1 = Amount of loans granted (million ECU).
2 = Number of jobs created/to be created.

Business and innovation centres

514.   Preparatory work on four new European business and innovation centres was launched in Crete, Galicia, Frankfurt/Oder and Zwickau while eight new proposals concerning Spain (two), France (two), Italy (one), Germany (one), and Portugal (two), are being appraised.

The reorganization of the European Business and Innovation Centre Network[1] was completed. Rapid progress was made in implementing the network's planned work programme of services for these centres.

'Europartenariat', a periodic event designed to help SMEs to forge contacts, was held in Portugal in June 1991 and was pronounced highly successful. The same applies to the Europartenariat organized for companies in the new German *Länder* and the associated conference, which took place on 2 and 3 December 1991 in Leipzig.

---

[1]   Eighteenth General Report, point 355.

Other studies and technical assistance

515.   The Commission financed several studies which examined regional problems at Community level in greater detail, in particular in the area of education and health infrastructures, and analysed the regional impact of developments outside the Community, such as for example the flow of migrants from Central and Eastern Europe. The Commission also financed two studies designed to encourage participation of the social partners (employers' and workers' organizations) in Community regional schemes.

Seed capital

516.   The Commission continued to implement the Community pilot scheme to stimulate the creation of seed-capital funds for investment in new businesses launched in 1989 for a period of five years. [1] All the funds selected, 15 of which are in assisted regions, are now operational and have formed themselves into a network. An extension of the pilot scheme is also planned in order to cover the new German *Länder*.

Work relating to the Aegean island regions of Greece

517.   Together with the Greek authorities the Commission has undertaken a general study of the socioeconomic problems of Greece's Aegean islands. On 23 October the Greek authorities sent the Commission a draft programme of specific measures in this connection which they would like to see implemented over the period 1992-96. At the end of the year, the Commission drafted an interim report for the Council and Parliament on the situation in these islands and the present state of the Commission's deliberations on the subject.

---

[1]   Point 299 of this Report.

Section 12

Measures to assist the Community's remoter regions

518.   The institutions continued and developed the work on implementing a Community approach to its remoter regions begun in December 1989 with the adoption of the Poseidom programme. [1] The aim of this approach is to ensure that the regions concerned take full advantage of the internal market and European integration despite the difficulties caused by their considerable isolation and insular nature while at the same time recognizing their special situation compared with the rest of the Community. These principles were established in the 'Declaration on the outermost regions of the Community' adopted by the Intergovernmental Conference and annexed to the new Treaty on European union.

519.   The Council's adoption of 'frameworks' for the application of Community policies in the Canary Islands, the Azores and Madeira continued the implementation of the Community's approach towards the remoter regions. The Commission intends to implement these frameworks in parallel so that the special measures planned for each region in the Poseidom, Poseican and Poseima action programmes are operational before 31 December 1992 and has sent its initial proposals to the Council. Moreover, the Commission has ensured that the general approach of these programmes has been taken into account in the general proposals presented under the various Community policies, for example on air transport or in the Council's work on an overall agreement on the abolition of tax frontiers.

520.   In 1991, the Council also adopted a new Decision on the association of the overseas countries and territories with the EEC, [2] the new features of which were drawn up in line with the policy towards the remoter regions, particularly with regard to regional cooperation between overseas departments, overseas countries and territories and African and Caribbean States in the Caribbean and the Indian Ocean.

521.   The Commission also continued its work on the drafting of common measures for the Community market in bananas, a crop of great economic and social importance for most of the remoter regions.

---

[1]   Programme of options specific to the remote and insular nature of the French overseas departments, OJ L 399, 30.12.1989; Twenty-third General Report, points 490 and 491.
[2]   Point 984 of this Report.

522. Efforts to help the economies of those regions, all of which come under Objective 1, to catch up, led to the implementation of operational programmes under the Community support frameworks and the adoption by the Commission of the first operational programmes under the Regis Community initiative,[1] specifically designed for the remoter regions.

The French overseas departments

523. In December, the Council adopted Regulation (EEC) No 3763/91[2] introducing specific measures in respect of certain agricultural products for the benefit of the French overseas departments, following the issuing of opinions by the Economic and Social Committee and Parliament on 30 October[3] and 22 November[4] respectively. The proposal, which was adopted by the Commission on 13 May,[5] was the subject of consultations on several occasions with the French authorities concerned under the Commission/ Member State/regions partnership. This Regulation implements most of the agricultural measures under Poseidom. It contains a series of measures on the special conditions governing the provision of certain supplies to the overseas departments and on support for particular types of production in those departments. Other measures to improve production conditions and the quality of products complete the package.

524. Pending application of the special measures provided for in the Regulation, the Commission took appropriate steps to guarantee the supply of cereals to the overseas departments during 1991 so as to fulfil their consumer needs.

525. On the taxation front, in accordance with the Council Decision of 21 December 1989,[6] a plan to impose dock dues on oil products in French Guiana was notified to the Commission, which raised no objection.

The Canary Islands (Spain)

526. On 26 June the Council adopted Regulation (EEC) No 1911/91 on the application of the provisions of Community law to the Canary Islands[7] and Decision 91/314/EEC

---

[1] OJ C 196, 4.8.1990; Twenty-fourth General Report, point 419.
[2] OJ L 356, 24.12.1991; Bull. EC 12-1991; Commission proposal: OJ C 149, 8.6.1991; Bull. EC 5-1991, point 1.2.104.
[3] OJ C 14, 20.1.1992; Bull. EC 10-1991, point 1.2.129.
[4] OJ C 326, 16.12.1991; Bull. EC 11-1991, point 1.2.140.
[5] JO C 149, 8.6.1991; Bull. EC 5-1991, point 1.2.104.
[6] OJ L 399, 30.12.1989; Twenty-third General Report, points 490 and 492.
[7] OJ L 171, 29.6.1991; Bull. EC 6-1991; point 1.2.119; Commission proposal: OJ C 67, 15.3.1991; Twenty-fourth General Report, point 424.

setting up a programme of options specific to the remote and insular nature of the Canary Islands (Poseican). [1] These texts take account of all the main points in the opinions issued by Parliament and the Economic and Social Committee on 17[2] and 30 May[3] respectively. The Regulation amends the arrangements laid down for the Canary Islands at the time of Spain's accession to the Community by establishing conditions for the integration of the Canary Islands into the customs union, the common agricultural policy and the common fisheries policy and adjustment of their special tax arrangements. On the basis of this Regulation, the Poseican programme sets out the principles for the application of common policies in an amended form in those sectors where this is required to take account of constraints and handicaps resulting from the special geographical and historical position of the Canary Islands.

527.   The Commission commenced the implementation of these new arrangements for the Canary Islands on 24 September when it decided not to object to the system of exemptions from the new Canary Islands 'arbitrio' on imports and production notified by Spain under Article 5 of the new Regulation.

The Azores and Madeira (Portugal)

528.   On 26 June, the Council adopted the programme of options specific to the remote and insular nature of Madeira and the Azores (Poseima),[4] following the issuing of opinions by Parliament and the Economic and Social Committee on 17[5] and 30 May[6] respectively. This programme, based on the same principles as Poseidom and Poseican, is made up of various measures, either general or specific to particular sectors, designed to apply Community policies in an amended form to take account of the constraints and the particular characteristics of these regions, in particular in the areas of agriculture, taxation, customs, energy and craft industries.

529.   Pending application of the special supply measures provided for under Poseima, the Commission took appropriate steps to guarantee supplies of cereals to Madeira and the Azores during 1991 to fulfil their consumer needs.

---

1   OJ L 171, 29.6.1991; Bull. EC 6-1991, point 1.2.120.
2   OJ C 158, 17.6.1991; Bull. EC 5-1991, points 1.2.95 and 1.2.96.
3   OJ C 191, 22.7.1991; Bull. EC 5-1991, point 1.2.96.
4   OJ L 171, 29.6.1991; Bull. EC 6-1991, point 1.2.121; Commission proposal: OJ C 67, 15.3.1991; Twenty-fourth General Report, Point 424.
5   OJ C 158, 17.6.1991; Bull. EC 5-1991, point 1.2.97.
6   OJ C 191, 22.7.1991; Bull. EC 5-1991, point 1.2.97.

Section 13

Agriculture[1]

Priority activities and objectives

530.   Implementation of the common agricultural policy in 1991 was dominated by three themes: first, the strict application of the adjustment measures defined in previous years and of the reform of the conditions for the use of the structural Funds; secondly, the continuing negotiations on agriculture in the GATT round and the intensified contacts between the Community and the countries of Central and Eastern Europe; and thirdly, the decision to launch a new discussion on the future of Community agriculture.

In the context of the agricultural markets, the first theme involved, in particular, the maintenance or reduction of institutional prices, the application of stabilizers and the strengthening of accompanying measures, such as set-aside, designed to influence production. At the same time, the new instruments for the application of the structural policy were phased in and used both to assist areas eligible under Objectives 1 and 5b and to speed up the development of agricultural structures.

With regard to the countries of Central and Eastern Europe, in particular Hungary, Poland and Czechoslovakia, negotiations were commenced to define cooperation procedures and explore the possibilities of increasing trade in certain areas. Following the breakdown of GATT negotiations in December 1990, technical discussions continued with a view to facilitating the search for agreement.

The situation regarding overproduction on several agricultural markets, the rapid increase in budgetary expenditure and the need to ensure the competitiveness of European agriculture while safeguarding social and economic equilibrium in rural areas led the Commission to propose a fresh general discussion on the future of the CAP and to present to the Council a series of guidelines for amending the policy as currently applied.[2] The Commission is proposing a general reduction in agricultural prices and adjustments to the current quota and intervention arrangements, in order to adapt production better to market requirements and to encourage more widespread preferential use of Community products. Compen-

---

[1]   For further details see *The Agricultural Situation in the Community — 1991 Report*, published in conjunction
     with this Report (available from the Office for Official Publications).
[2]   Supplement 5/91 — Bull. EC.

sation schemes to offset these price reductions would no longer be based on the quantities produced but on the areas under cultivation. The Commission believes that this system will preclude any incentive to produce more, while safeguarding the income of farmers by ensuring that the level of compensation varies depending on the region concerned and taking account of specific situations. These proposals are accompanied by measures to protect and conserve the environment, to encourage the afforestation of agricultural land and to improve the early retirement scheme.

531.   With a view to implementing this new approach, the Commission adopted proposals in October for Regulations relating to arable crops,[1] tobacco[2] and milk products,[3] as well as beef/veal[4] and sheepmeat,[5] together with proposals for Regulations on accompanying measures[6] dealing with the countryside environment, the afforestation of farmland and aid for early retirement.

Content of the agricultural policy

Agricultural prices for 1991/92

532.   On 13 and 18 June the Council formally adopted all of the agricultural prices for the 1991/92 agricultural year,[7] with the exception of the prices for nuts, adopted on 15 July.[8] On the whole, for the fourth year in succession, the Council kept to the approach adopted for the adjustment of the CAP and the guideline for agricultural expenditure.[9] Only a few price adjustments were made, which in general did not lead to changes in the institutional prices expressed in ecus (in countries with weak currencies); however, as a result of the agrimonetary adjustments, the decisions led to an average increase of 0.5% in prices expressed in national currencies.

---

[1]   OJ C 303, 22.11.1991; Bull. EC 10-1991, point 1.2.99.
[2]   OJ C 295, 14.11.1991; Bull. EC 10-1991, point 1.2.100.
[3]   OJ C 337, 31.12.1991; Bull. EC 10-1991, point 1.2.101.
[4]   OJ C 303, 22.11.1991; Bull. EC 10-1991, point 1.2.102.
[5]   OJ C 303, 22.11.1991; Bull. EC 10-1991, point 1.2.103.
[6]   OJ C 300, 21.11.1991; Bull. EC 10-1991, point 1.2.104.
[7]   OJ L 150, 15.6.1991; OJ L 162, 26.6.1991; OJ L 163, 26.6.1991; Bull. EC 6-1991, points 1.2.128 and 1.2.156; Commission proposal: OJ C 104, 19.4.1991; Bull. EC 3-1991, point 1.2.93.
[8]   OJ L 187, 13.7.1991; Bull EC 7/8-1991, point 1.2.209; Commission proposal: OJ C 104, 19.4.1991; Bull. EC 3-1991, point 1.2.93.
[9]   Twenty-fourth General Report, point 428.

Adjustment of the agricultural market organizations

533.   No major revisions were made to the market organizations in 1991 in conjunction with the price proposals; only a few adjustments were made, in particular in the milk and beef and veal sectors. A 2% general reduction in milk quotas was agreed and a system introduced for buying back milk quotas to build up the national reserves, so that Member States can redistribute and adjust quotas where necessary. The intervention arrangements for beef were changed.[1]

534.   In order to expedite the reduction in cereal production, the Council decided to supplement the scheme for the set-aside of arable land by introducing a voluntary programme whereby farmers can, for 1991/92, set aside at least 15% of the area which had been sown to cereals, oilseeds and protein crops in the previous year. In return, those farmers will receive an allowance per hectare set aside at least equal to the proportion of the premium granted and eligible for EAGGF financing under the set-aside Regulation, together with repayment of the basic co-responsibility levy payable on sales of cereals, which was increased from 3 to 5% this year.

535.   In order to bring the Community oilseed scheme into line with GATT rules (soya panel),[2] in December the Council, acting on a proposal from the Commission,[3] adopted new rules radically amending the system of support for soya beans, rapeseed and sunflower seed.[4]

Rural development

536.   The rural development schemes apply to all rural areas of the Community and involve assistance from the three structural Funds for regions whose development is lagging behind (Objective 1) and particularly vulnerable rural areas (Objective 5b), as well as horizontal measures to improve agricultural structures and the processing and marketing of agricultural and forestry products that are financed by the EAGGF Guidance Section (Objective 5a) applicable throughout the Community.

537.   Following the adoption in 1990 of the 44 Community support frameworks (CSFs)[5] for the areas eligible under Objectives 1 and 5b of the reform of the structural Funds,[6] the Commission continued its rural development policy and adopted almost all of the

---

[1]   OJ L 150, 15.6.1991; Bull. EC 6-1991, point 1.2.156.
[2]   Bull. EC 1/2-1990, point 1.2.100.
[3]   OJ C 255, 1.10.1991; Bull. EC 7/8-1991, point 1.2.164.
[4]   OJ L 356, 24.12.1991; Bull. EC 12-1991.
[5]   Twenty-fourth General Report, point 432.
[6]   OJ L 185, 15.7.1988; OJ L 374, 31.12.1988; Twenty-second General Report, points 533 and 534.

operational programmes under these CSFs, maintaining a balance between multifund and single-fund programmes. These programmes relate to agricultural development, restructuring and diversification schemes in Objective 1 and 5b areas and schemes under Objective 5a. The commitments of the EAGGF Guidance Section for schemes in Objective 1 areas totalled ECU 1 577 million at the end of 1991, i.e. 53.2% of the contribution proposed for the period 1989 to 1993.

538.   The Commission also adopted, on 13 March, a CSF for the five new German *Länder* and the eastern part of Berlin, [1] the EAGGF-Guidance contribution having been set at ECU 600 million.

539.   In the case of the Objective 5b areas, i.e. areas whose development is lagging behind, 74 programmes were approved, with allocations totalling ECU 1 665.2 million for the financing of new measures. The total allocation for Objective 5b amounts to ECU 2 607 million for the period 1989 to 1993. [2]

540.   Expenditure under Objective 5a was just under ECU 1 600 million, i.e. 57% of the amount earmarked for the same period. The implementation of measures continued on the basis of the legal texts revised at the end of 1989 and involves primarily the establishment of young farmers, compensatory allowances for less favoured areas and aids for the processing and marketing of agricultural products.

541.   Pursuant to Regulations (EEC) Nos 866/90 and 867/90 concerning Community aid for investments in the marketing and processing of agricultural products, [3] the Member States presented 92 sectoral programmes for which the corresponding multi-sectoral Community support frameworks have now been drawn up by Objective, distinguishing between regions whose development is lagging behind and other regions; [4] implementation of these CSFs will complete the process of substituting the new system for the old procedure laid down in Regulation (EEC) No 355/77. [5]

542.   The Commission also undertook a series of *ex ante* assessment studies of, first of all, the largest-volume CSFs for Objectives 5a and 5b and, secondly, several operational programmes. [6]

543.   On 15 March the Commission approved, on second reading, [7] a communication laying down guidelines for programmes under the Community initiative for rural

---

[1]   Point 408 of this Report.
[2]   OJ L 91, 6.4.1990; Twenty-fourth General Report, point 432.
[3]   OJ L 91, 6.4.1991, Bull. EC 3-1990, point 1.1.108.
[4]   OJ L 350, 19.12.1991; Bull. EC 12-1991.
[5]   OJ L 51, 23.2.1977; Eleventh General Report, point 310.
[6]   Point 402 of this Report.
[7]   OJ C 73, 19.3.1991; Bull. EC 3-1991, point 1.2.88.

development called Leader (Links between actions for the development of the rural economy).[1]

544.   On 30 January and 12 March respectively, the Economic and Social Committee[2] and Parliament[3] endorsed the proposal for a Regulation on the introduction and maintenance of agricultural production methods compatible with the requirements of the protection of the environment and the maintenance of the countryside.[4]

Quality of agricultural products

545.   Work to improve and recognize the quality of agricultural products and foodstuffs continued in 1991, and enjoyed the growing interest of farmers, the food industry and consumers.

546.   On 24 June, the Council adopted Regulation (EEC) No 2092/91 laying down organic production methods and arrangements for regular inspection of producers.[5] Proposals for regulations on designations of origin[6] and certificates of specific character for foodstuffs[6] were the subject of intense debate by Parliament and the Council. The Economic and Social Committee gave its opinion on the proposal regarding designations of origin on 3 July.[7] The purpose of the proposals is to protect either products the quality of which is linked to the geographical area whose name they bear, or products produced in a particular way which gives them a specific quality in the perception of consumers.

Management of the common agricultural policy

Market organizations

Crop products

547.   In 1990/91, production of cereals, particularly maize, was affected by drought and the Community harvest was therefore below the maximum guaranteed quantity (MGQ) (160 million tonnes, not including the former German Democratic Republic). This result

---

[1]   Twenty-fourth General Report, point 434.
[2]   OJ C 69, 18.3.1991; Bull. EC 1/2-1991, point 1.2.136.
[3]   OJ C 106, 22.4.1991; Bull. EC 3-1991, point 1.2.90.
[4]   OJ C 267, 23.10.1990; Twenty-fourth General Report, point 435.
[5]   OJ L 198, 22.7.1991; Bull. EC 6-1991, point 1.2.153; Commission proposal: OJ C 4, 9.1.1990.
[6]   OJ C 30, 6.2.1991.
[7]   OJ C 269, 14.10.1991; Bull EC 7/8-1991, point 1.2.171.

was also due to the cumulative effects of a sharp reduction (4.3%) in the area sown to cereals.

Initial estimates place the Community cereals harvest for 1991/92 (including the former German Democratic Republic) at around 178 million tonnes, as a result of a slight increase in the area sown and record yields of barley and common wheat in most southern regions. Durum wheat production was up by about 30% as a result of a substantial increase in the cultivated area in Spain, Greece and France. Introduction of the CAP in the territory of the former German Democratic Republic led to a considerable drop in the production of rye and oats.

Pursuant to the current system,[1] the additional co-responsibility levy for 1990/91 was set at 1.5% of the intervention price for common wheat, while no additional levy was fixed for 1991/92 because the maximum guaranteed quantity (MGQ) was not exceeded in 1990.

The Council fixed intervention prices for cereals for 1991/92[2] at the same level as for 1990/91,[3] with the exception of the intervention price for durum wheat, which was reduced by 3.5% in order to align it on the price of common wheat. The impact of this alignment was partially offset by an increase in aid, fixed at ECU 181.88/ha (+6.7%). In view of the alarming increase in intervention stocks of cereals, which total 18.7 million tonnes, including 8.5 million tonnes of common wheat, mostly situated in France and Germany, an additional temporary scheme for the set-aside of arable land was introduced in June for 1991/92.[4]

With the entry into force of the second stage of the transitional period of Portuguese accession,[5] aid was granted for cereals sold into intervention in order to offset the reduction in prices in Portugal as a result of their alignment on Community prices.

548.   Rice production in 1990 (2.37 million tonnes) was up on the previous year (1.85 million tonnes), when there was a sharp reduction in the cultivated area because of poor weather conditions in Spain. Producer prices reflected the abundance of the varieties in surplus (round, medium and long A grain rice) and remained below the intervention price, particularly in the case of round-grain varieties. Large quantities were offered for intervention from 1 January 1991, when intervention was opened. The breakdown of quantities taken over is as follows: 181 000 tonnes of paddy rice in Italy, 28 000 tonnes in Spain and 6 000 tonnes in France. According to estimates made in September, the overall area sown to rice this year will be about 2% less than in 1990. This reduction relates in particular to the areas sown to surplus varieties (round, medium

---

[1]   OJ L 22, 27.1.1990.
[2]   OJ L 162, 26.6.1991; Bull. EC 6-1991, point 1.2.128.
[3]   Twenty-fourth General Report, point 440.
[4]   OJ L 150, 15.6.1991; OJ L 162 and 163, 26.6.1991; Bull. EC 6-1991, point 1.2.156.
[5]   OJ L 302, 15.11.1985; Nineteenth General Report, points 730 and 731.

and long A grain rice), which will be about 11% down on the previous year (from 332 000 ha to 293 000 ha). However, cultivation of varieties in demand (Indica) should be clearly up on 1990/91 (from 35 000 ha to 65 000 ha).

549.   In the sugar sector, a production quota of 847 000 tonnes of white sugar was allocated to the new *Länder* of the German Democratic Republic. On 4 February the Council extended the current quota arrangements for sugar to the 1991/92 and 1992/93 marketing years,[1] while maintaining the current self-financing system whereby the costs of disposing of exportable quantities under Community guarantee are borne fully by the producers (beet growers and manufacturers). In addition, under the Act of Accession of Spain, the Council adopted proposals on the two-stage alignment of Spanish sugar and sugarbeet prices on the common prices, with the first stage covering 1991/92 and 1992/93 and the second stage running from 1993/94 to 1995/96.[2] The area under sugarbeet in 1990 (2 085 000 ha) increased in relation to 1989 by an amount which should not have been more than 1.6% but which in reality amounted to 12.4% because of German unification. The forecasts on plantings for 1991/92 suggest a reduction of 5.2% in relation to 1990/91. Sugar production in 1990/91 again increased sharply, because of favourable weather conditions. The average Community yield of sugar per hectare is 7.48 tonnes (8.12 tonnes/ha if the territory of the former German Democratic Republic is excluded, which beats the all-time record of the previous year (7.59 tonnes/ha)). Total Community production of white sugar has been fixed at 15.882 million tonnes, 1.610 million tonnes more than in 1989/90, of which 0.883 million tonnes were produced in the former German Democratic Republic.

550.   Community production of olive oil in 1990/91 is estimated at about 1 194 400 tonnes, as against 1 512 297 in 1989/90. There was little change in the area under olive trees, which available data put at 4.4 million hectares (of which 1.17 million are in Italy, 1.9 million in Spain, 0.7 million in Greece and 0.5 million in Portugal). Community consumption in 1989/90 amounted to 1 400 000 tonnes (75% of world consumption) and the forecast for 1990/91 made at the end of September was of the same order. Since the consumption aid scheme was introduced, consumption of oil in small containers, at 650 000 tonnes, accounts for most of the consumption in the Community of Ten. Farm consumption is still considerable. At the beginning of 1990/91, intervention stocks were 65 500 tonnes; at the end of the marketing year they were 30 000 tonnes.

A stabilizer was introduced in 1987/88, with an MGQ of 1.35 million tonnes. Although in that year the co-responsibility mechanism came into play, leading to a reduction of 31% in the aid, the MGQ was not reached in subsequent years and is unlikely to be reached in 1990/91. In view of the end of the transitional period in Spain and Portugal

---

[1]   OJ L 37, 9.2.1991; Bull. EC 1/2-1991, point 1.2.173; Commission proposal: OJ C 258, 13.10.1990; Bull. EC 7/8-1990, point 1.3.165.
[2]   OJ L 162, 26.6.1991.

on 31 December 1990 and the consequent total liberalization of the market in seed oils, the Council adopted measures in order to maintain the balance of the market in olive oil.[1]

551. After falling for two successive years, Community production of oilseeds in 1990/91 almost regained the level reached in 1987/88, i.e. 12 million tonnes, as against 10.5 million tonnes in 1989/90 (excluding the former GDR). However, in 1991/92 the area sown to oilseeds fell to an estimated 4.9 million ha, excluding the former GDR (5.3 million ha in 1990/91); production is expected to stabilize at a level of 12 million tonnes excluding the former GDR and reach 12.9 million tonnes including the new *Länder*. It is clear that the stabilizer mechanism, which was strengthened by the European Council in 1988,[2] has stabilized the area sown and checked the steady upward trend in production.

This mechanism, combined with the Council's decision to lower institutional prices by 1.5%, has led to renewed automatic cuts in institutional prices for rapeseed and sunflower seed for 1991/92, compared with 1990/91.

In December the Council adopted the Commission's proposal introducing a new support mechanism for producers of soya beans, rapeseed and sunflower seed.[3] The purpose of this new mechanism is to give effect to the conclusions of the GATT panel on oilseeds.

552. The latest data regarding the 1990 harvest (excluding Portugal) of all wines[4] suggest output will be 176 million hl, i.e. 3 million hl up on 1989. Due to weather conditions, the 1990/91 harvest, like the two previous ones, was relatively low compared with the production levels recorded over the last 10 years.

The 1991 harvest (for EUR 12), put at 165 million hl, is expected to be well down on 1990 as a result of the spring frosts. Considerable quantities were distilled under Community intervention measures (preventive, compulsory and support distillation and distillation under special price support measures for long-term storage-contract holders) during the 1990/91 marketing year (33 million hl compared with 24 million hl distilled in 1989/90). All forms of distillation were applied. Special provisions relating to management of the market in table wines (special distillation) were introduced in Portugal in 1991, whereas the Community rules on wine have applied in Spain from 1 March 1986. Market prices for table wine in the Community of Ten have been stable for a long period, with a very gentle downward trend. Price stability is even more marked in Spain, especially for red wine.

---

[1]   OJ L 130, 29.11.1990; Twenty-fourth General Report, point 443.
[2]   Bull. EC 6-1988, point 3.5.18.
[3]   Point 535 of this Report.
[4]   Rectified forward estimate established on 3 July 1991.

553.   In the fresh fruit and vegetables sector for 1991/92, the late frosts in spring 1991 over a large part of the Community cut some crops substantially, in particular apples (−32%), pears (−19%), nectarines (−11%) and apricots, except in Spain (Spain: +77%, other Member States: −17.4%). Production of apples is not expected to exceed 5.3 million tonnes, as against 7.8 million tonnes in 1990, with the production of pears at 2 million tonnes, while total production of peaches and nectarines, which has been increasing steadily since the early 1980s, amounted to 3.5 million tonnes in 1990 as against 3.7 million tonnes in 1989. Production of citrus fruit totalled 9 million tonnes for 1990/91, only slightly below the very high figure of 9.5 million tonnes in 1989/90. Marketing premiums for mandarins and certain varieties of oranges were reduced by one third. In July the Council amended the aid scheme for nuts and locust beans introduced in 1989.[1] The aid for improvement plans now varies according to the nature of the work envisaged so as to give priority to renewal or varietal conversion schemes for orchards. The Commission approved eight projects under the aid scheme to promote consumption of fresh apples and citrus fruit and the processing of apples.

554.   The Community harvest of fresh vegetables, which reached the record level of 44.1 million tonnes for the 1989/90 marketing year, stabilized in 1990/91 at 43.9 million tonnes (−0.5% compared with 1989/90 but +4.9% compared with the average for the period 1986 to 1988). No overall figure is available as yet for 1991/92. For 1991/92, the Council kept all the basic and buying-in prices at the levels obtaining in the Ten and aligned the prices in force in Spain and Portugal towards the common prices, in accordance with the rules laid down in the Act of Accession. Certain prices were subsequently cut after the intervention thresholds had been exceeded.

555.   With respect to tobacco, pending the substantial review of the market organization proposed by the Commission in October,[2] the Community policy to speed up improvements in the quality of production was continued, and even stepped up, by means of a review of the MGQs and the aids granted for the different varieties.

556.   Aid for hops was set at ECU 340 per hectare for all varieties. The Community is granting special aid of ECU 2 500/ha for a certain period and a maximum of 800 ha per Member State to encourage producers to convert areas sown to bitter varieties to varieties more suited to market requirements.

557.   For the Community, cotton is a minor crop in terms of area and number of producers; however, it does play an important socioeconomic role in the relatively less favoured areas of Greece and Spain where production is concentrated. In 1991 the Community had 311 500 ha under cotton, 233 000 ha of which were in Greece and

---

[1]   Point 532 of this Report.
[2]   OJ C 295, 14.11.1991; Bull. EC 10-1991, point 1.2.100.

78 500 ha in Spain, for an estimated total production of 889 000 tonnes of unginned cotton (626 000 tonnes in Greece, 263 000 tonnes in Spain). The Community produced 26% of its cotton fibre requirements in 1990, with consumption amounting to about 1 250 000 tonnes. Production has exceeded the MGQ (752 000 tonnes) each year since 1986/87, resulting in reductions in the guide price and aid. These reductions were fixed at ECU 239.65/tonne (25% of the guide price) for 1990/91 and ECU 67.19/tonne (7%) for 1991/92. The area sown to cotton, which increased steadily in previous years, actually fell by 40 000 hectares in 1991.

558.   After having increased over recent years, there was a sharp reduction in the areas sown to fibre flax in the Community in 1991 (79 000 ha in 1989 and 1990, 55 000 in 1991). Hemp is an extremely marginal crop, practically only harvested in France, on 4 000 hectares. Aid for these two fibre crops was maintained at the same level in 1991.

559.   In the seed sector, the Commission fixed the new reference prices for hybrid maize and hybrid sorghum in accordance with the rules. With 122 800 hectares sown to grasses (14% less than in 1990) and 131 800 hectares to legumes, seed multiplication can be considered to be in slight decline. The import/export ratio shows a production shortfall of some 20 000 tonnes.

Livestock products

560.   In the milk sector, the number of dairy cows continued to fall during 1991, to 22.9 million head, which corresponds to a 17% reduction since 1983. Output, which had remained more or less stable until 1990, is set to fall in 1991 as a result of the quota reduction, with milk collections totalling 96.8 million tonnes as against 98.9 million tonnes in 1990. Although consumption of certain milk products such as butter and milk powders is falling, total consumption continues to increase at a rate of 0.5% per year, particularly because of increased sales of cheese, but the imbalance in the use of milkfats and milk proteins is continuing to grow and poses serious difficulties. Problems with managing the market in milk required a 2% reduction in quotas in 1991.[1] The quota scheme was extended to Portugal and the new *Länder*,[1] and a new scheme for voluntary discontinuation of milk production was introduced involving the buying out of not more than 3% of quotas.[1]

561.   A cyclical upturn in Community beef and veal production took place in 1990 and 1991, resulting in a considerable increase in public intervention stocks. During this period, the demand for beef and veal collapsed under the joint effect of supplies of certain beef and veal at low prices but of a quality not suited to consumer tastes, and

---

[1]   OJ L 150, 15.6.1991; Bull. EC 6-1991, point 1.2.156.

the appearance of bovine spongiform encephalopathy ('mad cow' disease), particularly in the British Isles. This epizootic, together with the loss of certain outlets because of the Gulf War, substantially reduced Community exports of beef and veal to non-Community countries, due to the fear of contamination. As a result, intervention buying during 1990/91, of the order of 800 000 tonnes, was 4.5 times higher than withdrawals from the market during the previous marketing year. The 1991/92 thresholds for intervention measures were reduced by around 5% and buying-in prices brought into line with the market prices obtaining in the various countries. The level of buying-in prices for market support is now 25% lower than was the case five or six years ago. On the basis of the demographic progression in cattle numbers and general, long-term market trends, a cyclical downturn of beef and veal production from the present peak can be expected in the next six months or so.

562.   Community production of sheepmeat and goatmeat increased by 1.7% in 1991, to 1 211 000 tonnes, mainly as a result of increased output in the United Kingdom and Ireland. The number of sheep is falling (-0.8%), particularly in Germany and the United Kingdom, but consumption continues to increase. The reform of the market organization introduced by Regulation (EEC) No 3013/89[1] has applied since the beginning of 1990 and will be fully in place by the end of 1992 after a transitional period of three years. The main objective of the reform is to complete unification of the market regime by applying a single premium across the board, with differential rates for dairy farming and for meat production only. In 1991 the premium was paid by means of an initial advance in July and a second payment at the end of the year.

563.   The drop in prices for pigmeat at the end of 1990 required the introduction of private-storage aid schemes, under which 76 000 tonnes of pigmeat were placed in storage. Higher prices in the summer, together with a drop in the price of feedingstuffs, led to more acceptable commercial results. The market has held up reasonably well, partly because of a drop in production in the new *Länder* and of various diseases which temporarily reduced pig numbers. Imports into the Community from Hungary, Poland and Czechoslovakia continued under preferential arrangements involving quotas and a 50% reduction in levy.

564.   There is no internal market support for poultrymeat. The regulations governing trade with non-Community countries have been adapted to the world market situation and export refunds have declined, although destinations are still differentiated. In 1991 the concessions granted by the Community under the generalized system of preferences to developing countries and Hungary and Poland have been extended to Czechoslovakia and Bulgaria.

---

[1]   OJ L 289, 7.10.1989; Twenty-third General Report, point 578.

As in the case of pigmeat, these concessions consist of a 50% reduction in the levies on certain quantities of goose and duck. Following the adoption by the Council in June 1990 of a regulation on marketing standards for poultry, [1] on 5 June 1991 the Commission adopted the detailed implementing provisions. [2] These standards have applied since 1 July 1991.

565.   With regard to the egg sector, following the fall in production in 1989 (-4%), there has been an upturn in layer numbers since 1990. The sharp fall in production in the five new *Länder* has nevertheless enabled the increase in production to be absorbed. The situation on the Community market in 1991 has also generally been satisfactory. Market organization is the same as for poultrymeat and the same types of measures are in force. As regards trade, the internal and world market situation meant that refunds had to be maintained. On 15 May the Commission adopted the implementing rules [3] for the Council Regulation [1] to bring marketing standards for eggs more in line with current market requirements and consumer expectations.

Other work

Approximation of laws

566.   For the approximation of laws on public and animal health, feedingstuffs, plant health products and seeds and propagating material, see 'Harmonization of veterinary and plant health rules' in Chapter II, Section 2 ('Completing the internal market') of this Report. [4]

Agrimonetary measures

567.   The agrimonetary measures adopted by the Council for the 1991/92 marketing year [5] dismantled all the remaining monetary gaps in Germany, the Netherlands and the United Kingdom and three-quarters of the remaining gap in Greece, after automatic dismantling and alignment of green rates on the highest rate, and slightly reduced the applied monetary gaps in the milk, beef, cereals and sugar sectors in Spain. The agrimonetary situation has therefore improved considerably in 1991 in that there is no longer any distortion in the group of currencies held within the narrow margin of the EMS and the gaps for the currencies not held within that margin have been reduced.

---

[1]   OJ L 173, 6.7.1990; Twenty-fourth General Report, point 455.
[2]   OJ L 143, 7.6.1991; Bull. EC 6-1991, point 1.2.179.
[3]   OJ L 121, 16.5.1991; Bull. EC 5-1991, point 1.2.138.
[4]   Points 114 to 125 of this Report.
[5]   OJ L 150, 15.6.1991; Bull. EC 6-1991, point 1.2.128.

Food aid for the needy

568. The Community continued its programme[1] of food aid for the needy.[2] Since Germany, like last year, did not participate in the operation, about ECU 150 million was shared among the 11 other Member States to assist the distribution of foodstuffs through social and charitable organizations.

Income aid

569. The Commission approved the aid programmes submitted by Italy, Germany and Belgium in accordance with Regulation (EEC) No 768/89.[3] Two programmes for the Netherlands and France were approved in 1990,[4] the first year of application of the income support policy. The programme for Italy concerns only olive-oil producers in the south of the country. The first of the two programmes approved for the Federal Republic of Germany concerns all producers in Baden-Württemberg, irrespective of the type of holding, while the second programme applies only to areas of Rheinland-Pfalz which are not classified as less favoured areas, and concerns only arable land. The programme for Belgium covers the entire country and all types of holding. The estimated number of beneficiaries is 80 000 for the Italian programme, 30 000 for Baden-Württemberg, 4 000 for Rheinland-Pfalz and 8 000 for the Belgian programme.

Competition[5]

570. The Commission has paid special attention to the aids granted by Member States to their farmers and farming industries. When implementing this policy, it has generally given favourable decisions with respect to aid relating to environmental protection, plant health measures, research, information and training and compensation for disasters. The Article 93(2) procedure was initiated against four German schemes,[6] four Italian schemes,[7] two Spanish schemes,[8] two French measures,[9] one Greek scheme,[10] and one

---

[1]   Twenty-fourth General Report, point 458.
[2]   OJ L 352, 15.12.1987; Twenty-first General Report, point 588.
[3]   OJ L 84, 29.3.1989; Twenty-third General Report, point 562.
[4]   Twenty-fourth General Report, point 459.
[5]   For more information, see the chapter devoted to agriculture in the Commission's annual *Report on Competition Policy.*
[6]   OJ C 45, 21.2.1991; OJ C 32, 7.2.1991; OJ C 254, 28.9.1991.
[7]   OJ C 315, 14.12.1990; OJ C 165, 25.6.1991; OJ C 251, 26.9.1991; OJ C 246, 21.9.1991.
[8]   OJ C 45, 21.2.1991; OJ C 246, 21.9.1991.
[9]   OJ C 91, 25.3.1991; OJ C 165, 25.6.1991.
[10] OJ C 246, 21.9.1991.

TABLE 7

The agricultural management and regulatory committees

Committees	From 1 January to 31 December 1991			
	Meetings[1]	Favourable opinion	No opinion	Unfavourable opinion
Management Committee for Cereals	47	803	61	0
Management Committee for Pigmeat	12	23	1	0
Management Committee for Poultrymeat and Eggs	15	48	3	0
Management Committee for Fruit and Vegetables	13	87	3	0
Management Committee for Wine	30	74	5	0
Management Committee for Milk and Milk Products	29	198	44	0
Management Committee for Beef and Veal	27	144	9	0
Management Committee for Sheep and Goats	18	33	16	0
Management Committee for Oils and Fats	22	80	33	0
Management Committee for Sugar	51	127	3	0
Management Committee for Live Plants	4	5	0	0
Management Committee for Products Processed from Fruit and Vegetables	11	42	4	0
Management Committee for Tobacco	8	13	2	0
Management Committee for Hops	2	9	0	0
Management Committee for Flax and Hemp	5	4	1	0
Management Committee for Seeds	3	5	0	0
Management Committee for Dried Fodder	6	7	1	0
Management Committee for Agricultural Income Aids	4	0	0	0
Implementation Committee for Spirit Drinks	10	1	0	0
Implementation Committee for Aromatized Wine-based Drinks	1	2	0	0
Joint meetings of management committees[1]	4	9	0	0
Regulation 598/91 Committee	13	12	0	0
USSR Guarantee Committee	8	2	1	0
EAGGF Committee	15	20	0	0
Standing Committee on Feedingstuffs	4	6	0	0
Standing Veterinary Committee	22	134	1	0
Standing Committee on Seeds and Propagating Material for Agriculture, Horticulture and Forestry	5	21	0	0
Committee on Agricultural Structures and Rural Development	11	127	0	0
Community Committee on the Farm Accountancy Data Network	2	1	0	0
Standing Committee on Agricultural Research	3	2	0	0
Standing Committee on Plant Health	15	19	0	0
Standing Committee on Zootechnics	1	0	0	0
Standing Forestry Committee	8	0	0	0
Standing Committee on Organic Farming	1	1	0	0
Ad hoc Committee on the Supplementary Trade Mechanism	0	0	0	0

[1] Except those on trade mechanisms (11 meetings) and agrimonetary questions (8 meetings).

Belgian scheme.[1] The Commission sent a negative recommendation to France[2] and also to Belgium,[3] both concerning parafiscal charges. A formal decision with conditions was taken in a case concerning Italy.

Farm accountancy data network (FADN)

571. The management committee responsible for the general coordination and management of the network held two meetings in 1991 and visited Spain. A large number of economic analyses were based on FADN data. The proposals for the reform of the CAP prompted several analyses of income and the effects of the proposed reform on production. In addition, studies on the definition of economic indicators for agricultural holdings, the profitability of farms and production costs were carried out by outside consultancies following a call for tenders.

Advisory committees and relations with professional organizations

572. As in previous years, the advisory committees made up of representatives of the farming sector and consumer organizations, created at Community level, have been kept regularly informed of the application, development and future of the CAP.

Financing the common agricultural policy: the EAGGF

Guarantee Section

573. The 1991 budget, adopted on 13 December 1990,[4] provided EAGGF guarantee appropriations amounting to ECU 33 353 million, or 60% of the total budget (57% if

---

[1] OJ C 302, 22.11.1991.
[2] OJ L 123, 18.5.1991.
[3] OJ L 294, 25.10.1991.
[4] OJ L 30, 4.2.1991; Twenty-fourth General Report, point 993 *et seq.*

only the appropriations subject to the guideline are considered), broken down as follows:

EAGGF Guarantee Section
(subsection B1)   ECU 32 516 million

Other appropriations to which the detailed
rules for Guidance Section financing apply:

- Fisheries Guarantee Fund
  (Chapter B2-90)   ECU 27 million
- Reimbursement of Member States'
  expenditure on depreciation of stocks
  and disposal of butter
  (Chapter B0-10)   ECU 810 million

Guarantee Section total   ECU 33 353 million

The amounts of ECU 32 516 million and ECU 33 353 million include the appropriations set aside for the monetary reserve (ECU 1 000 million) and the appropriation entered in Chapter B0-40 for the second stage provided for in the Act of Accession of Portugal to the Community (ECU 97 million). The monetary reserve is entered in the budget to minimize the impact of any major and unforeseeable fluctuations in the exchange rate between the US dollar and the ecu compared with the rate used for the budget. It can be applied only in certain circumstances and is not included in the agricultural guideline fixed in the context of budgetary discipline. [1]

The guideline for 1991 was fixed at ECU 32 511 million and covers the appropriations entered in subsection B1, not including the reserve of 1 000 million, i.e. ECU 31 516 million.

The preliminary draft budget for 1992, adopted by the Commission on 30 April, was sent to the budgetary authority. [2] It took account of the Commission's price proposals and related measures for the 1991/92 marketing year. [3] The Council's decisions [4] led to smaller savings than those in the Commission's proposals, so on 2 July the Commission adopted a letter of amendment [5] expressing the Council's decisions in budgetary terms and adapting the proposed appropriations accordingly.

---

[1]   Twenty-second General Report, point 671.
[2]   Bull. EC 4-1991, point 1.5.7.
[3]   Bull. EC 3-1991, point 1.2.93.
[4]   Point 532 of this Report.
[5]   Bull. EC 7/8-1991, point 1.5.3.

TABLE 8

EAGGF-Guarantee appropriations, by sector

(million ECU)

	1989 expenditure	1990 expenditure	1991 appropri- ations[1]	Proposed 1992 appropri- ations[2]
Milk and milk products[3]	5 040.6	4 971.7	5 670	5 812
Cereals and rice[3]	3 340.3	3 950.2	5 477	6 597
Fruit and vegetables, wine, tobacco	3 305.1	3 230.3	4 382	4 652
Beef, sheepmeat, goatmeat and pigmeat	4 142.3	4 532.4	4 313	6 720
Olive oil, oilseeds and protein crops[3]	4 781.2	5 481.4	6 937	6 444
Sugar[3]	1 979.8	1 391.1	1 948	2 117
Other products	918.6	843.3	1 058	1 093
Refunds on processed products	552.1	511.5	724	672
Monetary compensatory amounts	364.3	307.5	245	73
Impact of accounts clearance decisions	−202.7	−377.9	token entry	token entry
Other:				
Interest payable to Member States following financial reform	48.5	66.6	60	96
Distribution of agricultural products to the needy	132.9	136.9	150	150
Fraud control	—	3.0	21	36
Rural development activities related to the operation of markets	—	—	334	397
Subtotal	24 403.0	25 048.0	31 319	34 859
Set-aside (share borne by Guarantee Section)	3.0	21.2	100	180
Provisional appropriations entered in Chapter B0-40 for the second stage of accession of Portugal	—	—	97	—
Total financed within guideline	24 406.0	25 069.2	31 516	35 039
Initial appropriations	26 761.0	26 501.0	31 516	35 039
Guideline	28 624.0	30 630.0	32 511	35 039
Fisheries	24.0	23.6	27	29
Depreciation of stocks and disposal of butter	1 442.9	1 360.7	810	810
Total	25 872.9	26 453.5	32 353[4]	35 878[4]

[1] Budget (OJ L 30, 4.2.1991).
[2] Preliminary draft budget, taking account of Letter of Amendment No 1.
[3] Including refunds for Community food-aid operations.
[4] Not including the additional ECU 1 000 million for the monetary reserve.

The breakdown of the appropriations for the Guarantee Section is as follows:

EAGGF Guarantee Section
(subsection B1)   ECU 36 039 million[1]

Other appropriations to which the detailed
rules for Guarantee Section financing apply:

- Fisheries Guarantee Fund
  (Chapter B2-90)   ECU 29 million
- Reimbursement of Member States'
  expenditure on depreciation of stocks
  and disposal of butter
  (Chapter B0-10)   ECU 810 million

Guarantee Section total   ECU 36 878 million[1]

The preliminary draft budget coincides exactly with the agricultural guideline, fixed at ECU 35 039 million for 1992.

With respect to the Community's own resources, agricultural levies and sugar sector levies will, according to the preliminary draft budget, yield an estimated ECU 1 353 million and ECU 1 236 million respectively in 1992.

The proceeds of the co-responsibility levy in the cereals sector and the financial contribution of milk producers in the milk products sector do not count as own resources but are treated as agricultural market intervention; these are estimated, for 1992, at ECU 1 161 million for cereals and ECU 323 million for milk and milk products.

574.   On 17 October, the Commission adopted the 20th financial report (1990) on the activities of the EAGGF Guarantee Section with a view to transmitting it to the Council and to Parliament.[2]

Guidance Section

575.   Since 1 January 1989 funding from the EAGGF Guidance Section has been provided as part of the general scheme of the structural Funds.[3] This is illustrated in the table showing the breakdown of 1990 appropriations by Objective for expenditure

---

[1]   Including the appropriation of ECU 1 000 million for the monetary reserve.
[2]   Bull. EC 10-1991, point 1.2.157.
[3]   OJ L 185, 15.7.1988; OJ 374, 31.12.1988; Twenty-second General Report, point 641.

qualifying for contributions from this Section, i.e. the adjustment of regions whose development is lagging behind (Objective 1), the adjustment of agricultural structures (Objective 5a), and the development of rural areas (Objective 5b). The appropriations entered in the 1991 budget totalled ECU 2 378 million for commitments (16.6% of the total for the structural Funds) and ECU 2 011 million for payments.[1] These appropriations are separate from those granted for fisheries measures, since financial management of the EAGGF Guidance Section for fisheries has been split off from that of the Guidance Section for agriculture since 1 January 1990. However, in the context of a transfer of appropriations within the total amount allocated to the structural Funds, the budget of the EAGGF Guidance Section for payment appropriations was increased to ECU 2 051 million. As a result of the implementation of the Community support frameworks for the regions covered by Objectives 1 and 5b, the draft budget for 1992 was increased to ECU 2 823.5 million for commitments and ECU 2 643.6 million for payments. The commitment appropriations account for 16% of the total for all the structural Funds.

TABLE 9

EAGGF Guidance Section — Agriculture: Summary of 1990 budget implementation
(Commitment appropriations)

(million ECU)

Type of financing	Total	Objective 1	Objective 5a	Objective 5b	Transitional
Direct	407.005	216.053	151.328	16.522	23.102
Regional	61.125	21.501		16.522	23.102
General	345.880	194.552	151.328		
Indirect	1 361.507	715.364	592.483	20.718	32.942
Regional	335.806	282.146		20.718	32.942
General	1 025.701	433.218	592.483		
Operational programmes	155.678	148.913		6.765	
Regional	135.610	128.845		6.765	
Marketing/processing	20.068	20.068			
Community initiatives	—	—		—	
Pilot projects, etc. (Article 22, Reg. 797/85; Article 8, Reg. 4256/88)	1.486	0.827			0.659
Global grant	—				
Total	1 925.676	1 081.157	743.811	44.005	56.703

---

[1]   OJ L 30, 4.2.1991; Twenty-fourth General Report, point 468.

The budget for the set-aside scheme, [1] financed equally by both Sections of the EAGGF, will be increased from ECU 200 million in 1991 to ECU 360 million in 1992. The 1992 draft budget provides ECU 180 million for agricultural income aids. Although the appropriations entered in the 1991 budget amounted to ECU 200 million, expenditure accounts for only 5% of that amount.

576. Pursuant to Article 25 of the coordinating Regulation (Regulation (EEC) No 4253/88[2]) the Commission adopted on 16 April the report on the EAGGF Guidance Section for 1989. [3]

International provisions

577. In 1991, continuing its humanitarian assistance under Operation Phare which was launched in 1990, and in addition to its programme of assistance for the development and privatization of agriculture in various countries in Central and Eastern Europe, the Community decided to grant additional food aid worth ECU 53 million to Romania. [4] It also extended its food-aid programmes to Bulgaria (ECU 28 million), Albania[4] and the USSR (ECU 250 million) and decided to guarantee food purchases by the Soviet Union up to a ceiling of ECU 500 million. [5]

---

[1]   OJ L 106, 21.4.1988; Twenty-second General Report, point 642.
[2]   OJ L 374, 31.12.1988; Twenty-second General Report, point 584.
[3]   Bull. EC 4-1991, point 1.2.79.
[4]   Point 818 of this Report.
[5]   Point 844 of this Report.

Section 14

Fisheries

Priority activities and objectives

578.   *On 4 December, the Commission adopted a report in accordance with Article 8 of Council Regulation (EEC) No 170/83*[1] *on the situation of fisheries in the Community, the economic and social development of coastal areas, the state of stocks and their probable development.*[2] *The report reviews the situation throughout the whole of the fisheries sector and lays down guidelines for the common fisheries policy for the period 1993 to 2002.*

The aim of the policy must be to assure the continuation of fishing activities, by a balanced and rational exploitation of the live resources of the sea. Striking the proper balance between resources and fishing effort will bring about socioeconomic changes to which the Community will have to find solutions, especially the social problems, as a contribution to economic and social cohesion.

On 11 March, under the reform of the structural Funds and more particularly to contribute to the achievement of Objective 5a, the Commission formally adopted the Community support frameworks for the improvement of the conditions under which fishery and aquaculture products are processed and marketed in the various Member States.[3]

The Commission also intensified its consultations with trade unions and industry federations in the fisheries sector and its exchanges of views and information with Parliament, for which it organized two seminars, one on the structural aspects of the common fisheries policy and the other on the Community's external fisheries relations.

579.   *In September, the Economic and Social Committee adopted an opinion*[4] *on the Commission's communication on the common policy,*[5] *in which it requested that more emphasis be given to the social aspects. In December, Parliament adopted a resolution on the same subject.*[6]

---

[1]   OJ L 24, 27.1.1983; Seventeenth General Report, point 466.
[2]   Bull. EC 12-1991.
[3]   OJ L 99, 19.4.1991; Bull. EC 3-1991, point 1.2.147.
[4]   OJ C 339, 31.12.1991; Bull. EC 9-1991, point 1.2.110.
[5]   Twenty-fourth General Report, point 471.
[6]   OJ C 13, 20.1.1992; Bull.EC 12-1991.

Internal resources and policy on conservation and monitoring

Community measures

580.   On 25 March, 29 July[1] and 3 December,[2] the Council amended Council Regulation (EEC) No 3926/90 fixing, for certain fish stocks and groups of fish stocks, the total allowable catches (TACs) for 1991 and certain conditions under which they may be fished.[3] In December it set TACs and quotas for 1992.[4] Under the Act of Accession, it also adopted in December three Regulations[4] fixing fishing possibilities in 1992 for vessels of Member States wishing to fish in Spanish and Portuguese waters and for Spanish and Portuguese boats wishing to fish in the waters of other Member States.

581.   On 22 February, Parliament adopted a resolution on establishing TACs and fishing quotas for Community waters for 1991.[5]

582.   In order to give better protection to juveniles and to reduce the impact of fishing on ecosystems, the Commission adopted on 6 June a proposal for a Regulation[6] amending   Council Regulation (EEC) No 3094/86   laying   down   certain   technical measures for the conservation of fishery resources[7] with the aim of making certain measures previously contained in the annual TAC and quota Regulations permanent.

583.   In April the Commission sent the Council a report on the use of selective trawls in the Norway lobster fishery in Zone 3, fulfilling the declaration made by the Commission when the Council adopted Regulation (EEC) No 4056/89.[8]

584.   The Commission also adopted, in June, a proposal[9] to consolidate Regulation (EEC) No 3094/86[10] to take account of the nine amendments and two corrections made to date.

585.   In order to adjust, simplify and clarify the technical measures for the conservation of fishery resources contained in Regulation (EEC) No 3094/86, the Council agreed an

---

[1]   Point 599 of this Report.
[2]   OJ L 343, 13.12.1991; Bull. EC 12-1991.
[3]   OJ L 378, 31.12.1990; Twenty-fourth General Report, point 472.
[4]   OJ L 367, 31.12.1991; Bull. EC 12-1991.
[5]   OJ C 72, 18.3.1991; Bull. EC 1/2-1991, point 1.2.211.
[6]   Bull. EC 6-1991, point 1.2.188.
[7]   OJ L 288, 11.12.1986; Bull. EC 10-1986, point 2.1.174.
[8]   OJ L 389, 30.12.1989.
[9]   Bull. EC 6-1991, point 2.1.189.
[10]   OJ L 162, 18.6.1986; Twentieth General Report, point 662.

11th amendment[1] on 28 October consisting of a package of technical measures set out in the Commission's proposals for the 10th, 11th and 12th amendments.[2]

586.   On 28 November the Council adopted Regulation (EEC) No 3500/91, representing the 10th amendment of Regulation (EEC) No 3094/86, in order to continue the 'mackerel box' provided for in Article 8 of the latter.[3]

587.   The Commission drew up a document on the discarding of fish as a common practice in Community fisheries, identifying the reasons for it and its effects, and proposing a strategy to deal with the problem.

588.   With a view to the gradual introduction of a Community scheme for the conservation and management of resources in the Mediterranean, on 28 November the Council also adopted Regulation (EEC) No 3499/91[4] introducing a set of projects on the structure of traditional fisheries, the adaptation of specialized fisheries, the monitoring of fishing activities, the development of a statistical network and the coordination of research and the use of scientific data.

589.   Under the fisheries and aquaculture research programme (FAR), a total of 128 research projects were selected and various schemes to coordinate research received financial support.

As the result of the Council's Decisions adopting the third framework programme in the field of research and technological development[5] and the specific programme in the field of agriculture and agro-industry, including fisheries,[6] the Commission issued a call for project proposals in research and technological development.[7]

National measures

590.   The Commission has taken note of 64 national conservation measures notified by the Member States. Of these, 43 have been the subject of observations made by the Commission or have been approved by it while 21 are still being examined.

---

[1]   Bull. EC 10-1991, point 1.2.162.
[2]   Twenty-fourth General Report, point 473; Bull. EC 6-1991, point 1.2.188.
[3]   OJ L 331, 3.12.1991; Bull. EC 11-1991, point 1.2.172; Commission proposal: Bull. EC 11-1991, point 1.2.172.
[4]   OJ L 331, 3.12.1991; Bull. EC 11-1991, point 1.2.175; Commission proposal: Bull. EC 7/8-1991, point 1.2.247.
[5]   OJ L 117, 8.5.1990; Twenty-fourth General Report, point 247.
[6]   OJ L 265, 21.9.1991; Bull. EC 9-1991, point 1.2.37.
[7]   OJ C 264, 10.10.1991.

Monitoring

591.   The Commission continued to monitor compliance with the TACs and quotas in Community waters and some international waters, having to close a total of 76 fisheries during the year following the exhaustion of a TAC or quota. The Commission opened a number of preliminary infringement procedures relating to overfishing. Procedures relating to overfishing in previous years (from 1985 to 1988) were continued in 1991.

592.   The Commission also monitored observance of conservation measures, fisheries agreements with non-member countries and international agreements and also continued its surveillance in the regulatory area of the Northwest Atlantic Fisheries Organization (NAFO).

593.   Within the framework of Council Decision 89/631/EEC,[1] the Commission continued to assess the eligibility of programmes presented by the Member States for the acquisition and improvement of means of surveillance and inspection.[2]

594.   Parliament delivered a favourable opinion[3] on the Commission's proposal on the checks and penalties applicable under the common agricultural and fisheries policies.[4]

External resources

595.   In November the Council adopted a Decision authorizing the Commission to negotiate fisheries agreements with Ecuador and Venezuela.[5]

596.   New protocols were concluded to the fisheries agreements with Senegal,[6] Morocco,[7] Mauritania[8] and São Tomé and Príncipe.[9]

597.   The Council also decided on the provisional application of the protocol with Morocco,[10] Guinea-Bissau,[11] the Comoros,[12] Mozambique and Guinea, and adopted

---

[1]   OJ L 364, 14.12.1989; Twenty-third General Report, point 598.
[2]   OJ C 37, 9.2.1991; Bull. EC 2-1991, point 1.2.213.
[3]   OJ C 72, 18.3.1991; Bull. EC 1/2-1991, point 1.2.138.
[4]   OJ C 137, 6.6.1990; Twenty-fourth General Report, point 476.
[5]   Bull. EC 11-1991, point 1.2.174.
[6]   OJ L 53, 27.2.1991; Bull. EC 1/2-1991, point 1.2.217; basic agreement: OJ L 226, 29.8.1980.
[7]   OJ L 78, 26.3.1991; Bull. EC 3-1991, point 1.2.150; basic agreement: OJ L 137, 2.6.1988; Twenty-second General Report, point 689.
[8]   OJ L 117, 10.5.1991; Bull. EC 4-1991, point 1.2.126.
[9]   OJ L 123, 18.5.1991; Bull. EC 5-1991, point 1.2.146.
[10]   OJ L 195, 18.7.1991; Bull. EC 7/8-1991, point 1.2.250.
[11]   OJ L 309, 11.11.1991.
[12]   Bull. EC 12-1991.

two Decisions on extension and amendment of the fisheries agreement with the United States of America[1] and the extension of the agreement with South Africa[2] respectively.

598.   The Joint Committees responsible for the management of the agreements with Morocco, the Seychelles and Mauritania met in Brussels on 19 March,[3] 15 April and 22/23 September respectively.

599.   On 25 March[4] and 29 July,[5] the Council amended Regulation (EEC) No 3926/90[6] fixing TACs and quotas for 1991, to take account of an agreement between the Community, Sweden and Norway laying down reciprocal fishing arrangements for 1991 in the Skagerrak, Kattegat, the North Sea and the Celtic Sea.

600.   On 15 July, the Council adopted Regulation (EEC) No 2156/91[7] amending Regulation (EEC) No 1866/86 on measures for the conservation of fishery resources in the waters of the Baltic Sea, the Belts and the Sound[8] in order to prohibit fishing with trawls, Danish seines and similar nets in the Oderbank zone. On 23 September the Council amended Community legislation on the conservation of fish stocks in the Antarctic[9] to take account of the recommendations adopted by the CCAMLR at its ninth meeting.[10]

601.   In April, the Council allocated additional catch quotas among Member States for vessels fishing in Swedish waters in 1991.[11] In July[12] and in December,[13] the Council amended the catch quotas laid down by Regulation (EEC) No 3928/90 for fishing in the Norwegian exclusive economic zone and the fishing zone around Jan Mayen.[14] Also in December, the Council amended Regulation (EEC) No 3927/90 laying down for 1991 certain measures for the conservation and management of fishery resources applicable to vessels flying the flag of Norway.[15] The Council adopted in December the allocation between Member States for 1992 of catch quotas in the waters of the Faeroes,[16]

---

[1]   OJ L 166, 28.6.1991; Bull. EC 6-1991, point 1.2.191.
[2]   OJ L 175, 4.7.1991; Bull. EC 6-1991, point 1.2.192.
[3]   Bull. EC 3-1991, point 1.2.151.
[4]   OJ L 82, 28.3.1991; Bull. EC 3-1991, point 1.2.148.
[5]   Bull. EC 7/8-1991, point 1.2.246.
[6]   OJ L 378, 31.12.1990; Commission proposal: Bull. EC 7/8-1991, point 1.2.246.
[7]   OJ L 201, 24.7.1991; Bull. EC 7/8-1991, point 1.2.248.
[8]   OJ L 162, 18.6.1986; Bull. EC 6-1986, point 2.1.216.
[9]   OJ L 271, 29.7.1991; Bull. EC 9-1991, point 1.2.114; Commission proposal: Bull. EC 4-1991, point 1.2.129.
[10]   Twenty-fourth General Report, point 483.
[11]   OJ L 102, 23.4.1991; Bull. EC 4-1991, point 1.2.125; Commission proposal: Bull. EC 3-1991, point 1.2.149.
[12]   OJ L 222, 10.8.1991; Bull. EC 7/8-1991, point 1.2.249.
[13]   OJ L 343, 13.12.1991; Bull. EC 12-1991.
[14]   OJ L 378, 31.12.1990; Twenty-fourth General Report, point 480.
[15]   OJ L 348, 17.12.1991; Bull. EC 12-1991.
[16]   OJ L 367, 31.12.1991; Bull. EC 12-1991.

Greenland,[1] the NAFO area,[1] Norway[1] and Sweden,[1] as well as Regulations laying down the conservation measures applying to vessels flying the Faeroese,[1] Norwegian[1] and Swedish[1] flags in Community fishing areas.

602.   The Community participated, either as a member or as an observer, in the work of a number of international fisheries organizations and in particular the Group to manage resources on the continental shelf off Guinea, formed by the Fishery Committee for the Eastern Central Atlantic (Cecaf), held from 4 to 7 February; the eighth annual meeting of the North Atlantic Salmon Conservation Organization (Nasco) from 11 to 14 June;[2] the meeting of the Inter-American Commission for Tropical Tuna (IACTT) held from 18 to 20 June; the 13th meeting of the Northwest Atlantic Fisheries Organization (NAFO) from 9 to 13 September, as a result of which the Commission in December adopted two proposals for Regulations fixing detailed rules for applying the monitoring measures introduced by NAFO;[3] the statutory meeting of the International Council for the Exploration of the Sea (ICES) held from 23 to 26 September; the meeting of the fishery resources committee of the General Fisheries Council for the Mediterranean (GFCM) from 28 to 31 October; the 10th meeting of the Commission for the Conservation of Antarctic Marine Living Resources (CCAMLR) from 21 October to 1 November; the 12th ordinary meeting of the International Commission for the Conservation of Atlantic Tunas from 11 to 15 November, and the meeting of the Commission for North-West Atlantic Fisheries held from 19 to 24 November.

Organization of markets

603.   On 28 November the Council adopted a Regulation[4] consolidating Council Regulation (EEC) No 3796/81 on the common organization of the market in fishery products,[5] designed to make Community law clearer and more transparent in this field.

604.   On 28 October the Council also adopted Regulation (EEC) No 3162/91[6] amending Regulation (EEC) No 104/76 laying down common marketing standards for shrimps, edible crabs and Norway lobsters.[7]

---

[1]   OJ L 367, 31.12.1991; Bull. EC 12-1991.
[2]   Bull. EC 6-1990, point 1.2.194.
[3]   Bull. EC 12-1991.
[4]   OJ L 354, 23.12.1991; Bull. EC 11-1991, point 1.2.176; Commission proposal: Bull. EC 3-1991, point 1.2.153.
[5]   OJ L 379, 31.12.1981.
[6]   OJ L 300, 31.10.1991; Bull. EC 10-1991, point 1.2.169.
[7]   OJ L 20, 28.1.1976.

605.   As part of measures for the management of the tuna market, financial compensation was paid to producers' organizations for tuna delivered to the canning industry for the periods 1 April to 30 June 1990,[1] 1 July to 30 September 1990,[2] 1 October to 31 December 1990[2] and 1 January to 31 March 1991.[3]

606.   To enable the Commission to obtain an overall view of the landings of fishery products throughout the Community, on 21 May the Council adopted a Regulation on the submission of data on the landings of fishery products in Member States.[4]

607.   In connection with the implementation of the common fisheries policy in the territory of the former German Democratic Republic, on 4 April the Commission adopted a Regulation[5] extending Regulation (EEC) No 3714/90 on transitional measures on trade in certain fishery products with the USSR after the unification of Germany,[6] on 28 June, a Regulation[7] amending Regulation (EEC) No 1106/90 on the communication of information for the purposes of the common organization of the market in fishery products,[8] in order to complete the list of representative ports in the whole of German territory, and on 16 October a Regulation[9] granting an export refund on carp originating in the former territory of the German Democratic Republic.

608.   In view of disturbances on the salmon market, the Commission initially adopted a Regulation laying down arrangements for retrospective Community surveillance in respect of imports of Atlantic salmon,[10] subsequently making these imports subject to a minimum price.[11]

609.   On 28 November, the Council adopted Regulations (EEC) Nos 3568/91, 3569/91 and 3570/91, fixing prices for fishery products for the 1992 season.[12]

---

[1]   OJ L 86, 6.4.1991; Bull. EC 4-1991, point 1.2.130.
[2]   OJ L 158, 22.6.1991; Bull. EC 6-1991, point 1.2.196.
[3]   OJ L 348, 17.12.1991; Bull. EC 12-1991.
[4]   OJ L 133, 28.5.1991; Bull. EC 5-1991, point 1.6.1; Commission proposal: Bull. EC 6-1991, point 2.6.4.
[5]   OJ L 85, 5.4.1991.
[6]   OJ L 353, 17.12.1990; Twenty-fourth General Report, point 23.
[7]   OJ L 168, 29.6.1991; Bull. EC 6-1991, point 1.2.197.
[8]   OJ L 111, 1.5.1990; Twenty-fourth General Report, point 484.
[9]   OJ L 287, 17.10.1991.
[10]   OJ L 151, 15.6.1991; Bull. EC 6-1991, point 1.2.195.
[11]   OJ L 308, 9.11.1991; OJ L 319, 21.11.1991.
[12]   OJ L 338, 10.12.1991; Commission proposals: Bull. EC 11-1991, point 1.2.171.

Structural policy

Fleet structure, aquaculture

610.   Under Regulation (EEC) No 4028/86 of 18 December 1986, as last amended by Regulation (EEC) No 3944/90,[1] the Commission granted total aid for the 1991 budget year of around ECU 22 million towards 591 projects for the modernization of fishing vessels, around ECU 8 million to 29 projects for the construction of fishing vessels and around ECU 39 million to 236 installation projects involving aquaculture and artificial reefs.

The Commission also granted total aid of approximately ECU 7 million to 32 projects for the equipping of fishing ports in 1991.

With regard to exploratory fishing as provided for in the same Regulation, the Commission granted incentive premiums amounting to approximately ECU 1.8 million to 12 projects submitted by Italy and Spain.

On 24 May, and updated by a decision of 10 December, the maximum total amount of eligible expenditure by Member States on measures to adjust capacity came to ECU 188.4 million.

The Commission approved total aid of around ECU 2 million for joint ventures.

The Commission granted total aid of around ECU 0.5 million to one project submitted by Italy for redeployment operations.

The Commission granted aid of around ECU 27.5 million under the same Regulation to 13 projects submitted by Italy, Portugal, France and Spain, for the creation of joint enterprises.

By way of specific measures under Regulation (EEC) No 4028/86, the Commission granted aid of ECU 0.6 million to a project submitted by Denmark to alleviate difficulties affecting the whiting fishery in the North Sea[2] and aid of ECU 1.6 million for a three-year measure submitted by Spain to back up the prohibition on alevin fishing.[3] The Commission also granted aid of around ECU 0.4 million to a project submitted by France for the market promotion of fresh sardines.

611.   Following the amendment of Regulation (EEC) No 4028/86[4] by Regulation (EEC) No 3944/90,[5] on 21 June the Commission adopted four new Regulations laying

---

[1]   OJ L 380, 31.12.1990; Twenty-fourth General Report, point 684.
[2]   Bull. EC 4-1991, point 1.2.133.
[3]   Bull. EC 7/8-1991, point 1.2.255.
[4]   OJ L 376, 31.12.1986; Twentieth General Report, point 684.
[5]   OJ L 380, 31.12.1990; Twenty-fourth General Report, point 489.

down detailed rules for implementing the amended Regulation with regard to exploratory fishing, joint enterprises, redeployment operations and joint ventures.[1]

612.   On the same date, the Commission adopted Decision 91/327/EEC fixing Commission guidelines on fishing zones, species and fishing gear and methods for exploratory
fishing voyages, redeployment operations and cooperation operations within the context
of joint ventures,[1] and Regulation (EEC) No 1960/91 laying down detailed rules for the
application of Article 43 of Regulation (EEC) No 4028/86 as regards Community
assistance granted in the form of interest-rate reductions or contributions to guarantee
funds.

613.   On 14 October, the Commission also approved an amendment to the German
multiannual guidance programme to bring the fishing fleet of the former German
Democratic Republic under the common fisheries policy structural regulations.[2]

Processing and marketing

614.   On 11 March, the Commission adopted the Community support frameworks for
the improvement of the processing and marketing of fishery and aquaculture products.
The Decision regarding Germany, which did not apply to the new *Länder*, was supplemented by the Commission Decision of 13 March on the establishment of the Community support framework for all structural measures on the territory of the former German
Democratic Republic.[3] The Commission Decision regarding Portugal was amended on
17 June 1991.[4]

The Community financial envelope currently allotted is approximately ECU 190 million
over three years (1991-93). Community aid, excluding that allocated for the new German
Länder, is some 70 % higher than that granted in the years before the application of the
reform of the structural Funds.

On the basis of the Community support frameworks and in accordance with the
Community priorities laid down, the Member States established 15 operational programmes of investment which were then approved by the Commission.

---

[1]   OJ L 181, 8.7.1991; Bull. EC 6-1991, point 1.2.198.
[2]   OJ L 295, 25.10.1991.
[3]   OJ L 114, 7.5.1991.
[4]   OJ L 191, 16.7.1991; Bull. EC 6-1991, point 1.2.200.

Socioeconomic aspects

615.   As part of the preparation for a new socioeconomic programme to offset the impact of the implementation of the common fisheries policy, the Commission took a series of decisions establishing concerted measures for the implementation of pilot schemes in the fisheries and aquaculture sector in Spain,[1] the United Kingdom,[2] Greece,[2] France,[3] Portugal, Denmark and Italy,[4] total aid amounting to ECU 0.35 million under Title X ('Specific measures') of Regulation (EEC) No 4028/86.[5]

State aids

616.   In accordance with Articles 92 and 93 of the EEC Treaty, the Member States notified 45 draft national aid schemes in the fisheries and aquaculture sector. The Commission also examined six aid schemes that were not notified.

By the end of December, the Commission had arrived at 29 final decisions. It did not raise objections to the implementation of 18 schemes. In respect of seven draft schemes it decided to open the examination procedure laid down in Article 93(2) of the Treaty and in the case of four others it terminated the procedure.

---

[1]   OJ L 231, 20.8.1991.
[2]   OJ L 307, 8.11.1991.
[3]   OJ L 307, 8.11.1991; Bull. EC 12-1991.
[4]   Bull. EC 12-1991.
[5]   OJ L 376, 31.12.1986; Twentieth General Report, point 684.

Section 15

Environment

Priority activities and objectives

617.   1991 has seen environment policy become inextricably linked to the overall economic policy thinking of the Community. The perception has grown that concerted action on environment issues is needed at the Community level. Commission initiatives are seen to be necessary to bring about the integration of environment considerations into other policy areas including agriculture, the internal market, transport and energy.

Linked very closely to energy policy issues and in response to the urgent problem of global warming, on 25 September the Commission approved a communication[1] to the Council on a Community strategy to limit carbon dioxide emissions and to improve energy efficiency and security of supply. It proposes introducing a carbon dioxide/energy tax as a means of attaining the target of stabilizing emissions. Confirming the need for national programmes to limit emissions of carbon dioxide and greenhouse gases, and endorsing the use of tax measures, the Council asked the Commission[2] to come up with proposals to put this strategy into effect, making it a principle to share the burden between the Member States.

In addition, on 12 December the Council recorded its agreement[3] on LIFE, a key financial instrument designed to strengthen the effectiveness of the structures for implementing the environment policy throughout the Community.

Significant progress was made in the legislative field as the Council adopted or agreed measures on the Community Norspa project,[4] waste water,[5] a Community eco-label,[6] the protection of natural habitats[7] and pollution by lorries.[8] Major new proposals were also made by the Commission on all aspects of environmental protection. At the same time the Commission continued to place great emphasis on implementation of the existing legislation.

---

[1]   Point 622 of this Report.
[2]   Bull. EC 12-1991.
[3]   Point 632 of this Report.
[4]   Point 633 of this Report.
[5]   Point 649 of this Report.
[6]   Point 637 of this Report.
[7]   Point 659 of this Report.
[8]   Points 662 and 663 of this Report.

On the international scene, in the run-up to the Rio de Janeiro UN Earth Summit[1] in June 1992, the Community was at the heart of the negotiations on climate change, biological diversity and tropical forests.[2] It also continued to play a leading role in helping the countries of Central and Eastern Europe to deal with their environmental problems. Similarly, the Commission was actively involved in the operations to clean up the marine pollution caused by the conflict in the Gulf. In particular, it followed up the conclusions adopted by the Council on 18 March[3] by deciding to grant support to help oil companies from the Community to extinguish the burning wells.[4]

Horizontal measures

Taking the environment into account in other policies

618.   As required by Article 130r of the Treaty , the Commission continued to take environmental protection requirements into account in its other policies, particularly agricultural policy. In this context, as part of the accompanying measures provided for in the communication on the development and future of the common agricultural policy[5] it expanded its proposal for a Regulation on the introduction and maintenance of agricultural production methods compatible with the requirements of the protection of the environment and the preservation of the countryside.[6]

619.   The Council adopted a series of legislative measures to reduce pollution by inputs used in agriculture, including Regulation (EEC) No 2092/91 of 24 June on organic production of agricultural products and indications referring thereto on agricultural products and foodstuffs[7] and Directive 91/414/EEC of 15 July concerning the placing of plant protection products on the market.[8] It also agreed on the proposal for a Directive on the protection of water against pollution by nitrates from agriculture.[9]

---

[1]   Point 626 of this Report.
[2]   Points 670 to 672 of this Report.
[3]   Bull. EC 3-1991, point 1.2.175.
[4]   Bull. EC 4-1991, point 1.2.136.
[5]   Point 530 of this Report; Supplement 5/91 — Bull. EC.
[6]   OJ C 267, 23.10.1990; Twenty-fourth General Report, point 498.
[7]   OJ L 198, 22.7.1991; Bull. EC 6-1991, point 1.2.153; Commission proposal: OJ C 4, 9.1.1990; Twenty-third General Report, point 183; OJ C 101, 18.4.1991; Bull. EC 3-1991, point 1.2.110.
[8]   OJ L 230, 19.8.1991; Bull. EC 7/8-1991, point 1.2.203; Commission proposal: OJ C 212, 9.9.1976, OJ C 89, 10.4.1989, OJ C 93, 11.4.1991; Bull. EC 3-1991, point 1.2.113.
[9]   Point 649 of this Report.

620.   In a resolution of 21 November,[1] Parliament asked the Commission to prepare a report on implementation of Directive 85/337/EEC on the assessment of the effects of certain public and private projects on the environment.[2]

621.   On 26 March the Commission adopted guidelines[3] for a new legislative model to reconcile environmental requirements and the requirements of the internal market, the second stage of which entails setting 'target' standards going beyond the immediately applicable standards.

Economic and fiscal instruments

622.   To follow up the conclusions[4] adopted by the Council in October 1990, when it identified four priority areas (energy and climate change, solid wastes, integration with other policies and water quality), the Commission continued to analyse the ways open to it to introduce economic and fiscal instruments as part of its environment policy. In response to the Council's conclusions to stabilize total CO_2 emissions in the EC at 1990 levels by 2000, on 14 October the Commission adopted a communication it had approved on 25 September on a Community strategy to limit carbon dioxide emissions and to improve energy efficiency.[5] This communication outlined a comprehensive strategy to meet the stabilization target set by the Council by means of voluntary, sectoral regulations, research and development programmes and fiscal measures, possibly in the form of a combined energy and carbon dioxide tax, backed up by national programmes.

623.   On 24 June the Council reached agreement[6] on the minimum excise duty rates to be imposed on petroleum products by the Member States as from 1 January 1993. In keeping with the principle of tax differentiation in favour of the environment, the Council decided to maintain a differential of ECU 50 between the minimum excise duty rates on leaded and unleaded petrol.

Public awareness, information and training

624.   Pending a decision on the site and starting date for the European Environment Agency,[7] the Commission set about a series of technical preparations in cooperation with the relevant bodies in the Member States. A resolution adopted by Parliament on 14 June deplored the Community's failure to decide on a seat for the Agency.[8]

---

[1]   OJ C 326, 16.12.1991; Bull. EC 11-1991, point 1.2.191.
[2]   OJ L 175, 4.7.1985.
[3]   Bull. EC 3-1991, point 1.2.156.
[4]   Twenty-fourth General Report, point 501.
[5]   Bull. EC 9-1991, point 1.2.116; Bull. EC 10-1991, point 1.2.194.
[6]   Bull. EC 6-1991, point 1.2.5.
[7]   OJ L 120, 11.5.1990; Twenty-fourth General Report, point 502.
[8]   OJ C 183, 15.7.1991; Bull. EC 6-1991, point 1.2.211.

625.   The Council adopted[1] a Directive harmonizing and rationalizing reports relating to the environment on 1 October.

International cooperation

626.   One of the Commission's priorities was to prepare for the United Nations Conference on Environment and Development to be held in Rio de Janeiro in June 1992. In particular, the Commission took part in two meetings of the Preparatory Committee for the Conference in Geneva, the first from 18 March to 5 April and the second from 12 August to 5 September. In addition, on 2 October the Commission approved a communication[2] entitled 'A common platform: guidelines for the Community for Unced 1992', in which it proposed the principles on which the Community and the Member States could base their position, and which was the subject of Council declarations on 28 November[3] and 12 December.[4] Parliament adopted a resolution[5] on the strategy of the United Nations Development Programme in this area. In May the Commission was represented at the 16th meeting of the Governing Council of the United Nations Environment Programme in Nairobi. Amongst other things, the meeting agreed to set up, on an experimental basis, a United Nations centre for emergency environmental assistance and to continue the preparations to set up an international centre for environmental technology.

627.   Earlier, on 26 February, the Commission signed,[6] on behalf of the Community, the Framework Convention of the United Nations Economic Commission for Europe on Environmental Impact Assessment in a Transboundary Context.[7]

628.   Where the Council of Europe is concerned, on 23 April the Commission put to the Council a proposal[8] authorizing the Commission to participate in the negotiations on the preparation of an International Convention on Damage Resulting from Activities Dangerous to the Environment.

629.   At regional level, the Conference of European Ministers for the Environment in Dobris (Prague) from 21 to 23 June was one of the outstanding events of the year. This Conference brought together representatives from virtually every European country,

---

[1]   Bull. EC 12-1991; Commission proposal: OJ 214, 29.8.1990; Twenty-fourth General Report, point 496.
[2]   Bull. EC 10-1991, point 1.2.193.
[3]   Bull. EC 11-1991, point 1.2.193.
[4]   Bull. EC 12-1991.
[5]   OJ C 326, 16.12.1991; Bull. EC 11-1991, point 1.2.190.
[6]   Bull. EC 1/2-1991, point 1.2.238.
[7]   Twenty-fourth General Report, point 508.
[8]   Bull. EC 4-1991, point 1.2.138.

plus the USA, Canada, Japan and 20 or so international organizations and financial institutions, to define a package of measures which, once implemented, should substantially bolster regional cooperation on environmental matters.

630.   The European Parliament recommended establishing permanent structured links between parliaments at pan-European level to deal with environmental matters. [1]

631.   As part of its cooperation with the countries of Central and Eastern Europe, the Community continued to provide support in the form of funding for several environmental projects under the Phare programme. [2] Finally, on a proposal from the Commission [3] endorsed by Parliament [4] and the Economic and Social Committee, [5] on 18 November the Council approved the Convention on the International Commission for the Protection of the Elbe. [6]

Financial instruments

632.   On 12 December the Council recorded its agreement [7] on a proposal for a Regulation establishing a financial instrument for the environment (LIFE), [8] the objective being to promote the development and implementation of the Community's environment policy and legislation by financing priority projects. After the Economic and Social Committee [9] and Parliament [10] had endorsed this proposal on 30 May and 13 September respectively, the Commission [11] amended its proposal accordingly on 1 October.

633.   On 4 March the Council adopted Regulation (EEC) No 563/91 on action by the Community for the protection of the environment in the Mediterranean region (Medspa). [12] Subsequently, on 19 December it adopted [13] a Regulation on action by the Community to protect the environment in the coastal areas and coastal waters of the Irish Sea, North Sea, Baltic Sea and North-East Atlantic Ocean (Norspa). Both these instruments will be incorporated in LIFE and will make a financial contribution to pilot

[1]   OJ C 326, 16.12.1991; Bull. EC 11-1991, point 1.2.192.
[2]   Point 818 of this Report.
[3]   OJ C 93, 11.4.1991; Bull. EC 3-1991, point 1.2.172.
[4]   OJ C 158, 17.6.1991; Bull. EC 5-1991, point 1.2.158.
[5]   OJ C 191, 22.7.1991; Bull. EC 5-1991, point 1.2.158.
[6]   OJ L 321, 29.11.1991; Bull. EC 11-1991, point 1.2.186.
[7]   Bull. EC 12-1991.
[8]   OJ C 44, 20.2.1991; Bull. EC 1/2-1991, point 1.2.220.
[9]   OJ C 191, 22.7.1991; Bull. EC 5-1991, point 1.2.163.
[10]   OJ C 267, 14.10.1991; Bull. EC 9-1991, point 1.2.124.
[11]   OJ C 277, 24.10.1991; Bull. EC 10-1991, point 1.2.191.
[12]   OJ L 63, 9.3.1991; Bull. EC 3-1991, point 1.2.173.
[13]   OJ L 370, 31.12.1991; Bull. EC 12-1991; Commission proposal: OJ C 21, 29.1.1991; Twenty-fourth General Report, point 527; OJ C 276, 23.10.1991; Bull. EC 9-1991, point 1.2.123.

or demonstration projects and to measures to improve the environment and strengthen cooperation in the regions in question.

Industry and the environment, civil protection

Environmental control of products, industrial installations and biotechnology

634. In the course of the year the Commission adopted a series of Directives adapting to technical progress for the 12th,[1] 13th,[2] 14th[3] and 15th[4] times Directive 67/548/EEC on the approximation of laws, regulations and administrative provisions relating to the classification, packaging and labelling of dangerous substances.[5] On 29 July the Council also adopted a common position[6] on the proposal[7] amending the same Directive for the seventh time, following which, on 11 December, the European Parliament gave its opinion (second reading).[8]

635. On 28 February the Economic and Social Committee endorsed[9] the proposal for a Regulation on the evaluation and the control of the environmental risks of existing substances.[10] The Parliament gave its opinion[11] on 9 October, which prompted the Commission to amend its proposal[12] on 12 December. Agreement was reached on a common position on the proposal[13] on 12 December. On 29 May the Economic and Social Committee also endorsed[14] the proposal for a Regulation concerning the export and import of certain dangerous substances,[15] as endorsed by Parliament[16] on 24 October. On 12 December the Council recorded its agreement[13] on the proposal which had been amended[17] by the Commission on 6 December.

---

1   OJ L 180, 8.7.1991; Bull. EC 3-1991, point 1.2.165.
2   OJ L 180, 8.7.1991; Bull. EC 3-1991, point 1.2.166.
3   OJ L 228, 17.8.1991; Bull. EC 7/8-1991, point 1.2.265.
4   Bull. EC 10-1991, point 1.2.182.
5   OJ L 196, 16.8.1967.
6   Bull. EC 7/8-1991, point 1.2.263.
7   OJ C 33, 13.2.1990; Twenty-third General Report, point 196.
8   OJ C 13, 20.1.1992; Bull. EC 12-1991.
9   OJ C 102, 18.4.1991; Bull. EC 1/2-1991, point 1.2.226.
10   OJ C 276, 5.11.1990; Twenty-fourth General Report, point 525.
11   OJ C 280, 28.10.1991; Bull. EC 10-1991, point 1.2.179.
12   OJ C 334, 28.12.1991; Bull. EC 12-1991.
13   Bull. EC 12-1991.
14   OJ C 102, 18.4.1991; Bull. EC 5-1991, point 1.2.152.
15   OJ C 17, 25.1.1991.
16   OJ C 305, 25.11.1991; Bull. EC 10-1991, point 1.2.183.
17   OJ C 6, 10.1.1992; Bull. EC 12-1991.

636. The Council authorized the Commission, on 28 January, to negotiate a draft OECD decision-recommendation concerning the joint review of existing chemical products and the reduction of the associated risks. [1]

637. On 11 February the Commission formally adopted[2] the proposal for a Council Regulation on a Community award scheme for an eco-label[3] which it had approved in November 1990. The Economic and Social Committee and Parliament endorsed this proposal on 25 September[4] and 10 December[5] respectively. The Commission duly amended its proposal[6] on 11 December and the Council recorded its agreement[7] on 11 December.

638. On 18 December the Commission approved[7] a proposal for a Council Regulation establishing a Community system for the assessment and improvement of the environmental performance of certain activities and for appropriate information for the public, the aim being to promote the widest possible use of the most efficient environmental management systems, including environmental auditing by industrial firms, and to encourage them to keep the public informed, with the aid of reports certified by authorized inspectors.

639. On 4 November the Council adopted[8] Decision 91/596/EEC concerning the summary notification format referred to in Article 9 of Directive 90/220/EEC on the deliberate release into the environment of genetically modified organisms. [9] On 21 May and 29 July respectively, the Commission adopted a Decision listing the Community legislation covered by Article 10 of Directive 90/220/EEC[10] and a Decision concerning the classification guidelines referred to in Article 4 of Directive 90/219/EEC on the contained use of genetically modified micro-organisms. [9]

[1]   Bull. EC 1/2-1991, point 1.2.225.
[2]   OJ C 75, 20.3.1991; Bull. EC 1/2-1991, point 1.2.235.
[3]   Twenty-fourth General Report, point 505.
[4]   OJ C 339, 31.12.1991; Bull. EC 9-1991, point 1.2.125.
[5]   OJ C 13, 20.1.1992; Bull. EC 12-1991.
[6]   OJ C 12, 18.1.1992; Bull. EC 12-1991.
[7]   Bull. EC 12-1991.
[8]   OJ L 322, 23.11.1991; Bull. EC 11-1991, point 1.2.181; Commission proposal: Bull. EC 7/8-1991, point 1.2.267.
[9]   OJ L 117, 8.5.1990; Twenty-fourth General Report, point 523.
[10] OJ L 239, 28.8.1991; Bull. EC 7/8-1991, point 1.2.266.

Emissions from industrial installations and products

640. On a proposal[1] submitted by the Commission on 18 March, the Council authorized[2] the Commission to participate in the negotiations for a Convention on the Transboundary Impact of Industrial Accidents under the auspices of the United Nations Economic Commission for Europe on 29 July.

Waste management

641. Work in the waste management field concentrated primarily on implementing the communication from the Commission on a Community strategy for waste management,[3] on which Parliament adopted a resolution[4] on 19 February. The Directive on hazardous waste, on which the Council recorded its agreement in December 1990, was formally adopted[5] on 12 December.

642. On 28 January the Council authorized[6] the Commission to negotiate a draft OECD decision-recommendation on the reduction of the transfrontier movements of waste, and, on 20 November, a draft OECD decision on the monitoring of waste intended for reprocessing.[7]

643. On 18 March the Council adopted Directive 91/156/EEC[8] amending Directive 75/442/EEC on waste.[9] The main purpose was to establish an integrated and adequate network of waste disposal facilities, to promote the disposal of waste as close as possible to the production site in order to limit the hazards inherent in moving waste and to promote clean technologies and recyclable products. This Directive will now form the framework for Community waste policy.

644. Directive 91/157/EEC on batteries and accumulators containing certain dangerous substances,[10] which governs the placing on the market of batteries containing mercury in particular, was adopted by the Council on 18 March.

---

[1]   Bull. EC 3-1991, point 1.2.162.
[2]   Bull. EC 7/8-1991, point 1.2.264.
[3]   Twenty-third General Report, point 537.
[4]   OJ C 72, 18.3.1991; Bull. EC 1/2-1991, point 1.2.230.
[5]   Bull. EC 12-1991; Commission proposal: OJ C 295, 19.11.1988; Twenty-second General Report, point 597; OJ C 326, 30.12.1989; Twenty-third General Report, point 240.
[6]   Bull. EC 1/2-1991, point 1.2.228.
[7]   Bull. EC 11-1991, point 1.2.189.
[8]   OJ L 78, 26.3.1991; Bull. EC 3-1991, point 1.2.167; Commission proposal: OJ C 295, 19.11.1988; Twenty-second General Report, point 597.
[9]   OJ L 194, 25.7.1975.
[10]   OJ L 78, 26.3.1991; Bull. EC 3-1991, point 1.2.163; Commission proposal: OJ C 6, 7.1.1989; Twenty-second General Report, point 600.

645.   On 17 April the Commission adopted a proposal for a Council Directive on the landfill of waste,[1] on which the Economic and Social Committee gave its opinion[2] on 27 November. The aim is to harmonize environmental and technical landfill standards to provide a high level of environmental protection, particularly of soil and groundwater.

646.   On 27 June, in response to the opinions adopted by Parliament and the Economic and Social Committee,[3] the Commission amended[4] its proposal for a Council Directive on civil liability for damage caused by waste.[5] In July the Economic and Social Committee endorsed[6] the proposal for a Council Regulation on the supervision and control of shipments of waste within, into and out of the European Community.[7] In February Parliament endorsed[8] the proposal for a Council Decision on the conclusion, on behalf of the Community, of the Convention on the Control of Transboundary Movements of Hazardous Wastes and their Disposal.[9]

647.   On 2 October the Commission adopted a proposal for a Directive on procedures for harmonizing the programmes for the reduction of pollution by titanium dioxide.[10] Its provisions are similar to those of Directive 89/428/EEC,[11] which was annulled[12] by the Court of Justice on 11 June. Moreover, this judgment gave rise to a declaration[13] by the Council and the representatives of the Governments of the Member States on 1 October.

On 22 October it amended[14] its proposal for a Directive on the disposal of polychlorinated biphenyls (PCBs) and polychlorinated terphenyls (PCTs).[15]

Civil protection

648.   The Council and the representatives of the Governments of the Member States meeting within the Council added an operational dimension to the response to the

---

[1]   OJ L 190, 22.7.1991; Bull. EC 4-1991, point 1.2.134.
[2]   Bull. EC 11-1991, point 1.2.182.
[3]   Twenty-fourth General Report, point 534.
[4]   OJ C 191, 23.7.1991; Bull. EC 6-1991, point 1.2.208.
[5]   OJ C 251, 4.10.1989; Twenty-third General Report, point 538.
[6]   OJ C 269, 14.19.1991; Bull. EC 7/8-1991, point 1.2.269.
[7]   OJ C 289, 17.11.1990; Twenty-fourth General Report, point 533.
[8]   OJ C 72, 18.3.1991; Bull. EC 1/2-1991, point 1.2.229.
[9]   Twenty-fourth General Report, point 533.
[10] OJ C 317, 7.12.1991; Bull. EC 10-1991, point 1.2.185.
[11] OJ L 201, 14.7.1989; Twenty-third General Report, point 514.
[12] OJ C 180, 11.7.1991.
[13] Bull. EC 10-1991, point 1.2.184.
[14] OJ C 299, 20.11.1991; Bull. EC 10-1991, point 1.2.186.
[15] OJ C 319, 12.12.1988; Twenty-second General Report, point 598.

resolution on the introduction of Community cooperation on civil protection[1] by adopting a resolution on 8 July on improving mutual aid between Member States in the event of a natural or technological disaster.[2]

Quality of the environment and natural resources

Protection of water, coastal areas, the environment and tourism

649.   The Council adopted Directive 91/271/EEC concerning urban waste water treatment[3] on 21 May and a Directive on the protection of waters against pollution caused by nitrates from agriculture[4] on 12 December. Also on 12 December, the Council adopted a resolution on Community policy on groundwater.[5]

650.   On the same date it asked the Commission to prepare an integrated strategy for the management of coastal waters.[5]

651.   On the basis of the Council's directives,[6] the Commission took part in the negotiations on a Protocol to the Barcelona Convention on the Protection of the Mediterranean Sea against Pollution resulting from Exploration and Exploitation of the Continental Shelf, Sea-bed and Substratum of the Mediterranean. On 18 September the Commission recommended the Council to authorize it to take part in the negotiations on the measures to reduce marine pollution within the same framework.[7] In response to a communication from the Commission,[8] on 29 July the Council authorized the Commission to take part in the negotiations on a Convention on the Protection of the Oder.[9]

652.   Parliament in turn adopted a resolution[10] on 9 July on the results of the North Sea Conferences,[11] in which it stressed the need to improve the procedures for dealing with infringements.

---

[1]   OJ C 176, 4.7.1987; Twenty-first General Report, point 154.
[2]   OJ C 198, 27.7.1991; Bull. EC 7/8-1991, point 1.2.289.
[3]   OJ L 135, 30.5.1991; Bull. EC 5-1991, point 1.2.149; Commission proposal: OJ C 300, 29.11.1989; Twenty-third General Report, point 515.
[4]   OJ L 375, 30.11.1991; Bull. EC 12-1991; Commission proposal: OJ C 54, 3.3.1989; Twenty-second General Report, point 572; OJ C 51, 2.3.1990; Twenty-fourth General Report, point 517.
[5]   Bull. EC 12-1991.
[6]   Bull. EC 1/2-1991, point 1.2.221.
[7]   Bull. EC 9-1991, point 1.2.117.
[8]   Bull. EC 5-1991, point 1.2.157.
[9]   Bull. EC 7/8-1991, point 1.2.278.
[10]   OJ C 240, 16.9.1991; Bull. EC 7/8-1991, point 1.2.277.
[11]   Twenty-fourth General Report, point 511.

653.   In June the Commission published its eighth report on bathing water quality (for 1989-90).

Protection of nature, the environment and agriculture

654.   To pave the way for effective implementation of the Community legislation on the conservation of flora and fauna, on 10 July the Commission adopted a proposal for a Council Directive laying down minimum standards for keeping animals in zoos.[1] The Economic and Social Committee gave its opinion[2] on 27 November.

655.   On 13 November the Commission adopted a proposal for a Council Regulation establishing rules on the possession and sale of specimens of species of wild fauna and flora.[3] The proposal provides for the implementation of a range of provisions governing the trading inside and outside the Community of wild animals and plants and includes the provisions of Regulation (EEC) No 3626/82 on the implementation of the Washington Convention.[4] A proposal for a regulation to amend Annex A of the abovementioned Regulation was adopted on 17 December.[5] To allow hunting of selected species under certain conditions, on 6 March the Commission adopted a proposal[6] for a Directive amending Directive 79/409/EEC on the conservation of wild birds.[7] The Economic and Social Committee endorsed this proposal[8] on 29 May. On 6 March the Commission adopted a Directive amending the annexes to Directive 79/409/EEC to include 31 species or subspecies native to Spain and Portugal.[9] On 13 September Parliament adopted a resolution on the trade in exotic birds,[10] in which it called for an outright ban on such imports into the Community.

656.   On 4 November the Council adopted Regulation (EEC) No 3254/91 prohibiting the use of leghold traps in the Community and the introduction into the Community of pelts and manufactured goods of certain wild animal species originating in countries which catch them by means of leghold traps or trapping methods which do not meet international humane trapping standards.[11]

---

[1]   OJ C 249, 24.9.1991; Bull. EC 7/8-1991, point 1.2.271.
[2]   Bull. EC 11-1991, point 1.2.184.
[3]   Bull. EC 11-1991, point 1.2.179.
[4]   OJ L 384, 31.12.1982; Twenty-first General Report, point 516.
[5]   OJ L 349, 18.12.1991; Bull. EC 12-1991.
[6]   OJ L 115, 8.5.1991; Bull. EC 3-1991, point 1.2.168.
[7]   OJ L 103, 25.4.1979, OJ L 106, 16.4.1986; Twentieth General Report, point 570.
[8]   OJ C 191, 22.7.1991; Bull. EC 5-1991, point 1.2.154.
[9]   Bull. EC 3-1991, point 1.2.169.
[10] OJ C 267, 14.10.1991; Bull. EC 9-1991, point 1.2.121.
[11] OJ L 308, 9.11.1991; Bull. EC 11-1991, point 1.2.183; Commission proposal: OJ C 134, 31.5.1989; Twenty-third General Report, point 532; OJ C 97, 13.4.1991; Bull. EC 3-1991, point 1.2.170.

657.   Under the Regulation on action by the Community relating to the environment (ACE),[1] in the course of the year the Commission granted financial aid totalling ECU 14 015 000 to 18 projects to promote the conservation of biotopes of particular importance for the Community.

On the basis of the Council's directives,[2] the Commission participated in the negotiations to draft an Agreement on the Conservation of Small Cetaceans in the Baltic and the North Seas, which was signed in Geneva in September.

658.   Another Convention negotiated by the Commission on the strength of negotiating directives issued by the Council[3] — the Convention on the Protection of the Alps — was signed in Salzburg on 7 November at the second Conference of the Ministers for the Environment of the Alpine countries, after the Council, on 4 November, had adopted[4] the Commission proposal on the conclusion of this Convention.[5]

659.   In response to Parliament's opinion,[6] on 8 February the Commission amended[7] its proposal for a Council Directive on the protection of natural and semi-natural habitats and of wild fauna and flora,[8] on which agreement had been reached in the Council[9] on 12 December. On 29 October the Commission also adopted a communication on the establishment of a European Alternative Test Method Evaluation Centre.[10]

Action by the Community relating to nature conservation (Acnat)

660.   On 9 December the Council adopted[11] the Regulation on action by the Community relating to nature conservation (Acnat). The Council in turn reached agreement on this proposal on 14 June. The Community's contribution to measures to maintain or re-establish biotopes or habitats of importance to the Community and to schemes to conserve or re-establish endangered species was set at ECU 50 million spread over two years.

---

[1]   OJ L 207, 29.7.1987; Twenty-first General Report, point 486.
[2]   Bull. EC 7/8-1991, point 1.2.273; Commission recommendation: Bull. EC 5-1991, point 1.2.155.
[3]   Bull. EC 5-1991, point 1.2.156; Commission recommendation: Bull. EC 3-1991, point 1.2.171.
[4]   Bull. EC 11-1991, point 1.2.185.
[5]   Bull. EC 10-1991, point 1.2.188.
[6]   Twenty-fourth General Report, point 527.
[7]   OJ C 75, 20.3.1991; Bull. EC 1/2-1991, point 1.2.234.
[8]   OJ C 247, 21.9.1988; Twenty-second General Report, point 592.
[9]   Bull. EC 12-1991.
[10]   Bull. EC 10-1991, point 1.2.187.
[11]   OJ L 370, 31.12.1991; Bull. EC 12-1991; Commission proposal: OJ C 137, 6.6.1990; Twenty-fourth General Report, point 529; OJ C 47, 23.2.1991; Bull. EC 1/2-1991, point 1.2.232.

Urban environment, air quality, transport, noise

Urban environment

661.   On 5 July the Economic and Social Committee endorsed[1] the Green Paper on
the urban environment.[2] To give firmer shape to some of the conclusions reached and
measures proposed, on 28 January the Council formally adopted[3] the resolution which
it approved[2] in December 1990. Parliament in turn adopted a resolution on 12 September calling for measures in this field, particularly on urban tourism and public transport.[4]

Air quality

662.   On 26 June the Council adopted Directive 91/441/EEC[5] amending Directive 70/220/EEC on the approximation of the laws of the Member States relating to
measures to be taken against air pollution by emissions from motor vehicles.[6] This set
new limit values for emissions of pollutants and particulates (from diesel engines).

663.   On 1 October the Council adopted Directive 91/542/EEC[7] amending Directive 88/77/EEC on the measures to be taken against the emission of gaseous pollutants
from diesel engines for use in vehicles. This provides for a two-stage reduction in the
limit values for emissions of three gaseous pollutants (carbon monoxide, hydrocarbons
and oxides of nitrogen) from commercial vehicles and for the introduction of new
measures to control emissions of particulates from such vehicles.

664.   The Commission in turn adopted a proposal for a Council Directive[8] on 30 April
with a view to reducing the sulphur content of industrial, bunker and heating gas oils
in two stages to not more than 0.2% by weight as from 1 October 1994 and 0.1% as
from 1999. The Economic and Social Committee gave its opinion[9] on this proposal on
30 October.

---

[1]   OJ C 269, 14.10.1991; Bull. EC 7/8-1991, point 1.2.274.
[2]   Twenty-fourth General Report, point 536.
[3]   OJ C 33, 8.2.1991; Bull. EC 1/2-1991, point 1.2.233.
[4]   OJ C 267, 14.10.1991; Bull. EC 9-1991, point 1.2.120.
[5]   OJ L 242, 30.8.1991; Bull. EC 6-1991, point 1.2.202; Commission proposal: OJ C 81, 30.3.1990;
      Twenty-fourth General Report, point 519.
[6]   OJ L 81, 14.4.1970; Fourth General Report, point 28.
[7]   OJ L 295, 25.10.1991; Bull. EC 10-1991, point 1.2.176; Commission proposal: OJ C 187, 27.7.1990;
      Twenty-fourth General Report, point 520; Bull. EC 3-1991, point 1.2.158.
[8]   OJ C 174, 5.7.1991; Bull. EC 4-1991, point 1.2.135.
[9]   OJ C 14, 20.1.1992; Bull. EC 10-1991, point 1.2.181.

665.   On 24 June the Commission also adopted another proposal for a Directive,[1] this time on air pollution by ozone, on which the Economic and Social Committee gave its opinion[2] in December. The main aim was to establish a common ozone pollution monitoring, information-exchange, and warning procedure to protect human health and vegetation. On 6 November it sent the Council a proposal[3] for amendment of Regulation (EEC) No 3528/86 on the protection of the Community's forests against pollution.[4]

666.   On 23 September the Council adopted[5] a Decision on the negotiation of a Protocol to the Convention on Long-range Transboundary Air Pollution,[6] concerning the control of emissions of volatile organic compounds or their transboundary fluxes. On 23 October the Commission put to the Council a proposal for a Decision on the signing of this Protocol.[7] On 17 July it also submitted a proposal for a Decision on accession by the European Economic Community to the Protocol to the same Convention concerning the control of emissions of nitrogen oxides or their transboundary fluxes.[8] The Economic and Social Committee endorsed this proposal[9] on 27 November.

Noise

667.   On 10 April the Commission adopted[10] a proposal for a Directive to supplement Directive 89/629/EEC on the limitation of noise emission from civil subsonic jet areoplanes.[11] This provides, in particular, for the phasing out of the noisiest aeroplanes covered by Chapter 2 of the Convention on International Civil Aviation. The proposal was endorsed by the Economic and Social Committee in September[12] and by Parliament in December.[13] On 16 December the Council recorded its agreement.[13]

1   OJ C 192, 23.7.1991; Bull. EC 6-1991, point 1.2.207.
2   Bull. EC 12-1991.
3   OJ C 312, 3.12.1991; Bull. EC 11-1991, point 1.2.109.
4   OJ L 362, 17.11.1986; Twentieth General Report, point 571.
5   Bull. EC 9-1991, point 1.2.118; Commission proposal: Bull. EC 5-1991, point 1.2.150.
6   OJ L 171, 27.6.1981; Fifteenth General Report, point 335.
7   Bull. EC 10-1991, point 1.2.178.
8   OJ C 230, 4.9.1991; Bull. EC 7/8-1991, point 1.2.262.
9   OJ C 230, 4.9.1991; Bull. EC 11-1991, point 1.2.180.
10   OJ C 111, 26.4.1991; Bull. EC 4-1991, point 1.2.137.
11   OJ L 363, 13.12.1989; Twenty-third General Report, point 522.
12   OJ C 339, 31.12.1991; Bull. EC 9-1991, point 1.2.119.
13   OJ C 13, 20.1.1992; Bull. EC 12-1991.

Global environment, climate change, geosphere and biosphere

668.   On 4 March the Council adopted Regulation (EEC) No 594/91 implementing in the Community the Montreal Protocol on Substances that Deplete the Ozone Layer,[1] as revised by the parties to the Protocol in London in June 1990, which provides, in particular, for an end to the use of chlorofluorocarbons (CFCs) by June 1997. On 12 December it also adopted a Decision[2] on the conclusion of the amendment to the Montreal Protocol, as adopted at the London Conference.[3]

669.   Quotas for imports of chloroflurocarbons into the Community from 1 July 1991 to 31 December 1992 were set by a Commission Decision[4] adopted on 15 July.

670.   At its meeting in Luxembourg in June the European Council expressed its support[5] for the pilot project for the preservation of tropical forests which the Commission had prepared in conjunction with the Brazilian authorities and the World Bank with a view to safeguarding the Amazonian Forest in Brazil. It confirmed that the Community would make a financial contribution of USD 15 million to the preliminary phase of this project. At its annual summit meeting in London in July the Group of Seven in turn expressed its support for this programme,[6] called on the World Bank to continue the preparations in conjunction with the Commission and likewise granted financial support towards the preliminary phase. The programme was presented at a first meeting of potential contributors, one of which is the Community, held on 7 and 8 December under the auspices of the World Bank. The meeting resulted in firm commitments totalling USD 250 million by the main participants, including several Member States of the Community. The Commission was also represented at the 10th World Forestry Congress convened by the United Nations Food and Agriculture Organization (FAO) in September.[7]

671.   On 29 July the Council issued the Commission with directives for the negotiations on an International Convention on Biological Diversity under the auspices of the United Nations Environment Programme.[8] This Convention is scheduled for signature at the United Nations Conference on Environment and Development in Rio de Janeiro in 1992.[9]

---

[1]   OJ L 67, 14.3.1991; Bull. EC 3-1991, point 1.2.160; Commission proposal: OJ C 86, 4.4.1990; Twenty-fourth General Report, point 539.
[2]   Bull. EC 12-1991; Commission proposal: OJ C 11, 17.1.1991; Twenty-fourth General Report, point 539.
[3]   OJ L 11, 17.1.1991; Twenty-fourth General Report, point 539.
[4]   OJ C 193, 17.7.1991; Bull. EC 7/8-1991, point 1.2.268.
[5]   Bull. EC 6-1991, point I.36.
[6]   Point 853 of this Report.
[7]   Bull. EC 9-1991, point 1.2.122.
[8]   Bull. EC 7/8-1991, point 1.2.272; Commission proposal: Bull. EC 5-1991, point 1.2.153.
[9]   Point 626 of this Report.

672.   On 4 February the Council accepted[1] the Commission's proposal authorizing it to participate, on behalf of the Community, in the negotiations on a framework Convention on Climatic Change, once again under the auspices of the United Nations.

---

[1]   Bull. EC 1/2-1991, point 1.2.223.

Section 16

Consumers

Priority activities and objectives

673.   The Council's agreement on a common position on the general product safety Directive represented a decisive step forward in the Community's consumer protection strategy, [1] *as did the adoption by the Commission of a proposal for a Directive on the approximation of the Member States' legislation on comparative advertising.* [2] *Moreover, the inclusion in the Treaty on European union, on which the European Council reached agreement in Maastrict in December, of provisions to increase the Community's responsibilites in the field of consumer protection, will broaden its scope in this area.*

The Commission stepped up its efforts to integrate the consumer dimension into the other Community policies, by taking consumers' views into account in matters relating to safety and the transparency of information, in particular in the work on animal and plant health legislation, the harmonization of legislation on foodstuffs, pharmaceuticals and chemicals, and technical harmonization and standardization. Consumers' views were also taken into consideration in matters relating to health, foodstuffs policy, the environment, biotechnology, energy and financial institutions.

In addition to these general activities, the Commission continued and stepped up the implementation of the three-year action plan (1990-92) [3] *in all four areas concerned, namely consumer representation, consumer information and education, consumer health and safety and consumer transactions.*

Consumer representation

674.   The Consumer Consultative Council (CCC), [4] composed of representatives of the main European consumers' organizations and of national organizations, the disabled and the elderly, continued to deliver opinions on matters of relevance to consumers.

---

[1]   Point 681 of this Report.
[2]   Point 686 of this Report.
[3]   Twenty-fourth General Report, point 541.
[4]   Twenty-fourth General Report, point 542.

675.   At national level, the Commission increased its financial support to consumer organizations, particularly in southern Europe and Ireland, and extended the scope of its activities to include the organizations of the former German Democratic Republic.

676.   In March the Commission set up two groups,[1] one of which is the Users' Liaison Group,[2] to advise on payment systems in the internal market.

Consumer information and education

677.   Two new consumer information centres were opened,[3] with Commission support, in Gronau (Germany) and Barcelona (Spain). These pilot projects are designed to provide better information for consumers who make cross-border purchases.

678.   A Eurobarometer survey conducted in the Member States showed that user/consumer confidence in the single market is not unbounded, particularly with regard to cross-frontier transactions. Further price surveys were also carried out in the border areas of the Community and within the Member States in order to provide consumers with better information about price differences for certain consumer goods and services.

679.   On 26 September the Economic and Social Committee adopted an own-initiative opinion on completion of the internal market and consumer protection,[4] in which it stressed the role of the consumer organizations.

Health, physical safety and quality

680.   On 21 March the Commission adopted a communication[5] on the Ehlass (European home and leisure accident surveillance system) demonstration project, in which it reports on the work done, briefly states the new guiding principles and specifies how they are to be implemented in the event of the project being continued beyond the initial 31 December 1991 deadline. On the basis of this communication, significant progress was made this year in the harmonization of data collection and processing and in financial management.

---

[1]   Twenty-fourth General Report, point 129.
[2]   Twenty-fourth General Report, point 555.
[3]   Twenty-fourth General Report, point 543.
[4]   OJ C 339, 31.12.1991; Bull. EC 9-1991, point 1.2.127.
[5]   OJ L 296, 27.10.1990; Twenty-fourth General Report, point 547.

681.   On 15 October the Council agreed[1] on a common position on an amended proposal for a general product safety Directive,[2] which concerns a harmonized, effective approach by Member States to product safety and the possibility, in the event of grave and immediate risk, for the Commission to intervene at Community level by issuing a communication to the Member States. The Council adopted its common position[3] on 23 December.

682.   The Community system for the rapid exchange of information (RES) on the dangers arising from the use of consumer products[4] continued to function efficiently, and the introduction of a standard format for information on non-food products, which the Member States have undertaken to communicate, has facilitated the use of the system.

683.   On 5 February the Commission adopted a proposal[5] for a sixth amendment to Council Directive 76/768/EEC on the approximation of the laws of the Member States relating to cosmetic products[6] with a view to further harmonization of national instruments relating to the free circulation of cosmetics. The Economic and Social Committee delivered its opinion in July.[7]

Directive 76/768/EEC was adapted to technical progress for the 13th time[8] on 12 March. Parliament[9] and the Economic and Social Committee[10] also delivered opinions on the proposal for a Directive consolidating all the amendments made to Directive 76/768/EEC to date.[11]

684.   In the context of implementation of the toy safety Directive,[12] the European Committee for Standardization (CEN) continued its work on revising certain existing standards and on preparing a standard for chemical toys other than chemistry sets. The European Committee for Electrotechnical Standardization (Cenelec) also began work on drafting a European standard for electrical toys.

685.   The proposal for a Directive on the liability of suppliers of services,[13] which is designed to provide protection against damage to the physical integrity of persons and

---

[1]   Bull. EC 10-1991, point 1.2.195.
[2]   OJ C 156, 27.6.1990; Twenty-fourth General Report, point 545.
[3]   Bull. EC 12-1991.
[4]   OJ L 173, 6.7.1990; Twenty-fourth General Report, point 546.
[5]   OJ L 52, 28.2.1991; Bull. EC 1/2-1991, point 1.2.239.
[6]   OJ L 262, 27.9.1976; Tenth General Report, point 124.
[7]   Bull. EC 7/8-1991, point 1.2.284.
[8]   OJ L 91, 12.4.1991; Bull. EC 3-1991, point 1.2.176.
[9]   OJ C 48, 25.2.1991; Bull. EC 1/2-1991, point 1.2.240.
[10]   OJ C 102, 18.4.1991; Bull. EC 1/2-1991, point 1.2.240.
[11]   OJ C 322, 21.12.1990; Twenty-fourth General Report, point 549.
[12]   OJ L 187, 16.7.1988; Twenty-second General Report, point 602.
[13]   OJ C 12, 18.1.1991; Twenty-fourth General Report, point 551.

private property, was the subject of an Economic and Social Committee opinion[1] on 3 July.

Transactions involving consumers

686.   On 22 May 1991 the Commission approved[2] a proposal for a Directive amending Directive 84/450/EEC on misleading advertising.[3] This sets out the rules for comparative advertising in all Member States, defined as any advertising which 'identifies goods or services of the same kind offered by a competitor', provided that it refers to relevant and objectively verifiable features, that it does not mislead and that it does not discredit competitors. The Economic and Social Committee delivered a favourable opinion[4] in December.

687.   The proposal for a Council Directive prohibiting unfair terms in consumer contracts[5] was endorsed[6] by the Economic and Social Committee on 24 April. Parliament likewise endorsed[7] the proposal in first reading on 20 November.

---

[1]   Bull. EC 7/8-1991, point 1.2.286.
[2]   OJ C 180, 11.7.1991; Bull. EC 5-1991, point 1.2.164.
[3]   OJ L 250, 19.9.1984; Eighteenth General Report, point 399.
[4]   Bull. EC 12-1991.
[5]   OJ C 243, 28.9.1990; Twenty-fourth General Report, point 554.
[6]   OJ C 159, 17.6.1991; Bull. EC 4-1991, point 1.2.139.
[7]   OJ C 326, 16.12.1991; Bull. EC 11-1991, point 1.2.194.

Section 17

Transport

Priority activities and objectives

688.   It is a time of unprecedented change and dynamism for transport policy: with the advent of the single market, transport clearly has a strategic role to play in enabling the free movement of goods and persons. In general, therefore, the Commission has this year given absolute priority to the completion of the single market in transport services. It has drafted and introduced a set of measures providing access to the market for all transport operators regardless of nationality and supporting this liberalization with harmonization rules under which healthy competition can develop between carriers while other objectives can be achieved, particularly in relation to safety, environmental protection, passenger comfort and the working conditions of transport employees. At the end of this year, almost all the measures for creating a single market in transport services have either been adopted or presented for adoption by the Commission. However, the external relations aspect of Community transport policy has yet to be finalized.

In particular, the Commission has presented a third package of legislative measures which constitute the final stage in the liberalization necessary for creating a single market in air transport.[1] Moreover, the new Directive on the development of the Community railways, adopted by the Council in July,[2] is a milestone in the development of a sector hitherto characterized by a lack of transparency in relations between the railways and the Member States.

Infrastructure

Transport networks

689.   Community master plans are being drawn up for each of the modes of transport concerned, i.e. high-speed rail, combined transport, motorways and inland waterways.

---

[1]   Point 724 of this Report.
[2]   Point 696 of this Report.

These initiatives have been strongly encouraged by Parliament which, in its resolution of 9 July, called for account to be taken of the safety and environmental protection aspects.[1] The harmful effects of certain modes of transport also led Parliament to propose, on 11 September, the drafting of a framework programme for technical harmonization, developing environment-friendly infrastructure and promoting research and development in this field.[2]

In the field of high-speed rail transport, real progress has been achieved on technical harmonization and decisions have been taken on extending the network to include the EFTA countries. A working document setting out the initial conclusions on the definition of the European combined-transport network and the conditions for its proper operation has also been drafted, as has a study for a Community master plan. Furthermore, at the prompting of the transport ministers, a working party on inland waterways has been set up.

Financial support for projects of Community interest

690.   On the basis of Regulation (EEC) No 3359/90 for an action programme in the field of transport infrastructure,[3] the Commission adopted on 7 November a Decision granting Community financial support to 23 transport infrastructure projects of European interest.[4] This year, a total of ECU 128 million has been earmarked for this purpose.

Multimodal transport

Development of combined transport

691.   On 27 March the Council formally adopted Directive 91/224/EEC[5] amending Directive 75/130/EEC on the establishment of common rules for certain types of combined carriage of goods between Member States.[6] The new Directive provides for the

---

[1]   OJ C 240, 16.9.1991; Bull. EC 7/8-1991, point 1.2.104.
[2]   OJ C 267, 14.10.1991; Bull. EC 9-1991, point 1.2.46.
[3]   OJ L 326, 24.11.1990; Twenty-fourth General Report, Point 559.
[4]   Bull. EC 11-1991, point 1.2.63.
[5]   OJ L 103, 25.4.1991; Bull. EC 3-1991, point 1.2.68; Commission proposal: OJ C 34, 14.2.1990; Twenty-fourth General Report, point 587.
[6]   OJ L 48, 22.2.1975.

liberalization of initial and terminal road journeys, exempts such journeys from tariff regulations, provides access to the combined transport market for own-account operators and extends the allowable distances for road journeys connecting with inland waterway transport.

Abolition of border controls

692.   On 7 November the Council adopted Regulation (EEC) No 3356/91[1] amending Regulation (EEC) No 4060/89 with respect to the elimination of frontier controls on commercial vehicles used for the intra-Community carriage of dangerous goods and perishable foodstuffs.[2]

Summer time arrangements

693.   On 9 July the Commission adopted a proposal for a sixth Council Directive on summer time arrangements for 1993 and 1994.[3] The Economic and Social Committee delivered its opinion on 27 November,[4] as did Parliament on 13 December.[5]

Observation of the markets

694.   On 29 May[6] the Economic and Social Committee adopted a favourable opinion on the proposal from the Commission concerning the European system for observing the markets in the inland carriage of goods.[7] Parliament delivered an opinion on 13 December.[8]

---

[1]   OJ L 318, 20.11.1991; Bull. EC 11-1991, point 1.2.64; Commission proposal: OJ C 117, 1.5.1991; Bull. EC 4-1991, point 1.2.53.
[2]   OJ L 390, 30.12.1989; Twenty-third General Report, point 188.
[3]   OJ C 219, 22.8.1991; Bull. EC 7/8-1991, point 1.2.105.
[4]   Bull. EC 11-1991, point 1.2.65.
[5]   OJ C 13, 20.1.1992; Bull. EC 12-1991.
[6]   OJ L 191, 22.7.1991; Bull. EC 5-1991, point 1.2.67.
[7]   OJ C 29, 5.2.1991; Twenty-fourth General Report, point 560.
[8]   Bull. EC 12-1991.

Inland transport

Railways

695.   On 20 June the Council adopted Regulation (EEC) No 1893/91 [1] amending Regulation (EEC) No 1191/69 on action by Member States concerning the obligations inherent in the concept of a public service in transport by rail, road and inland waterway. [2] This Regulation introduces the principle of terminating public service obligations and provides for their replacement, where the public interest warrants maintaining unprofitable transport services, by public service contracts negotiated between governments and transport undertakings. It provides that, for the supply of certain services or in the interests of certain social categories of passengers, the Member States may retain the right to maintain or impose certain public service obligations. It also introduces the principle of separate accounting for State-imposed public service activities and commercial activities undertaken by transport companies.

696.   On 29 July the Council formally adopted Directive 91/440/EEC on the development of the Community's railways. [3] The purpose of this Directive is to make relations between the railways and the public authorities more transparent and to ensure the financial, administrative, economic and accounting independence of the railway undertakings. It provides, in particular, for improvement of the financial situation of such undertakings and for separation of the accounts for infrastructure-related and operational activities. It also provides that international groupings of Community railways should be granted the right of access to and transit through the rail networks of the Member States in which the constituent undertakings are established and the right of transit through other Member States for the purposes of operating international transport services. Finally, it provides for Community railways to be granted the right of access to and transit through the entire Community network for the purposes of operating international combined goods-transport services.

---

[1]   OJ L 169, 29.6.1991; Bull. EC 6-1991, point 1.2.84; Commission proposal: OJ C 34, 14.2.1990; Twenty-third General Report, point 624; Bull. EC 3-1991, point 1.2.67.
[2]   OJ L 156, 28.6.1969.
[3]   OJ L 237, 24.8.1991; Bull. EC 7/8-1991, point 1.2.108; Commission proposal: OJ C 34, 14.2.1990; Twenty-fourth General Report, point 561; OJ C 87, 4.4.1991; Bull. EC 3-1991, point 1.2.71.

Road transport

Market access

697. On 4 February the Council adopted Regulation (EEC) No 296/91[1] amending Regulation (EEC) No 4059/89 laying down the conditions under which non-resident carriers may operate national road haulage services within a Member State.[2] In the wake of German unification, the cabotage quota for the carriage of goods by road in 1991 was increased. Under the same Regulation, the Commission decided on 10 April to increase the Community cabotage quota for road haulage services by 10% for 1991/92.[3]

698. To complete the liberalization of the road haulage market, the Commission adopted on 16 October a proposal for a Regulation laying down the definitive system under which non-resident carriers may operate national road haulage services within a Member State.[4] This will replace the transitional system introduced by Regulation (EEC) No 4059/89[2] when the latter expires.

699. On 24 July the Commission proposed that the Council introduce a system of Community authorizations for access to the market for international carriage of goods by road.[5] These authorizations are based on qualitative criteria and replace the current system of quantitative restrictions. On 16 December the Council approved this proposal for a Regulation.[6]

700. On 16 December[6] the Council also approved a proposal for a Regulation on common rules for the international carriage of passengers by coach and bus.[7]

Taxation

701. On 24 April the Economic and Social Committee delivered a favourable opinion[8] on the amended proposal for a Council Directive on the charging of transport infrastructure costs to heavy goods vehicles.[9]

---

[1]   OJ L 36, 8.2.1991; Bull. EC 1/2-1991, point 1.2.97; Commission proposal: Twenty-fourth General Report, point 564.
[2]   OJ L 390, 30.12.1989; Twenty-third General Report, point 629.
[3]   OJ L 102, 23.4.1991; Bull. EC 4-1991, point 1.2.54.
[4]   OJ C 317, 7.12.1991; Bull. EC 10-1991, point 1.2.54.
[5]   OJ C 238, 13.9.1991; Bull. EC 7/8-1991, point 1.2.103.
[6]   Bull. EC 12-1991.
[7]   OJ C 301, 26.11.1988; Twenty-second General Report, point 723.
[8]   OJ C 159, 17.6.1991; Bull. EC 4-1991, point 1.2.52.
[9]   OJ C 75, 20.3.1991; Twenty-fourth General Report, point 569.

702.   On 13 September the Commission approved its 14th report to the Council and Parliament on expenditure relating to the use of rail, road and inland waterway transport infrastructure.

Technical aspects

703.   On 4 February the Council formally adopted Directive 91/60/EEC[1] amending Directive 85/3/EEC on the weights and dimensions of certain road vehicles in respect of the maximum authorized dimensions of road trains.[2] Since 1 October the maximum length of road trains has been set at 18.35 m, the maximum load length at 15.65 m and the maximum total load length including the distance between the tractor unit and the trailer at 16 m.

704.   On 25 April[3] and 11 June[4] respectively, the Economic and Social Committee and Parliament delivered favourable opinions on the proposal for a Directive[5] amending Council Directive 85/3/EEC on the weights and dimensions of certain road vehicles with a view to defining a parametric equivalent to air suspension systems.[2] On 13 November the Commission amended its proposal accordingly,[6] and the Council reached a political agreement on the proposal on 16 December.[7]

On 16 December the Council formally adopted the Directive on the compulsory use of safety belts in vehicles of less than 3.5 tonnes. It lays down the principle that the driver and passengers of a vehicle of less than 3.5 tonnes must use safety belts, or, in the case of children, child restraint systems adapted to their size and weight, where their seat is so equipped. Member States may lay down in their territory more flexible rules in respect of children.[8]

705.   The Council twice amended Directive 77/143/EEC on the approximation of the laws of the Member States relating to roadworthiness tests for motor vehicles and their trailers.[9] On 27 March and 21 June respectively it adopted Directive 91/225/EEC,[10]

---

[1]   OJ L 37, 9.2.1991; Bull. EC 1/2-1991, point 1.2.96; Commission proposal: OJ C 316, 16.12.1989; Twenty-third General Report, point 632; OJ C 268, 24.10.1990; Twenty-fourth General Report, point 570.
[2]   OJ L 2, 3.1.1985; Eighteenth General Report, point 493.
[3]   OJ C 159, 17.6.1991; Bull, EC 4-1991, point 1.2.56.
[4]   OJ C 183, 15.7.1991; Bull. EC 6-1991, point 1.2.89.
[5]   OJ C 292, 22.11.1990; Twenty-fourth General Report, point 570.
[6]   OJ C 313, 4.12.1991; Bull. EC 11-1991, point 1.2.66.
[7]   Bull. EC 12-1991.
[8]   OJ L 373, 31.12.1991; Bull. EC 12-1991; Commission proposals: OJ C 298, 23.11.1988; Twenty-second General Report, point 735; OJ C 308, 8.12.1990; Twenty-fourth General Report, point 592.
[9]   OJ L 47, 12.2.1977, Tenth General Report, point 448.
[10]   OJ L 103, 23.4.1991; Bull. EC 3-1991, point 1.2.70; Commission proposal: OJ C 74, 22.3.1989; Twenty-third General Report, point 633.

which aims to standardize tests on commercial vehicles so as to ensure the same safety and environmental standards in all Member States, and Directive 91/328/EEC which extends the scope of this legislation to private cars.[1]

706.   On 4 July the Commission adopted two proposals for amendments to the above-mentioned Directive on roadworthiness tests for motor vehicles and their trailers. The purpose was firstly to specify the criteria used in tests on braking systems and the components of such systems which should be tested[2] and, secondly, to lay down limit values for exhaust emissions.[3] On 18 December the Economic and Social Committee delivered an opinion on both proposals.[4] On 25 July the Commission also adopted a proposal for a Directive on speed limitation devices.[5] This Directive would make it compulsory to install and use, on heavy goods vehicles weighing more than 12 tonnes and on motor coaches or buses weighing more than 5 tonnes and registered on or after 1 January 1985, devices limiting the maximum speed of the vehicle to certain harmonized levels. The Economic and Social Committee and Parliament gave their opinions on 27 November[6] and 13 December[7] respectively and on 16 December the Council reached a political agreement on the proposal.[4]

707.   Following up its report on the carriage of dangerous goods and hazardous waste,[8] the Commission adopted on 12 June a proposal for a Directive[9] on the appointment of an officer for the prevention of the risks inherent in the carriage of dangerous goods in undertakings which transport such goods, and on the vocational qualification of such officers. On 27 November the Economic and Social Committee delivered a favourable opinion.[10]

Road safety

708.   In view of the opinion expressed by Parliament,[11] on 25 March the Commission amended its proposal for a Directive[12] on speed limits for certain categories of motor vehicles.[13]

---

[1]   OJ L 178, 6.7.1991; Bull. EC 6-1991, point 1.2.87; Commission proposal: OJ C 133, 31.5.1986; Twentieth General Report, point 706; OJ C 183, 11.7.1987; Twenty-first General Report, point 637.
[2]   OJ C 189, 20.7.1991; Bull. EC 7/8-1991, point 1.2.109.
[3]   OJ C 189, 20.7.1991; Bull. EC 7/8-1991, point 1.2.110.
[4]   Bull. EC 12-1991.
[5]   OJ C 225, 30.8.1991; Bull. EC 7/8-1991, point 1.2.112.
[6]   Bull. EC 11-1991, point 1.2.67.
[7]   OJ C 13, 20.1.1992; Bull. EC 12-1991.
[8]   Twenty-first General Report, point 520.
[9]   OJ C 185, 17.7.1991; Bull. EC 6-1991, point 1.2.86.
[10]   Bull. EC 11-1991, point 1.2.68.
[11]   OJ C 260, 15.10.1990; Twenty-fourth General Report, point 593.
[12]   OJ C 96, 12.4.1991; Bull. EC 3-1991, point 1.2.69.
[13]   OJ C 33, 9.2.1989; Twenty-third General Report, point 651.

709.   On 21 June the Council and the representatives of the governments of the Member States adopted a resolution calling on the Commission to implement a Community action programme on road safety aimed at undertaking common initiatives and comparing national experience in the campaign against road accidents.[1]

Inland waterways

710.   On 8 February, in order to reduce the structural overcapacity of vessels registered in the former German Democratic Republic at the time of unification, the Commission adopted Regulation (EEC) No 317/91[2] amending Regulation (EEC) No 1102/89[3] laying down certain measures for implementing Council Regulation (EEC) No 1101/89 on structural improvements in inland waterway transport.[3] The Regulation lays down the procedures for administering the additional scrapping scheme concerning vessels from the former German Democratic Republic.

711.   On 16 December the Council adopted a Directive on the mutual recognition of national boatmasters' certificates for the carriage of goods and passengers by inland navigation.[4]

712.   On 16 December, with a view to liberalizing inland waterway cabotage within the Community, the Council adopted a Regulation laying down the conditions under which non-resident carriers may transport goods and passengers by inland waterway within a Member State.[5]

Social conditions

713.   On 25 September[6] the Economic and Social Committee adopted a favourable opinion on the proposal for a Directive on admission to the occupation of road haulage and road passenger transport operator.[7] Parliament endorsed the proposal in December.[8]

---

[1]   OJ C 178, 9.7.1991; Bull. EC 6-1991, point 1.2.88.
[2]   OJ L 37, 9.2.1991; Bull. EC 1/2-1991, point 1.2.98.
[3]   OJ L 116, 28.4.1989; Twenty-third General Report, point 634.
[4]   OJ L 373, 31.12.1991; Bull. EC 12-1991; Commission proposal: OJ C 120, 7.5.1988; Twenty-second General Report, point 738.
[5]   OJ L 373, 31.12.1991; Bull. EC 12-1991; Commission proposal: OJ C 330, 20.12.1985; Nineteenth General Report, point 632.
[6]   OJ C 339, 31.12.1991; Bull. EC 9-1991, point 1.2.48.
[7]   OJ C 286, 14.11.1990; Bull. EC 10-1990, point 1.3.189.
[8]   OJ C 13, 20.1.1992; Bull. EC 12-1991.

714. On 7 October[1] the Council approved the proposal for a Directive on the mutual recognition of national skippers' licences for inland waterway vessels carrying goods.[2]

Sea transport

Application of the 1986 regulations

715. Under Regulation (EEC) No 4055/86 applying the principle of freedom to provide services to maritime transport, the Commission continued its discussions with the Member States with a view to amending bilateral maritime transport agreements involving cargo sharing.[3]

716. In order to promote the principle of freedom to provide services and of free access to cargoes in ocean trades, the Commission continued discussions with third countries, in particular Kenya, the Republic of Korea and Japan. Significant progress was made in November with the implementation of an administrative agreement on door-to-door services between the Community and the Korean authorities with a view to allowing Community shipowners to have access to this kind of traffic. On the basis of Regulation (EEC) No 2641/84,[4] and in response to a complaint by the European Community Shipowners' Association (ECSA), the Commission initiated an examination[5] of the Japanese Harbour Management Fund and the port charge imposed by Japan.

The Community helped organize a conference for the purposes of revising the United Nations Convention on a Code of Conduct for Liner Conferences, and contributed greatly to its success. At the conclusion of the conference the Commission took steps to reopen the dialogue with the countries of Central and West Africa.

717. Sea transport was also covered in a number of cooperation agreements concluded with third countries, including several Latin American countries.

718. The Commission also continued looking into a number of complaints and individual requests for exemptions on the basis of Regulation (EEC) No 4056/86.[3]

---

[1]   Bull. EC 10-1991, point 1.2.59.
[2]   OJ C 120, 7.5.1988; Twenty-second General Report, point 738.
[3]   OJ L 378, 31.12.1986; Twentieth General Report, point 711.
[4]   OJ L 252, 20.9.1984.
[5]   OJ C 40, 16.2.1991.

Increased competitiveness for the Community fleet

719.   On 22 February,[1] in the light of the opinion expressed by Parliament,[2] the Commission amended the proposals for Regulations it had adopted in 1989 concerning the establishment of a Community shipping register, the definition of a Community shipowner, and the application of the principle of freedom to provide services to maritime transport within Member States.[3]

720.   On 4 March the Council adopted Regulation (EEC) No 613/91 on the transfer of ships from one register to another within the Community, the purpose of which is to improve the operating conditions and competitiveness of the Community merchant fleet.[4] The Commission amended for the third time[5] its proposal for a Regulation establishing a Community register.[3]

Safety at sea

721.   On 21 January, in order to ensure a coherent and complete coverage of the European maritime area and to compensate for the lack of radionavigation aids in certain areas, the Commission adopted a proposal for a Decision on the Loran-C radionavigation system.[6] In this Decision the Commission calls on the Member States to participate in agreements on the establishment of Loran-C terrestrial radionavigation chains covering Northern Europe, the Iberian Peninsula and the Mediterranean. On 24 April the Economic and Social Committee delivered a favourable opinion,[7] as did Parliament on 8 October.[8] On 17 December the Council approved the proposal in principle.[5]

---

[1]   OJ C 73, 19.3.1991; Bull. EC 1/2-1991, point 1.2.100.
[2]   OJ C 295, 26.11.1990; Twenty-fourth General Report, point 576.
[3]   OJ C 263, 16.10.1989; Twenty-third General Report, point 637.
[4]   OJ L 68, 15.3.1991; Bull. EC 3-1991, point 1.2.72; Commission proposal: OJ C 153, 22.6.1990; Twenty-fourth General Report, point 576.
[5]   Bull. EC 12-1991.
[6]   OJ C 53, 28.2.1991; Bull. EC 1/2-1991, point 1.2.99.
[7]   OJ C 159, 17.6.1991; Bull. EC 4-1991, point 1.2.57.
[8]   OJ C 280, 28.10.1991; Bull. EC 10-1991, point 1.2.60.

Air transport

Implementation of the common policy

722.   As a result of the adoption by the Council in July 1990 of the second air transport package, the Commission adopted the first measures implementing Council Regulations (EEC) No 2342/90 and (EEC) No 2343/90, particularly in respect of complaints regarding air fares.[1] It also examined State aids and other injections of capital into airlines.

723.   On 4 February the Council adopted two Regulations, one on air cargo services[2] and the other concerning a denied-boarding compensation system in scheduled air transport.[3]

Finalization of the common policy

724.   On 17 July the Commission adopted three proposals for Regulations constituting the third and final stage in the liberalization of air transport with a view to completing the single market.[4] The first of these proposals defines the Community requirements to be met by airlines in order to obtain certificates authorizing them to operate, without restrictions based on nationality, in Community territory. The second proposal aims to liberalize the conditions under which air carriers are granted access to intra-Community routes. It provides, in particular, for full fifth-freedom liberalization, authorizes cabotage and abolishes capacity sharing. The last proposal promotes the general application of the principle of double disapproval of air fares and rates by the Member States when new ones are proposed by air carriers.

725.   Furthermore, on 25 September,[5] the Economic and Social Committee delivered an opinion on the proposal for a Council Regulation on common rules for the allocation of slots at Community airports.[6] The Committee requested that the allocation policy take account of all air carriers. On 13 December Parliament delivered its opinion on the proposal.[7]

---

[1]   OJ L 217, 11.8.1990; Twenty-fourth General Report, point 584.
[2]   OJ L 36, 8.2.1991; Bull. EC 1/2-1991, point 1.2.102; Commission proposal: OJ C 88, 26.4.1990; Twenty-fourth General Report, point 578.
[3]   OJ L 36, 8.2.1991; Bull. EC 1/2-1991, point 1.2.101; Commission proposal: OJ C 129, 24.5.1990; Twenty-fourth General Report, point 579.
[4]   OJ C 258, 4.10.1991; Bull. EC 7/8-1991, point 1.2.102.
[5]   OJ C 339, 31.12.1991; Bull. EC 9-1991, point 1.2.50.
[6]   OJ C 43, 19.2.1991; Twenty-fourth General Report, point 583.
[7]   OJ C 13, 20.1.1992; Bull. EC 12-1991.

Technical aspects

726.   On 16 December[1] the Council adopted a Regulation on the harmonization of technical requirements and procedures applicable to civil aircraft. This Regulation had originally been put forward as a proposal for a Directive, but the Ministers had requested at the Council meeting held on 20 and 21 June that it be transformed into a proposal for a Regulation.

Air safety

727.   Safety is a vital element of air transport policy. On 4 September, in the context of the liberalization of air transport, the Commission adopted a communication analysing the aspects relating to air incidents and accidents and suggesting a number of Community measures to be taken in this field.[2]

Social conditions

728.   On 16 December the Council adopted a Directive on mutual acceptance of personnel licences for the exercise of functions in civil aviation.[3]

Research and technological development

729.   Under the Euret Community research programme,[4] a call for proposals was issued and 42 proposals for shared-cost research projects were received, involving 309 firms.[5] After assessment by independent experts, nine of these projects were adopted, from nine consortia made up of a total of 120 firms and relating to research in rail, air, sea and multimodal transport. Furthermore, four concerted action projects were launched relating to cost-benefit analysis for the construction of new roads, trends in demand for the carriage of goods, evaluation of the driving safety of car-trailer combinations and evaluation of the safety of road trains.

---

[1]   OJ L 373, 31.12.1991; Bull. EC 12-1991; Commission proposal: OJ C 270, 26.10.1991; Twenty-fourth General Report, point 585.
[2]   Bull. EC 9-1991, point 1.2.45.
[3]   OJ L 373, 31.12.1991; Bull. EC 12-1991; Commission proposals: OJ C 10, 16.1.1990; Twenty-fourth General Report, point 598; OJ C 175, 6.7.1991; Bull. EC 6-1991, point 1.2.91
[4]   OJ L 8, 11.1.1991; Twenty-fourth General Report, point 599.
[5]   OJ C 9, 15.1.1991.

Transport and the environment

730.   On 16 April the Commission adopted a proposal for a Directive limiting the use of aircraft falling within Chapter 2 of Annex 16 to the Chicago Convention.[1] On 16 December,[2] in the light of the opinion delivered by Parliament on 13 December,[3] the Council approved the proposal.

International cooperation

Transit through non-Community countries

731.   The Commission continued its negotiations on transit with Austria, Switzerland and Yugoslavia on the basis of the negotiating directives adopted by the Council and its conclusions on those negotiations.[4]

732.   The agreement with Yugoslavia was signed on 24 June after a political agreement had been reached by the Council on 20 June.[5] However, in view of recent events in Yugoslavia it has not yet been ratified. On 12 June the Commission also adopted a proposal for a Decision on the conclusion of that Agreement,[6] on which the Economic and Social Committee delivered an opinion on 27 November.[7]

733.   After a number of meetings for the purpose of advancing the negotiations with Austria and Switzerland,[8] on 21 October the Council gave its approval in principle to the conclusion of Alpine transit agreements with those two countries.[9] The agreements were initialled on 3 December.[2] They provide, in particular, for the promotion of conventional rail transport and of combined road/rail transport. In the case of Austria the existing bilateral traffic quota arrangements are replaced by a new system involving 'ecopoints' under which the number of authorizations for journeys by Community vehicles in transit through Austria depends upon the reduction in the amount of pollution caused.

---

[1]   Point 667 of this Report.
[2]   Bull. EC 12-1991.
[3]   OJ C 13, 20.1.1992; Bull. EC 12-1991.
[4]   Twenty-second General Report, point 751.
[5]   Bull. EC 6-1991, point 1.2.93.
[6]   OJ C 181, 12.7.1991; Bull. EC 6-1991, point 1.2.93.
[7]   Bull. EC 11-1991, point 1.2.73.
[8]   Bull. EC 1/2-1991, point 1.2.104; Bull. EC 4-1991, point 1.2.59.
[9]   Bull. EC 10-1991, point 1.2.53.

734.   On 24 January[1] and 10 July[2] Parliament adopted two resolutions on relations with the EFTA countries in the field of transport, while its resolution of 11 June concerned relations with Central and East European countries.[3]

735.   The Commission and Parliament jointly organized a pan-European conference on transport which was held in Prague from 29 to 31 October.[4] A statement was adopted at the end of the conference defining the objectives of a pan-European transport policy and describing the means to be deployed in order to achieve them.

Air traffic rights

736.   On 24 July[5] the Commission proposed to the Council that the civil aviation agreement between the European Economic Community, the Kingdom of Norway and the Kingdom of Sweden should be concluded.[6] On 27 November the Economic and Social Committee delivered a favourable opinion on the proposal.[7]

---

[1]   OJ C 48, 25.2.1991; Bull. EC 1/2-1991, point 1.2.103.
[2]   OJ C 240, 16.9.1991; Bull. EC 7/8-1991, point 1.2.116.
[3]   OJ C 183, 15.7.1991; Bull. EC 6-1991, point 1.2.92.
[4]   Bull. EC 10-1991, point 1.2.61.
[5]   Bull. EC 7/8-1991, point 1.2.115.
[6]   Twenty-fourth General Report, point 590.
[7]   Bull. EC 11-1991, point 1.2.72.

Section 18

Energy

Priority activities and objectives

737.   In May the Council adopted the Directive on the transit of natural gas through grids, marking the first step towards completion of the internal market in energy. With a view to completion of the internal gas and electricity market, the Commission this year proposed new guidelines to the Council based on a progressive approach and freedom from rigid mechanisms and excessive regulation. This new approach will be in three successive stages. The first stage will consist of the implementation of the three Directives already adopted. The second, designed with subsidiarity in mind, will seek to make further progress in three main areas: the liberalization of production and construction of power lines and gas pipelines, the introduction of separate management of the various activities of vertically integrated companies, and the limited introduction of third-party access to networks. The third stage will be defined in the light of the experience gained from 1 January 1996.

738.   The European Energy Charter signed by the 38 signatory countries at the closing conference on 17 December in The Hague introduces long-term cooperation in Europe in the energy sector based on the equality of rights and obligations. It refers to the complementary relationships which exist and attempts to create an awareness of common responsibility for supply and environmental problems.

739.   An important step towards the promotion of energy efficiency in the Community was taken with the adoption of the SAVE programme by the Council on 29 October.

740.   Efforts towards achieving further integration of policies on energy and the environ-ment also continued. In order to stabilize overall CO_2 emissions in the Community at their 1990 level by the year 2000, on 14 October the Commission adopted a communication to the Council on the strategy to be followed to achieve this objective, in particular through further improvements in energy efficiency and the introduction of an energy/carbon dioxide tax.

Internal energy market

741.   On 23 October the Commission adopted general guidelines for the completion of the internal market in gas and electricity.[1] Three stages are planned. The first involves the implementation of the three directives on electricity transit, natural gas transit and price transparency. The second stage, beginning on 1 January 1993, will seek to end exclusive rights. The third stage, beginning on 1 January 1996, is to be defined in due course in the light of experience.

742.   On 31 May the Council adopted Directive 91/296/EEC on the transit of natural gas through grids.[2] This Directive is to be implemented in accordance with the above-mentioned guidelines.

743.   On 3 December the Commission approved a report on energy investment projects in the Community.[3] The document, which is based on the situation on 1 January 1990, is aimed at defining ways of improving the application of Council Regulation (EEC) No 1056/72, as agreed by the Council during its discussion of the proposal amending that Regulation.[4]

Energy and Community cohesion

744.   On 8 May the Commission approved a communication defining the framework, the scope and the objective of regional energy planning in the Community and proposing guidelines for the period 1991 to 1993.[5] The main aims are to improve the information base for and analysis of the energy situation in the regions and to improve the decision-making process on matters of energy policy and planning at subnational level, in particular in order to make the best possible use of local energy resources and to use energy more efficiently.

745.   Under the Community plan for regional energy planning, which has been extended to include urban energy planning, the Commission decided to grant financial support totalling some ECU 3.6 million to carry out 50 studies selected following an invitation to submit proposals published in January.[6]

---

[1]   Bull. EC 10-1991, point 1.2.64.
[2]   OJ L 147, 12.6.1991; Bull. EC 5-1991, point 1.2.72; Commission proposal: OJ C 247, 28.9.1989; Twenty-third General Report, point 673; OJ C 268, 24.10.1990; Twenty-fourth General Report, point 604.
[3]   Bull. EC 12-1991.
[4]   Twenty-fourth General Report, point 603.
[5]   Bull. EC 5-1991, point 1.2.73.
[6]   OJ C 12, 18.1.1991.

Energy and the environment

746.   In order to stabilize overall CO_2 emissions in the Community at 1990 levels by 2000, on 14 October the Commission adopted a communication[1] on the strategy to be followed, which concentrates on further improving energy efficiency and the introduction of a new, fiscally neutral energy/carbon dioxide tax, the detailed arrangements of which will be defined in cooperation with the Member States. The Council approved this approach on 13 December.

747.   At international level, in Unctad, the Commission is continuing to work towards the preparation of a convention on climatic protection and of a programme aimed at sustainable energy consumption.

748.   In June Parliament made recommendations,[2] in a series of resolutions on energy and the environment, for the effective reduction of pollutant emissions, particularly through the use of tax measures.

749.   In July the Economic and Social Committee adopted an own-initiative opinion[3] in which it called for priority to be given to the problem of climatic change as a result of global warming and the implementation of specific strategies at Community level.

750.   Following its communication on energy and the environment,[4] the Commission asked the main European energy associations to start work on industrial codes of behaviour for better environmental protection. Codes of behaviour were drawn up in 1990 and 1991 by the electricity, coal, oil and gas industries in the Community.

Promotion of energy technologies

751.   Under the Thermie programme,[5] the Commission, as of 1 January, established a network of 35 organizations for the promotion of energy technologies (Opets). These Opets cover practically all the regions of the Community and may be either public or private sector organizations. Their purpose is to help the Commission to implement its programme to promote innovatory energy technologies. The Commission also decided,[6] on 6 August, to give financial support amounting to ECU 89 580 360 to 128 projects or

---

[1]   Point 622 of this Report.
[2]   OJ C 183, 15.7.1991; Bull. EC 6-1991, point 1.2.96.
[3]   OJ C 269, 14.10.1991; Bull. EC 7/8-1991, point 1.2.122.
[4]   Twenty-third General Report, point 657.
[5]   OJ L 185, 17.7.1990; Twenty-fourth General Report, point 608.
[6]   Bull. EC 7/8-1991, point 1.2.123.

project phases concerning the rational utilization of energy (54 projects), renewable energy sources (44), solid fuels (5) and oil and gas (25). In December, it adopted three new decisions[1] on the granting of financial support totalling ECU 25 941 311.

Community energy strategy and objectives for 1995

752.   The Commission carried out an analysis of the Member States' energy programmes with regard to the objectives for 1995 in order to pinpoint subjects which might be reviewed in detail, as referred to in a communication[1] of 13 December. It also continued its exploratory investigations with a view to identifying the priority themes which will provide a basis for new energy objectives beyond 1995.[2]

Relations with third countries producing or importing energy

753.   The annual ministerial meeting of the Governing Board of the International Energy Agency (IEA) was held on 3 June in Paris[3] and was attended by Mr Cardoso e Cunha. It was marked by the accession of France and Finland to the Agency and by agreement to informal dialogue between the members of the Agency and the oil-producing countries.

754.   On a proposal from the Commission,[4] the Council approved the conclusion of an agreement in the form of an exchange of letters amending the cooperation agreement between the European Atomic Energy Community (Euratom) and the Government of Canada on the peaceful uses of atomic energy.[5] This agreement, which was signed on 15 July,[6] is aimed at laying down conditions for Canada to supply tritium and related equipment to Euratom for use in its fusion programme.

755.   On 16 December, on the basis of a Commission proposal, the Council gave the Commission negotiating directives for a new agreement on nuclear cooperation between Euratom and the United States.[1] This proposal is concerned with the provisions on

---

[1]   Bull. EC 12-1991.
[2]   Twenty-fourth General Report, point 609.
[3]   Bull. EC 6-1991, point 1.2.98.
[4]   Bull. EC 1/2-1991, point 1.2.110.
[5]   OJ 60, 24.11.1959.
[6]   OJ C 215, 17.8.1991; Bull. EC 7/8-1991, point 1.2.125.

non-proliferation and industrial and commercial cooperation and establishes in particular a link with the important related aspects of health and environmental protection,
research and development and fusion.

756.   On 17 June the Commission was authorized by the Council to negotiate three
cooperation agreements between Euratom and the USSR on controlled nuclear fusion,
nuclear safety, and matters relating to exchanges of nuclear materials.[1]

757.   Under the umbrella of the 24 Western countries (G24) associated with the Phare
programme, international energy cooperation programmes with the Central and East
European countries were stepped up considerably in 1991. Within the G24 forum, the
Commission organized several coordination meetings with the International Energy
Agency, the World Bank, the European Investment Bank and the United States in order
to prepare the energy assistance strategy. The Phare programme[2] furthermore provides
for an overall budget in 1991 of some ECU 5 million for each recipient country for
technical assistance programmes in the field of energy such as the drafting and planning
of energy policy, energy supply and demand, the tariffs and pricing system, energy
savings, interconnection of Eastern and Western grids, training, environmental protection, restructuring of the energy industry and nuclear safety. An appropriation of
ECU 11.5 million was also released for a specific regional nuclear safety programme in
Bulgaria.

758.   An energy programme totalling ECU 115 million for the Soviet Union[3] as part
of the technical assistance programme is intended for the introduction of measures to
reshape the institutions and the legal framework, the rational utilization of energy, the
electricity, oil and gas sectors and nuclear safety.

759.   Furthermore, energy cooperation continued with the countries of Asia and Latin
America and the Mediterranean countries. A budget of ECU 8 million this year made
it possible to fund more than 60 cooperation programmes.

760.   During a visit to the People's Republic of China in April, Mr Cardoso e Cunha
signed an agreement to provide China with Community support for the energy sector
in 1991.[4]

[1]   Bull. EC 6-1991, point 1.2.99; Commission proposal: Twenty-fourth General Report, point 613.
[2]   Point 818 of this Report.
[3]   Point 820 of this Report.
[4]   Bull. EC 4-1991, point 1.2.62.

European Energy Charter

761.   Following on from the conclusions of the Charter for a new Europe adopted at the CSCE Summit,[1] on 13 February the Commission proposed to the Council[2] a draft Charter laying down the principles, objectives and ways of achieving pan-European cooperation in the field of energy in the form of a code of conduct which signatory countries would agree to observe and enforce. The Council expressed its support for the draft and asked all of the European countries, including the Soviet Union, and all of the non-European countries of the Group of 24 to negotiate the Charter.[3] At the first preparatory conference in Brussels,[4] the Economic and Social Committee unreservedly welcomed the Commission's proposal,[5] as did the European Parliament, which felt the Charter should in particular be regarded as an integral part of an effective common energy policy.[6] On 3 December, on a proposal from the Commission,[7] the Council authorized the Commission[8] to negotiate concerning the responsibilities of the Community and, on behalf of the Community, concerning the Charter and the specific cooperation agreements.

The Charter, which was the subject of a European Parliament resolution in December,[9] was adopted by the 38 signatory countries at the closing conference on 16 and 17 December in The Hague. Based on equality of rights and obligations, the Charter has the following practical objectives: the expansion of trade, particularly through the free play of market forces; freedom of access to resources and the development of infrastructures; cooperation and coordination, particularly through coordination of energy policies, technology transfer and the harmonization of technical specifications and safety rules; and energy efficiency and environmental protection. In addition to this declaration of principle, there will be a legally binding basic agreement, which will later lead to the adoption of sectoral protocols to initiate the practical stage of cooperation.

---

[1]   Twenty-fourth General Report, point 871.
[2]   Bull. EC 1/2-1991, point 1.2.106.
[3]   Bull. EC 6-1991, point 1.2.95.
[4]   Bull. EC 7/8-1991, point 1.2.117.
[5]   OJ C 269, 14.10.1991; Bull. EC 7/8-1991, point 1.2.118.
[6]   OJ C 240, 16.9.1991; Bull. EC 7/8-1991, point 1.2.119.
[7]   Bull. EC 10-1991, point 1.2.68.
[8]   Bull. EC 12-1991.
[9]   OJ C 13, 20.1.1992; Bull. EC 12-1991.

Sectoral aspects

Oil and petroleum products

762. The introduction of a contingency scheme by the International Energy Agency on 17 January, together with the commencement of hostilities against Iraq, was instrumental in calming the oil markets, which remained stable until the end of the conflict.

763. The dialogue between producers and consumers was relaunched at the Franco-Venezuelan conference in July in which the Commission participated.

764. The Council continued its examination of the Commission's proposals on action to be taken in the event of supply difficulties and on oil stocks. On 31 May it said it supported a Community mechanism linked to that of the International Energy Agency. In the conclusions[1] adopted on 29 October it restated the need for a new approach to the management of oil crises in the context of the IEA, to which the Community should accede. It outlined the proposed procedure whereby Community action would be complementary to that of the IEA, in which the Community would speak with one voice.

Natural gas

765. In October the Commission adopted general guidelines for the completion of the internal market in energy, particularly gas.[2]

766. On 31 May the Council adopted the Directive on the transit of natural gas through grids,[3] the aim of which is to help further integrate the European energy market by abolishing obstacles to increases in natural gas exchanges between grids.

767. On 18 March it also adopted Council Directive 91/148/EEC repealing Directive 75/404/EEC on the restriction of the use of natural gas in power stations.[4]

---

[1]   Bull. EC 10-1991, point 1.2.63.
[2]   Point 741 of this Report.
[3]   Point 742 of this Report.
[4]   OJ L 75, 21.3.1991; Bull. EC 3-1991, point 1.2.76; Commission proposal: OJ C 203, 14.8.1990; Twenty-fourth General Report, point 619.

Solid fuels

768.   In 1991 the Commission authorized the granting of aid by Germany,[1] Belgium,[2] France[3] and Spain[4] to their coal industries for 1991 and by Germany[5] and Portugal[3] for 1990 pursuant to Council Decision No 2064/86/ECSC establishing Community rules for State aid to the coal industry.[6] Furthermore, the Commission authorized the granting of additional aid by Germany[7] for 1989. The financial measures planned by the Member States were authorized on condition that the aid meets the objectives of Decision No 2064/86/ECSC and the criteria for granting aid set out in that Decision. The Commission included as a condition of authorization in the case of Spain a request for the submission of strategic plans for each company as part of the plan to reduce compensatory payments made to electricity producers.

769.   In accordance with Decision No 2064/86/ECSC, on 28 June the Commission adopted its annual report on the application of Community rules for State aid to the coal industry in 1989.[8] On 14 November it adopted the 1990 report.[9] On 11 November it also adopted a mid-term report[10] on the experience gained and the problems encountered since the introduction of the Community rules.

770.   On 19 March the Commission approved (first reading) the annual report on the market for solid fuels in the Community in 1990 and the outlook for 1991.[11] On 22 March the ECSC Consultative Committee expressed its opinion on the report, of which the Commission approved a revised version[12] on 27 September. The ECSC Consultative Committee expressed a further opinion[13] on 1 October and the report was formally adopted by the Commission[14] on 13 December.

---

[1]   Bull. EC 7/8-1991, point 1.2.124.
[2]   OJ L 226, 14.8.1991.
[3]   OJ L 193, 17.7.1991.
[4]   OJ L 324, 26.11.1991.
[5]   OJ L 226, 14.8.1991; Bull. EC 1/2-1991, point 1.2.108.
[6]   OJ L 177, 1.7.1986; Twentieth General Report, point 737.
[7]   OJ L 105, 25.4.1990; Bull. EC 1/2-1991, point 1.2.108.
[8]   Bull. EC 6-1991, point 1.2.97.
[9]   Bull. EC 11-1991, point 1.2.75.
[10]   Bull. EC 11-1991, point 1.2.74.
[11]   Bull. EC 3-1991, point 1.2.75.
[12]   Bull. EC 9-1991, point 1.2.54.
[13]   Bull. EC 10-1991, point 1.2.66.
[14]   Bull. EC 12-1991.

Electricity

771.   In October the Commission adopted general guidelines[1] for the completion of the internal market in energy, particularly electricity.

772.   The Commission continued its work in the context of the Community action programme for improving the efficiency of electricity use (PACE),[2] in particular as regards standards for the electrical efficiency of domestic appliances, Community labelling procedures and schemes for increasing efficiency in other specific sectors such as industry and commercial premises.

773.   Contacts with the EFTA countries continued in order to study the possibility of applying Community law to electricity in their territories.

774.   The electricity sector was a priority area for relations with the Central and East European countries, in particular in the framework of the Phare programme, technical assistance to the Soviet Union, coordination of aid given by the Group of 24, and the negotiations on the European Energy Charter.

775.   On 10 December Parliament adopted a resolution[3] establishing principles for pan-European cooperation on energy and for supplying the countries of Central and Eastern Europe with electricity.

Nuclear energy

776.   Following the publication in 1990 of the Community's illustrative nuclear programme,[4] pursuant to Article 40 of the Euratom Treaty, the Commission has been following closely the efforts being made by the various economic operators in the Community nuclear industry to reach a joint decision on the specifications of future reactors. This approach, which was recommended by the Commission, should facilitate the adoption of standard rules on safety at Community level and the creation of a single market in nuclear power plant components.

777.   In the context of aid to the countries of Central and Eastern Europe and the USSR, the Commission worked intensively to direct technical assistance programmes

---

[1]   Point 741 of this Report.
[2]   OJ L 157, 9.6.1989; Twenty-third General Report, point 681.
[3]   OJ C 13, 20.1.1992; Bull. EC 12-1991.
[4]   Twenty-fourth General Report, point 625.

towards those measures best suited to improving the safety of nuclear power stations of Soviet design.

New and renewable energy sources

778.   The Commission launched a study on the long-term prospects for renewable sources of energy in the European Community and the Central and East European countries, except the Soviet Union, for 1995, 2000 and 2010. As part of its efforts to gain more knowledge about these sources of energy, it continued work, in cooperation with the national statistical offices, on the introduction of systematic gathering of statistics on renewable energy sources.

779.   The Commission also helped to set up a database on products and services offered by European industry in the field of photovoltaic energy, a study on the use of active solar energy in Europe, the publication of a guide to small-scale hydroelectric schemes for non-specialists and a guide on the treatment of solid municipal waste.

780.   Finally, the Commission continued its work on the development of biomass, in particular biofuels, with the threefold aim of diversification of energy supply, redirection of the common agricultural policy and compliance by the Community with its commitments in respect of greenhouse gas emissions.

Energy savings and rational use

781.   On 29 October the Council adopted[1] the programme on the promotion of energy efficiency in the Community (SAVE)[2] after the Economic and Social Committee and Parliament had given their opinions in March[3] and July[4] respectively. The aim of the programme is to reduce energy intensity per unit of GNP by 20% over the next five years.

782.   On 19 December the Council adopted[5] a common position on the first Directive provided for in the SAVE programme concerning the efficiency requirements for new hot-water boilers fired with liquid or gaseous fuels.[6]

---

[1]   OJ L 307, 8.11.1991; Bull. EC 10-1991, point 1.2.62; Commission proposal: OJ C 301, 30.11.1991; Twenth-fourth General Report, point 628.
[2]   Specific actions for vigorous energy efficiency.
[3]   OJ C 120, 6.5.1991; Bull. EC 3-1991, point 1.2.74.
[4]   OJ C 240, 16.9.1991; Bull. EC 7/8-1991, point 1.2.120.
[5]   Bull. EC 12-1991.
[6]   Bull. EC 12-1991; Commission proposal: OJ C 292, 22.11.1990; Twenty-fourth General Report, point 628.

783.   On 26 July the Commission adopted, under the same programme, a proposal for a Directive on the indication of the consumption of energy and other resources by domestic appliances by means of labelling and standard product information.[1] Its aim is to promote rational energy use and to ensure that action taken by the Member States in this area does not hinder intra-Community trade. The Economic and Social Committee gave its opinion on the proposal in December.[2]

784.   Furthermore, the Commission, in cooperation with the International Energy Agency, organized an international conference on least-cost planning methods on 23 and 24 October in Copenhagen.

Euratom Supply Agency

785.   In 1991, as in previous years,[3] users of natural uranium, enriched uranium and services for the nuclear fuel cycle, with the exception of the reprocessing of highly enriched uranium, had an adequate, diversified supply at their disposal. The Community depended on imports for more than 70% of its supplies of natural uranium. Of the eight external supplier countries, none accounted for more than 25% of total supplies.

The supply of natural and enriched uranium and of services for the whole fuel cycle in the Community is reasonably secure in the short to medium term. The shortfall of uranium production in relation to demand in countries with a market economy is likely to continue to be covered by the further running down of stocks and by increased supply from the Soviet Union. In the longer term, the low price of uranium is continuing to cause companies to close down, which might lead to a reduction in the number of sources of supply and possibly a risk to the security of supply. The Agency takes the view that this can best be guaranteed by the conclusion of long-term contracts at prices which at least cover production costs, thereby ensuring market stability and the diversification of sources. Specific contracts could be considered for unforeseen needs.

786.   As in 1990, the primary market, both in natural uranium and in enrichment services, again remained quiet. Only six long-term contracts for uranium procurement, compared with four in 1990, and one long-term contract for enrichment services were concluded out of a total of 81 contracts for the supply of natural uranium and 121 contracts for the supply of enrichment services and special fissile materials. On the secondary market, most transactions by the Agency were for swap transactions and loans and, to a lesser extent, spot purchases.

---

[1]   OJ C 235, 10.9.1991; Bull. EC 7/8-1991, point 1.2.121.
[2]   Bull. EC 12-1991.
[3]   Twenty-fourth General Report, point 629.

787.   As regards enriched uranium, there continues to be an excess of production capacity. High availability in the Soviet Union together with surplus stocks of enriched uranium kept spot prices relatively low. World spot market prices picked up again somewhat during the second half of the year.

788.   The Agency closely monitored the situation with regard to supplies to Community users to enable the Community to take appropriate action if necessary. Discussions within the Agency's Consultative Committee in 1991 essentially focused on supplies both by means of procurement and by means of swaps and loans of material from the Soviet Union.

Section 19

Euratom safeguards

789.   In 1991 the Euratom Safeguards Directorate conducted physical and accounting checks on average stocks of 203 tonnes of plutonium, 13 tonnes of highly enriched uranium and 200 000 tonnes of low enriched uranium, natural uranium, depleted uranium, thorium and heavy water. These materials were held in over 800 nuclear installations in the Community and gave rise to some 600 000 operator entries concerning physical movements and stocks. As in the past, the checks also covered equipment subject to external commitments under cooperation agreements with non-member countries. The anomalies and irregularities detected by the Directorate were followed up rigorously by additional inspections; some of these are still being looked into.

790.   In December the Euratom Safeguards Directorate submitted its second report,[1] covering the period 1989-90, on its activities in connection with the nuclear fuel cycle for civil use, including research and other related activities. The report also contains an analysis of the various operational aspects and sets out guidelines for the years ahead.

791.   In view of the constant increase in plutonium stocks and plutonium recycling in MOX fuels, thought has had to be given to more modern safeguard techniques, and following discussions with the International Atomic Energy Agency (IAEA) and operators the measures to be deployed in the fuel fabrication plants under construction (Siemens-MOX, MDF-Sellafield) were determined.

792.   In 1991, sophisticated safeguards arrangements were implemented by Euratom at the La Hague UP_3 reprocessing plant. This large-scale operation at a modern installation of an imposing size was followed up this year by the introduction of similar arrangements at the Thorp reprocessing plant in the United Kingdom which will come into service in 1992. The arrangements in question are designed to improve safeguards in real time, keep costs within reasonable bounds and reduce the need for growing numbers of safeguard inspectors to carry out inspections in complex installations.

---

[1]   First report: Twenty-fourth General Report, point 634.

793.   As in 1990[1] special attention was paid to on-site laboratories with a view to reducing costs, delays and the hazards associated with the transport of samples. The laboratory project at the Sellafield site is the furthest advanced; safety studies and detailed plans were completed and the premises are already being prepared.

794.   The safeguards initiated on the territory of the former German Democratic Republic following reunification were stepped up, reaching a normal level of intensity. Discussions continued concerning the implementation of the particular safeguards provisions required by Articles 7 and 8 of Regulation (Euratom) No 3227/76 in respect of these installations in 1992.[2]

During the year consultations also took place with the IAEA with a view to reconciling Euratom safeguards methods with the new criteria laid down by the IAEA for the period 1991-95.

---

[1]   Twenty-fourth General Report, point 637.
[2]   OJ L 363, 31.12.1976.

Section 20

Nuclear safety

Priority activities and objectives

795.   *The main feature of this year was the Community's increased involvement in the field of nuclear safety in Central and Eastern Europe and the Soviet Union. The need to give this matter urgent attention was explicitly acknowledged by the G7 annual summit[1] in London from 15 to 17 July. Within its sphere of responsibility the Commission continued to perform its role of coordinating international efforts to raise the level of nuclear safety throughout Europe, particularly as regards plant safety, worker training and informing the public. These activities were carried out in close cooperation with the other international organizations responsible, and in particular with the International Atomic Energy Agency (IAEA). In addition, in the radiation protection field the Community began work on a revision of Community regulations to take account of the latest scientific developments and the requirements associated with the completion of the single market.*

Radiation protection

796.   On 13 September Parliament delivered an opinion[2] on the proposal for a Directive[3] amending Directive 80/836/Euratom[4] laying down the basic standards for the health protection of the general public and workers against the dangers arising from ionizing radiation as regards prior authorization of the shipment of radioactive waste.

797.   The Commission accorded greater urgency to the preparation of a proposal amending Directive 80/836/Euratom[4] laying down the basic standards for the health protection of the general public and workers against the dangers arising from ionizing radiation, in order to bring it into line with the latest scientific findings set out in the

---

[1]   Point 853 of this Report.
[2]   OJ C 267, 14.10.1991; Bull. EC 9-1991, point 1.2.126.
[3]   OJ C 210, 23.8.1990; Twenty-fourth General Report, point 651.
[4]   OJ L 246, 17.9.1980; Fourteenth General Report, point 265.

Recommendations of the International Commission on Radiological Protection published in April. The group of scientific experts provided for under Article 31 of the
Euratom Treaty delivered its opinion on the matter in December.

798.   On 26 July the Commission adopted a recommendation[1] spelling out the detailed
procedures for the application of the third and fourth paragraphs of Article 33 of the
Euratom Treaty, in particular with regard to the drawing up and harmonization of the
appropriate provisions, laid down by legislation, regulation or administrative action, to
ensure compliance with basic Community standards on radiation protection. Under the
same article of the Treaty the Commission also issued eight recommendations on draft
regulations submitted by Belgium, Greece, Spain and the Netherlands.

799.   On 19 April the Commission published a communication[2] on the implementation
of Directive 89/618/Euratom[3] on informing the general public about the health protection measures to be applied and the steps to be taken in the event of a radiological
emergency.

800.   It also adopted, on 22 January, Regulation (EEC) No 146/91[4] establishing a list
of products excluded from the application of Council Regulation (EEC) No 737/90[5] on
the conditions governing imports of agricultural products originating in third countries
following the accident at the Chernobyl power station.

801.   In accordance with its Decision[6] of 20 December 1989 the Commission continued
its discussions with the Member States with a view to resuming inspections under
Article 35 of the Euratom Treaty to verify the operation and efficiency of facilities for
monitoring radioactivity levels.

802.   Acting under Article 37 of the Euratom Treaty, the Commission delivered two
opinions concerning plans for the discharge of radioactive waste from different types of
nuclear installations.

803.   On 28 November the Council adopted the specific programme in the field of
nuclear fission safety,[7] which is part of the framework programme of research and
technological development (1990-94) and includes a research project on radiation
protection for the period 1992-93, for which an amount of ECU 29 million is to be set
aside from an overall budget of ECU 36 million.

---

[1]   OJ L 238, 27.8.1991; Bull. EC 7/8-1991, point 1.2.281.
[2]   OJ C 103, 19.4.1991.
[3]   OJ L 357, 17.12.1989; Twenty-third General Report, point 693.
[4]   OJ L 17, 23.1.1991; Bull. EC 1/2-1991, point 1.2.236.
[5]   OJ L 82, 29.3.1990; Twenty-fourth General Report, point 639.
[6]   Twenty-third General Report, point 697.
[7]   Point 342 of this Report.

Plant safety

804. The specific programme in the field of nuclear fission safety[1] adopted by the Council as part of the framework programme of research and technological development (1990-94) also contains a section on reactor safety, for which an amount of ECU 7 million has been earmarked.

Radioactive waste

805. On 11 July the European Parliament adopted a resolution on the revision of the Euratom Treaty[2] in which it called for the implementation of a common European strategy on radioactive waste management and more stringent provisions governing the right of the communities concerned to receive information.

International action

806. On 17 June the Council adopted a Decision setting out guidelines for the Commission for the negotiation of three cooperation agreements between the Community and the Soviet Union in the fields of nuclear safety, controlled nuclear fusion and matters relating to trade in nuclear materials.[3] In the context of the discussions on the nuclear safety agreement, the Commission decided to set up a working party to prepare a joint EC-USSR analysis of the future safety of nuclear power stations and its impact on the development of nuclear energy.[4]

On 5 June, with a view to improving nuclear safety in the countries of Central and Eastern Europe and the Soviet Union, the Commission set out the main lines of Community assistance,[5] which it agreed to direct towards certain specific objectives. In this connection, on 31 July it approved aid of ECU 11.5 million to improve safety at the Kozloduy nuclear power plants in Bulgaria, which were also the subject of a resolution[6] adopted by Parliament on 11 July. In addition, on 27 and 28 June the Commission held a meeting in Brussels between representatives of the authorities responsible for nuclear safety in the Central and East European countries and their

---

[1] Point 342 of this Report.
[2] OJ C 240, 16.9.1991; Bull. EC 7/8-1991, point 1.2.282.
[3] Bull. EC 6-1991, point 1.2.99.
[4] OJ C 204, 3.8.1991.
[5] Bull. EC 6-1991, point 1.2.206.
[6] OJ C 240, 16.9.1991; Bull. EC 7/8-1991, point 1.2.283.

counterparts in the Member States of the Community. The former expressed a definite interest in placing cooperation with the Community on an institutional footing, going beyond management of the specific problems associated with the Soviet VVER power stations.

807.   In May, as part of its assistance to the USSR, the Commission supplied 650 high-quality dosimeters intended for communities in areas affected by the Chernobyl accident.

808.   The Commission and the Member States played a major part in the preparation, proceedings and drafting of conclusions of the 'International Conference on the Safety of Nuclear Power: Strategies for the Future' held from 2 to 6 September in Vienna. Its conclusions were endorsed by the IAEA General Conference on 20 September and pave the way for an international framework convention on nuclear safety. The Commission is closely involved in the preliminary stages of the drafting of this convention.

809.   The Commission actively participated in a number of IAEA activities, including the international evaluation of the radiological consequences of the Chernobyl accident, the special project on the safety of the VVER-230 reactors, two Asset (Assessment of Safety-Significant Event Team) missions to the Soviet power plants at Kola and Novovoronezh and a Rapat (Radiation Protection Advisory Team) mission to Poland. It also cooperated with the IAEA and WHO in connection with the international programme on the health effects of the Chernobyl accident and with the International Centre for Radiation Health Issues on topics of common interest.

Chapter III

External relations

Section 1

Priority activities and objectives

810.   *More than ever this year, the Community has expressed its desire to strengthen its links with the countries of Central and Eastern Europe: on 16 December the 'Europe agreements' with Hungary, Poland and Czechoslovakia were signed. These agreements will enable those countries to take part in the process of European integration and will help them to progress towards their ultimate objective, which is to become full members of the Community. In addition to the progressive establishment of a free trade area, these agreements contain provisions on commercial, economic and financial cooperation, lay down the procedures for a genuine, institutionalized political dialogue and establish the framework for restoring cultural exchanges throughout Europe. Exploratory talks were started at the end of the year with Bulgaria and Romania with a view to opening negotiations on identical agreements. Once the independence of the Baltic States had been recognized by the Community, the Council gave the Commission negotiating directives for a trade and cooperation agreement with each of those countries and for an identical agreement with Albania. The programme of Community assistance to support the process of political and economic reform undertaken by the countries of Central and Eastern Europe (Operation Phare) underwent further developments: it was extended to include the Baltic States and Albania. For 1991 a total of ECU 785 million was allocated to the programme and earmarked for all the countries concerned except the Baltic States, which have this year been recipients of technical assistance granted to the Soviet Union and its republics. In addition, the Commission has actively pursued its role of coordinating economic assistance within the Group of 24. Furthermore, besides its existing commitments within the context of the International Monetary Fund, the Community has been*

undertaking a wide-ranging programme of support for the balance of payments in certain countries. Its purpose is to back up the adjustment and reform programmes undertaken by the recipient countries, namely Czechoslovakia, Bulgaria, Romania and Hungary. In spite of the uncertainties arising from the upheavals which have taken place since the summer in the Soviet Union, the Community's activity in respect of that country and its republics has centred on implementing the conclusions of the December 1990 European Council (Rome II). The necessary steps were taken to supply, free of charge, food products worth ECU 250 million, much of which was dispatched before the end of the year. The technical assistance programme, worth ECU 400 million, was launched and the Council approved a credit guarantee for ECU 500 million for the purchase of agricultural and food products. Moreover, in view of the food shortages, the Soviet Union was granted a loan of ECU 1 250 million, the first instalment of which (ECU 500 million) was made available in December. Finally, as a result of the Maastricht European Council on 9 and 10 December, the Council decided to grant emergency aid worth ECU 200 million principally to the cities of Moscow and St Petersburg.

During 1991 negotiations continued apace between the Community and the EFTA countries with a view to creating a European Economic Area. A joint ministerial meeting was held in May and overall political agreement was reached at the October Council meeting in Luxembourg. The final conclusion of the negotiations was postponed until early 1992 in order to enable the negotiators to make appropriate judicial arrangements: in December the Court of Justice of the European Communities gave its opinion that an independent Court for the European Economic Area would be incompatible with the EEC Treaty. The Community and the EFTA countries reaffirmed their political will to conclude the Agreement on the European Economic Area early in 1992 and to ensure that it entered into force on 1 January 1993.

Relations between the Community and the United States entered a new phase with the adoption in November 1990 of the Transatlantic Declaration, and throughout 1991 bilateral relations between the two parties developed within a strengthened institutional context. The same is true of relations with Canada, based on a similar declaration adopted jointly with that country. There have been regular, intensive contacts between the Community and the two countries concerned and full use has been made of the procedures set up by the Transatlantic Declarations. This has made it possible to promote Community interests, to consolidate bilateral relations and, in general, to strengthen transatlantic solidarity. The principles governing both declarations have been applied to fields in which cooperation and consultation needed to be widened and reinforced, particularly political and economic cooperation, education, scientific cooperation and a number of fields such as financial services, competition policy and environmental protection, standards, tests and certificates.

Relations between the Community and Japan have similarly been strengthened and deepened. As a result of a number of high-level meetings, a declaration was adopted, similar to those governing Community-US relations and Community-Canada relations, aimed in particular at stepping up cooperation in a number of fields of common interest. Mechanisms for regular consultation and dialogue have also been set up. Despite such progress, the ongoing and increasing trade deficit with Japan remains a matter of major concern. If there is to be a greater European presence on the Japanese market, both sides must make an effort to open up that market to Community exports and investments and to increase sales of European products.

Community activity has been greatly influenced by such developments as the Gulf War, the Middle East Peace Conference and the situation in Yugoslavia. Following the Gulf War, the Community expressed its solidarity with the countries and peoples most severely affected, by granting aid worth ECU 600 million to Turkey, Jordan and Egypt and to Israel and the Occupied Territories. Furthermore, following the informal European Council in April, the Heads of State or Government decided to grant emergency aid worth ECU 150 million to Iraqi refugees and displaced persons, and in particular the Kurds. ECU 100 million of this aid was granted from the Community budget. In addition, the embargo applied to Kuwait was lifted, and the embargo in respect of Iraq was progressively eased. At a later stage, the Council gave the Commission negotiating directives for a free trade agreement with the Gulf Cooperation Council (GCC). At the instigation of the Community, an international conference was held to find a peaceful solution to the problems which have arisen in Yugoslavia. The worsening of the political and institutional crisis and the ongoing civil war have obliged the Community to adopt a number of sanctions against Yugoslavia including an arms embargo, the suspension of financial aid — including aid under Operation Phare — termination of the cooperation agreement and the ECSC agreement, suspension of the generalized preferences and the imposition of restrictions on textile imports. In December, however, positive measures were introduced in respect of Bosnia-Hercegovina, Croatia, Macedonia and Slovenia, which have cooperated in seeking a peaceful solution under the Hague Peace Conference. A Community emergency aid programme for the victims of the fighting was also launched.

The EC International Investment Partners instrument was adopted in 1991. Its purpose is to make it easier to set up joint ventures between businesses based in the Community and the Mediterranean countries and also in Asian and Latin American countries. The new guidelines adopted last year for improving the instruments for financial and technical cooperation with the countries of Asia and Latin America have been translated into operational terms in the form of a proposed Regulation which the Council has approved. It provides for a significant increase in aid, in particular for regional integration, the environment and economic cooperation. Furthermore, the Council extended to the countries of Central America the scheme of generalized preferences already granted to the Andean countries, to help them in their fight against drugs.

Even before the Lomé Convention entered into force on 1 September, work was being done on programming Community aid and, thanks to close cooperation with the

European Investment Bank and the Member States, and to intensive dialogue with the countries concerned, the indicative programmes have been finalized. The Commission has also proposed a batch of measures to alleviate the debt of the ACP States, including cancellation of the obligation to replenish Stabex resources under the Third Lomé Convention. This step has already been approved by the Council. The new association arrangements for the overseas countries and territories also became applicable this year and will remain in force for 10 years. The arrangements contain a good number of improvements: some of these already appear in the Fourth Lomé Convention, while the others relate to the particular status of the overseas countries and territories. The arrangements are based on a partnership between the Commission, the Member State concerned and the overseas countries and territories, the purpose of which is to permit a three-way dialogue on questions of common interest. The funds allocated under the seventh EDF represent an increase of 40% over the previous exercise.

Finally, the Community has continued its efforts to supply food aid. In November it became a member of the United Nations Food and Agriculture Organization (FAO). This is a particularly important step since the Community is the first regional economic grouping to become a member of a United Nations specialized agency. In addition to its normal activities in the field of emergency and food aid, the Community proposed a special programme for Africa, intended in particular to help the countries of the Horn of Africa, southern Africa and the Sahel, which are suffering from a serious drought. Under the programme 600 000 tonnes of grain equivalent were to be provided. Furthermore, to make Community humanitarian aid more efficient and give it a higher profile, the Commission decided to set up a European Office For Emergency Humanitarian Aid to enhance the Community's presence in the field and to provide better coordination among donors.

Where multilateral relations are concerned, the Community has persisted in its efforts to ensure that the Uruguay Round of trade negotiations reaches a successful conclusion. However, it was not possible, before the end of the year, to achieve the overall, balanced result for which the Maastricht European Council had hoped.

In 1991 the number of diplomatic missions accredited to the European Communities by non-member countries rose to 144.

The Commission, for its part, set up delegations in Lima, Valletta, Moscow, Port-au-Prince, Santo Domingo and Windhoek. It is preparing to set up delegations in Buenos Aires, Prague and Sofia and to open an Office in Hong Kong. This will bring the number of its external delegations in foreign countries to 107.

Section 2

Relations with the Soviet Union and the countries of Central and Eastern Europe

Assistance for economic restructuring

Coordination of the Group of 24

811. The Commission continued to coordinate economic assistance from the 24 Western countries and took steps to increase the number of recipient countries. The Group of 24 has so far contributed a total of ECU 26 million to the countries of Central and Eastern Europe, in addition to the sums contributed by the international financial institutions.

The Community, in conjunction with the Group of 24, sought to prevent a deterioration in the balance of payments from jeopardizing reform in the countries of Central and Eastern Europe, which are facing severe external pressures, by concentrating its efforts on a large-scale special programme to bolster the balance of payments as a complement to commitments made within the framework of the International Monetary Fund (IMF).[1] At the Commission's suggestion USD 1 billion in financial assistance was granted to Czechoslovakia, USD 500 million to Hungary, USD 800 million to Bulgaria and USD 1 billion to Romania. The Community undertook to contribute about half of all this aid, signing loan agreements with Czechoslovakia on 29 May for ECU 375 million, Bulgaria on 25 July for ECU 240 million, Hungary on 5 July for ECU 180 million and Romania on 28 November for ECU 190 million, and paid the first tranche on 14 August. On 5 June the Commission adopted a communication taking stock of the assistance granted so far and laying down the guidelines for its future operations in this field.[2]

812. In addition to this medium-term support, the Community continued to finance economic restructuring projects and programmes, to which it allocated a total of ECU 785 million in addition to EIB loans totalling ECU 405 million and ECSC loans for financing investment in the coal and steel industries.

---

[1] Point 73 of this Report.
[2] Bull. EC 6-1991, point 1.3.9.

813. On 10 September Parliament delivered an opinion[1] on the proposal to establish a reinsurance pool for export credits for Central and Eastern Europe.[2]

814. As a result of its progress in the implementation of reforms, Romania was made eligible for economic assistance by the Group of 24,[3] whereas previously it had only been eligible for humanitarian assistance under the Phare programme.[4] On 29 April the Commission amended for the second time,[5] in order to cover Romania, the draft Decision authorizing borrowing on the capital market with a view to granting loans to finance investment in the coal and steel sector in Hungary and Poland,[6] which it had previously amended to include Bulgaria, Czechoslovakia and Yugoslavia.[7] The ECSC Consultative Committee delivered a favourable opinion on 7 June,[8] and the Council gave its approval on 11 November.[9] The Council extended to Bulgaria, Czechoslovakia[6] and Romania[10] its Decision 90/62/EEC providing the Community guarantee to the EIB against losses under loans for projects in Poland and Hungary.[11]

815. Following recent changes in Albania and the government's reforms to pave the way for democracy and economic liberalization, the Group of 24 decided in September to help the country establish a market economy and to extend to it their coordinated assistance, in the light of a Commission report regarding a package of measures to meet Albania's chief needs in terms of food and medical aid, assistance to the government, technical assistance for economic restructuring and macroeconomic assistance.

816. Similarly, from 8 to 14 September a Commission identification mission visited Estonia, Latvia and Lithuania in order to assess the progress of political and economic reform in these States and determine priorities for external assistance.[12] The Commission responded to the Group of 24's decision of 25 September to extend assistance to the three States by tabling a package of measures aimed at providing a framework for coordinated economic assistance to the countries concerned in the fields of training, finance, agriculture and industrial restructuring.

At their meeting on 11 November the Ministers of the Group of 24 decided to suspend coordinated assistance to Yugoslavia because of the escalating conflict and failure to comply with the political and economic conditions for such assistance.

---

[1] OJ C 267, 14.10.1991; Bull. EC 9-1991, point 1.3.15.
[2] OJ C 302, 1.12.1990; Twenty-fourth General Report, point 668.
[3] Bull. EC 1/2-1991, point 1.3.9.
[4] OJ L 257, 21.9.1990; Twenty-fourth General Report, point 669.
[5] Bull. EC 4-1991, point 1.3.7.
[6] Twenty-fourth General Report, point 668.
[7] Twenty-fourth General Report, point 51.
[8] Bull. EC 6-1991, point 1.3.12.
[9] Bull. EC 11-1991, point 1.3.12.
[10] Bull. EC 5-1991, point 1.3.7.
[11] OJ L 42, 16.2.1990; Twenty-fourth General Report, point 668.
[12] Bull. EC 9-1991, point 1.3.12.

Operation Phare

817. In accordance with the decision of the Group of 24,[1] the Council decided on 23 December to extend the Phare programme to cover Albania and the Baltic States[2] and to amend Council Regulation (EEC) No 2698/90 on economic aid accordingly.[3]

818. The 1991 budget for the Phare programme totalled ECU 785 million. Bulgaria, Czechoslovakia, Hungary, Poland, Romania and Yugoslavia were all eligible although aid to the latter country was suspended in the autumn; 80 new technical and financial assistance programmes were approved in late December.[4] The programmes were chosen in the light of the experience gained from the implementation of aid in 1989 and 1990,[5] the general guidelines laid down by the Commission on 15 May[6] and the indicative programmes agreed with the recipient countries for 1991 and 1992; they put the emphasis on breaking up monopolies, privatization, the restructuring of nationalized firms, the fostering of small and medium-sized enterprises, and the development of the financial sector, the private-sector company and the labour market. Funds were also granted for structural reform programmes in such sectors as agriculture, energy, the environment, research and health, and for technical assistance for the modernization of infrastructure in sectors such as telecommunications and transport. This year saw the launch of the first regional cooperation programmes bringing together several countries of Central and Eastern Europe in the fields of statistics, standards, customs, government and environmental protection. The Tempus programme of higher-education exchanges, and ACE, an economic research programme, were renewed. As in the previous year, some of the Phare resources were allocated for humanitarian aid, which consisted of ECU 20 million for medicinal products to Romania and Bulgaria,[7] the continuation of the operation on behalf of children in Romania and emergency food and medical aid for Albania.

819. A resolution adopted by Parliament on 10 October welcomed the extension of the Phare programme to the Baltic States, called for the programme to emphasize research, management and energy as well as culture and the environment and for greater account to be taken of the social dimension.[8]

---

[1] Point 816 of this Report.
[2] OJ L 357, 28.12.1991; Bull. EC 12-1991; Commission proposal: OJ C 313, 4.12.1991; Bull. EC 11-1991, point 1.3.11.
[3] OJ L 257, 21.9.1990; Twenty-fourth General Report, point 669.
[4] Bull. EC 1/2-1991, point 1.3.13; Bull. EC 4-1991, point 1.3.8; Bull. EC 5-1991, point 1.3.6; Bull. EC 7/8-1991, point 1.3.9.
[5] Bull. EC 7/8-1991, point 1.3.8.
[6] Bull. EC 5-1991, point 1.3.5.
[7] OJ L 67, 14.3.1991; Bull. EC 3-1991, point 1.3.8; Commission proposals: OJ C 22, 30.1.1991; Twenty-fourth General Report, point 669.
[8] OJ C 280, 20.10.1991; Bull. EC 10-1991, point 1.3.5.

TABLE 10

Operation Phare: Financial aid granted

(million ECU)

Beneficiary	Sectors										Total
	Other	Agri-culture	Edu-cation	Environ-ment	Financial system	Indus-try	Infra-structure	SMEs	Social	Humani-tarian aid	
Albania	1.0	—	0	0	—	—	—	—	0	10	11
Bulgaria	—	25	5	7.5	10	20	5	—	2.5	20	95
Czecho-slovakia	20	0	9	5	—	19	11	20	15	0	99
Hungary	13.0	13	12	10	9	47	7	4	0	0	115
Poland	10.5	17	14.5	35	16	50	10	6	38	0	197
Romania	22	34	10	—	—	—	9	—	25	45.5	134.5
Yugoslavia	—	0	6	0	0	0	0	0	0	8.5	14.5
Regional cooperation	39	0	20.5	20	0	4.5	15	20	0	0	119
Total	105.5	89	77	77.5	35	140.5	57	50	80.5	73	785

NB: 0 = No financial aid granted.
— = Financial aid granted, but minimal amounts.

Technical assistance to the USSR

820.   At its meeting in Rome on 14 and 15 December 1990 the European Council decided to back the Soviet Government's economic reform and recovery efforts by granting ECU 400 million in technical assistance for 1991.[1] Five priority sectors were targeted: training in public administration and business management, energy, transport, financial services and the distribution of foodstuffs. On 15 July the Council adopted Regulation (EEC, Euratom) No 2157/91 in respect of this assistance.[2] The dialogue that the Commission had opened with the Soviet authorities in January regarding the procedures for the implementation of aid in the five priority sectors led, despite delays owing to political events at the beginning of the year in the Baltic States, to the adoption by the Commission, on 4 September, of an indicative programme that had previously been signed with the Soviet authorities.[3] Founded on the principles of decentralized

---

[1]   Twenty-fourth General Report, point 684.
[2]   OJ L 201, 24.7.1991; Bull. EC 7/8-1991, point 1.3.5; Commission proposal: OJ C 140, 30.5.1991; Bull. EC 5-1991, point 1.3.16.
[3]   Bull. EC 9-1991, point 1.3.8.

cooperation, the programme is designed to promote the changes necessary for the transition to a market economy through a massive transfer of know-how. Notwithstanding further delays resulting from August's political upheavals in the USSR, financing decisions adopted by the Commission during the last quarter of the year enabled operations planned under sectoral programmes to begin.[1] In so doing, the Commission played a leading part in Western efforts to speed economic and political reform in the country.

Trade arrangements

821.   The gradual liberalization, begun in 1990, of quantitative restrictions on products originating in the countries of Central and Eastern Europe was actively continued this year. The arrangements already granted to Bulgaria, Czechoslovakia, Hungary and Poland (the elimination of specific quantitative restrictions and the suspension of 'non-specific' quantitative restrictions) were extended to Romania by Council Regulation (EEC) No 2727/90 and entered into force on 1 May,[2] at the same time as the trade and cooperation Agreement with that country.[3] Furthermore, as the Community's relations with the Baltic States and Albania developed, the Council adopted on 23 December a Regulation[4] again amending Regulation (EEC) No 3420/83.[5] The Regulation lays down rules for imports of products originating in the Baltic States and extends to them and Albania liberalization measures or the suspension of quantitative restrictions already accorded to other countries of Central and Eastern Europe. It also extends the validity of the suspension of non-specific quantitative restrictions for all the countries concerned until 31 December 1992.

822.   The Council continued the operation begun in 1990 in respect of the Soviet Union[6] and, on 15 July, liberalized with effect from 1 August all specific quantitative restrictions still affecting that country,[7] thereby anticipating the gradual dismantling provided for in the trade and cooperation Agreement with that country.[8]

---

[1]   Bull. EC 9-1991, point 1.3.9.
[2]   OJ L 262, 26.9.1990; Twenty-fourth General Report, point 670.
[3]   Point 839 of this Report.
[4]   OJ L 362, 31.12.1991; Bull. EC 12-1991; Commission proposal: Bull. EC 11-1991, point 1.3.14.
[5]   OJ L 346, 8.12.1983; Seventeenth General Report, point 631.
[6]   OJ L 138, 31.5.1990; Twenty-fourth General Report, point 670.
[7]   OJ L 201, 24.7.1991; Bull. EC 7/8-1991, point 1.3.7; Commission proposal: Bull. EC 5-1991, point 1.3.18.
[8]   OJ L 68, 15.3.1990; Twenty-fourth General Report, point 685.

Bilateral relations

General aspects

823.   The Community continued to contribute significantly to the process of political and economic reform under way in the Soviet Union and the countries of Central and Eastern Europe, through technical assistance, food aid, the continuation and extension of Operation Phare, [1] and the negotiation of a series of agreements aimed at strengthening links between these countries and the Community. In accordance with the guidelines it adopted in January 1990, [2] the Commission worked to normalize trade relations and complete the network of commercial and economic cooperation agreements with the Central and East European countries. The trade and commercial and economic cooperation Agreement with Romania was concluded by the Council, on behalf of the European Economic Community, in March and by the Commission, on behalf of the European Atomic Energy Community, on 5 March; [3] the Commission also proposed that the Council mandate it to open negotiations with a view to the conclusion of a similar agreement with Albania.

'Europe agreements' with Poland, Czechoslovakia and Hungary were signed on 16 December [4] after the Council had, on 15 April [5] and 30 September, [6] relaxed the negotiating directives given to the Commission. Parliament, [7] the Economic and Social Committee [8] and the ECSC Advisory Committee [9] adopted resolutions on these negotiations. Pending ratification, the trade provisions of the Europe agreements will be implemented by means of interim agreements. The Europe agreements will provide the means of establishing special links reflecting geographical proximity, shared values and growing interdependence. Extensive political and economic reform in the Central and East European countries is a prerequisite for these agreements. The Europe agreements negotiated with Poland, Czechoslovakia and Hungary share a common framework tailored to the special circumstances of each partner. They include provisions on political dialogue and provide for the gradual introduction of free trade in industrial products, although trade in agricultural and fishery products is subject to special provisions. There are provisions on the movement of workers, services and capital. The economic integration of the associated countries will depend on the gradual approximation of

---

[1]   OJ L 375, 23.12.1989; Twenty-third General Report, point 786.
[2]   Twenty-fourth General Report, point 672.
[3]   Point 839 of this Report.
[4]   Bull. EC 12-1991.
[5]   Bull. EC 4-1991, point 1.3.4.
[6]   Bull. EC 9-1991, point 1.3.16.
[7]   OJ C 129, 20.5.1991; Bull. EC 4-1991, point 1.3.5.
[8]   OJ C 339, 31.12.1991; Bull. EC 9-1991, point 1.3.14.
[9]   Bull. EC 6-1991, point 1.3.10.

legislation. In order to support economic restructuring, economic, scientific and technical cooperation will be stepped up and diversified; it will embrace industry, technical standards, energy, the environment, transport, telecommunications, training, science and technology, the aim being to encourage investment. The Community is planning a flexible and non-binding multiannual financial framework to succeed Phare after 1992. The associated countries will continue to have access to EIB investment loans. Cultural cooperation programmes should also serve to restore cultural links across Europe.

824.   The Commission also gave practical assistance to the countries of Central and Eastern Europe by financing studies on the steel and mining situations in Poland, Czechoslovakia, Hungary, Yugoslavia and Romania. At the same time it decided to organize seminars in this context in order to help those countries to switch to a market economy.

Specific aspects

Albania

825.   At the request of the Albanian authorities and in order to normalize the Community's relations with Albania, on 24 July the Commission proposed to the Council,[1] which gave its approval on 23 September,[2] that negotiations be opened with a view to the conclusion of a non-preferential trade and cooperation agreement, without a financial commitment or protocol.

826.   In January and March the Commission demonstrated its solidarity by granting ECU 1.5 million to meet the immediate needs, in terms of food and shelter, of Albanian refugees in Greece and Italy.[3] Following Mr Andriessen's visit to Tirana on 22 July,[4] the Commission made two emergency aid grants of ECU 500 000, plus ECU 1.5 million in humanitarian aid for the purchase of immediately and urgently needed medicines and medical equipment, so bringing the aid total to ECU 4 million.

827.   After the visit on 24 June of Mr Pashko, the Deputy Prime Minister and Minister for the Economy,[5] the Commission adopted on 24 July a proposal for a Regulation concerning the delivery of 50 000 tonnes of breadmaking wheat worth ECU 5 million.[6]

---

[1]   Bull. EC 7/8-1991, point 1.3.11.
[2]   Bull. EC 9-1991, point 1.3.19.
[3]   Bull. EC 1/2-1991, point 1.3.69; Bull. EC 3-1991, point 1.3.49.
[4]   Bull. EC 7/8-1991, point 1.3.10.
[5]   Bull. EC 6-1991, point 1.3.14.
[6]   OJ C 211, 13.8.1991; Bull. EC 7/8-1991, point 1.3.12.

In September Parliament endorsed the proposal, but wanted the delivery increased to 100 000 tonnes.[1] On 1 October the Council complied with this request by adopting Regulation (EEC) No 2938/91 concerning the supply of 100 000 tonnes of breadmaking wheat as emergency food aid.[2] In late August the Commission had also moved to respond to Albania's immediate plight by approving the delivery by Hungary, under the Phare budget, of 50 000 tonnes of breadmaking wheat in the Community's first triangular operation with a country of Central or Eastern Europe.

828.   On 4 September the Commission adopted a communication taking stock of the measures already taken and proposing other measures to meet the forecast wheat shortfall,[3] and Parliament adopted a number of resolutions regarding the situation in Albania.[4]

829.   On 23 December the Council amended Regulation (EEC) No 2698/90 in order to include Albania in the list of aid recipients.[5] On the same day it also adopted a Regulation providing emergency food aid worth ECU 35 million.[6]

Bulgaria

830.   Mr Andriessen was in Sofia on 10 and 11 March,[7] and President Zhelev visited the Commission on 13 and 14 November.[8] Mr Popov, the Prime Minister, had previously visited Brussels, on 29 April,[9] as had Mr Ludzhev, the Deputy Prime Minister, on 29 January.[10] During his visit on 2 July,[11] Mr Kostov, the Minister for Finance, signed a contract for a medium-term loan to Bulgaria of ECU 290 million,[12] which was in addition to the Community's guarantee to the EIB for loans given for projects in that country.[13]

---

[1]   OJ C 267, 14.10.1991; Bull. EC 9-1991, point 1.3.20.
[2]   OJ L 280, 8.10.1991; Bull. EC 10-1991, point 1.3.6.
[3]   Bull. EC 9-1991, point 1.3.18.
[4]   OJ C 72, 18.3.1991; Bull. EC 1/2-1991, point 1.3.16; OJ C 106, 22.4.1991; Bull. EC 3-1991, point 1.3.9; OJ C 183, 15.7.1991; Bull. EC 6-1991, point 1.3.13.
[5]   Point 817 of this Report.
[6]   OJ L 362, 31.12.1991; Bull. EC 12-1991.
[7]   Bull. EC 3-1991, point 1.3.7.
[8]   Bull. EC 11-1991, point 1.3.15.
[9]   Bull. EC 4-1991, point 1.3.9.
[10]   Bull. EC 1/2-1991, point 1.3.17.
[11]   Bull. EC 7/8-1991, point 1.3.15.
[12]   Point 830 of this Report.
[13]   Twenty-fourth General Report, point 668.

Baltic States

831.   Having officially recognized the independence of the Baltic States, the Community undertook a series of operations to assist these countries. After a meeting between Mr Andriessen and the Estonian, Latvian and Lithuanian Governments,[1] the Commission took stock of all three countries' aid needs.[2] On 25 September the Group of 24 decided to bring the Baltic States under the umbrella of Western economic assistance to the countries of Central and Eastern Europe. The Council therefore amended, on 23 December, Regulation (EEC) No 2698/90, adding the Baltic States to the list of those eligible with effect from 1 January 1992.[3] In 1991 ECU 15 million from the technical assistance resources for the Soviet Union was used to finance projects in the Baltic States in three sectors: agriculture, transport and the environment. On a proposal from the Commission,[4] the Council adopted negotiating directives on 4 November with a view to drawing up a trade and cooperation agreement with each of the Baltic States.[5] These first-generation agreements will cover industrial, agricultural and, in the case of Lithuania, Euratom products.

The Baltic States were also included in the list of countries eligible for triangular operations under Regulation (EEC) No 3281/91 amending Regulation (EEC) No 599/91 on credit guarantees and Decision 91/658/EEC on the medium-term loan to the Soviet Union. On 23 December the Council adopted a Regulation providing the Baltic States with ECU 45 million of emergency food aid.[6]

832.   Parliament adopted on 13 June a resolution on the situation in the Baltic States[7] and, on 12 September, a resolution on relations between these States and the Soviet Union.[8]

Hungary

833.   On 8 March Mr Andriessen visited Budapest,[9] where he had a meeting with Mr Antall, the Prime Minister, who subsequently visited the Commission on 29 Octo-

---

[1]   Bull. EC 9-1991, point 1.3.11.
[2]   Bull. EC 9-1991, point 1.3.12.
[3]   Point 817 of this Report.
[4]   Bull. EC 10-1991, point 1.3.11.
[5]   Bull. EC 11-1991, points 1.3.16 to 1.3.18.
[6]   OJ L 362, 31.12.1991; Bull. EC 12-1991; Commission proposal: Bull. EC 12-1991.
[7]   OJ C 183, 15.7.1991; Bull. EC 6-1991, point 1.3.21.
[8]   OJ C 267, 14.10.1991; Bull. EC 9-1991, point 1.3.7.
[9]   Bull. EC 3-1991, point 1.3.7.

ber.[1] Mr Kupa, the Minister for Finance, visited the Commission on 26 March,[2] and Ms Papandreou was in Budapest from 19 to 21 September.[3]

834.   The contract for the second tranche of medium-term financial assistance to Hungary was signed in Brussels on 29 January,[4] and on 5 July Mr Christophersen, for the Community, and Mr Botos, Minister of State, representing Hungary, signed a new contract for a medium-term loan.[5]

835.   The Europe agreement establishing an association between the Community and Hungary was signed on 16 December.[6]

Poland

836.   President Walesa visited the Commission on 3 April and 3 July.[7] Mr Andriessen visited Warsaw in March, where he had talks with President Walesa.[8] Mr Christophersen,[9] Sir Leon Brittan,[10] Ms Papandreou[3] and Mr Van Miert[11] also visited Poland. The visit to the Commission on 9 October of the Polish Prime Minister, Mr Bielecki, provided an opportunity to review the overall situation in his country.[12] On 10 September Parliament adopted a resolution on industrial and infrastructure investment in Poland.[13]

837.   The Europe agreement establishing an association between the Community and Poland was signed on 16 December.[6]

Romania

838.   On 13 February the Foreign Minister, Mr Nastase, had talks in Brussels with Mr Andriessen,[14] who paid an official visit to Romania on 11 and 12 March.[8]

---

[1]   Bull. EC 10-1991, point 1.3.14.
[2]   Bull. EC 3-1991, point 1.3.13.
[3]   Bull. EC 9-1991, point 1.2.67.
[4]   OJ L 375, 31.12.1990; Bull. EC 1/2-1991, point 1.3.18.
[5]   Bull. EC 7/8-1991, point 1.3.16.
[6]   Point 823 of this Report.
[7]   Bull. EC 4-1991, point 1.3.3; Bull. EC 7/8-1991, point 1.3.17.
[8]   Bull. EC 3-1991, point 1.3.7.
[9]   Bull. EC 6-1991, point 1.3.17.
[10]   Bull. EC 5-1991, point 1.3.11.
[11]   Bull. EC 9-1991, point 1.2.51.
[12]   Bull. EC 10-1991, point 1.3.4.
[13]   OJ C 267, 14.10.1991; Bull. EC 9-1991, point 1.3.23.
[14]   Bull. EC 1/2-1991, point 1.3.20.

839. The trade and commercial and economic cooperation Agreement signed in October 1990[1] was concluded in March[2] and entered into force on 1 May; the first meeting of the Joint Committee set up under this Agreement took place in Brussels on 30 May.[3] The Agreement is backed up by medium-term financial assistance totalling ECU 375 million,[4] and the Community's guarantee to the EIB for loans for projects in Romania.[5]

Czechoslovakia

840. President Havel visited the Commission on 20 March[6] and Mr Andriessen was in Prague from 8 to 10 March,[7] where he was co-chairman for the first meeting of the EC-Czechoslovakia Joint Committee set up under the trade and cooperation Agreement.[8] Sir Leon Brittan,[9] Mr Dondelinger,[10] Mr Schmidhuber, Ms Scrivener and Mr Van Miert also visited Prague in the course of the year.

841. A contract for a medium-term loan of ECU 375 million by the Community to Czechoslovakia was signed on 29 May,[11] this being additional to the Community's guarantee to the EIB for loans for projects in Czechoslovakia.[12]

842. The Europe agreement establishing an association between the Community and Czechoslovakia was signed on 16 December.[13]

Soviet Union

843. Apart from the establishment of technical assistance,[14] the Community took a range of measures aimed at helping the Soviet Union to confront the economic problems facing it and to support it in the economic and political process now under way.

---

[1]   Twenty-fourth General Report, point 680.
[2]   OJ L 79, 26.3.1991; Bull. EC 1/2-1991, point 1.3.19.
[3]   Bull. EC 5-1991, point 1.3.12.
[4]   Point 812 of this Report.
[5]   Point 814 of this Report.
[6]   Bull. EC 3-1991, point 1.3.6.
[7]   Bull. EC 3-1991, point 1.3.7.
[8]   OJ L 291, 23.10.1990; Twenty-fourth General Report, point 683.
[9]   Bull. EC 5-1991, point 1.3.15.
[10]   Bull. EC 5-1991, point 1.3.14.
[11]   Point 811 of this Report.
[12]   Twenty-fourth General Report, point 668.
[13]   Point 823 of this Report.
[14]   Point 820 of this Report.

844.   On 5 March the Council adopted Regulations (EEC) No 598/91 granting ECU 250 million as emergency food aid[1] and No 599/91 introducing a credit guarantee of ECU 500 million over three years for exports of agricultural products and foodstuffs from the Community to the Soviet Union.[1] The latter Regulation was amended on 18 June to take account of an alteration to the repayment schedules,[2] and on 8 July the Community concluded with the Soviet authorities an Agreement in the form of an exchange of letters implementing the amended Regulation.[3]

In September, after the failed coup in the Soviet Union, Mr Andriessen travelled to Moscow, where he had meetings with President Gorbachev and Mr Silayev, Prime Minister of the Russian Republic, who formally requested additional food aid.[4] Following a Commission report on the measures already taken and the prospects for further aid,[5] the Council, on 22 October, amended[6] Regulation (EEC) No 599/91[1] for the second time in order to permit the development of triangular operations with the countries of Central and Eastern Europe. On 7 October the Council decided in principle to grant the Soviet Union a credit facility of ECU 1.25 billion for the purchase of food and pharmaceutical products. This is in addition to the ECU 750 million already granted by the Community and brings total Community aid to ECU 2 billion. This decision forms part of a Group of 7 operation amounting to about ECU 6 billion (USD 7.5 billion), of which the Community is contributing a third of the total. On 16 December the Council adopted the decision regarding this medium-term loan of ECU 1.25 billion, to be paid in three tranches, in order to enable the Soviet Union and its republics to import food and agricultural products and medical supplies; 50% of the total may be used in triangular operations.[7] On the same date the Council decided to grant emergency aid worth ECU 200 million for Moscow and St Petersburg and adopted an initial Regulation covering ECU 95 million.[8] The Commission adopted measures for the implementation of the credit guarantee: Regulation (EEC) No 2150/91,[9] as amended by Regulation (EEC) No 3363/91,[10] lays down conditions for the agreement to be concluded with a syndicate of banks and Regulation (EEC) No 3281/91 sets a 25% ceiling on the guarantee for purchases by the Soviet Union of food products from Bulgaria, Czechoslovakia, Hungary, Poland, Romania, Yugoslavia, Estonia, Latvia and Lithuania.[11]

---

[1]   OJ L 67, 14.3.1991; Bull. EC 3-1991, point 1.3.8; Commission proposal: OJ C 22, 30.1.1991; Bull. EC 12-1990, point 1.4.2.
[2]   OJ L 158, 22.6.1991; Bull. EC 6-1991, point 1.3.18; Commission proposal: OJ C 122, 8.5.1991; Bull. EC 4-1991, point 1.3.12.
[3]   OJ L 202, 25.7.1991; Bull. EC 7/8-1991, point 1.3.6; Commission proposal: Bull. EC 6-1991, point 1.3.19.
[4]   Bull. EC 9-1991, point 1.3.4.
[5]   Bull. EC 9-1991, point 1.3.10.
[6]   OJ L 310, 12.11.1991; Bull. EC 10-1991, point 1.3.8; Commission proposal: Bull. EC 9-1991, point 1.3.10.
[7]   OJ L 362, 31.12.1991; Bull. EC 12-1991; Commission proposal: OJ C 320. 11.12.1991; Bull. EC 11-1991, point 1.3.3.
[8]   OJ L 356, 29.12.1991; Bull. EC 12-1991; Commission proposal: OJ C 11, 17.1.1992; Bull. EC 12-1991.
[9]   OJ L 200, 23.7.1991.
[10]   OJ L 318, 20.11.1991; Bull. EC 11-1991, point 1.3.5.
[11]   OJ L 310, 12.11.1991; Bull. EC 11-1991, point 1.3.8.

26 November saw the signing of an agreement between the Community, represented by Mr Delors, and the Soviet Union, represented by Mr Silayev, Chairman of the Inter-Republican Economic Committee, establishing guarantee procedures and the list of products that might be purchased, an agreement between the Commission and a Deutsche Bank-led syndicate of banks setting out the terms of the Community guarantee, and an agreement between this syndicate and the Vnesheconombank.[1]

845.   Bilateral meetings increased appreciably during the year. Mr Delors hosted meetings with Mr Pavlov, the Soviet Prime Minister, and Mr Silayev on 29 April[2] and 26 November respectively,[3] and met Mr Gorbachev in June;[4] he also met, in Brussels in September, the Vice-Chairman of the Committee for the management of the economy of the USSR,[5] and the Ministers for the Economy of the Soviet republics.[6]

---

[1]   Bull. EC 11-1991, point 1.3.7.
[2]   Bull. EC 4-1991, point 1.3.11.
[3]   Bull. EC 11-1991, point 1.3.6.
[4]   Bull. EC 6-1991, point 1.3.8.
[5]   Bull. EC 9-1991, point 1.3.5.
[6]   Bull. EC 9-1991, point 1.3.6.

Section 3

European Free Trade Association

Relations with EFTA

846.   Using as a basis the negotiating directives adopted by the Council on 18 June 1990,[1] the Commission continued negotiations with EFTA throughout the year for the establishment of a European Economic Area (EEA). The negotiations were conducted at regular ministerial meetings[2] and meetings of senior officials on specialized subjects.

The Luxembourg European Council of 28 and 29 June[3] welcomed the parties' undertaking to bring the negotiations to a rapid conclusion. At the close of a final ministerial meeting held on 21 October,[4] the Council approved the content of the agreement which had been negotiated, as well as the compromise reached on outstanding issues, notably transit, fisheries and the cohesion fund. Active efforts to finalize matters continued, with a view to the signing of the Agreement at the beginning of 1992, subject to a formula being found to resolve the legal problem raised by the Court of Justice in its Opinion 1/91 of 14 December.[5]

The Agreement will be an important component of Europe's structure in that the European Economic Area it establishes will combine with the single market to bring about free movement of goods, persons, services and capital between the Community and the EFTA countries on the basis of the relevant established Community rules and practices and increase cooperation with regard to flanking policies and economic and social cohesion. Additional negotiating directives, adopted by the Council on 27 March,[6] provided the basis for the negotiation of an annex extending freedom of movement to ECSC products.

847.   Parliament reiterated its support for the establishment of the EEA by adopting two resolutions on the subject, one on 14 March[7] and the other on 14 June,[8] and by proposing the creation of a joint EEC-EFTA parliamentary delegation.

---

1   Twenty-fourth General Report, point 688.
2   Bull. EC 5-1991, point 1.3.1; Bull. EC 6-1991, point 1.3.2.
3   Bull. EC 6-1991, points I.1 and I.23.
4   Bull. EC 10-1991, point 1.3.1.
5   Bull. EC 12-1991.
6   Bull. EC 3-1991, point 1.3.2; Commission proposal: Bull. EC 1/2-1991, point 1.3.2.
7   OJ C 106, 22.4.1991; Bull. EC 3-1991, point 1.3.1.
8   OJ C 183, 15.7.1991; Bull. EC 6-1991, point 1.3.4.

Bilateral relations with the EFTA countries

848.   On 31 July[1] the Commission adopted an opinion, as requested by the Council, on Austria's application for accession.[2] It considered from an economic standpoint that the Community should accept the application, but emphasized that from the political standpoint Austria's permanent neutrality gave rise to problems. Subject to the outcome of the Intergovernmental Conferences, it did not consider that these would prove insurmountable during negotiations for accession.

849.   On 1 July[3] Sweden submitted an official application for accession to the European Communities, and the Council decided to set in motion the procedures laid down in the Treaties, notably by taking the step of requesting a Commission opinion on the matter.

850.   Bilateral relations between the Community and the individual EFTA countries were dominated by the negotiations on a European Economic Area.[4] An air transport agreement establishing common rules was concluded between Norway and Sweden and the Community.[5] Agreements were also concluded with all the EFTA countries to bring them into the Community's Erasmus programme from the 1992/93 academic year.[6] The outcome of negotiations with Switzerland and Austria on trans-Alpine transit was approved by the Council on 21 October.[7]

851.   A large number of visits and meetings at all levels took place throughout the year. The Austrian Chancellor, Mr Vranitzky, visited the Commission on 18 February,[8] and was followed in April and November by Mr Mock, Austria's Foreign Minister.[9] Several members of Finland's new government visited Brussels. They included the Prime Minister, Mr Aho (16 September[10]), and the Foreign Minister, Mr Väyrynen (6 June[11]). Norway's Prime Minister, Mrs Brundtland, had talks with Mr Delors in Brussels on 8 May.[12] The President of the Swiss Confederation, Mr Cotti, met Mr Delors in Brussels on 23 September.[13]

---

[1]   Bull. EC 7/8-1991, point 1.3.2.
[2]   Twenty-third General Report, point 782.
[3]   Bull. EC 7/8-1991, point 1.3.3.
[4]   Point 846 of this Report.
[5]   Point 736 of this Report.
[6]   Point 475 of this Report.
[7]   Point 733 of this Report.
[8]   Bull. EC 1/2-1991, point 1.3.4.
[9]   Bull. EC 11-1991, point 1.3.1.
[10]   Bull. EC 9-1991, point 1.3.1.
[11]   Bull. EC 6-1991, point 1.3.6.
[12]   Bull. EC 5-1991, point 1.3.4.
[13]   Bull. EC 9-1991, point 1.3.3.

Mr Andriessen paid official visits to Finland (4 April[1]) and Norway (5 and 6 April[2]). Other Members of the Commission also visited various EFTA countries during the course of the year and had talks on specific bilateral issues and the negotiations then in progress.

852.   Meetings of the Joint Committees for the EEC-Austria/ECSC-Austria and EEC-Switzerland/ECSC-Switzerland free trade Agreements took place in Brussels in February. A meeting of the EEC-Iceland Joint Committee took place in Reykjavik in September.

---

[1]   Bull. EC 4-1991, point 1.3.1.
[2]   Bull. EC 4-1991, point 1.3.2.

Section 4

Relations with the United States, Japan and other industrialized countries

Western Economic Summit

853. The 17th Western Economic Summit was held in London from 15 to 17 July.[1] At the close of the summit Mr Delors issued a statement covering all the issues discussed. An economic declaration, a political declaration on the strengthening of the international order and a declaration on sales of conventional weapons and the non-proliferation of nuclear, chemical and biological weapons were also adopted in the course of the meeting. On the economic front, participants decided to hold an annual high-level meeting with the Soviet Union; they also agreed on a support plan for the Soviet Union, under which it would become an associate member of the IMF and the World Bank, aid would be provided for reforms and cooperation would be established to help the Soviet Union with the conversion of the arms industry, food distribution, nuclear safety and transport. On the question of support for the countries of Central and Eastern Europe, the participants agreed to open their markets to those countries' products and services, including iron and steel, textiles and agricultural products. They also pledged to do their utmost to bring the Uruguay Round negotiations to a successful conclusion.

United States

854. The strengthening of EC-US relations and the stepping-up of bilateral dialogue and consultation, provided for in the Transatlantic Declaration adopted in November 1990,[2] continued throughout the year. The successive Presidents of the Council, Mr Santer and Mr Lubbers, together with Mr Delors, met President Bush on 11 April[3] and 9 November respectively.[4] There were also meetings between EC Foreign Ministers and US Secretary of State, James Baker. The Commission and the US administration met

---

[1]   Bull. EC 7/8-1991, points 1.3.32 and 2.2.2 to 2.2.4.
[2]   Twenty-fourth General Report, point 693.
[3]   Bull. EC 4-1991, point 1.3.29.
[4]   Bull. EC 11-1991, point 1.3.39.

in Brussels on 21 December,[1] the two sides led respectively by Mr Delors and Mr Baker; Mr Lubbers was present at part of the meeting. In addition to these regular meetings, provision for which was included in the Transatlantic Declaration, there were numerous *ad hoc* ministerial-level meetings, and the extensive network of contacts at technical level continued to expand.

At these *ad hoc* meetings, particular emphasis was laid on developing further sectoral cooperation in areas of common interest. The ongoing dialogue on industrial and food standards was expanded to cover new areas such as food labelling and health requirements for fishery products. The meeting between Mr Bangemann and US Secretary of Commerce, Mr Mosbacher, on 21 June[2] emphasized the strengthening of the dialogue and provided an opportunity to identify specific areas for cooperation. Exploratory talks were held to prepare for the negotiation of mutual recognition agreements between the EC and the USA on product testing and certification. Prominent among the new subjects of regular dialogue or active cooperation was competition policy; an agreement aimed at preventing jurisdictional conflict in the application of anti-trust rules was signed on 23 September.[3] Furthermore, a joint declaration on cooperation on securities was signed in September by Sir Leon Brittan on behalf of the Community.[4] Other subjects were data privacy and new technologies, and economic measures to protect the environment. These activities constitute more than exchanges of views and experience. They seek to reduce the number of potential legal and regulatory problems and, in time, to promote greater regulatory convergence. This aim is of special importance in view of the substantial volume of trade in goods and services and of direct investment between the Community and the USA. Collaboration on pre-normative research in science and technology was stepped up, with meetings of the Joint Consultative Group chaired by Mr Pandolfi and Dr Bromley, President Bush's Science Adviser, held in February[5] and November.[6] A number of technical-level discussions in individual sectors also took place.

855.   While the unilateral elements of the US Omnibus Trade and Competitiveness Act of 1988 continued to be a source of concern to the Community,[7] US trade barriers and unfair practices were the subject of a new (1991) Commission report[8] published in April, setting out the difficulties faced by the Community in its economic relations with the USA. These include 'Buy American' restrictions in procurement by the federal and state authorities, 'national security' and other discriminatory provisions applied to foreign

---

[1]   Bull. EC 12-1991.
[2]   Bull. EC 6-1991, point 1.3.35.
[3]   Point 246 of this Report.
[4]   Bull. EC 9-1991, point 1.3.32.
[5]   Bull. EC 1/2-1991, point 1.2.88.
[6]   Bull. EC 11-1991, point 1.2.52.
[7]   Twenty-fourth General Report, point 693.
[8]   Bull. EC 4-1991, point 1.3.30.

investment, US legislation with extraterritorial effect and the fragmentation of the US market in such areas as standards, testing and certificates, and banking and financial services.

856.   As in 1990, the US Administration implemented the Omnibus Trade and Competitiveness Act of 1988 with relative restraint and reaffirmed its commitment to the conclusion of the Uruguay Round multilateral trade negotiations. In June the US Congress extended for another two-year term the authority of the US President to conclude international agreements such as those negotiated within GATT using the 'fast-track' procedure.

857.   A number of trade issues in the telecommunications and information technology sectors were discussed in the Uruguay Round and at bilateral level. Meetings were held at which the EC sought US commitments concerning open procurement by US telecommunications carriers.

The USA has also continued to raise issues relating to access to the single Community market for high-technology products. There have also been consultations, at the Community's request, with a view to ensuring non-discriminatory implementation of the newly extended US-Japan agreement on semiconductors.

In parallel, cooperation on research in information technology is among the areas under examination by the Joint Consultative Group, and US and EC manufacturers made good progress in building up cooperation in the semiconductor sector.

In October a panel established at the Community's request under the GATT procurement code held its first meeting to examine the procurement of a sonar mapping system by the National Science Foundation.

The Community also requested the setting-up of a GATT panel on the US harbour maintenance fee, a measure which discriminates against Community exports.

The trade embargo imposed by the USA on certain Community tuna products was found by a specially established GATT panel to be unlawful.

The USA continued to apply retaliatory measures such as those imposed in January 1989[1] in response to the Directive prohibiting the use in livestock farming of certain substances having a hormonal effect.[2] The removal of certain US slaughterhouses from the approved list allowing exports to the Community was the subject of an exchange of letters in May at ministerial level which set out a programme to resolve this dispute. The agreement concluded in 1987 with the USA following the most recent enlargement

---

[1]   Twenty-third General Report, point 754.
[2]   OJ L 382, 31.12.1985; Nineteenth General Report, point 203.

of the Community, which had been extended for a year at the end of 1990,[1] was reviewed in September, as proposed, and the Community decided independently to extend the agreement for a further year. The USA requested consultations under Article XXIII(1) of the GATT on their exports of corn gluten feed to the Community; a memorandum of understanding on this subject was concluded to resolve the problem, however. In December the Council amended certain measures concerning the Community oilseed arrangements in the light of the panel findings adopted by the GATT Council in January 1990.[2] Bilateral discussions are continuing between the Commission and the US administration on issues relating to a proposed EC-US wine agreement and the protection and recognition of spirit appellations.

858.   On 4 February[3] the Council adopted a decision on the negotiating directives for new arrangements for trade in civil aircraft with the USA and other parties to the GATT.[4]

Japan

859.   The year was marked by closer relations between the Community and Japan as they strove to improve cooperation, particularly in the economic, industrial, scientific and political fields. Several meetings at the highest level were held, which led to the adoption of an EC-Japan joint declaration[5] similar to those governing relations between the Community and the USA[6] and Canada.[7]

860.   In May[8] Mr Delors visited Japan, accompanied by Mr Andriessen. He met the Emperor and the Prime Minister, Mr Kaifu, to whom he expressed his desire that the talks on relations between the Community and Japan should produce substantial results and lead to practical cooperation in a variety of areas.

Sir Leon Brittan, on a visit to Tokyo on 28 February and 1 March,[9] had talks with prominent figures, including the Governor of the Bank of Japan, and the Minister for International Trade and Industry, Mr Nakao. Mr Nakao visited the Commission on 5 June for discussions with Mr Andriessen, Mr Bangemann and Mr Pandolfi.[10]

---

[1]   Twenty-fourth General Report, point 697.
[2]   Point 535 of this Report.
[3]   Bull. EC 1/2-1991, point 1.3.106.
[4]   Twenty-fourth General Report, point 699.
[5]   Bull. EC 7/8-1991, point 1.3.33.
[6]   Twenty-fourth General Report, point 693.
[7]   Twenty-fourth General Report, point 712.
[8]   Bull. EC 5-1991, point 1.3.41.
[9]   Bull. EC 3-1991, point 1.3.26.
[10]   Bull. EC 6-1991, point 1.3.36.

Mr Christophersen met Mr Katsumura, Deputy Minister for Economic Affairs, on 5 February.[1]

861.   On 18 July a first summit meeting was held between the Community and Japan in The Hague,[2] at the end of which a joint declaration on relations between the Community and Japan calling for greater cooperation and dialogue between the two was adopted. The declaration set out the general principles and objectives of the proposed cooperation and dialogue, and proposed annual consultations between the President of the European Council, the President of the Commission and the Prime Minister of Japan to supplement the existing consultative machinery.

Mr Andriessen visited Tokyo on 25 and 26 November to meet ministers in the new Japanese Government. The meetings provided an opportunity to take stock of the international situation and bilateral relations, and to lay down guidelines for future EEC-Japan relations in the spirit of the joint declaration.

862.   The Japanese economy continued to grow, although at a slower pace (3.5%, even 3% in the second half of the year). This expansion was led by domestic demand; net exports made a negative contribution to growth, which meant that Japan's trade surplus with the rest of the world was cut by about a third and the current account by over a half. However, this trend appeared to be going into reverse and the OECD forecast increases in the trade and current account surpluses in 1991 and 1992. The EC trade deficit with Japan, down in 1990 by 8.7% to ECU 23 496 million, worsened again. In the first half of the year it grew by 26.2% as a result of an increase in Japanese exports to the EC (up 9.35%) and a slowdown in EC exports to Japan (lower by 7.55%).

The unresolved issues of market access, agricultural and industrial, and barriers, tariff and non-tariff, continued to be the subject of regular negotiations in the Market Access Group of the Uruguay Round. These problems were also discussed during bilateral meetings between the Commission and the Japanese authorities. A number of bilateral meetings, dealing primarily with leather goods and footwear, were held during the year, with the aim of developing arrangements which would allow the Community industry to expand its sales in Japan considerably.

863.   On 31 July the Community and Japan agreed on a solution for trade in motor vehicles.[3] Its objective is to liberalize the Community market as part of the completion of the single market, while avoiding market distortion by exports from Japan.

---

[1]   Bull. EC 1/2-1991, point 1.3.31.
[2]   Bull. EC 7/8-1991, point 1.3.33.
[3]   Point 1060 of this Report.

864. The Commission continued and stepped up its efforts to promote EC exports to Japan. This second year of the campaign launched in 1990[1] to increase exports in specific sectors of EC industry saw the implementation of a number of practical promotional operations.

The informal discussions with the Japanese authorities aimed at establishing coordination between the Commission's export promotion programme for Japan and the Japanese measures to promote imports into Japan, which started last year,[1] continued at a technical level.

865. On 17 October the 11th series of discussions on competition matters took place in Tokyo between the Commission and representatives of the Fair Trade Commission and the Ministry of International Trade and Industry (MITI). They provided an opportunity for discussion of recent developments in Japanese and Community competition policy and the international dimension of competition issues.

With a view to identifying specific areas of cooperation on the environment, two meetings were held at expert level, one in Brussels in March and a second in Tokyo in June, preparatory to a high-level meeting in January 1992.

The first ever high-level meeting between the Commission and Japan on development aid issues took place in Tokyo on 24 and 25 October. The two sides exchanged views on their respective development assistance policies and on the general framework in which cooperation could take place.

Other industrialized countries

Canada

866. This year marked the 15th anniversary of the signing of the 1976 Framework Agreement for Commercial and Economic Cooperation and the first year of operation of the declaration on EC-Canada relations, which was adopted in November 1990[2] to supplement the 1976 Framework Agreement. A good number of high-level meetings took place in this connection: on 29 January between Mr Andriessen and Luxembourg's Foreign Minister, Mr Poos, and the Canadian Secretary of State, Mr Clark, the first meeting of this nature under the declaration;[3] on 12 April Mr Delors and European Council President, Mr Santer, paid a visit to Ottawa to meet the Prime Minister, Mr

---

[1]   Twenty-fourth General Report, point 709.
[2]   Twenty-fourth General Report, point 712.
[3]   Bull. EC 1/2-1991, point 1.3.34.

Mulroney, [1] the first of the regular meetings between the Canadian Prime Minister and the Presidents of the European Council and the Commission provided for in the declaration. In this connection, Mr Mulroney, Mr Delors and Mr Andriessen met on 17 November. [2] They discussed the Uruguay Round and the situation in Yugoslavia and the Soviet Union. On 12 July [3] the annual ministerial consultations between Canada and the Commission were preceded by the ninth meeting of the Joint Cooperation Committee, set up under the 1976 Framework Agreement. The discussions focused on fisheries problems and the potential for wider cooperation in science and technology. A joint declaration on environmental cooperation was adopted.

867. The Community maintained its position as Canada's second-largest trade and investment partner. Bilateral trade stood at an estimated ECU 18 billion, with a trade surplus of almost ECU 2 billion for the Community. In July the Canadian International Trade Tribunal decided to prolong the countervailing duty that has blocked Community beef and veal exports to Canada since 1986, although in 1987 a GATT panel condemned the duty as contrary to Canadian obligations under the GATT. [4] Talks continued on a possible agreement on reciprocal recognition and protection of wines and spirits appellations. [5] Following the Council's adoption of Regulation (EEC) No 3254/91 providing for a ban from 1 January 1995 on imports of certain fur products from countries, such as Canada, which still use leghold traps or methods not conforming to internationally agreed humane trapping standards at that date, [6] Canada claimed that the deadline had been set too close to allow a phasing-out of these practices.

Fisheries were the focal point of talks and considerable progress was made in finding solutions for the remaining contentious issues.

868. In May [7] the Council approved the conclusion of a Euratom-Canada agreement on the peaceful uses of atomic energy, which was signed in July.

Australia

869. The ninth EC-Australia ministerial consultations, which were held in Canberra on 20 May, [8] highlighted the development of closer bilateral relations as a result of the extension of cooperation to new areas such as science and technology, industry, trade

---

1   Bull. EC 4-1991, point 1.3.32.
2   Bull. EC 11-1991, point 1.3.41.
3   Bull. EC 7/8-1991, point 1.3.36.
4   Twenty-fourth General Report, point 714.
5   Twenty-second General Report, point 910; Twenty-fourth General Report, point 714.
6   Point 656 of this Report.
7   Point 754 of this Report.
8   Bull. EC 5-1991, point 1.3.43.

relations and of the closer consultations on energy, development assistance and the environment. An open exchange of views during the Uruguay Round negotiations showed that both parties were anxious for them to succeed, even though significant differences on agriculture remain. Reform of the common agricultural policy, Australian industrial policy, the completion of the single market and the geopolitical situation in Europe, Asia and the Pacific were also discussed at length. An exchange of letters providing for closer collaboration in the field of the environment was signed by Mr Andriessen and Senator Evans.

870.   Various members of the government visited the Commission: Mr Beddall, Minister for Small Business,[1] Mr Blewett, Minister responsible for trade negotiations, Mr Crean, Minister for Primary Industries and Energy, and Ms Kelly, Minister for the Environment.

New Zealand

871.   Normal good relations between the Community and New Zealand were further consolidated by a visit by Mr Andriessen to New Zealand from 16 to 18 May[2] when he met the Prime Minister, Mr Bolger, the Minister of Foreign Affairs, Mr McKinnon and the Minister of Commerce, Mr Burdon. The discussions focused on the multilateral trade negotiations, agriculture, and reform of the common agricultural policy, which are all issues of importance for New Zealand's economy. With the aim of extending the scope of bilateral relations, Mr Andriessen and the Deputy Prime Minister, Mr McKinnon, signed an arrangement providing for closer cooperation in the fields of science and technology.

South Africa

872.   The Community and its Member States are still committed to a policy of complete abolition of apartheid by peaceful means and its replacement by a democratic system in which all South Africans can participate in peace and harmony, regardless of colour and race. In line with the guidelines set out by the Rome European Council of 15 December 1990,[3] the Community has pursued a policy of encouraging change in South Africa through a gradual review of the existing restrictive measures.

On 25 February representatives of the governments of the Member States meeting within the Council adopted Decision 91/114/EEC lifting the ban on new investment in

---

[1]   Bull. EC 1/2-1991, point 1.3.33.
[2]   Bull. EC 5-1991, point 1.3.44.
[3]   Bull. EC 12-1990, point I.29.

South Africa.[1] Following President De Klerk's initiative in proposing the repeal of the statutory pillars of apartheid, the Group Areas Act and the Land Acts, the Commission adopted on 26 March[2] a draft Decision to repeal trade restrictions on certain steel products and a proposal for a Regulation to repeal trade restrictions on gold coins (Krugerrands), adopted in 1986.[3] On 15 April the Twelve decided in principle to lift these restrictive measures, subject to a reservation pending parliamentary consultations entered by one Member State. Parliament adopted a resolution on the subject on 16 May.[4]

873.   During a visit to Brussels on 10 June,[5] Mr Mandela, Vice-President of the ANC, had talks with Mr Delors on the proposed lifting of sanctions and on the Community's positive measures to aid victims of apartheid.

[1]   OJ L 59, 6.3.1991; Bull. EC 1/2-1991, point 1.3.32.
[2]   Bull. EC 3-1991, point 1.3.27.
[3]   OJ L 268, 19.9.1986, OJ L 305, 31.10.1986.
[4]   OJ C 158, 17.6.1991; Bull. EC 5-1991, point 1.3.42.
[5]   Bull. EC 6-1991, point 1.3.38.

Section 5

Relations with Mediterranean and Middle East countries

Mediterranean countries

874.   Against the backdrop of a worsening economic and political situation in the countries in the region due to the Gulf War, the Commission presented a package of measures to the Council concerning the implementation of the December 1990 decision on a new Mediterranean policy, [1] on which the Economic and Social Committee adopted a second supplementary opinion on 27 November. [2]

875.   On 19 February it adopted a proposal for a Regulation concerning financial cooperation in respect of all the Mediterranean non-member countries, supplementing the financial protocols concluded between the Community and each of the countries involved. [3] On 22 May it adopted a communication on the implementation of trade arrangements [4] and presented a proposal for a Council Regulation amending the arrangements applying to imports into the Community of certain agricultural products originating in Mediterranean non-member countries. [5] On 29 May the Commission put forward a proposal to the Council laying down the rules and arrangements for administering the financial cooperation provided for in the abovementioned protocols. [6]

876.   On 12 July Parliament adopted a resolution calling on the Council to give greater priority to the new Mediterranean policy. [7]

---

[1]   Twenty-fourth General Report, point 718.
[2]   Bull. EC 11-1991, point 1.3.27.
[3]   OJ C 68, 16.3.1991; Bull. EC 1/2-1991, point 1.3.22.
[4]   Bull. EC 5-1991, point 1.3.22.
[5]   Bull. EC 5-1991, point 1.3.23.
[6]   Bull. EC 5-1991, point 1.3.21.
[7]   OJ C 240, 16.9.1991; Bull. EC 7/8-1991, point 1.3.20.

Turkey

877. In line with the Commission's communication of June 1990,[1] relations between the Community and Turkey were given fresh impetus.

878. The focus of discussion of the EC-Turkey Association Council, which met in Brussels on 30 September,[2] was the state of the association since the last meeting of the Council in 1986.[3]

879. The EC-Turkey Joint Parliamentary Committee met in Brussels in March[4] and December and in Istanbul in July. The main topic discussed was the development of relations betwen the Community and Turkey.

880. During his visit to Brussels in July, Mr Ekrem Pakdemirli, Turkish Deputy Prime Minister, met Mr Andriessen and Mr Bangemann. Mr Van Miert visited Turkey in August to discuss cooperation in the field of transport. The proposal for a Decision on the conclusion of a cooperation agreement in the field of medical and health research was approved by Parliament in September.[5] A financing agreement for vocational training programmes was signed on 30 September by Mr Matutes and Mr Safa Giray, Turkish Foreign Minister, who also met Mr Andriessen and Mr Bangemann for an exchange of views on EEC-Turkey relations.

881. Regulation (EEC) No 3557/90[6] on financial assistance for the countries most directly affected by the Gulf crisis was implemented. Of the ECU 105 million allocated by the Community from March onwards to help refugees from Iraq in the aftermath of the war, more than ECU 37 million was committed for use in Turkey or on the border between Turkey and Iraq.

Cyprus

882. Ms Papandreou visited Cyprus on 18 and 19 March to discuss various aspects of bilateral relations.[7] On 25 April Mr Nemitsas, the Cypriot Minister for Commerce and

---

[1] Twenty-fourth General Report, point 719.
[2] Bull. EC 9-1991, point 1.3.31.
[3] Twentieth General Report, point 850.
[4] Bull. EC 3-1991, point 1.3.25.
[5] Point 330 of this Report.
[6] OJ L 347, 12.12.1990; Twenty-fourth General Report, point 734.
[7] Bull. EC 3-1991, point 1.3.22.

Industry, had talks with Mr Andriessen and Mr Matutes in Brussels.[1] They discussed the GATT negotiations and Cyprus' application for accession.[2]

883.   On 19 March Parliament adopted a resolution on the application of UN resolutions on Cyprus.[3] On 12 September[4] it adopted a resolution on the Community's participation in the international conference on the Cyprus question.

Malta

884.   Once Parliament had given its assent, on 17 April,[5] the Council adopted on 25 April[6] Decision 91/246/EEC concerning the conclusion of the protocol extending the first stage of the Association Agreement[7] until 31 December 1991, with an automatic extension beyond that date.

885.   Mr Cardoso e Cunha visited Malta on 11 and 12 July.[8] He met Mr Tabone, President of Malta, and Mr Adami, Prime Minister, with whom he discussed the country's accession to the Community and the development of trade relations between Maltese and Community small businesses. Mr Adami paid a visit to the Commission on 23 July[9] during which he reviewed with Mr Delors the whole gamut of relations between Malta and the Community.

886.   The Commission opened a Delegation in Valletta. The President of Malta, the Prime Minister and the Foreign Minister attended the opening ceremony.

Andorra

887.   On 12 July the EEC-Andorra Joint Committee adopted various decisions designed to implement the provisions of the agreement in the form of an exchange of letters between the Community and the Principality of Andorra, signed in Luxembourg on 28 June 1990.[10]

---

[1]   Bull. EC 4-1991, point 1.3.21.
[2]   Twenty-fourth General Report, point 722.
[3]   OJ C 106, 22.4.1991; Bull. EC 3-1991, point 1.3.23.
[4]   OJ C 267, 14.10.1991; Bull. EC 9-1991, point 1.3.27.
[5]   OJ C 129, 20.5.1991; Bull. EC 4-1991, point 1.3.23.
[6]   OJ L 116, 9.5.1991; Bull. EC 4-1991, point 1.3.23; Commission proposal: OJ C 311, 12.12.1990; Twenty-fourth General Report, point 725.
[7]   OJ L 61, 14.3.1971; Fifth General Report, point 410.
[8]   Bull. EC 7/8-1991, point 1.3.26.
[9]   Bull. EC 7/8-1991, point 1.3.27.
[10]   Twenty-fourth General Report, point 726.

Yugoslavia

888.   Relations wih Yugoslavia have been severely affected by the serious crisis there.[1] Owing to the uncertainty surrounding the future of the Yugoslav Federation following the declarations of independence by Slovenia and Croatia, the third financial protocol,[2] which was signed in Brussels on 24 June, has not been sent to Parliament and the procedure for concluding the agreement has been suspended, as have cooperation under the second financial protocol and technical assistance schemes provided for under Phare.[3]

889.   The worsening political and institutional crisis in Yugoslavia, the continuing civil war, which the UN Security Council described as a threat to international peace and security, the effects of the civil war on economic and trade relations, both between the Yugoslav republics and with the Community, led the Council and the representatives of the Member States on 11 November[4] to suspend the application of EEC[5] and ECSC agreements with Yugoslavia with immediate effect. As a result of this decision the trade concessions provided for by the agreements were suspended. Yugoslavia was also withdrawn from the list of beneficiary countries under the system of generalized preferences. On 25 November the Council denounced the agreements in accordance with the procedure provided for by them.[6]

890.   On 2 December, in order to offset the adverse effects of these measures on those republics which had cooperated in seeking a political solution during the Hague Conference on Yugoslavia, the Council and the representatives of the Member States adopted corrective positive measures: most of the preferential arrangements established under the Cooperation Agreement were restored for Bosnia-Hercegovina, Croatia, Macedonia and Slovenia.[7] The Council also called on the Commission to resume the technical assistance intended for Yugoslavia under the Phare programme with these four republics. The Council similarly called on the European Investment Bank to resume with these four republics the financial cooperation provided for under the second EC-Yugoslavia financial protocol. On 17 December the Commission presented a proposal to the Council to re-establish the generalized tariff preferences for agricultural products in respect of the four republics and it also adopted a decision on financing a European emergency aid plan for victims of the fighting.[8]

---

[1]   Point 1093 of this Report.
[2]   Bull. EC 6-1991, point 1.3.29.
[3]   Point 818 of this Report.
[4]   OJ L 315, 15.11.1991; Bull. EC 11-1991, point 1.3.20.
[5]   OJ L 41, 14.2.1983.
[6]   OJ L 325, 27.11.1991; Bull. EC 11-1991, point 1.3.21.
[7]   OJ L 342, 12.12.1991; Bull. EC 12-1991.
[8]   Bull. EC 12-1991.

891.   On 14 November the Culture Ministers of the Member States meeting within the Council published a declaration on conserving Yugoslavia's cultural heritage.[1]

892.   Parliament adopted resolutions on the situation in Yugoslavia on 11 September,[2] 10 October,[3] and 22 November.[4]

San Marino

893.   On the basis of the negotiating directives adopted by the Council,[5] a draft agreement providing for the establishment of a customs union between the two sides was initialled in Brussels on 4 July.[6] It includes provisions in the area of cooperation and in the social field.

894.   On 4 November[7] the Commission adopted a proposal for a Decision on the conclusion of the agreement, which was signed on 16 December.

Maghreb (Algeria, Morocco, Tunisia),
Mashreq (Egypt, Jordan, Lebanon and Syria) and Israel,
West Bank and Gaza Strip (the Occupied Territories)

895.   Implementation of the third financial protocols continued satisfactorily.[8] As at 31 December the bulk of the funds earmarked under the protocols, namely ECU 1 215 million, i.e. 75% of the total ECU 1 618 million, had been allocated through financing decisions. The protocol with Syria was signed in Brussels on 7 February[9] but has not yet been implemented since Parliament has not given its assent to the proposal on the conclusion of the protocol.[10] Israel is entitled only to EIB loans under its financial protocol, but cooperation activities were also financed, as in previous years, from Community budget funds. In view of the new political climate created by the end of the Gulf War, the Commission resumed normal relations with Israel in the field of scientific cooperation, which had been partially suspended in 1990[11] because of the closure by the Israeli authorities of universities in the Occupied Territories.

[1]   Bull. EC 11-1991, point 1.3.25.
[2]   OJ C 267, 4.10.1991; Bull. EC 9-1991, point 1.3.25.
[3]   OJ C 280, 28.10.1991; Bull. EC 10-1991, point 1.3.16.
[4]   OJ C 326, 16.12.1991; Bull. EC 11-1991, point 1.3.24.
[5]   Twenty-fourth General Report, point 727.
[6]   Bull. EC 7/8-1991, point 1.3.28.
[7]   OJ C 302, 22.11.1991; Bull. EC 11-1991, point 1.3.35.
[8]   Twenty-second General Report, point 928.
[9]   Bull. EC 1/2-1991, point 1.3.26.
[10]   OJ C 16, 24.1.1990; Twenty-fourth General Report, point 729.
[11]   Twenty-fourth General Report, point 729.

TABLE 11

Third financial protocols

Breakdown at 31 December 1990 of financing decisions in respect of the
Maghreb and Mashreq countries and Israel (Commission and EIB)

Sector	Amount (million ECU)	%
Agriculture	272	22.4
Energy	97	8.0
Industry	326	26.8
Distributive trades	19	1.6
Infrastructure	425	35.0
Education and training[1]	43	3.5
Health and environment	10	0.8
Scientific cooperation	23	1.9
Total	1 215	100.0

[1] Project-linked training operations are included in the relevant project sector.

896. During the course of the year the fourth financial protocols were negotiated and signed with the Maghreb and Mashreq countries and Israel,[1] in accordance with the Council's comprehensive decision on implementing the Community's new Mediterranean policy.[2]

897. On 22 July[3] the Council adopted Decision 91/408/EEC on financial aid for Israel and the Palestinian population of the Occupied Territories, which is intended to alleviate the adverse effects of the Gulf War. It takes the form of a loan of ECU 160 million and interest-rate subsidies of ECU 27.5 million for Israel and grants totalling ECU 60 million for the Palestinian population of the Occupied Territories.

898. Besides this special assistance, the Community continued its development aid programme for the Occupied Territories, which this year amounted to some ECU 10 million.[4] This direct aid is in addition to that already channelled via the UNRWA, which was also substantially increased owing to the particularly difficult

---

[1] Bull. EC 6-1991, point 1.3.26.
[2] Twenty-fourth General Report, point 718.
[3] OJ L 227, 15.8.1991; Bull. EC 7/8-1991, point 1.3.19; Commission proposal: OJ C 68, 16.3.1991; Bull. EC 1/2-1991, point 1.3.23; OJ C 111, 26.4.1991; Bull. EC 4-1991, point 1.3.19.
[4] Bull. EC 5-1991, point 1.3.38.

TABLE 12

Fourth financial protocols

(million ECU)

Country	Budget resources		EIB loans		Total	
	Amount	Growth (%)	Amount	Growth (%)	Amount	Growth (%)
Morocco	218	+ 26	220	+ 46	438	+ 35
Algeria	70	+ 25	280	+ 53	350	+ 46
Tunisia	116	+ 25	168	+ 28	284	+ 27
Egypt	258	+ 29	310	+ 24	568	+ 27
Jordan	46	+ 24	80	+ 27	126	+ 26
Syria	43	+ 19	115	+ 5	158	+ 8
Lebanon	24	+ 20	45	− 15	69	− 5
Israel	—	—	82	+ 30	82	+ 30
Total	775	+ 26	1 300	+ 30	2 075	+ 28

economic situation in the region. In this connection, in order to promote agricultural exports to the Community, which until then had come under the preferential arrangements introduced in 1986,[1] on 29 April the Council adopted Regulation (EEC) No 1134/91 improving these arrangements as from 1 January 1992.[2]

899. On 10 September Parliament adopted a resolution on this issue.[3]

900. Following the Luxembourg European Council's agreement in June, on 23 September the Council adopted Decision 91/510/EEC granting a medium-term loan to Algeria for balance-of-payments support.[4] On 11 July Parliament adopted a resolution on the development of democracy in Algeria.[5]

901. The ninth meeting of the EEC-Israel Cooperation Council,[6] the first meeting of the EEC-Jordan Cooperation Council[7] and the seventh meeting of the EEC-Egypt Cooperation Council[8] were held in Brussels in May, November and December respectively.

---

[1] OJ L 306, 1.11.1986.
[2] OJ L 112, 4.5.1991; Bull. EC 4-1991, point 1.3.28; Commission proposal: Bull. EC 1/2-1991, point 1.3.25.
[3] OJ C 267, 14.10.1991; Bull. EC 9-1991, point 1.3.30.
[4] Point 77 of this Report.
[5] OJ C 240, 16.9.1991; Bull. EC 7/8-1991, point 1.3.24.
[6] Bull. EC 5-1991, point 1.3.26.
[7] Bull. EC 11-1991, point 1.3.31.
[8] Bull. EC 12-1991.

902.   Mr Delors paid an official visit to Egypt in November[1] and Mr Matutes to Israel in July[2] and to Kuwait in November.[3] During the year the Commission played host to Mr Boussena, Algerian Minister for Industry and Mines, Mr Filali,[4] Moroccan Minister for Foreign Affairs, Mr Alaoui, Moroccan Minister for Mines and Energy, Mr Benyahia, Tunisian Minister for Foreign Affairs,[5] Mr Ganzouri, Egyptian Deputy Prime Minister, Mr Makramallah, Egyptian Minister for International Cooperation, Mr al-Shara,[6] Syrian Minister for Foreign Affairs and Mr Baqjaji,[7] Syrian Minister for Planning.

903.   On 4 November the Foreign Ministers of the Community and the Arab Maghreb Union met informally for the second time in Brussels.[8] The two sides decided to strengthen relations and institutionalize their meetings, which will now be held at political level at least twice a year.

904.   Parliament adopted resolutions on the situation of the Western Sahara on 18 April[9] and 12 September.[10]

Middle East countries

905.   At the end of the opening session of the Middle East Peace Conference, held in Madrid from 30 October to 14 November, the Community was given a leading role in the multilateral negotiations which will take place subsequently.[11]

906.   The second meeting of the Joint Cooperation Council established by the Cooperation Agreement[12] between the European Economic Community and the States of the Gulf Cooperation Council (GCC) was held in Luxembourg on 11 May.[13] There was a comprehensive exchange of views on the role of international cooperation, in particular between the Community and the GCC, with regard to development aid for the Arab world. The two sides resolved to give fresh impetus to their relations, for example in

---

[1]   Bull. EC 11-1991, point 1.3.28.
[2]   Bull. EC 7/8-1991, point 1.3.25.
[3]   Bull. EC 11-1991, point 1.3.37.
[4]   Bull. EC 6-1991, point 1.3.27.
[5]   Bull. EC 5-1991, point 1.3.29.
[6]   Bull. EC 5-1991, point 1.3.40.
[7]   Bull. EC 3-1991, point 1.3.24.
[8]   Bull. EC 11-1991, point 1.3.36.
[9]   OJ C 129, 20.5.1991; Bull. EC 4-1991, point 1.3.24.
[10]   OJ C 267, 14.10.1991; Bull. EC 9-1991, point 1.3.29.
[11]   Bull. EC 10-1991, point 1.3.15.
[12]   OJ L 54, 25.2.1989; Twenty-third General Report, point 814.
[13]   Bull. EC 5-1991, point 2.3.1.

the field of energy and industrial cooperation, which would be given practical expression at the second industrial conference in Doha (Qatar) at the beginning of 1992.[1]

907.   Negotiations with a view to a free trade agreement continued on the basis of new directives adopted by the Council on 1 October[2] following a communication from the Commission on 30 May.[3]

908.   The complete embargo on trade with Iraq and Kuwait[4] was maintained throughout the duration of the war. On 4 March, following the liberation of Kuwait, and in the framework of UN Security Council resolutions, the Council adopted Regulation (EEC) No 542/91 raising the embargo on trade with Kuwait;[5] Decision 91/125/ECSC was also adopted as regards products subject to the ECSC Treaty.[6] On 27 March Regulation (EEC) No 542/91 was amended by Regulation (EEC) No 811/91, which introduced the possibility, under tight control, of supplying products intended strictly for medical purposes.[7] The embargo was relaxed following Iraq's acceptance of the terms of UN Security Council Resolution 687 concerning cease-fire conditions and in view of the deterioriating situation of the civilian population. Regulation (EEC) No 1194/91[8] and Decision 91/265/ECSC[9] were adopted to allow trade in foodstuffs and basic necessities with the civilian population and to authorize Iraqi oil exports so that Iraq could pay for the purchase of the products authorized.

On 12 July the Commission presented a proposal to the Council to adopt a Regulation prohibiting the honouring of Iraqi claims with regard to contracts and transactions affected by UN Security Council Resolution 661 in respect of the embargo, thereby ruling out any retroactive compensation for Iraq for the adverse effects of the embargo.[10]

909.   On 8 April, in the first few weeks after the end of the war an informal meeting of the European Council was held in Luxembourg.[11] The Council decided to provide ECU 150 million of emergency aid for the Kurdish and other refugees in the region, ECU 100 million of which would come from the Community budget. On 16 April the Commission decided to establish an appropriation for this amount,[12] supplementing the ECU 5 million of emergency aid already allocated on 3 April.[13]

---

[1]   Twenty-fourth General Report, point 733.
[2]   Bull. EC 10-1991, point 1.3.17.
[3]   Bull. EC 5-1991, point 1.3.33.
[4]   OJ L 213, 9.8.1990; OJ L 304, 1.11.1990; Twenty-fourth General Report, point 734.
[5]   OJ L 60, 7.3.1991; Bull. EC 3-1991, point 1.3.15.
[6]   OJ L 60, 7.3.1991; Bull. EC 3-1991, point 1.3.16.
[7]   OJ L 83, 28.3.1991; Bull. EC 3-1991, point 1.3.17; Commission proposal: Bull. EC 3-1991, point 1.3.17.
[8]   OJ L 115, 8.5.1991; Bull. EC 5-1991, point 1.3.35; Commission proposal: Bull. EC 4-1991, point 1.3.16.
[9]   OJ L 127, 23.5.1991; Bull. EC 5-1991, point 1.3.34.
[10] OJ C 204, 3.8.1991; Bull. EC 7/8-1991, point 1.3.21.
[11] Bull. EC 4-1991, point 1.3.13.
[12] Bull. EC 4-1991, point 1.3.15.
[13] Bull. EC 4-1991, point 1.3.14.

910. The Community also played a full part in anti-pollution operations in the Gulf.[1]

911. Throughout the year Parliament continued to adopt resolutions on the situation in the Gulf and the consequences of the war.[2]

Euro-Arab Dialogue

912. The decisions taken by the Euro-Arab ministerial conference in Paris in December 1989[3] and the General Committee of the Euro-Arab Dialogue in Dublin in June 1990[4] to reactivate the Dialogue were suspended because of the Gulf War and changes which had taken place within the Arab League. Work should resume shortly, the Arab side having made it quite clear that it does not wish to break off the Dialogue again, to which both it and the Community attach the greatest importance.

---

[1] Point 617 of this Report.
[2] OJ C 48, 25.2.1991; Bull. EC 1/2-1991, point 1.3.27; OJ C 72, 18.3.1991; Bull. EC 1/2-1991, points 1.3.28 and 1.3.29; OJ C 106, 22.4.1991; Bull. EC 3-1991, point 1.3.18; OJ C 129, 20.5.1991; Bull. EC 4-1991, point 1.3.17; OJ C 140, 16.9.1991; Bull. EC 7/8-1991, point 1.3.22; OJ C 326, 16.12.1991; Bull. EC 11-1991, point 1.3.38.
[3] Twenty-third General Report, point 816.
[4] Twenty-fourth General Report, point 736.

Section 6

Relations with the countries of Asia and Latin America

Asia

South Asia

913.   The successful transition to democracy of Bangladesh, with its 110 million inhabitants the largest of the LLDCs, has intensified relations with the Community.

The Community made substantial commitments to the relief and rehabilitation efforts of the new government following the catastrophic cyclone of 29 and 30 April. In line with the conclusions adopted on 14 May,[1] a decision was taken by the representatives of the Member States meeting within the Council to allocate special aid of ECU 60 million in addition to food aid and emergency aid granted under other headings.[2] Substantial Community resources were also provided in support of new investment in cyclone protection and cyclone shelters and to alleviate the macroeconomic impact on the country of the cyclone and the Gulf War. Parliament expressed its solidarity with the victims on 16 May.[3]

In October, an EC fact-finding mission of ministerial representatives led by the Netherlands Minister for Development Cooperation, Mr Jan Pronk, representing the Presidency of the Council, visited Bangladesh. It discussed with the new democratic government the role of Community assistance following the disaster.

914.   On 13 June, following the assassination of Mr Rajiv Gandhi, Parliament condemned terrorism and political violence in India and saluted the government's determination to continue with the elections.[4] Mr Andriessen visited India from 25 to 29 October and had talks with Prime Minister P.V. Narasimha Rao.[5] The discussions mainly concerned the Uruguay Round, intellectual property and the implementation of textile agreements.

---

[1]   Bull. EC 5-1991, point 1.3.47.
[2]   Points 1015 and 1020 of this Report.
[3]   OJ C 158, 17.6.1991; Bull. EC 5-1991, point 1.3.48.
[4]   OJ C 183, 15.7.1991; Bull. EC 6-1991, point 1.3.41.
[5]   Bull. EC 10-1991, point 1.3.22.

915.   On 21 February Parliament adopted a resolution on the earthquake in Pakistan and Afghanistan.[1]

Association of South-East Asian Nations

916.   The ninth meeting of the EEC-Asean Joint Cooperation Committee took place in Kuala Lumpur in February, preceded by two subgroup meetings on trade and on science and technology. The participants noted the expansion of EC-Asean trade and the large number of activities and programmes undertaken since the previous Committee meeting in 1988.[2] Agreement was reached on the need to strengthen industrial and investment cooperation between the Community and Asean.

917.   The ninth annual meeting of Asean and Community Foreign Ministers was held in Luxembourg on 30 and 31 May, followed on 1 June by a special meeting of ministers responsible for economic affairs. At this meeting, at which the Commission was represented by Mr Matutes, the ministers took stock of their bilateral relations and exchanged views on various regional and international political issues. Ministers agreed to negotiate a new cooperation agreement, taking into account the changes which had taken place since the signing of the 1980 Agreement.[3] The issues of human rights and the environment (particularly tropical forests) were also discussed at length.

918.   In July, at the Asean post-ministerial conference held in Kuala Lumpur following the 24th ministerial meeting of the Asean countries, the Community participated for the first time as a full dialogue partner in debates on Asian and Pacific matters.[4] In this context, Mr Matutes was able to speak on behalf of the Community in the plenary session, both on prospects for trade and economic relations with the Pacific region and on the Community's relations with the South Pacific. Mr Matutes welcomed the Thai Prime Minister's proposal for an Asean free trade area by 2000 and stated the Commission's readiness to cooperate with Asean on this issue provided that the move contributed to strengthening the open multilateral trading system. The content of the new cooperation agreement was also discussed and the meeting resulted in a better understanding of the two parties' positions.

919.   Mr Matutes paid an official visit to the Philippines on 15 and 16 May to inaugurate, in the presence of President Corazon Aquino, the Commission's new Delegation in Manila.[5] On 30 October, meanwhile, Mr Andriessen visited Malaysia, where he

---

[1]   OJ C 72, 18.3.1991; Bull. EC 1/2-1991, point 1.3.35.
[2]   Twenty-second General Report, point 942.
[3]   OJ L 144, 10.6.1980; Twenty-fourth General Report, point 690.
[4]   Bull. EC 7/8-1991, point 1.3.37.
[5]   Bull. EC 5-1991, point 1.3.51.

discussed problems concerning the Uruguay Round and the protection of intellectual property with members of the Malaysian Government.[1]

920. Mr Matutes also visited Singapore on 17 May and met Mr Wong Kan Seng, Singapore's Foreign Minister, and Mr Mah Bow Tan, Minister for Trade and Industry.[2] He discussed with them various proposals by Singapore for economic cooperation, preference being ultimately given to a scheme for setting up an EEC-Singapore regional environmental protection centre.

From 30 October to 2 November Mr Matutes visited Indonesia, where he had talks on economic development and the management of the country's forestry resources.[3]

921. On 12 September, Parliament adopted a resolution on the need for cooperation with the Asean countries to be stepped up and supplemented with a more precisely targeted bilateral approach including the protection of the environment and tropical forests.[4]

China

922. Relations with China developed during the year in line with the Twelve's decision of 22 October 1990 on progressive normalization of bilateral relations,[5] after the Madrid European summit had imposed sanctions against China following the events there in June 1989.[6]

923. A meeting of the EEC-China Joint Committee was held on 23 and 24 October in Beijing with Mr Andriessen and the Minister for Foreign Economic Relations and Trade, Mr Li Lanqing, as co-chairmen. Its main theme was the Community's growing trade deficit with China, and particularly the fall in imports from the Community. A memorandum on cooperation in the information technology and telecommunications sectors was also signed. Mr Andriessen also held talks with the Prime Minister, Mr Li Peng, in which he raised the question of respect for human rights in China. High-level talks between Mr Andriessen and Mr Li Lanqing also took place during the visit. China's Deputy Prime Minister, Mr Zhu Rongji, visited the Commission on 12 April,[7] followed by the Deputy Foreign Minister, Mr Tian Zengpei, on 10 June.[8]

---

[1] Bull. EC 10-1991, point 1.3.23.
[2] Bull. EC 5-1991, point 1.3.52.
[3] Bull. EC 11-1991, point 1.3.42.
[4] OJ C 267, 14.10.1991; Bull. EC 9-1991, point 1.3.33.
[5] Twenty-fourth General Report, point 745.
[6] Twenty-third General Report, point 828.
[7] Bull. EC 4-1991, point 1.3.35.
[8] Bull. EC 6-1991, point 1.3.39.

924.   An EEC-China biotechnology centre was inaugurated in Beijing on 1 November.

Korea

925.   At the seventh round of high-level talks[1] between the Commission and the Republic of Korea in Seoul on 27 May, the Community delegation was headed by Mr Andriessen and the Korean delegation by the Foreign Minister, Mr Lee Sang Ock.[2] The discussions mainly concerned the protection of intellectual property, international matters of common interest such as the Uruguay Round negotiations, and developments in Eastern and Central Europe and in the Korean peninsula.

926.   Intellectual property was also the principal topic of discussions between Mr Andriessen and the President of the Republic, Mr Roh Tae Woo. On 29 October the Commission was authorized by the Council to negotiate an agreement on this subject with Korea.[3] On 6 December the Commission adopted a proposal for a decision concerning the agreement in the form of an exchange of letters.[4]

On 3 December the Commission proposed that the Council lift the suspension of generalized preferences which had been applied to Korea because of its discrimination against the Community.[5]

927.   Bilateral meetings took place in Seoul in March between Sir Leon Brittan and the Deputy Prime Minister and Minister responsible for Economic Planning, Mr Choi Gak Kyu, the Foreign Minister, Mr Lee Sang Ock, the Trade and Industry Minister, Mr Lee Pong Suh, and the Finance Minister, Mr Chung Young Eui.[6] Trade and Industry Minister Mr Lee Pong Suh in turn met Mr Andriessen and Sir Leon Brittan in Brussels on 24 and 25 June.[7]

Other Asian countries

928.   Following the decision to set up a joint programme for the repatriation and reintegration of Vietnamese asylum-seekers returning to Viet Nam from their first countries of asylum in South-East Asia,[8] the Commission adopted a financing decision

---

[1]   Sixth round: Twenty-third General Report, point 830.
[2]   Bull. EC 5-1991, point 1.3.49.
[3]   Bull. EC 10-1991, 1.2.38.
[4]   Bull. EC 12-1991.
[5]   OJ C 334, 28.12.1991; Bull. EC 12-1991.
[6]   Bull. EC 3-1991, point 1.3.29.
[7]   Bull. EC 6-1991, point 1.3.40.
[8]   Twenty-fourth General Report, point 748.

for the programme on 15 February[1] and work started in April. The programme was endorsed in May at the fourth meeting of the Steering Committee for the International Conference on Indochinese Refugees and an expanded programme for the years 1992 to 1994 was put before the members of the Conference in October. In April the Commission invited a group of 12 Vietnamese officials to a special training course on Community institutions and a workshop on the Community was held in Hanoi in September.

929.   Mr Andriessen visited Hong Kong on 28 May[2] and met the Governor, Sir David Wilson, for further talks on the Uruguay Round negotiations.[3]

930.   On 25 November, the Council authorized the Commission to negotiate an agreement on trade and economic cooperation with the Mongolian People's Republic.[4]

Trade arrangements for Asian State-trading countries

931.   Imports from Asian State-trading countries (China, North Korea, Mongolia and Viet Nam) of products not liberalized at Community level continued to be subject to arrangements differing substantially from one Member State to another, as it had not yet proved possible to harmonize all the import arrangements for such products. The import quotas to be opened by the Member States in 1991 were set by the Council on 11 November.[5]

Latin America

Relations with regional bodies

932.   The first institutionalized ministerial conference between the Community and its Member States and the Rio Group[6] was held in Luxembourg on 26 and 27 April.[7] It formed part of the political dialogue between the two regions which was launched by the declaration adopted in Rome on 20 December 1990.[8] At the close of the conference a political and economic communiqué was adopted.

---

[1]   Bull. EC 1/2-1991, point 1.3.36.
[2]   Bull. EC 5-1991, point 1.3.50.
[3]   Previous talks: Twenty-fourth General Report, point 747.
[4]   Bull. EC 11-1991, point 1.3.43.
[5]   OJ L 369, 31.12.1991; Bull. EC 11-1991, point 1.3.86.
[6]   Argentina, Brazil, Bolivia, Chile, Colombia, Ecuador, Mexico, Paraguay, Peru, Uruguay and Venezuela.
[7]   Bull. EC 4-1991, point 1.3.34.
[8]   Twenty-fourth General Report, point 750.

933. Continuing the dialogue begun in San José, Costa Rica, in 1984,[1] the seventh ministerial conference (San José VII) between the Community and its Member States and the countries of Central America and Panama, with Colombia, Mexico and Venezuela as cooperating countries, was held in Managua, Nicaragua, on 18 and 19 March.[2] At the close of the conference, a joint political declaration and a joint economic communiqué were adopted. Community aid (all aid combined) to Central America under the 1986 Agreement[3] reached a total of ECU 117 million, the highest so far. The Joint Committee set up by the Agreement held its fifth meeting in Brussels on 25 and 26 November.

Two ministerial meetings were held in New York on 26 September during the session of the United Nations General Assembly, one between the Community and the Rio Group, the other between the Troika and Ministers from Central America.

934. On 11 March the Commission adopted a Decision approving an exchange of letters formalizing relations with the Secretariat of the Latin American Integration Association (LAIA) in the fields of technical cooperation, consultation and exchanges of information, and cultural cooperation.[4]

935. Following in the footsteps of LAIA, the OAS[5] and the ILCA,[6] the Latin American Council of the Latin American Economic System (SELA) granted the European Community permanent observer status.

936. The Commission began work in preparation for the third EEC-Andean Pact Joint Committee meeting and on the negotiating directives for a new and expanded cooperation agreement.

937. During an official visit on 29 April by the Foreign Ministers of the Mercosur (Southern Cone Common Market) Group[7] and the Secretary-General of LAIA, the Commission reiterated its support for the process of integration in the Southern Cone and decided to conclude an interinstitutional agreement on technical assistance between the Commission and the relevant body of Mercosur, following the ratification of the Treaty of Asunción establishing a common market between the countries concerned.

938. On 16 December[8] the Council amended Council Regulation (EEC) No 3833/90[9] on the tariff preference arrangements applied to Colombia, Bolivia, Ecuador and Peru,

---

[1]   Eighteenth General Report, point 707.
[2]   Bull. EC 3-1991, point 1.3.28.
[3]   OJ L 172, 30.6.1986; Twentieth General Report, point 889.
[4]   Bull. EC 3-1991, point 1.3.30.
[5]   Organization of American States.
[6]   Instituto Latinoamericano de la Cooperación para la Agricultura.
[7]   Paraguay, Brazil, Uruguay and Argentina.
[8]   Bull. EC 12-1991; Commission proposal: OJ C 194, 25.7.1991; Bull. EC 6-1991, point 1.3.56.
[9]   OJ L 308, 8.11.1991; Twenty-fourth General Report, point 758.

extending them to Costa Rica, El Salvador, Guatemala, Honduras, Nicaragua and Panama for a period of three years.

939.   Parliament passed a resolution on 22 February calling on the Commission to step up its development aid programmes and cooperation with Central American regional organizations and institutions. [1]

Bilateral relations

940.   The first meeting of the Joint Committee set up under the trade and cooperation Agreement with Argentina[2] was held in Buenos Aires in December.

941.   On his visit to Bolivia in April,[3] Mr Matutes confirmed the Community's decision to support the Bolivian Government in implementing the development plan it had drawn up.

942.   While in Central America for the ministerial conference in Managua,[4] Mr Matutes paid visits to Costa Rica, Guatemala, El Salvador and Nicaragua.[5] On a visit to the Commission in February, Nicaragua's President Violeta Chamorro discussed the external debt problems facing Nicaragua.[6]

943.   On a visit to Strasbourg on 16 and 17 April,[7] Chile's President Patricio Aylwin met the Presidents of the European Parliament, the Council and the Commission, and also Mr Matutes, and expressed satisfaction at the forthcoming entry into force of the framework cooperation agreement between the Community and Chile,[8] following its endorsement by Parliament[9] in February and the Decision on its conclusion in March.[10] The first meeting of the Joint Committee took place in Santiago in December.[11] Parliament adopted two resolutions, one on economic relations between the Community and Chile,[12] and the other on the disastrous effects of the heavy rains in the north of the country.[13]

[1]   OJ C 72, 18.3.1991; Bull. EC 1/2-1991, point 1.3.37.
[2]   OJ L 295, 26.10.1990; Twenty-fourth General Report, point 759.
[3]   Bull. EC 4-1991, point 1.3.37.
[4]   Point 933 of this Report.
[5]   Bull. EC 3-1991, point 1.3.32.
[6]   Bull. EC 1/2-1991, point 1.3.42.
[7]   Bull. EC 4-1991, point 1.3.38.
[8]   Twenty-fourth General Report, point 760.
[9]   OJ C 72, 18.3.1991; Bull. EC 1/2-1991, point 1.3.38.
[10]   OJ L 79, 26.3.1991; Bull. EC 3-1991, point 1.3.31.
[11]   Bull. EC 12-1991.
[12]   OJ C 72, 18.3.1991; Bull. EC 1/2-1991, point 1.3.39.
[13]   OJ C 240, 16.9.1991; Bull. EC 7/8-1991, point 1.3.41.

The President of Venezuela, Mr Carlos Andrés Pérez, paid an official visit to the Commission on 27 May, during which various matters of common interest were raised.[1]

944.   Bilateral relations between the Community and Ecuador were discussed during a visit to the Commission by President Rodrigo Borja in February,[2] and Parliament adopted a resolution on the disastrous situation in the Pastaza area.[3]

945.   A framework cooperation agreement between the Community and Mexico was initialled in Brussels on 13 February, signed in Luxembourg on 26 April[4] and concluded by the Council on 7 October.[5] This third-generation agreement, which expands prospects for cooperation in a large number of fields, was endorsed by Parliament in September,[6] when it also adopted a resolution on economic relations between the Community and Mexico.[7]

946.   In April Mr Matutes paid a visit to Peru, where he met President Alberto Fujimori.[8] Mr Fujimori, in return, paid an official visit to the Commission in October.[9] In February Parliament called for humanitarian and economic aid to be given following the cholera epidemic;[10] the Commission allocated some ECU 2 million in emergency aid.[11]

947.   Acting on a mandate from the Council,[12] the Commission conducted negotiations with the Government of Paraguay with a view to concluding a framework agreement, which was initialled on 15 July,[13] and on 7 November it proposed that the Council conclude the agreement.[14] During the first official visit by a member of the Paraguayan Government to the Commission, in September,[15] the Minister for Industry and Commerce, Mr Ubaldo Scavone, sought support for industrial restructuring being undertaken in Paraguay.

948.   In October Parliament passed a resolution on the peace process under way in El Salvador.[16]

---

[1]   Bull. EC 5-1991; point 1.3.45.
[2]   Bull. EC 1/2-1991, point 1.3.40.
[3]   OJ C 240, 16.9.1991; Bull. EC 7/8-1991, point 1.3.42.
[4]   Bull. EC 4-1991, point 1.3.39.
[5]   OJ L 340, 11.12.1991; Bull. EC 10-1991, point 1.3.24.
[6]   OJ C 267, 14.10.1991; Bull. EC 9-1991, point 1.3.34.
[7]   OJ C 267, 14.10.1991; Bull. EC 9-1991, point 1.3.35.
[8]   Bull. EC 4-1991, point 1.3.40.
[9]   Bull. EC 10-1991, point 1.3.21.
[10]   OJ C 72, 18.3.1991; Bull. EC 1/2-1991, point 1.3.43.
[11]   Point 1020 of this Report.
[12]   Bull. EC 3-1991, point 1.3.34.
[13]   Bull. EC 7/8-1991, point 1.3.43.
[14]   OJ C 309, 29.11.1991; Bull. EC 11-1991, point 1.3.48.
[15]   Bull. EC 9-1991, point 1.3.36.
[16]   OJ C 280, 28.10.1991; Bull. EC 10-1991, point 1.3.25.

949.   A new, third-generation framework agreement on cooperation with Uruguay was signed on 4 November in Brussels,[1] on the occasion of a visit by Uruguay's Foreign Minister, Mr Hector Gros. The agreement was negotiated by the Commission in accordance with the directives given to it by the Council,[2] and had been initialled in June.[3]

Cooperation with the countries of Asia and Latin America

950.   Following the Council agreement in December 1990, new guidelines proposed by the Commission to improve financial and technical cooperation instruments[4] entered into force in 1991, providing for a significant increase in overall Community assistance from 1991 to 1996. Putting these guidelines into effect, the Commission sent a proposal to the Council in April[5] for replacing Council Regulation (EEC) No 442/81,[6] which focuses exclusively on financial and technical aid. Following Parliament's opinion on 10 September,[7] the Commission modified its proposal on 9 October to take account of the amendments proposed, in particular concerning the environment and cooperation on science and technology.[8] The Council endorsed the proposal on 28 November.[9]

951.   Financial and technical cooperation with Latin America, which represents the main instrument of aid to the region, amounted to ECU 133.3 million. The main economic cooperation activities were geared to trade promotion (ECU 5.7 million) and training (ECU 8.2 million); ECU 2 million was devoted to regional integration, ECU 3.8 million to energy cooperation, ECU 5.5 million to investment promotion, ECU 10 million to aid for the development of democracy in the region, and ECU 15.6 million to supporting voluntary repatriation programmes for refugees returning to Nicaragua, Guatemala and El Salvador, and also a programme for repatriation to Chile.

[1]   Bull. EC 11-1991, point 1.3.49.
[2]   Bull. EC 3-1991, point 1.3.35.
[3]   Bull. EC 6-1991, point 1.3.44.
[4]   Twenty-fourth General Report, point 763.
[5]   OJ C 119, 4.5.1991; Bull. EC 4-1991, point 1.3.41.
[6]   OJ L 48, 21.2.1981; Fifteenth General Report, point 674.
[7]   OJ C 267, 14.10.1991; Bull. EC 9-1991, point 1.3.37.
[8]   OJ C 284, 31.10.1991; Bull. EC 10-1991, point 1.3.26.
[9]   Bull. EC 11-1991, point 1.3.50.

952.   On 16 May the Commission presented a proposal[1] to extend the export earnings stabilization system for the least developed ALA countries[2] to the year 2000, and Parliament endorsed the proposal in December.[3]

953.   Under the existing system, in the meantime, the Commission received six transfer requests relating to losses in 1990 from Nepal and Bangladesh, the only countries involved in the system following Haiti's accession to the Lomé Convention, and its removal from the list of Compex beneficiaries and inclusion on the list of Stabex beneficiaries.[4] Five requests were deemed inadmissible; the sixth resulted in a transfer of ECU 64 213 to Nepal.

954.   On 16 December the Council adopted the Regulation on the EC International Investment Partners facility, which is aimed at promoting investment in the Asian, Latin American and Mediterranean countries, notably in the form of joint ventures.[5]

---

[1]   OJ C 147, 6.6.1991; Bull. EC 5-1991, point 1.3.54.
[2]   OJ L 43, 13.2.1987; Twenty-first General Report, point 861.
[3]   OJ C 13, 20.1.1992; Bull. EC 12-1991.
[4]   OJ L 18, 24.1.1991; Bull. EC 1/2-1991, point 1.3.53.
[5]   Bull. EC 12-1991; Commission proposal: Twenty-fourth General Report, point 765; OJ C 314, 5.12.1991; Bull. EC 11-1991, point 1.3.51.

Section 7

Relations with the African, Caribbean and Pacific countries and the overseas countries and territories

Implementation of the new Lomé Convention

955.   The main development in relations between the Community and the ACP States was the entry into force on 1 September[1] of the fourth Lomé Convention.[2] This followed the deposit of the instruments of ratification by all Member States. A Decision concluding this Convention had been adopted by the Council on 25 February.[3] The need to complete those formalities, to which Parliament had drawn the Member States' attention in July,[4] was vital as the programming of Community aid had already reached a very advanced stage in most ACP States with the exception of the new signatories and those countries whose internal situation made it impossible to hold proper consultations on the guidelines for Lomé IV.

Building on the work already under way on the operational front,[5] the Commission was able, for virtually all ACP States, through intensive discussions with them and close collaboration with the EIB and Member States, to define the aid guidelines for the next five years and to complete the formalities for the signature of the indicative programmes for these States. Under Lomé IV a total of ECU 4.4 billion is made available in programmable aid in the form of grants or risk capital. It did not, however, prove possible to complete the programming exercise for a small number of States with serious political and economic problems.

956.   Continuity in cooperation was also assured by two successive extensions, the first until 30 June[6] and the second until 30 September,[7] of the transitional measures intro-

---

[1]   Bull. EC 9-1991, point 1.3.39.
[2]   Twenty-third General Report, point 846.
[3]   Bull. EC 1/2-1991, point 1.3.47.
[4]   OJ C 240, 16.9.1991; Bull. EC 7/8-1991, point 1.3.50.
[5]   Twenty-fourth General Report, point 772.
[6]   OJ L 58, 5.3.1991; Bull. EC 1/2-1991, point 1.3.48; Commission proposal: Bull. EC 1/2-1991, point 1.3.48.
[7]   OJ L 170, 29.6.1991; Bull. EC 6-1991, point 1.3.48; Commission proposal: Bull. EC 5-1991, point 1.3.57.

duced by Regulation (EEC) No 714/90.[1] These provide a basis for implementing the greater part of the results obtained during the negotiations without waiting for the conclusion of the ratification process.

957. Similarly, for the sake of continuity in trade, the Council extended until 28 February 1992,[2] pending the entry into force of the Convention, Regulation (EEC) No 715/90 on the arrangements applicable to agricultural products and certain goods resulting from the processing of agricultural products originating in the ACP States or in the overseas countries and territories.[3] This Regulation was also amended[4] by the Council to take account of Namibia's accession to the Lomé Convention.[5]

958. On 29 July and 30 September respectively, the Council adopted the following Decisions to allow the seventh European Development Fund to get under way: a Decision on the adoption of the Financial Regulation applicable to cooperation on development financing,[6] a Decision adopting the rules of procedure[7] for the Committee set up under Article 28 of the internal agreement of 16 July 1990 on the financing and administration of Community aid under Lomé IV,[8] and a Decision adopting the EDF Committee's rules of procedure.[9]

959. On 4 December the Commission adopted a study report evaluating the measures taken within the Community and at international organization level to provide Community back-up for the process of structural adjustment in the ACP States.[10]

960. Confirmation of Europe's solidarity with the African continent was given at the highest level, notably during an official visit to Senegal by Mr Delors and Mr Marín from 30 April to 3 May.[11] The linkage between greater democracy and economic and social development was underlined on that occasion, as was the firm relationship between Europe and Africa, which was going through a period of serious political and economic difficulties.

---

[1] OJ L 84, 30.3.1990; Twenty-fourth General Report, point 766.
[2] OJ L 58, 5.3.1991; Bull. EC 1/2-1991, point 1.3.51; Commission proposal: Bull. EC 1/2-1991, point 1.3.51.
[3] OJ L 84, 30.3.1990; Twenty-fourth General Report, point 786.
[4] OJ L 36, 8.2.1991; Bull. EC 1/2-1991, point 1.3.52.
[5] Twenty-fourth General Report, point 768.
[6] OJ L 266, 21.9.1991; Bull. EC 7/8-1991, point 1.3.47; Commission proposal: OJ C 165, 6.7.1990; Bull. EC 6-1990, point 1.4.33; OJ C 267, 23.10.1990; Bull. EC 9-1990, point 1.2.34.
[7] Bull. EC 7/8-1991, point 1.3.49; Commission proposal: Bull. EC 4-1991, point 1.3.42.
[8] Twenty-fourth General Report, point 771.
[9] Bull. EC 9-1991, point 1.3.39; Commission proposal: Bull. EC 4-1991, point 1.3.42.
[10] Bull. EC 12-1991.
[11] Bull. EC 5-1991, point 1.3.55.

Similarly, the Council decided on 28 November to assist Angola in its efforts to reconstruct its society and economy and to coordinate such assistance through existing cooperation channels.[1]

961.   Assistance for ACP States was one of the numerous topics touched upon during the many official visits as part of bilateral relations with Mali,[2] Zimbabwe,[3] Haiti,[4] Benin,[5] Mozambique,[6] the Dominican Republic,[7] Tanzania,[8] Madagascar,[9] Mauritius,[10] the Seychelles,[11] the Comoros,[12] Swaziland[13] and Ethiopia.[14]

962.   Parliament adopted resolutions on the economic and political situation in Zaire, Madagascar and Suriname.[15]

963.   Another expression of European solidarity with the ACP States was the adoption on 16 January of a Commission communication on the relief of ACP debt to the Community.[16] This reflects the operational repercussions of the guidelines already adopted by the Commission[17] and will involve the cancellation of special loans with the exception of those given to profit-oriented businesses, the removal of the obligation for all but the least developed States to contribute to the replenishment of Stabex resources, including transfers under the first, second and third Lomé Conventions which have not yet been repaid, and the recycling of repayments in respect of risk capital made available to ACP States under the present and previous Lomé Conventions.

On 7 November the Council agreed to cancel the ACP States' obligation to replenish Stabex resources under the first three Lomé Conventions as this obligation had already been abolished under Lomé IV.[18]

964.   In view of the fact that some ACP States, notably Somalia and Liberia, had not yet ratified the fourth Lomé Convention but were in serious difficulties which warranted

---

[1]   Bull. EC 11-1991, point 1.3.57.
[2]   Bull. EC 6-1991, point 1.3.54.
[3]   Bull. EC 1/2-1991, points 1.3.39 and 1.3.40; Bull. EC 7/8-1991, point 1.3.57.
[4]   Bull. EC 1/2-1991, point 1.3.60; Bull. EC 7/8-1991, point 1.3.58; Bull. EC 10-1991, point 1.3.30.
[5]   Bull. EC 1/2-1991, point 1.3.57.
[6]   Bull. EC 1/2-1991, point 1.3.58.
[7]   Bull. EC 1/2-1991, point 1.3.59; Bull. EC 12-1991.
[8]   Bull. EC 4-1991, point 1.3.48.
[9]   Bull. EC 4-1991, point 1.3.49.
[10]   Bull. EC 4-1991, point 1.3.50.
[11]   Bull. EC 4-1991, point 1.3.51; Bull. EC 11-1991, point 1.3.61.
[12]   Bull. EC 5-1991, point 1.3.63.
[13]   Bull. EC 5-1991, point 1.3.64.
[14]   Bull. EC 10-1991, point 1.3.32.
[15]   OJ C 326, 16.12.1991; Bull. EC 11-1991, points 1.3.63, 1.3.59 and 1.3.62.
[16]   Bull. EC 1/2-1991, point 1.3.46.
[17]   Twenty-fourth General Report, point 769.
[18]   Bull. EC 11-1991, point 1.3.54.

immediate Community assistance the Commission adopted, on 8 November, a proposal for a Decision of the ACP-EEC Council of Ministers granting aid from the emergency and refugee aid funds left over from Lomé III. On 18 November the Council approved this aid[1] and on 11 December adopted the draft conclusions of the ACP-EEC Committee of Ambassadors on the question of transfers from the national indicative programmes under Lomé II and III.[2]

Trade cooperation

965. The development of trade and services, including tourism, which is one of Lomé IV's priorities, formed part of the aforementioned programming exercise at both national and regional level. Emphasis was laid on the need for coordinated trade strategies, optimum use of human resources and greater quality and competitiveness of products. The use of modern marketing techniques in production-oriented sectors and support services for external trade business and regional integration were key concerns.

966. Through annual integrated programmes the Commission also financed the attendance of 300 persons at trade fairs and events, trade missions and workshops. Some 40 ACP States were recipients of this form of aid which may also be used for the production of literature. Assistance was also given to Aproma (staples) and COLEACP (fruit, vegetables and flowers) to sell their products.

Stabex

967. Stabex operations in 1991 concerned the ACP countries' export earnings in 1990,[3] the first year covered by Lomé IV. The continuing and unprecedented slump in coffee and cocoa prices again led to a huge shortfall between available resources and total eligible transfers.[4] A total of 33 ACP States are eligible for 67 transfers totalling ECU 1 241 million if account is taken of the reduction authorized by the Lomé Convention to cover the shortfall in resources, which in this case amounts to ECU 384 million. On 24 September[5] the Commission allocated ECU 483.7 million for such a transfer subject to the release of ECU 100 million in additional resources by the ACP-EEC Committee of Ambassadors, acting on the authorization of the ACP-EEC Council of Ministers.

---

[1]   Bull. EC 11-1991, point 1.3.55.
[2]   Bull. EC 12-1991.
[3]   Bull. EC 4-1991, point 1.3.44.
[4]   Twenty-second General Report, point 1006; Twenty-third General Report, point 848; Twenty-fourth General Report, point 775.
[5]   Bull. EC 9-1991, point 1.3.42.

Table 13 gives a breakdown of operations by recipient country.

TABLE 13

Stabex transfers for 1990

Beneficiary countries	Product	Amount of transfer (ECU)
Sudan	Groundnut products	2 109 071
	Cotton products	18 949 680
	Hides and skins	2 768 785
	Gum arabic	2 910 847
	Sesame	3 233 020
	Oil cake	1 781 197
Mauritania	Squid	9 583 712
Mali	Cotton	329 852
Burkina Faso	Hides and skins	386 502
Cape Verde	Hides and skins	7 053
	Bananas	108 606
Sierra Leone	Coffee	2 041 855
Côte d'Ivoire	Cocoa products	16 677 301
	Coffee products	74 494 439
Ghana	Cocoa products	6 889 065
Togo	Cocoa products	1 724 659
	Coffee	3 505 259
Benin	Palm products	253 402
Cameroon	Cocoa products	39 080 820
	Coffee	28 307 419
Central African Republic	Coffee	6 101 469
	Cotton	629 984
Equatorial Guinea	Cocoa products	2 101 595
	Coffee	195 886
São Tomé and Príncipe	Cocoa	994 574
Rwanda	Coffee	15 363 630
	Hides and skins	967 433
	Pyrethrum	241 103
Burundi	Coffee	16 247 958
	Tea	301 049
Ethiopia	Coffee	58 456 423
	Hides and skins	6 132 026
Kenya	Coffee	29 870 422
Uganda	Coffee	36 283 936
	Cotton	701 713
Tanzania	Coffee	19 104 450
	Tea	9 749
	Sisal	64 031
Madagascar	Coffee	18 989 063
	Vanilla	1 693 310
	Cloves	757 227
	Essential oils	115 256
Comoros	Vanilla	1 392 804
	Cloves	942 073
Malawi	Tea	1 705 852
Haiti	Cocoa	1 411 489
	Coffee	9 842 250
	Essential oils	396 643
Dominica	Bananas	673 209

Grenada	Cocoa	618 472
	Bananas	274 633
	Nutmeg	1 133 528
Papua New Guinea	Cocoa products	6 754 994
	Coffee	7 563 555
	Copra products	3 322 667
	Palm products	7 307 497
Solomon Islands	Cocoa products	363 379
	Copra products	3 555 653
	Palm products	675 471
Tuvalu	Copra products	15 836
Kiribati	Copra products	396 292
Vanuatu	Copra products	1 702 208
Tonga	Copra products	471 594
	Bananas	518 072
Samoa	Cocoa products	357 736
	Copra products	1 626 494
	Oil cake	190 848
	Total	483 678 080

968.   On 21 January[1] the Council amended Regulation (EEC) No 429/87[2] in the light of Haiti's signature of the fourth Lomé Convention to allow it to be a beneficiary of the Stabex system.

Sysmin

969.   A total of ECU 18 million from the sixth EDF was allocated to a project in Papua New Guinea[3] but a planned project in Liberia had to be cancelled.

Sugar Protocol

970.   On 23 September the Council adopted a Decision on the conclusion of an agreement in the form of an exchange of letters on the guaranteed prices for sugar for the 1989/90, 1990/91 and 1991/92 delivery periods.[4] The agreed prices are identical to those applying to Community producers.

---

[1]   OJ L 18, 24.1.1991; Bull. EC 1/2-1991, point 1.3.53.
[2]   OJ L 43, 13.2.1987; Twenty-first General Report, point 861.
[3]   Twenty-fourth General Report, point 777.
[4]   Bull. EC 9-1991, point 1.3.43.

971. In April the Commission proposed that the Council should reject, subject to further examination, applications by Zambia and Papua New Guinea to join the Sugar Protocol. [1]

972. The Community also decided to introduce a marketing premium of ECU 30 million for a period of three years (1989/90, 1990/91 and 1991/92) to maintain the supply of raw sugar to Community refineries and to help the ACP States adapt their industries to market conditions.

973. In December, acting on a proposal from the Commission, [2] the Council authorized the Commission [3] to renegotiate the International Sugar Agreement. [4]

Industrial cooperation

974. Industrial cooperation in 1991 took the form of proposals for new aid programmes to further the development of the private sector in a number of ACP States including Burundi, Congo, Guinea-Bissau, Mali and Niger.

975. The Commission has been examining various aspects of cooperation, and will undertake a study of the means of safeguarding and guaranteeing investment in the ACP States, which forms a cornerstone of the new Convention. The statute and internal and financial regulations governing the operations of the Centre for the Development of Industry were also adopted. The Commission organized the fourth Community-Central Africa industrial forum in November.

Financial and technical development

976. A preliminary evaluation of programming in 1991 showed that the Lomé IV approach had been amply followed, with more widespread use made of sectoral policy aid and more coordinated concentration of instruments on the same development objectives. Rural development, road and socioeconomic infrastructure and the development of human resources are the main areas of focus for such aid. [5] The new priorities laid down by the Convention, in particular environmental protection and the role of

---

[1] Bull. EC 4-1991, point 1.3.45.
[2] Bull. EC 11-1991, point 1.3.72.
[3] Bull. EC 12-1991.
[4] OJ L 58, 3.3.1988; Twenty-second General Report, point 985.
[5] Bull. EC 3-1991, point 1.3.37.

women in development, have generally been taken into account. Decentralized cooperation and the private sector are also important aspects.

977.   Programming has made use of all the Convention's instruments in all ACP States where this has proved possible. On 2 October[1] and 18 December[2] the Commission decided to suspend the programming of aid for Haiti and Togo respectively in view of the political events there. In the case of the 35 States deemed eligible for structural adjustment aid clearly defined guidelines were laid down for its use. This interdependence between programming and adjustment formed the backdrop for the implementation of the Convention's provisions on eligibility, distribution of aid over a two-year period, priority sectors for Community assistance and discussion of reforms undertaken by the ACP States in question. It also played a part in the forging of closer relations with the Member States and institutions such as the International Bank for Reconstruction and Development (IBRD) and the International Monetary Fund (IMF) and in the Community's participation in wider initiatives, in particular the special programme of assistance for Africa (SPA) run by the World Bank. The Community will also allocate ECU 1 billion from Lomé IV to the adjustment measures in countries which are eligible under this programme.

The Commission's approach has been shaped by a number of factors considered essential from the viewpoint of Lomé IV: the social aspects of adjustment (mainly health and education), the observance of long-term objectives, the tailoring of the pace of reforms to each State's constraints and the regional dimension of adjustment.

As regards the type of instruments used, aid will be given in the form of import programmes. The counterpart funds generated by such programmes will in future form part of the macroeconomic, financial and monetary conditions of the ACP States concerned. On 27 May[3] the Council adopted a resolution on the use of counterpart funds generated by development aid instruments in which it defines the general principles guiding Community and Member States' policy in this area. Table 14 gives a breakdown by sector of funds provided.

978.   On 8 March[4] the Commission approved a report, 'From Lomé III to Lomé IV — review of aid from the Lomé Conventions at the end of 1989', in which it analyses commitments and payments and the reasons for any delays which may have been discovered.

---

[1]   Bull. EC 10-1991, point 1.3.28.
[2]   Bull. EC 12-1991.
[3]   Bull. EC 5-1991, point 1.3.75.
[4]   Bull. EC 3-1991, point 1.3.37.

TABLE 14

Lomé I, II and III financing decisions (EDF and EIB[1]) for ACP States, by sector, at 31 December

	Commitments (million ECU)							% of total commitments
	1976-86	1987	1988	1989	1990	1991[2]	Total	
Development of production	4 200.98	1 378.52	1 268.47	563.26	157.81	6.03	7 575.07	46.72
Industrialization	2 362.32	492.41	373.91	262.11	79.76	−16.08	3 554.43	21.92
Tourism	43.83	0.61	13.96	9.07	0.38	−0.07	67.78	0.4
Rural production	1 794.83	886.71	880.61	292.08	77.66	22.18	3 954.07	24.4
Economic infrastructure, transport and communications	1 583.66	521.69	206.54	275.18	148.31	137.5	2 873.08	17.73
Social development	1 093.23	176.30	273.15	179.48	56.21	13.49	1 791.86	11.04
Education and training	530.48	47.67	67.39	58.16	30.51	1.36	735.57	4.53
Health	152.53	78.18	60.69	50.55	7.48	6.16	355.59	2.19
Water engineering, urban infrastructure and housing	410.22	50.45	145.06	70.77	18.22	5.97	700.69	4.13
Trade promotion	90.59	27.51	20.13	14.23	37.34	9.11	198.91	1.22
Emergency aid	344.60	22.15	34.18	33.53	39.11	27.31	500.88	3.08
Stabex	1 117.75	269.03	553.49	274.03	216.09	349.09	2 779.48	17.12
RRP[3]	100.00	0.05	0.07	0.13	−0.8	−1.08	98.37	0.6
Refugee aid	0.00	0.86	18.63	31.98	—	6.1	57.57	0.35
Other	187.59	9.20	20.88	11.94	124.41	0.19	354.21	2.18
Total	8 718.40	2 405.41	2 395.54	1 383.77	992.49	567.26	16 229.43	100.00

[1] For EIB operations, see the Bank's annual report.
[2] As at 1 September 1991.
[3] Rehabilitation and recovery plan.

979. On 15 April[1] it adopted the balance sheets and management accounts of each of the funds running in 1990 (fourth, fifth and sixth EDFs) and a statement of transfers of funds during the financial year.

Regional cooperation

980. Under Lomé IV the objective of regional cooperation is to support sectoral policies coordinated at regional level in order to encourage the creation of viable, cohesive economic areas.

---

[1]   Bull. EC 4-1991, point 1.3.46.

981. The programming process, in which the new concept of regional economic integration has been substantially incorporated, has been completed for four of the eight ACP regions.

The Commission has been looking at this aspect and has adopted a programme of guidelines for initiatives to be taken in the wake of intergovernmental conferences. Under the special programme of assistance (SPA) it put forward a discussion paper on regional economic integration and structural adjustment to the donor community in Tokyo in October.

Institutional relations

982. The annual meeting of the ACP-EEC Council of Ministers was held in Brussels on 6 and 7 May.[1] Discussions centred largely on financial cooperation, and in particular on matters relating to the evaluation of financial and technical cooperation, indebtedness, structural adjustment and the implementation of the new general conditions for EDF contracts. Other matters discussed concerned sugar (guaranteed prices, special measures, the compensation system, access to the Portuguese market and the accession of Papua New Guinea and Zambia to the Sugar Protocol),[2] transitional measures pending the entry into force of Lomé IV, Community operations to help non-ACP countries, Stabex, and the international cocoa and coffee Agreements. The ACP side presented a statement on indebtedness and the Commission filed a report on measures to combat AIDS.

983. The ACP-EEC Joint Assembly held its two annual sessions in Kampala from 24 February to 1 March[3] and in Amsterdam from 23 to 27 September.[4] Discussions at the first session were dominated by the ACP countries' indebtedness, the impact of the Gulf crisis on their social and economic situation and measures to combat AIDS. One of the main questions discussed at the Amsterdam session was that of intra-ACP services and trade. Other matters under discussion were implementation of the Commission's anti-famine programme[5] and the relationship between democracy, human rights and development.

---

[1] Bull. EC 5-1991, point 1.3.61.
[2] Point 971 of this Report.
[3] OJ C 216, 19.8.1991; Bull. EC 3-1991, point 1.3.16.
[4] Bull. EC 9-1991, point 1.3.45.
[5] Point 1016 of this Report.

Overseas countries and territories

984.   A Decision on the association of the overseas countries and territories (OCTs) with the European Economic Community and a Decision of the representatives of the governments of the Member States of the European Coal and Steel Community, meeting within the Council, on the arrangements for trade in ECSC products between the Community and the OCTs were adopted on 25 July.[1] These new arrangements reflect certain features of Lomé IV and include the extension of their duration to 10 years, the improvement of the Stabex and Sysmin mechanisms, decentralization of cooperation and greater emphasis on environmental protection and the role of women. They also include numerous innovations specific to the OCTs and concern the rules applicable to the establishment and provision of services, access to the services of the Centre for the Development of Industry (CDI) or the Euro-Info-Centres, and trade rules based on the principle of free access subject to certain conditions. At the institutional level it was agreed to establish a three-way partnership between the Commission, the Member State and the OCT under which matters of mutual interest can be discussed. In terms of financial cooperation a sum of ECU 140 million has been made available under the seventh EDF (a 40% increase). The French OCTs will receive ECU 40.2 million, the Dutch OCTs ECU 30.3 million and the United Kingdom OCTs ECU 15.5 million.

985.   In December the Council adopted, under the new rules, the general regulations, general conditions and procedural rules on conciliation and arbitration for works, supply and service contracts financed by the EDF.[2]

986.   Pending the entry into force on 20 September of these new association arrangements, the Council and the representatives of the Governments of the Member States extended, on 6 September,[3] the measures provided for in Decisions 86/283/EEC and 86/284/ECSC governing the association rules for the preceding period.[4] On 22 July[5] the Council allocated the unexpended balance of the funds earmarked for Stabex under these Decisions.

---

[1]   OJ L 263, 19.9.1991; Bull. EC 7/8-1991, point 1.3.46; Commission proposal: OJ C 95, 11.9.1991; Twenty-fourth General Report, point 786.
[2]   Bull. EC 12-1991; Commission proposal: Bull. EC 7/8-1991, point 1.3.53.
[3]   OJ L 255, 12.9.1991; Bull. EC 9-1991, points 1.3.40 and 1.3.41.
[4]   OJ L 175, 1.7.1986; Twentieth General Report, point 943.
[5]   Bull. EC 7/8-1991, point 1.3.52.

Section 8

General development cooperation

Cooperation through the United Nations

United Nations Conference on Trade and Development

987.   The Trade and Development Board held its annual two meetings, in March and September. During the second part of the 37th session, in March, the Board continued its discussions on trade matters, and more especially the problems linked with protectionism and structural adjustment, and also the aspects of the Uruguay Round of more specific relevance to the developing countries. The first part of the 38th session was held in September and was given over to examining the 1991 report on trade and development, interdependence in trade, development financing and the international monetary system, and also the debt and development problems of the countries concerned. The Board also held a special meeting in December to prepare for the eighth Conference, which was originally scheduled for the end of the year, but was postponed until the beginning of 1992.

988.   On 31 October the Commission adopted a communication on guidelines for a Community position at this Conference;[1] the Council adopted these guidelines on 2 December.[2]

989.   A number of meetings of the most important specialized committees were held this year, dealing more especially with technology transfer, tariff preferences and economic cooperation between developing countries.

990.   In May and June the Conference for reviewing the United Nations Convention on the Code of Conduct for Liner Conferences was held.

---

[1]   Bull. EC 10-1991, point 1.3.47.
[2]   Bull. EC 12-1991.

United Nations Industrial Development Organization

991.   The Commission took part as an observer in the eighth session of the Industrial Development Board, which was held from 1 to 5 July, and in the fourth session of the General Conference, held from 18 to 22 November.

In addition to the matters customarily discussed, such as the adoption of the 1992 and 1993 budgets, the discussions focused mainly on the restructuring of the Secretariat. At the General Conference, the Commission gave an account of its industrial cooperation activities with the developing countries.

World Food Programme

992.   The Community allocated ECU 165 million, including transport costs, to the World Food Programme (WFP). This aid was used to meet the needs of various development projects and the International Emergency Food Reserve, and to contribute to the programmes to help refugees.

World Food Council

993.   The 17th ministerial session of the World Food Council (WFC), which was held in Elsinore, Denmark, at the beginning of June, was given over mainly to examining the implementation of the Cairo Declaration, which focuses on four general problems to be tackled: famine, chronic hunger, malnutrition and deficiency diseases.[1] With this in mind, and also taking into consideration the fact that world economic prospects were less encouraging than a year ago, and expressing the fear that events in Eastern Europe might have adverse consequences for the developing countries, the Council did its best to encourage dialogue and cooperation between these countries on political reforms linked with food security. While stressing the importance of the Uruguay Round negotiations in this context, the Council raised again the idea of a 'new green revolution' based on science, technology and research, and called for greater coordination between the United Nations agencies and the various programmes concerning food security in the world.

United Nations Food and Agriculture Organization

994.   The negotiations conducted over a number of years with the FAO in order to determine the Community's status were finally concluded in November at the FAO

---

[1]   Twenty-third General Report, point 870.

ministerial Conference[1] with the recognition of the Community as a member *sui generis*, which would state its views through the Commission on all matters coming within its sphere of competence.The Member States will still be responsible for dealing with all institutional or budgetary matters, since the Commission has right of representation only within the context of Community policies, such as forestry or development. On 25 November, the Council, acting on a proposal from the Commission,[2] decided officially to request that the Community be made a member.[3] The official ceremony took place on 26 November.[4] The Community's membership is of particular importance in that the Community is the first regional economic integration organization to join a United Nations specialized agency.

Generalized tariff preferences

995.   On 3 December[5] the Council and the representatives of the Member States' governments decided to extend into 1992 the Regulations and Decisions in force in 1991 concerning the opening of the Community's generalized tariff preferences.[6] These measures extending the *status quo* will make it possible to await the implementation of a revised scheme, which will be proposed by the Commission on the basis of the outcome of the Uruguay Round negotiations and the guidelines it has already proposed for 1990-2000; these are partly based on the need to take into account the ability of certain beneficiary countries to make their own contribution towards liberalizing trade.[7] The Economic and Social Committee delivered a favourable opinion on these guidelines in January.[8]

996.   On 3 December the Commission also proposed to amend these Regulations and Decisions in order to extend the benefits of the scheme to Albania and the Baltic States and to suspend them in the case of Korea, unless that country takes measures to end its discriminatory treatment of the Community with regard to intellectual property.[9] A further amendment was adopted by the Council on 23 December[10] to take into account

---

[1]   Bull. EC 11-1991, point 1.3.64.
[2]   OJ C 292, 9.11.1991; Bull. EC 10-1991, point 1.3.46.
[3]   Bull. EC 11-1991, point 1.3.64.
[4]   Bull. EC 11-1991, point 1.3.66.
[5]   OJ L 341, 12.12.1991; Bull. EC 12-1991; Commission proposal: OJ C 228, 3.9.1991; Bull. EC 7/8-1991, point 1.3.60.
[6]   OJ L 370, 31.12.1990; Twenty-fourth General Report, point 795.
[7]   Twenty-fourth General Report, point 794.
[8]   OJ C 69, 18.3.1991; Bull. EC 1/2-1991, point 1.3.62.
[9]   OJ C 334, 28.12.1991; Bull. EC 12-1991.
[10] OJ L 362, 31.12.1991; Bull. EC 12-1991.

the preferential system in the 'Europe agreements' with Poland, Hungary and Czecho-slovakia.[1]

997.   On 16 December[2] the Council decided that the arrangements for generalized tariff preferences for agricultural products applicable to Bolivia, Colombia, Ecuador and Peru should be extended to include the Central American countries to further their efforts to combat drug abuse.[3]

Commodities and world agreements

998.   The radical changes in the allocation of market shares, combined with Brazil's inability to formulate its policy, yet again hindered the negotiation of a new International Coffee Agreement. Consequently, acting upon the decision[4] by the International Coffee Council to extend the 1983 Agreement[5] until 30 September 1992, the Council decided on 17 June that the Community should accept the extension of the Agreement.[6] At its annual meeting, held from 23 to 27 September,[7] the International Coffee Council decided to set up a working party to hold discussions on the new agreement. On 8 October Parliament adopted a resolution on the situation on the world coffee market.[8]

999.   With the International Cocoa Agreement[9] extended without economic provisions until September 1992, the International Cocoa Council met in March[10], September[11] and December[12] to study the situation; serious financial difficulties had arisen as a result of certain producer countries' payment arrears, and there was a structural imbalance at world level between supply and demand. The Cocoa Council also decided to set up a working group to examine the possibility of concluding a new agreement.

1000.   The International Tropical Timber Organization (ITTO), whose Council and technical committees met in Quito from 29 May to 6 June[13] and in Yokohama from 28 November to 6 December[12] continued preparing the technical programmes and drafting standards governing the exploitation of tropical forests.

---

[1]   Point 823 of this Report.
[2]   Bull. EC 12-1991; Commission proposal: OJ C 194, 25.7.1991; Bull. 6-1991, point 1.3.56.
[3]   OJ L 370, 30.12.1990; Twenty-fourth General Report, point 797.
[4]   Twenty-fourth General Report, point 797.
[5]   OJ L 308, 9.11.1983; Seventeenth General Report, point 732.
[6]   OJ L 175, 4.7.1991; Bull. EC 6-1991, point 1.3.58.
[7]   Bull. EC 9-1991, point 1.3.49.
[8]   OJ C 280, 28.10.1991; Bull. EC 10-1991, point 1.3.36.
[9]   OJ L 69, 12.3.1987; Twentieth General Report, point 919.
[10]   Bull. EC 3-1991, point 1.3.45.
[11]   Bull. EC 9-1991, point 1.3.48.
[12]   Bull. EC 12-1991.
[13]   Bull. EC 6-1991, point 1.3.57.

1001.   On 18 March[1] the Council adopted a Decision on the notification of the application by the Community of the 1989 International Agreement on Jute and Jute Products.[2]

1002.   On 25 March the Council also adopted two Decisions accepting on behalf of the Community the terms of reference of the International Study Group on Tin[3] and the International Study Group on Copper[4], and also, on 14 October, Decision 91/537/EEC on the acceptance of the terms of reference of the International Study Group on Nickel.[5]

1003.   In the context of the Community's participation in the Common Fund for Commodities, the Commission paid the contributions for São Tomé and Príncipe, Equatorial Guinea and Togo.[6]

Protecting the environment

1004.   The matter of environmental protection was systematically raised at bilateral or regional cooperation meetings with developing countries and the Community played an active part in the preparations for the United Nations Conference on the Environment and Development, due to open in Rio de Janeiro on 2 June 1992.[7]

For the Asian and Latin American countries, 45 % of the total budget allocated to the developing countries concerned, which rose from ECU 8 million in 1990 to ECU 11 million in 1991, was used to implement pilot cooperation projects with governmental and non-governmental organizations in Asia and Latin America with the particular aims of integrating environment and development, tackling urban development and the control of urban pollution, conserving natural resources and safeguarding their biodiversity, protecting tropical forests and promoting information regarding the environment. Even greater emphasis was placed on environmental protection in these countries in 1991 as a result of the priority accorded to it in the new guidelines for financial and technical cooperation with the developing countries of Asia and Latin America for 1991-95.[8] The Mediterranean environmental technical assistance pro-

---

[1]   OJ L 75, 21.3.1991; Bull. EC 3-1991, point 1.3.42.
[2]   Twenty-fourth General Report, point 804.
[3]   OJ L 89, 10.4.1991; Bull. EC 3-1991, point 1.3.43; Commission proposal: Twenty-third General Report, point 877.
[4]   OJ L 89, 10.4.1991; Bull. EC 3-1991, point 1.3.44; Commission proposal: Twenty-fourth General Report, point 800.
[5]   OJ L 293, 24.10.1991; Bull. EC 10-1991, point 1.3.38; Commission proposal: Bull. EC 9-1991, point 1.3.50.
[6]   Twenty-fourth General Report, point 789.
[7]   Point 626 of this Report.
[8]   Twenty-fourth General Report, point 763.

gramme (Metap) made a major contribution towards environmental protection in the Mediterranean countries.

1005.   Conservation of tropical forests was a new priority this year. In particular, following the recommendations by the European Council held in Dublin in June 1990, projects geared to the protection of tropical forests were financed by the Community budget. The Commission also took part, in conjunction with the World Bank and the Brazilian authorities, in the drawing-up of a pilot programme for the conservation of tropical forests in Brazil; it was accepted by the European Council held in Luxembourg in June and Community funds amounting to USD 15 million were earmarked for it.

Drug abuse control

1006.   After the European Council, meeting in Luxembourg in June,[1] had approved the setting-up of a European unit to monitor drug problems and asked the European Committee to Combat Drugs (ECCD) to make the necessary preparations, the Commission adopted, on 27 November, a proposal for Regulation setting up this unit.[2] The European Council also asked the ministers with responsibility for combating international drug abuse to draw up specific proposals for establishing 'Europol'. In preparation for the European Council in Maastricht, the ministers involved in the Trevi Group adopted at their meeting in The Hague on 3 December a report which advocated setting up Europol in stages, the first of which would comprise the EDUs (European drugs units). The European Council requested the ministers to take measures, in conjunction with the Commission, to make Europol operational.

1007.   Again this year the Community continued with operations implementing the North-South cooperation programme for combating drug abuse, which is potentially aimed at all developing countries in two complementary spheres, namely the reduction of demand and the provision of alternatives to the production of illicit crops. New operations to prevent or reduce drug abuse were launched in Asia, Latin America and Africa. Even though this programme has been extended to cover more countries, it still falls far short of the aid requirements of the countries concerned. The fourth Lomé Convention nevertheless provides new opportunities for financing operations to control drug abuse, particularly in the health sector and in the regional cooperation context.[3] Given the extent of the drug problem in the ACP countries, increased attention will have to be paid to it in the coming years.

---

[1]   Bull. EC 6-1991, point I.18.
[2]   Point 211 of this Report.
[3]   Point 955 of this Report.

1008.   A new East-West dimension was added to the North-South dimension. At the first pan-European ministerial conference on drugs in Oslo on 9 and 10 May, an outline for new cooperation with the Central and East European countries was put forward. The Commission subsequently set in train various forms of cooperation on drug abuse with these countries and started talks with Hungary, Poland, Czechoslovakia and Bulgaria in order to analyse their priority requirements.

1009.   Community assistance is coordinated increasingly closely with that of the Member States and of the United States and other developed countries within the Dublin Group; the Commission is endeavouring in this way to implement the objectives of the European programme to combat drug abuse decided on at the end of 1990. [1] Furthermore, in order to halt the spread of illicit crops and the production of drugs and psychotropic substances, the Council decided in December that the arrangements for generalized tariff preferences already granted to Bolivia, Colombia, Ecuador and Peru should be extended to the countries of Central America. [2] Work began at the end of the year on a new agreement between the Commission and the United Nations Drug Control Programme which would lay the foundations for more extensive cooperation.

AIDS

1010.   All the funds allocated from the fifth EDF to the Commission programme for combating AIDS were committed; pending the mobilization of the seventh EDF, a carry-over sum of ECU 4 million from the sixth EDF was allocated to the programme. [3] The annual allocation of ECU 5 million made available for the programme and covering all the developing countries and the financing of regional projects was raised to ECU 8 million for 1991. [4]

Food aid

1011.   On 18 March the Commission adopted Decision 91/187/EEC on the establishment of overall quantities of food aid for 1991 and a list of products to be supplied as food aid. [5] When preparing the preliminary draft budget for 1991, the only source of

---

[1]   Twenty-fourth General Report, point 806.
[2]   Point 938 of this Report.
[3]   Twenty-first General Report, point 843.
[4]   Twenty-second General Report, point 988.
[5]   OJ L 92, 13.4.1991; Bull. EC 3-1991, point 1.3.46.

financing for food aid, the Commission had set amounts which would make it possible to grant the same quantities of cereals and sugar as in 1990, smaller quantities of butteroil (12 000 tonnes instead of 18 000 tonnes) and milk (83 500 tonnes instead of 94 100 tonnes), but larger quantities of vegetable oil (60 000 tonnes instead of 50 000 tonnes) and other products (ECU 50 million instead of ECU 40 million). The list of products remained the same, and non-governmental organizations and international organizations were still able to purchase produce, particularly fruit and vegetables, locally in the developing countries. Owing to the insufficient allocations for transport, it was decided not to supply all the planned quantities of milk products and to make an initial transfer of funds to help cover the costs of transporting the aid.

1012.   On 16 January[1] the Commission adopted a report in which it took stock of food aid policy and management in 1987 and 1988, and assessed the results of the implementation of Regulation (EEC) No 2200/87 laying down general rules for the mobilization of aid.[2] The report for 1989 was adopted on 3 May.[3]

Standard food aid

1013.   In accordance with Regulation (EEC) No 1930/90 on food aid policy and management, the Commission set the overall quantities of food aid, a large proportion of which was programmed by country (direct aid) and by international or non-governmental organization (indirect aid).[4] Proposals for the allocation of aid were put to the Food Aid Committee for its opinion before adoption by the Commission. Table 15 gives the breakdown of these operations.

1014.   Within the limits of these quantities, the Commission decided to finance three new multiannual programmes: for Burkina Faso (1991-94: 7 000 tonnes of cereals) in order to support that country's efforts to increase food security; for UNRWA[5] (1991-92 — 6 330 tonnes of cereals, 1 696 tonnes of vegetable oil, 4 123 tonnes of skimmed-milk powder, 2 502 tonnes of sugar, ECU 5.8 million of other products) to enable it to maintain its food programmes until the end of 1992; and for Tunisia (1991-96: 3 000 tonnes of skimmed-milk powder) in order to support projects forming part of the country's strategy to become self-sufficient in milk. These new programmes are in addition to the three already in progress for Cape Verde,[6] India and China. In addition to these allocations, various operations were undertaken, for a total of ECU 5 million,

---

[1]   Bull. EC 1/2-1991, point 1.3.64.
[2]   OJ L 204, 25.7.1987; Twenty-first General Report, point 845.
[3]   Bull. EC 5-1991, point 1.3.68.
[4]   OJ L 174, 7.7.1990; Twenty-fourth General Report, point 810.
[5]   United Nations Relief and Works Agency for Palestine Refugees in the Near East.
[6]   Twenty-fourth General Report, point 812.

TABLE 15

Allocation of food aid, 1991

	Cereals	Milk powder	Butter-oil	Vegetable oil	Sugar	Other products (million ECU)
			(tonnes)			
Africa	349 800	1 300	300	7 300	400	8.5
Indian and Pacific Oceans	12 000	—	—	—	—	—
Caribbean	10 000	—	—	—	—	—
Mediterranean	110 000	3 000	—	8 000	—	—
Latin America	59 251	2 680	—	5 800	—	3.075
Asia	210 000	5 000	1 667	1 500	—	—
Total direct aid	751 051	11 980	1 967	22 600	400	11.575
Total indirect aid	608 949	50 823	5 000	37 400	14 600	38.425
Grand total	1 360 000	62 803	6 967	60 000	15 000	50.0

as part of the implementation of the early-warning system programmes for UNRWA and the FAO;[1] the operations also involved storage facilities in Mali and Bangladesh, for the UNHCR[2] in Mozambique, Côte d'Ivoire and Sudan, and also for non-governmental organizations in Burundi, Togo, Mozambique, Peru and Guatemala. Furthermore, an amount of ECU 5 000 000 was used by international and non-governmental organizations to purchase foodstuffs and seeds as part of cofinancing. Most of this aid (ECU 3.7 million) went to Africa.

Emergency food aid

1015. The total amount of ECU 78 609 000 which the Commission channelled into emergency food aid over the year was large, owing mainly to the situation in Africa south of the Sahara and the devastation caused by the cyclones in Bangladesh. The emergency aid supplied is described below:

Sudan: 50 000 tonnes of cereals and ECU 2 million for other products;

Ethiopia: 60 000 tonnes of cereals and 2 000 tonnes of vegetable oil;

Bangladesh: 65 000 tonnes of cereals and 1 500 tonnes of vegetable oil;

Burkina Faso: 8 000 tonnes of cereals;

---

[1]   United Nations Food and Agriculture Organization.
[2]   Office of the United Nations High Commissioner for Refugees.

Cameroon: 2 800 tonnes of cereals;

UNRWA: 20 000 tonnes of cereals, 3 300 tonnes of vegetable oil and ECU 1.5 million for other products;

Kurdish refugees (WFP): 18 000 tonnes of cereals, 1 080 tonnes of vegetable oil and ECU 0.4 million for other products;

ICRC[1]: 22 329 tonnes of cereals, 2 960 tonnes of vegetable oil and ECU 1.6 million for other products;

NGOs: 3 260 tonnes of cereals;

UNHCR: ECU 0.15 million for various foodstuffs.

Special programme for Africa

1016.   In order to combat the serious drought in the Horn of Africa, southern Africa and certain Sahelian countries, and to help the victims of civil wars, the Commission proposed to the Council on 17 April that a special programme for Africa[2] should be implemented, with additional emergency food aid of 600 000 tonnes in cereals equivalent to be supplied in the proportions of 200 000 tonnes by the Member States and 400 000 tonnes by the Community as such, by means of a special budget. The breakdown of the ECU 140 million entered in the 1991 budget is as follows: Ethiopia: ECU 59.43 million; Sudan: ECU 42.16 million; Somalia: ECU 9.48 million; Liberia: ECU 7.64 million; Malawi: ECU 3.85 million; Angola: ECU 4.85 million; Mozambique: ECU 2.68 million; Mauritania: ECU 3.96 million; Niger: ECU 3.73 million; and logistic support: ECU 2.22 million. At the end of the year all the funds had been allocated and almost all the products distributed.

Emergency aid

1017.   In order to make the Community's humanitarian assistance more visible and more effective, the Commission decided on 6 November to set up a European Office for Emergency Humanitarian Aid, in the form of a specialized department of the Commission.[3] The role of this Office will be to enhance the Community's presence on the ground, improve coordination with the Member States, other donors, NGOs and

---

[1]   International Committee of the Red Cross.
[2]   Bull. EC 4-1991, point 1.3.52.
[3]   Bull. EC 11-1991, point 1.3.70.

specialized international agencies, and to facilitate mobilization of the necessary budgetary resources.

1018. On a more general level, the Commission adopted a communication on 25 November pinpointing the main aspects involved in the possible untying of Member States' bilateral aid. [1]

1019. The Council referred in a resolution adopted on 28 November to the importance of effective coordination of emergency aid. [2]

1020. The Commission granted emergency aid amounting to a total of ECU 195 million for the victims of disasters in the developing countries and other non-Community countries. This sum comprises ECU 56 million from the European Development Fund and ECU 139 million from the budget. The EDF funds were used mainly to help the victims of fighting and drought in Africa, with 88 % of the contributions, namely ECU 49.1 million, going to six countries and to the neighbouring regions also affected, as follows: Somalia, ECU 11.2 million; Sudan, ECU 14.5 million; Ethiopia, ECU 7.7 million; Liberia, ECU 9.3 million; Angola, ECU 3 million; and Mozambique, ECU 3.4 million. The funds from the Community budget, which were raised by ECU 100 million in order to meet the needs of refugees from Iraq, went mainly (to the tune of ECU 117 million) to the victims of the Gulf crisis and made it possible to mobilize 330 planes and supply 1.5 million blankets, 64 000 tents and 60 000 tonnes of food. The remainder was granted to help people affected by events in the Soviet Union (ECU 5 million), Albania (ECU 2.5 million)[3] and Yugoslavia (ECU 12 million), cholera in South America, particularly Peru (ECU 1.8 million), the cyclones and flooding in Bangladesh (ECU 2.4 million), the eruption of Pinatubo in the Philippines (0.9 million), the fighting in Cambodia (ECU 1.5 million), and also the victims of the earthquakes in Peru (ECU 0.22 million), Afghanistan and Pakistan (ECU 0.5 million) and Costa Rica, Panama and Guatemala (ECU 0.45 million).

Cooperation through non-governmental organizations

1021. The funds earmarked for development cooperation with the non-governmental organizations (NGOs) amounted for the year to ECU 104.2 million. At 31 December, ECU 93.88 million had been committed for 503 development projects being cofinanced in 78 African, Asian and Latin American countries. The sum of ECU 10.32 million had

---

[1]   Bull. EC 11-1991, point 1.3.71.
[2]   Bull. EC 11-1991, point 1.3.69.
[3]   Point 826 of this Report.

been committed for a large number of operations aimed at increasing European public awareness of development issues. This year block grants increased yet again; they numbered 120 and amounted to ECU 13.2 million.

Of the appropriations allocated to the budget heading established in 1986 to help the people of Chile (ECU 5 million), the ECU 3 million available for the NGOs was fully committed.[1] New budget headings were also opened for NGO operations in Viet Nam and Cambodia (ECU 2 million and ECU 0.5 million) and the corresponding commitments were made.

1022.   On 22 February[2] and 3 December[3] respectively the Commission adopted the reports on cooperation with European NGOs in the 1989 and 1990 financial years. The NGOs held their 17th annual meeting in April.[4]

Human rights and development

1023.   In March the Commission adopted a communication in which it proposed a line of conduct concerning the relationship between development cooperation policies, observance and promotion of human rights and support for democratic processes in the developing countries.[5] The Council and the Member States' representatives approved this communication in November[6] and asked the Commission to report on the proposed guidelines, which recommend the adoption of sanctions in the event of serious human rights infringements. Parliament adopted a resolution on this subject.[7]

---

[1]   Twentieth General Report, point 938.
[2]   Bull. EC 1/2-1991, point 1.3.70.
[3]   Bull. EC 12-1991.
[4]   Bull. EC 4-1991, point 1.3.56.
[5]   Bull. EC 3-1991, point 1.3.41.
[6]   Bull. EC 11-1991, point 1.3.67.
[7]   OJ C 326, 16.2.1991; Bull. EC 11-1991, point 1.3.68.

Section 9

Multilateral trade negotiations — Uruguay Round

1024.   The Community pursued with determination its efforts in the Uruguay Round negotiations. However, despite the real progress made at the end of the year and the resolve, expressed by the Heads of State or Government meeting at the European Council in Maastricht on 9 and 10 December, to see the discussion lead to a substantial and balanced outcome, it has proved impossible to reach an agreement concluding the talks.

At its meeting on 23 December the Council took note of a compromise proposal presented by Mr Arthur Dunkel, the GATT Director-General, and examined in particular the solution proposed for the agricultural aspect. It took the view that, as it stood, the solution called into question the very basis of the common agricultural policy and could not therefore be accepted. It accordingly asked the Commission to negotiate the necessary improvements and called on the principal trade partners concerned, in particular the United States and Japan, to join in the effort so that all parties might derive greater mutual advantages from the outcome of the negotiations.

Section 10

Commercial policy

Implementing the common commercial policy

Commercial policy instruments and import and export arrangements

1025.   At the end of the Gulf conflict and in accordance with the resolutions adopted by the United Nations Security Council, the Council gradually relaxed the trade embargo initially imposed on Iraq and Kuwait. [1]

1026.   On 23 January the Commission adopted its eighth annual report on the Community's anti-dumping and anti-subsidy activities in 1989; [2] it also contains, for the purposes of comparison, information on the number of investigations and reviews initiated and concluded in the years 1985 to 1988. The ninth annual report was adopted on 31 May. [3] While dealing essentially with the same activities carried out by the Community in 1990, it also provides statistics for the period 1986 to 1989, together with an appraisal of anti-dumping activities over the past 10 years and their repercussions for trade.

1027.   During the year, definitive anti-dumping duties were imposed on the following: imports of aspartame originating in the United States or Japan; [4] espadrilles originating in the People's Republic of China; [5] certain types of welded tubes, of iron or non-alloy steel, originating in Turkey or Venezuela; [6] linear tungsten halogen lamps originating in Japan; [7] audio tapes in cassettes originating in Japan or the Republic of Korea; [8] barium chloride originating in the People's Republic of China; [9] small-screen colour television receivers originating in Hong Kong, the People's Republic of China or the Republic of Korea; [10] certain types of erasable programmable read-only memories

[1]   Point 908 of this Report.
[2]   Bull. EC 1/2-1991, point 1.3.74.
[3]   Bull. EC 5-1991, point 1.3.79.
[4]   OJ L 134, 29.5.1991; Bull. EC 5-1991, point 1.3.82.
[5]   OJ L 166, 28.6.1991; Bull. EC 6-1991, point 1.3.64.
[6]   OJ L 91, 12.4.1991; Bull. EC 4-1991, point 1.3.60.
[7]   OJ L 14, 19.1.1991; Bull. EC 1/2-1991, point 1.3.75.
[8]   OJ L 119, 14.5.1991; Bull. EC 5-1991, point 1.3.80.
[9]   OJ L 60, 7.3.1991; Bull. EC 3-1991, point 1.3.52.
[10] OJ L 195, 18.7.1991; Bull. EC 7/8-1991, point 1.3.66.

known as Eproms originating in Japan;[1] video tapes in cassettes originating in the People's Republic of China;[2] urea originating in Venezuela;[3] gas-fuelled, non-refillable pocket flint lighters originating in Japan, the People's Republic of China, the Republic of Korea or Thailand;[4] oxalic acid originating in India or the People's Republic of China.[4]

1028. In certain cases, the Commission accepted undertakings from exporters to increase their prices, particularly for the following: welded wire-mesh originating in Yugoslavia;[5] certain types of erasable programmable read-only memories known as Eproms originating in Japan;[6] ferro-silicon originating in Brazil;[7] gas-fuelled, non-refillable pocket flint lighters in the case of a Thai exporter.[8] The Commission also accepted undertakings under an anti-subsidy proceeding concerning imports of polyester fibres and polyester yarns originating in Turkey.[9]

In some cases it was considered unnecessary to introduce protective measures, and investigations concerning imports of the following were terminated: thin polyester film originating in the Republic of Korea;[10] Atlantic salmon originating in Norway;[11] cotton terry-towelling articles (bathrobes, toilet and kitchen linen) originating in Turkey;[12] potassium permanganate originating in the Soviet Union;[13] Portland cement originating in Yugoslavia;[14] audio tapes in cassettes originating in Hong Kong;[15] self-propelled hydraulic excavators originating in Japan;[16] dihydrostreptomycin originating in Japan;[17] polyester yarns (man-made staple fibres) originating in the Republic of Korea;[18] urea originating in Trinidad and Tobago.[19]

1029. A number of anti-dumping measures expired, notably those concerning the following: imports of clogs originating in Sweden;[20] self-propelled hydraulic excavators

---

[1]   OJ L 65, 12.3.1991; Bull. EC 3-1991, point 1.3.53.
[2]   OJ L 293, 24.10.1991; Bull. EC 10-1991, point 1.3.52.
[3]   OJ L 272, 28.9.1991; Bull. EC 9-1991, point 1.3.57.
[4]   OJ L 326, 28.11.1991; Bull. EC 11-1991, point 1.3.55.
[5]   OJ L 123, 18.5.1991; Bull. EC 5-1991, point 1.3.87.
[6]   OJ L 65, 12.3.1991; Bull. EC 3-1991, point 1.3.60.
[7]   OJ L 111, 3.5.1991; Bull. EC 4-1991, point 1.3.70.
[8]   OJ L 326, 28.11.1991.
[9]   OJ L 272, 28.9.1991; Bull. EC 9-1991, point 1.3.62.
[10] OJ L 151, 15.6.1991; Bull. EC 6-1991, point 1.3.66.
[11] OJ L 69, 16.3.1991; Bull. EC 3-1991, point 1.3.61.
[12] OJ L 17, 23.1.1991; Bull. EC 1/2-1991, point 1.3.88.
[13] OJ L 14, 19.1.1991; Bull. EC 1/2-1991, point 1.3.86.
[14] OJ L 16, 22.1.1991; Bull. EC 1/2-1991, point 1.3.87.
[15] OJ L 119, 14.5.1991; Bull. EC 5-1991, point 1.3.80.
[16] OJ L 36, 8.2.1991; Bull. EC 1/2-1991, point 1.3.89.
[17] Bull. EC 12-1991.
[18] OJ L 276, 3.10.1991; Bull. EC 9-1991, point 1.3.61.
[19] OJ L 272, 28.9.1991; Bull. EC 9-1991, point 1.3.57.
[20] OJ C 34, 9.2.1991; Bull. EC 1/2-1991, point 1.3.85.

originating in Japan;[1] certain categories of glass originating in Bulgaria, Czechoslovakia, Hungary, Romania, Turkey or Yugoslavia;[2] copper sulphate originating in Yugoslavia;[3] certain types of freezer originating in Yugoslavia;[4] acrylic fibres originating in Israel, Romania or Turkey;[5] and electronic typewriters originating in Japan, though only as regards the undertakings given by Tokyo Juki Industrial Co. Ltd.[6]

1030.   On 7 October[7] and 19 December[8] the Council adopted two Regulations amending the annexes to Regulation (EEC) No 288/82 on common rules for imports and dealing respectively with products subject to quantitative restrictions in the various Member States, particularly as regards Japan (Annex I), and products subject to surveillance (Annex II).[9]

1031.   The Commission extended the validity of retrospective Community surveillance measures concerning imports of certain products originating in Japan[10] and imports into the Community of footwear originating in any non-member country.[11] Prior surveillance was introduced for imports of diammonium hydrogenorthophosphate originating in non-member countries.[12] In adopting Regulation (EEC) No 2014/91, the Commission re-established the levying of customs duties on certain products originating in Yugoslavia.[13]

Treaties and trade agreements

1032.   Pursuant to Decision 69/494/EEC,[14] the Council authorized the extension or automatic renewal for a further year of a number of trade agreements concluded between Member States and other countries, inasmuch as they did not constitute an obstacle to implementation of the common commercial policy.[15]

---

1   OJ L 36, 8.2.1991; Bull. EC 1/2-1991, point 1.3.89.
2   OJ C 55, 2.3.1991; Bull. EC 3-1991, point 1.3.62.
3   OJ C 117, 1.5.1991; Bull. EC 5-1991, point 1.3.89.
4   OJ C 251, 26.9.1991; Bull. EC 9-1991, point 1.3.64.
5   OJ C 251, 26.9.1991; Bull. EC 9-1991, point 1.3.63.
6   OJ L 96, 12.4.1991.
7   OJ L 284, 12.10.1991; Bull. EC 10-1991, point 1.3.50.
8   Bull. EC 12-1991.
9   OJ L 35, 9.2.1982; Sixteenth General Report, point 624.
10 OJ L 6, 9.1.1991: Bull. EC 1/2-1991, point 1.3.90.
11 OJ L 6, 9.1.1991; Bull. EC 1/2-1991, point 1.3.91.
12 OJ L 43, 16.2.1991; Bull. EC 1/2-1991, point 1.3.96.
13 OJ L 185, 11.7.1991; Bull. EC 7/8-1991, point 1.3.77.
14 OJ L 326, 29.12.1969.
15 OJ L 54, 28.2.1991; Bull. EC 1/2-1991, point 1.3.98; OJ L 83, 3.4.1991; Bull. EC 3-1991, point 1.3.69; OJ L 90, 11.4.1991; Bull. EC 4-1991, point 1.3.74; OJ L 202, 25.7.1991; Bull. EC 7/8-1991, point 1.3.81; OJ L 272, 28.9.1991; Bull. EC 9-1991, point 1.3.65.

1033.   On 25 March it also authorized the automatic renewal or maintenance in force of a number of friendship, trade and navigation treaties and similar agreements concluded between Member States and other countries.[1]

Export credits

1034.   Negotiations continued in the OECD on the guidelines for officially supported export credits (the 'Consensus') with a view to improving transparency and discipline in the field of export credits, including aid credits. The guidelines were amended as a result. The amendments, adopted by the Council on 16 December,[2] provide in particular for a more frequent recourse to non-subsidized interest rates and greater discipline in both tied and partially untied aid credit in respect of certain countries and for commercially viable projects.

1035.   Pending a Council decision on its November 1990 proposal concerning a reinsurance pool for export credits to Central and East European countries,[3] on which Parliament delivered its opinion on 10 September,[4] the Commission participated in the technical work of a group of experts on harmonizing the major principles of credit insurance.

1036.   On 21 October[5] the Council extended until 15 October 1992 the Decision implementing the Arrangement on guidelines for officially supported export credits.[6]

Export promotion

1037.   Activities to promote exports to non-member country markets focused on two priority areas — Asia and the Pacific, and Central and Eastern Europe.

1038.   Participation in major international conferences and exhibitions in Asia was particularly encouraged in the form of Community pavilions bringing together Member State industry representatives and the Commission. The organization of seminars of a scientific, sector-based or general nature held in parallel with the exhibitions generally gave a boost to the Community dimension of these activities and highlighted the synergy between R&D and industry fostered by this dimension and by the cooperation activities launched on the Commission's initiative.

---

[1]   OJ L 82, 28.3.1991; Bull. EC 3-1991, point 1.3.68.
[2]   Bull. EC 12-1991.
[3]   OJ C 302, 1.12.1990; Twenty-fourth General Report, point 837.
[4]   OJ C 267, 14.10.1991; Bull. EC 9-1991, point 1.3.15.
[5]   Bull. EC 10-1991, point 1.3.68.
[6]   Twelfth General Report, point 452.

1039.   As in 1990,[1] the Community was also represented at another type of event, designed more for exploratory and information purposes and targeted more specifically at Central and East European countries. A week-long trade forum, the third in the Marketplace series, was held from 26 to 29 November in Prague and Bratislava and brought together over a hundred potential partners to discuss five themes — agrifoodstuffs, biotechnology, the engineering and electronics industries and telecommunications.

1040.   Under a new budget heading specifically established to finance the promotion of exports of textiles and footwear, a project exploring the potential for developing exports of textiles and clothing to Mexico and South Korea was launched. In addition, to promote exports of footwear in particular to Asean countries, European manufacturers organized an exhibition in Singapore.

Two further initiatives got under way: a technical conference in Singapore on biotechnology and its application in a number of industries, and a market study on consumer product distribution systems in Korea.

Individual sectors

Steel

External element of the steel plan

1041.   The rules governing imports of ECSC steel products into the Community (formal arrangements for some suppliers, basic prices for the rest) are basically those dating from 1978[2] and there was little change on 1990.[3] Imports for 1991 totalled 11 million tonnes, down on the 1990 figure of 11.6 million tonnes.

On the basis of the negotiating directives adopted by the Council on 8 April,[4] the Commission approved on 30 July[5] the arrangements whereby five non-member countries (Czechoslovakia, Hungary, Poland, Romania and, for iron and steel products only, Brazil, through an exchange of letters extending the 1990 arrangement) undertook to limit their exports to the Community market.[4] Similar arrangements for Bulgaria were adopted by the Commission on 18 October.[6] Exports of Brazilian pig iron are now

---

[1]   Twenty-fourth General Report, point 839.
[2]   OJ L 196, 13.5.1978; Twelfth General Report, points 125 and 953.
[3]   Twenty-fourth General Report, point 840.
[4]   Bull. EC 4-1991, point 1.3.79.
[5]   Bull. EC 7/8-1991, point 1.3.83.
[6]   Bull. EC 10-1991, point 1.3.71.

subject only to a consultation clause identical to that which has covered all products of Korean origin for the past two years. There are now no special arrangements for EFTA countries. Given the marked 15% rise in quantities in 1990 coupled with a cut in the range of products covered, it was decided not to change the content of the arrangements for 1991.

Multilateral steel consensus in the context of GATT

1042.   On the initiative of the US authorities, exploratory talks have been under way since September 1990 in an attempt to reach an international agreement on relaxing trading conditions for steel products. The talks have drawn partly on the strict disciplines negotiated between the Community and the USA as part of the bilateral agreement signed in 1989.[1] A number of meetings involving the majority of steel-producing countries have enabled significant progress to be made on a large number of points, although certain major policy issues are still outstanding.

External element of the 1992 steel plan

1043.   In talks on the external element for 1991, the Member States stated their intention to end the arrangements for voluntary restraint of imports in 1992. This is in line with the 1989 bilateral agreement between the Community and the USA. Talks on putting this agreement on a multilateral footing are currently under way in Geneva.

Autonomous arrangements

1044.   On 22 July the representatives of the Member States meeting within the Council adopted Decision 91/463/ECSC maintaining 1990 levels for the tonnages of steel products allowed onto the markets of the five Member States which had maintained autonomous quotas with regard to certain Central and East European countries.[2]

1045.   On 6 September the Commission adopted two Decisions on the conclusion of Protocols with Poland[3] and Hungary[4] respectively on trade and commercial and eco-

---

[1]   OJ L 368, 18.12.1989; Twenty-third General Report, point 742.
[2]   Bull. EC 7/8-1991, point 1.3.83.
[3]   OJ L 322, 23.11.1991; Bull. EC 9-1991, point 1.3.22.
[4]   OJ L 340, 11.12.1991; Bull. EC 9-1991, point 1.3.21.

nomic cooperation as regards ECSC products. On 12 December a similar Decision was adopted in respect of the Czech and Slovak Federal Republic.[1] All quantitative restrictions imposed on these countries will have been lifted by the date the Protocols come into force.

1046.   The Council authorized the Commission to negotiate an agreement on trade and economic and commercial cooperation with Romania covering ECSC products.[2] On 16 December the Commission put before the Council three proposals for Decisions on the conclusion of interim association agreements and back-up measures between the European Economic Community and the European Coal and Steel Community and Hungary, Poland and the Czech and Slovak Federal Republic, and three Decisions on their conclusion on behalf of the European Coal and Steel Community.[2]

Relations with the USA

1047.   Since 1982 the main exporting countries' access to the US market has been restricted.[3] In 1989, on the basis of a programme for the liberalization of trade in steel, the US authorities renewed the relevant quotas for the last time until March 1992.[4]

As agreed bilaterally between the USA and the Community in 1989,[4] discussions involving the Community and 18 other steel-producing nations got under way within GATT on a multilateral agreement to liberalize trade in steel.[5]

Shipbuilding

1048.   The negotiations begun in 1990 within the OECD on an international agreement on adherence to normal and fair conditions of competition in the shipbuilding sector were actively pursued in 1991.[6] Despite the complexity of the issues at stake, further progress was made and all parties to the negotiations undertook to bring about a rapid settlement of those issues still outstanding.

[1]   Bull. EC 12-1991.
[2]   Bull. EC 11-1991, point 1.3.92.
[3]   Sixteenth General Report, point 637; Twentieth General Report, point 821.
[4]   OJ L 368, 18.12.1989; Twenty-third General Report, point 742.
[5]   Point 1042 of this Report.
[6]   Twenty-fourth General Report, point 844.

Textiles

Extending the MFA

1049.   On 31 July the GATT Textiles Committee adopted the decision and Protocol extending the Multifibre Arrangement (MFA) for a period of 17 months from 1 August 1991 to 31 December 1992. On 25 November the Council adopted a Decision on the conclusion of this Protocol pending the outcome of the Uruguay Round on multilateral trade in textiles. [1]

1050.   On 11 June Parliament adopted a resolution on renewal of the MFA and the need for a productive outcome in the Uruguay Round negotiations on textiles. [2]

Bilateral agreements with non-member countries

1051.   On the basis of the directives which it received from the Council on 13 May, [3] the Commission initialled exchanges of letters with all the non-member supplier countries, with the exception of India, Pakistan and Brazil, extending until 31 December 1992 the bilateral agreements due to expire on 31 December 1991. On 13 November the Council decided to apply provisionally the exchanges of letters for 1992. [4]

1052.   The bilateral agreements on trade in textiles renegotiated in 1986 [5] or negotiated subsequently under the MFA operated satisfactorily throughout the year. [6] The Council decided to apply provisionally the agreed minutes amending the agreements with Indonesia, [7] Malaysia [8] and Thailand. [9]

1053.   On 19 December the Council adopted a Regulation on common rules for imports of certain textile products originating in third countries aimed at implementing from 1 January 1992 all the provisions administering the agreements initialled and ensuring that the quantitative restrictions agreed upon for 1992 are complied with. [10]

1054.   The Textiles Committee, set up in 1978, assisted the Commission in administering the agreements and contributed to the preparation of several rounds of consultations

[1]   OJ L 327, 29.11.1991; Bull. EC 11-1991, point 1.3.88.
[2]   OJ C 183, 15.7.1991; Bull. EC 6-1991, point 1.3.72.
[3]   Bull. EC 5-1991, point 1.3.91.
[4]   Bull. EC 11-1991, point 1.3.89.
[5]   Twentieth General Report, point 804.
[6]   Twenty-fourth General Report, point 848.
[7]   OJ L 100, 20.4.1991; Bull. EC 4-1991, point 1.3.77.
[8]   OJ L 100, 20.4.1991; Bull. EC 4-1991, point 1.3.78.
[9]   OJ L 256, 13.9.1991; Bull. EC 7/8-1991, point 1.3.84.
[10]   Bull. EC 12-1991.

held during the year with various supplier countries.[1] The consultations resulted in the introduction of five new quantitative limits at regional and Community level, compared with four in 1990, and the settlement of other matters, in particular those linked to the introduction of the Harmonized System.

1055.   On 17 December the Commission adopted a proposal for a Council Regulation on common rules for imports of textile products originating in Estonia, Latvia or Lithuania.[2]

1056.   On 16 December[3] the Council adopted a Regulation to implement from 1 January 1991 the quantitative adjustments approved for 1991 on the basis of the Council Directives of 4 December 1990 adopted in the wake of German unification.[4] These adjustments are based on a standard formula which also takes account of the traditional trade links between the relevant countries and the former German Democratic Republic.

1057.   On a proposal from the Commission,[5] on 3 June the Council also adopted a Decision on the conclusion of the Agreement with the Soviet Union on trade in textiles.[6]

1058.   As part of negotiations on textile protocols to the association agreements with Czechoslovakia, Hungary and Poland, the Commission, having received the Council's mandate on 8 July, concluded a protocol with each of these countries amending for 1992 the textile agreements in force pending the negotiation of a fixed arrangement for trade in textiles during 1992. In its Regulation of 23 April, the Commission also increased the quantitative limits applicable to these countries.[7]

Under operation Phare,[8] the Council decided to adjust certain quantitative limits for Bulgaria and Romania.

Arrangements with preferential countries

1059.   Under its textile policy, the Commission continued and concluded consultations with Turkey and proposed on 12 July that the Council conclude the new arrangement for trade in clothing products.[9] This will replace the previous arrangement, which expired on 31 December 1990.[10]

---

[1]   OJ L 365, 25.12.1978; Twelfth General Report, point 454.
[2]   Bull. EC-12-1991.
[3]   OJ L 352, 21.12.1991; Bull. EC 12-1991; Commission proposal: Bull. EC 11-1991, point 1.3.90.
[4]   Twenty-fourth General Report, point 24.
[5]   Bull. EC 3-1991, point 1.3.72.
[6]   OJ L 164, 26.6.1991; Bull. EC 6-1991, point 1.3.73.
[7]   OJ L 111, 3.5.1991; Bull. EC 4-1991, point 1.3.76.
[8]   Point 818 of this Report.
[9]   Bull. EC 7/8-1991, point 1.3.85.
[10]   Twenty-first General Report, point 744.

On 28 October the Council authorized the Commission to negotiate the renewal of the textile arrangements with the other preferential countries.[1] Agreements were renewed with Malta, Egypt and Tunisia.

Automobiles

1060.   The Community and Japan reached a solution on trade in motor cars which, in close cooperation with the relevant parties, is aimed at liberalizing progressively and fully the Community's import arrangements for motor cars without disrupting the market, and at introducing a transitional period enabling Community production to attain adequate levels of international competitiveness.[2] During this period, from 1 January 1993 to 31 December 1999, the Japanese Government will, as part of cooperation measures, continue to monitor its exports to the Community and to the five currently 'protected' markets (France, Italy, the United Kingdom, Spain and Portugal) in particular.

1061.   As regards relations with other countries, the Commission began consultations with the USA on securing an amendment to the current method of calculating CAFE (Corporate average fuel efficiency), which is judged to be discriminatory. It also informed Austria that it believed the size of the subsidy granted to a multi-purpose vehicle assembly joint venture was unjustifiably high and could distort trade and competition.

Other products

1062.   On 4 February,[3] following a communication from the Commission,[4] the Council authorized the Commission to open negotiations with the USA and other parties to the GATT Agreement on trade in civil aircraft for the conclusion of new arrangements on international trade in this field.

---

[1]   Bull. EC 10-1991, point 1.3.69.
[2]   Bull. EC 7/8-1991, point 1.3.34.
[3]   Bull. EC 1/2-1991, point 1.3.106.
[4]   Twenty-fourth General Report, point 851.

Section 11

International organizations and conferences

United Nations

General Assembly

1063.   The 46th session of the United Nations General Assembly, which began on 23 September, was marked by an event of major political significance: the three Baltic States and the Democratic People's Republic of Korea and the Republic of Korea were admitted as members of the United Nations. The upheavals in East-West relations were reflected in a general shift in favour of a new world order in which conflicts would be settled peacefully by negotiation under the auspices of the United Nations. Major challenges had to be faced, such as ethnic conflict and nationalist separatist movements. Freedom and democracy were given world-wide support; extensive discussions were held on the promotion of human rights and the United Nations' role in this. As a result of the change in the international situation, China, France and South Africa announced that they would shortly sign the nuclear Non-Proliferation Treaty. Considerable support was shown for the proposal for a register of arms supply operations.

The new international political context and the fuller and more active role being played by the United Nations in economic development highlighted the process of restructuring the organization to enable it to meet international challenges more effectively.

The statement made by the EC Presidency on behalf of the Community and the Member States dealt with the following four topics: the need for countries to act responsibly in political, economic and military matters; the challenges posed by sustainable development and the eradication of poverty; the observance of human rights; the need to restructure the United Nations and streamline its operations.

The Commission was represented by Mr Andriessen and Mr Matutes. They took the opportunity offered by the General Assembly meeting to have talks, as part of European political cooperation, with the US Secretary of State and with the Foreign Ministers of Japan and a large number of developing countries in Asia, North Africa, Latin America and the Gulf.

On 3 December the General Assembly approved by acclamation the election of its sixth Secretary-General, Mr Boutros Boutros Ghali, for a five-year period starting on 2 January 1992.

Economic and Social Council

1064. The annual spring session of the Economic and Social Council (Ecosoc), held in New York from 13 to 31 May, tackled a large number of topics of interest to the Community, such as the situation of women, racism and racial discrimination, human rights and social development. The Community Presidency, in a statement on the problem of human rights, stressed the Community's awareness of the economic difficulties of the developing countries and emphasized the link between democracy and development, referring to the fourth Lomé Convention, the 1993 single market and the progress made in the Community on social issues, particularly the action taken by the Community to help the elderly, the handicapped and young people. The second regular session of Ecosoc, held in Geneva from 3 to 26 July, introduced a number of reforms in order to give new impetus to Ecosoc's activities. The discussions focused on East-West relations and their impact on the developing countries, the economic effects of the Gulf crisis and the report of the South Commission. As usual, the Community was the Group of 77's main discussion partner, generally supported by the Central and East European countries. The main political issue put to this Ecosoc session was Israel's admission to the United Nations Economic Commission for Europe (ECE), to which only the Islamic countries were opposed.

1065. The 46th annual session of the Economic Commission for Europe was held in Geneva from 9 to 19 April.[1] What emerged from the discussions was the need to concentrate efforts on the ECE's priorities, namely the environment, transport, the improvement of trade, statistics and economic analysis, together with the role played by the ECE in supporting the transition to a market economy under way in the Central and East European countries.

Convention on the Law of the Sea

1066. The 1982 Convention will not enter into force until it has been ratified by 60 parties. So far it has been ratified by 49 countries all of which, except Yugoslavia and Iceland, are developing countries. Within the Preparatory Commission, the industrialized countries, including the Community, are striving to obtain improvements to the

---

[1] Bull. EC 4-1991, point 1.3.80.

rules governing exploitation of the sea-bed so that the Convention can become universally acceptable. At the same time the United Nations Secretary-General has invited a number of States that are particularly concerned to a round of consultations, in which the United States has been taking part and the first stage of which ended in December 1991. The results suggest that a compromise between the Group of 77 and the industrialized countries can be found before the Convention enters into force.

United Nations Environment Programme

1067.   The Commission continued to take part in the work of UNEP, and more especially the preparations for the Conference on the Environment and Development (Unced), to be held in Rio de Janeiro in June 1992.[1] It also attended the Nairobi meeting in May, and the 16th session of UNEP's Governing Council, at which it was decided to set up an experimental centre for emergency environmental assistance.

International Monetary Fund and the World Bank

1068.   The International Monetary Fund and the World Bank (IBRD) held their annual meetings in Bangkok on 13 and 14 October.[2] The Community was represented by Mr Wim Kok, President of the Council, and Mr Christophersen, Commission Vice-President. Representatives of the Commission also took part in the discussions of the Group of Ten, which met before the plenary session, and of the Interim Committee of the IMF's Board of Governors, the Development Committee and the World Bank's Board of Governors.

General Agreement on Tariffs and Trade

1069.   The 47th session of the GATT Contracting Parties was held in Geneva from 3 to 5 December.[3] During this session, the Contracting Parties granted the Czech and Slovak Federal Republic a temporary derogation from its obligations under Article II of the GATT, pending the conclusion of the negotiations under Article XXVIII which will enable it to revise its tariff.

This derogation, which was fully supported by the Community, is needed so that the country can restructure its tariff protection in order to make the transition to a market

---

[1]   Point 626 of this Report.
[2]   Point 65 of this Report.
[3]   Bull. EC 12-1991.

economy. The old tariff, which was designed for a planned economy, was unsuited to meeting the challenges of free trade.

During the period in question, the GATT Council held a number of meetings to examine various trade issues which had been put to it. The Council began substantive talks on the interaction between trade and environment and ways of preventing disputes in this sphere, by means of discussions aimed at clarifying, interpreting or possibly amending certain provisions of the General Agreement.

A number of trade disputes put to the Council were referred to panels for examination. The Council was also asked to look into cases where the implementation of panels' reports concerning the Community, the United States and Japan had been linked with the outcome of the Uruguay Round.

1070. As part of GATT's trade policy review mechanism (TPRM), which was one of the main achievements of the Uruguay Round mid-term review and under which the Council examines, at regular special meetings, the impact of the trade policy and trading practices of each of its members on the multilateral trading system, the Council conducted a detailed study in April of the trade arrangements of the Community and other countries.

1071. The Committee on Trade and Development examined, among other matters, developments in international trade and the progress being made in the Uruguay Round.

1072. The Committees on the codes on non-tariff measures (subsidies, dumping, technical standards, government procurement, trade in civil aircraft and import licensing) held regular meetings on the administration of the agreements. In particular, the Airbus dispute between the United States and the Community was discussed by the Subsidies Committee and the Civil Aircraft Committee. At a meeting of the latter the Community proposed that negotiations should be initiated in order to extend and improve the civil aircraft code on a reciprocal basis and cover this type of trade more fully. [1]

1073. A working party set up by the GATT Council examined the free trade Agreement between the United States and Canada.

1074. With the accession of El Salvador, GATT now has 102 Contracting Parties; seven more countries have applied for membership and examination of their applications is under way. The Council of the European Communities decided on 28 January to conclude the protocol on Venezuela's accession to GATT. [2]

---

[1] Point 1062 of this Report.
[2] Bull. EC 1/2-1991, point 1.3.113; Commission proposal: Twenty-fourth General Report, point 864.

Organization for Economic Cooperation and Development

1075. In 1991 the OECD, while continuing the activities relating to the industrialized countries' economies, stepped up its efforts to develop the dialogue with the non-member economies, particularly the Central and East European countries, and also to examine the new dimensions of trade policy in the 1990s.

1076. At their annual meeting, held on 4 and 5 June, the ministers reaffirmed the top priority which they attached to rapid conclusion of the Uruguay Round of trade negotiations and their determination to combat protectionism in all its forms; they also stressed that their aim, following the recent economic slow-down, was to return to the path of sustained, non-inflationary growth. [1]

1077. Following its meeting on 4 and 5 June, the OECD Council of Ministers adopted, on 12 December, a third revised decision on national treatment, which provides for more effective machinery for examining the exceptions put forward by the member countries. This decision provides expressly for its adoption by the Community as such, and this will take effect when the Community procedures have been completed. The Community has already endorsed the policy declaration on national treatment adopted by the OECD in 1976. The Commission, for its part, proposed to the Council on 18 November that the third revised decision should be incorporated in Community legislation. [2]

Conference on Security and Cooperation in Europe

1078. Following the Paris Summit in November 1990 and the signing by the Heads of State or Government of the participating States and the European Community of the Paris Charter for a New Europe, [3] CSCE activities gathered momentum, both at intersessional meetings and in newly set-up CSCE institutions.

1079. As regards the intersessional meetings provided for in Basket II of the Helsinki Final Act, [4] the meeting on the peaceful settlement of disputes held in Valletta from 15 January to 8 February succeeded, for the first time under the CSCE process and after two failed attempts, in reaching conclusions on dispute settlement procedures under the CSCE. [5] The symposium on cultural heritage held in Cracow from 28 May to 7 June examined the cultural features which the participating States have in common and in

---

[1]   Bull. EC 6-1991, point 1.3.79.
[2]   Bull. EC 11-1991, point 1.3.98.
[3]   Twenty-fourth General Report, point 871.
[4]   Ninth General Report, points 510 to 512.
[5]   Bull. EC 1/2-1991, point 1.3.114.

its conclusions set out guidelines for consolidating cultural cooperation within the CSCE.[1] The meeting held in Geneva from 1 to 19 July on national minorities dealt with an important but sensitive issue in relations between the participating States. Although the outcome fell short of most of the delegations' expectations, the Geneva conclusions nevertheless signified some progress on the complex issue of minorities. The Conference on the Human Dimension,[2] the third meeting of this type since the CSCE meeting in Vienna in 1989,[3] was held in Moscow from 10 September to 4 October and had as its backdrop the dramatic events which had occurred in the Soviet Union shortly before. The conference strengthened and extended the human dimension machinery by establishing a monitoring and investigation system which can be set in train even against the wishes of the State concerned.

An expert-level seminar on democratic institutions was held in Oslo from 4 to 15 November. It gave rise to a wide-ranging exchange of views on the importance of the democratic tradition, the independence of the judiciary, the rule of law and the establishment of national centres for democratic institutions.[4]

The discussions at these five intersessional meetings, in which the Community played an important role, within the limits of its ability to establish common positions, demonstrated the importance of the matters examined but also the difficulties encountered by the participating States in working out common guidelines and specific commitments in the relevant spheres.

1080. The Committee of Senior Officials met on four occasions to work out the new institutions' method of operation, and to prepare for meetings of CSCE Foreign Ministers as a Council. It also held five extraordinary sessions in Prague in July, August, September, October and November to discuss the crisis in Yugoslavia. On each of these occasions, it appealed to all the parties concerned to declare or maintain a cease-fire and expressed its full and absolute support for the European Community's efforts to achieve a peaceful settlement of the crisis, and, at its last meeting, the course of action advocated by the United Nations in Yugoslavia.

1081. The CSCE Council, attended by the Foreign Ministers of the participating States and Mr Andriessen, held its first meeting in Berlin on 19 and 20 June.[5] At this meeting Albania was accepted as a member, and at an extraordinary session preceding the meeting on the human dimension in Moscow the Council decided to admit the three Baltic States, raising the number of CSCE participants from 34 to 38. The Council also held political consultations on all aspects of the CSCE process, adopted various measures

---

[1]   Bull. EC 6-1991, point 1.3.77.
[2]   Bull. EC 10-1991, point 1.3.72.
[3]   Twenty-third General Report, point 908.
[4]   Bull. EC 11-1991, point 1.3.94.
[5]   Bull. EC 6-1991, point 1.3.76.

aimed at giving added impetus to the future work of the CSCE in the light of the Paris Charter and held wide-ranging discussions on the crisis in Yugoslavia.

1082.   On 20 November the Commission adopted a communication in preparation for the next follow-up meeting, to be held in Helsinki from March onwards. The communication listed the topics on which further steps forward could be taken, such as science and technology, telecommunications, the environment, transport, human resources and immigration.[1]

Council of Europe

1083.   Over the year the Council of Europe acquired new members and continued to make a contribution to cooperation with, and assistance for, the Central and East European countries.

1084.   Czechoslovakia and Poland joined the Council of Europe at the February and November part-sessions of the Parliamentary Assembly respectively, bringing the number of members to 26. In January Bulgaria asked to be invited to join, and on 20 September Estonia, Latvia and Lithuania made the same request at the Parliamentary Assembly part-session, which they attended with special guest status.[2]

1085.   Cooperation with these countries and also with the USSR, Romania and Albania was extended, particularly in the context of the Demosthenes programme of assistance and training concerning the principles of pluralist democracy and human rights. The Commission took part in meetings on cooperation with these countries on the media and human rights.

1086.   With particular regard to cooperation between the Community and the Council of Europe the operational framework of the exchange of letters was supplemented by the appointment of the senior Commission official responsible for cooperation.[3] The Secretary-General of the Commission held the annual exchange of views with the ministers' delegates and the quadripartite meetings were held in May and November respectively; at these meetings the recent developments in pan-European cooperation with the Central and East European countries were discussed with particular reference to their accession to the Council of Europe and the association agreements concluded by some of them with the Community, and the situation in Yugoslavia and the Soviet

---

[1]   Bull. EC 11-1991, point 1.3.95.
[2]   Bull. EC 9-1991, point 1.3.70.
[3]   OJ L 273, 26.9.1987; Twenty-first General Report, point 902.

Union. The Commission was invited to attend the 88th and 89th meetings of the Committee of Ministers[1] and most of the specialist ministerial conferences, notably those held in Cyprus in September (media), in Vienna in October (education) and in Ankara in November (regional planning — Cemat).

---

[1]   Bull. EC 1/2-1991, point 1.3.115; Bull. EC 11-1991, point 1.3.97.

Chapter IV

Intergovernmental cooperation and human rights

Section 1

European political cooperation

1087.   The Gulf, Yugoslavia and the USSR were the three great challenges faced by the Community and its Member States. The following is a summary of the statements made in 1991 on behalf of the Community and its Member States on these and other issues.

A statement was issued in conjunction with the extraordinary ministerial meeting held on 4 January, which reiterated the firm commitment of the Community and its Member States in favour of the full and unconditional implementation of the relevant resolutions adopted by the UN Security Council since the onset of the Gulf crisis. [1] On 6 January a joint statement followed which expressed regret that Mr Tariq Aziz, the Minister for Foreign Affairs of Iraq, had declined to meet the 'troika' in Luxembourg on 10 January. [2] On 10 January concern and deep disappointment were expressed at the absence of any result from the meeting of 9 January between the American Secretary of State, Mr Baker, and Mr Tariq Aziz. [3] In conjunction with the extraordinary ministerial meeting held in Brussels on 14 January a joint statement was made which made it clear that the Community and its Member States had from the beginning of the Gulf crisis supported unreservedly the full and unconditional implementation of the relevant resolutions of the Security Council. In the face of the continued refusal of the Iraqi

---

[1]   Bull. EC 1/2-1991, point 1.4.4.
[2]   Bull. EC 1/2-1991, point 1.4.5.
[3]   Bull. EC 1/2-1991, point 1.4.8.

authorities to implement the resolutions of the Security Council, the Community and its Member States regretted to have to conclude that the conditions for a new European initiative did not exist at that moment.[1]

A statement was made on 17 January expressing deep regret that the use of force had become necessary to oblige Iraq to withdraw from Kuwait.[2] On the same day a joint statement was published reiterating the firm support of the Community and its Member States for the objectives contained in the relevant resolutions of the Security Council.[3] A statement was published on 19 February welcoming President Gorbachev's call for a full and unconditional withdrawal of the Iraqi troops from Kuwait.[4] A statement of 24 February deeply regretted the failure of Iraq to respond positively in accordance with the UN Security Council resolutions and hoped that the liberation of Kuwait could take place rapidly and with a minimum of loss of lives on both sides.[5]

On 28 February the Community and its Member States welcomed in a joint statement the suspension of military operations in the Gulf. They expressed their satisfaction that Kuwait had recovered its freedom and that international legality had been restored.[6]

1088.   The Community and its Member States expressed their deep concern in a joint statement of 22 January at the unscrupulous use of prisoners of war by Iraq. Such actions were condemned unreservedly. The Iraqi authorities were informed that the Community and the Member States held them responsible for all illegal acts constituting war crimes.[7] In two joint statements of 3 April[8] and 15 November[9] the Community and its Member States expressed their deep concern at the situation of the civilian population in Iraq, notably the Kurds and the Shi'ites.

1089.   A statement on the bombardment of Israel's territory by Iraqi missiles was published on 18 January. The unprovoked and entirely unjustified missile attack was strongly condemned.[10]

1090.   A joint statement on Israel's settlement policy was published on 3 May in which the Community and its Member States deplored the fact that the Israeli Government had given permission for the establishment of two new Israeli settlements in the Occupied Territories. They indicated that the initiative of the US Secretary of State,

---

[1]   Bull. EC 1/2-1991, point 1.4.11.
[2]   Bull. EC 1/2-1991, point 1.4.16.
[3]   Bull. EC 1/2-1991, point 1.4.17.
[4]   Bull. EC 1/2-1991, point 1.4.24.
[5]   Bull. EC 1/2-1991, point 1.4.25.
[6]   Bull. EC 1/2-1991, point 1.4.29.
[7]   Bull. EC 1/2-1991, point 1.4.19.
[8]   Bull. EC 4-1991, point 1.4.2.
[9]   Bull. EC 11-1991, point 1.4.11.
[10]   Bull. EC 1/2-1991, point 1.4.18.

Mr Baker, offered genuine prospects of peace in the region and that any establishment of new settlements in the Occupied Territories was especially harmful at such a time. [1]

1091. On 17 July a statement was issued in which the Presidency recalled the declaration by the European Council in Luxembourg (28 and 29 June) on the Middle East peace process, which confirmed the support of the Community and its Member States for the current initiative launched by the United States. [2] On 29 July a statement was made on the Middle East in which the Community and its Member States noted with satisfaction the emerging consensus on the initiative. [3] On 10 October they confirmed their full support for the process under way. [4]

1092. In a statement of 17 May on the situation in Western Sahara the Community and its Member States welcomed the adoption by the UN Security Council of Resolution 690 approving the report of the UN Secretary-General on the referendum to be held concerning the self-determination of the Sahrawi people. [5]

1093. The Community and its Member States followed with the greatest concern the situation in Yugoslavia. A joint statement of 26 March sought to encourage the resolution of the constitutional crisis by way of dialogue. [6]

On 8 May a further statement was published, referring to previous statements and approaches and stating firm opposition to the use of force. [7]

On 8 June the Community and its Member States published a joint statement in which they noted with satisfaction the outcome of the meeting of 6 June of the six presidents of the republics, which was perceived as being an encouraging step towards a return to constitutional order and a peaceful dialogue on the future structure of Yugoslavia. [8]

On 2 July a further statement was issued in which the Community and its Member States expressed their alarm at the resumption of hostilities in Slovenia. [9] Between 5 July and the end of September there were nine further statements: 5 July — announcement of the decision to organize a monitoring mission and arms embargo; [10] 10 July — stressed the need for full compliance of all parties with the Brioni Agreement; [11] 19 July — noting the Presidency's decision to withdraw the Yugoslav People's Army from the territory

---

[1] Bull. EC 5-1991, point 1.4.2.
[2] Bull. EC 7/8-1991, point 1.4.6.
[3] Bull. EC 7/8-1991, point 1.4.11.
[4] Bull. EC 10-1991, point 1.4.8.
[5] Bull. EC 5-1991, point 1.4.6.
[6] Bull. EC 3-1991, point 1.4.6.
[7] Bull. EC 5-1991, point 1.4.3.
[8] Bull. EC 6-1991, point 1.4.3.
[9] Bull. EC 7/8-1991, point 1.4.2.
[10] Bull. EC 7/8-1991, point 1.4.3.
[11] Bull. EC 7/8-1991, point 1.4.4.

of the Republic of Slovenia;[1] 6 August — deploring the absence of a cease-fire and urging acceptance of a cease-fire which the troika was trying to establish; also calling upon CSCE partners to support the latest initiatives of the Community and its Member States and noting that the WEU was taking stock of the situation and examining whether there was any contribution which it could make;[2] 20 August — expressing grave concern at the frequent infringements of the cease-fire and noting that negotiations should be based upon the principle that any change of borders by force was not acceptable;[3] 28 August — calling upon the Federal Presidency to put an immediate end to the illegal use of forces under its command, calling upon Serbia to lift its objection to the extension of the activities of the monitoring mission in Croatia and stating that an agreement on the monitoring of the cease-fire and its maintenance would allow the Community and its Member States to convene a peace conference and establish an arbitration procedure. In the absence, by 1 September, of an agreement on the monitoring of the cease-fire and on the peace conference, the Community and its Member States stated that they would consider additional measures, including international action;[4] 3 September — welcoming the fact that all Yugoslav parties had accepted the goals and instruments for a solution to the crisis as contained in the statement of 28 August and that, by signing the cease-fire agreement and the Memorandum of Understanding on the extension of the EC monitoring mission, they had demonstrated their commitment to cooperate to that end. The Community and its Member States undertook to convene under their aegis a Conference on Yugoslavia in the Peace Palace in The Hague on 7 September and at the same time set up an arbitration procedure;[5] 7 September — statement made at the opening of the Conference on Yugoslavia stating the aims of the Conference; 19 September — acknowledging Lord Carrington's invaluable contribution in bringing about a cease-fire and reiterating the basic principles subscribed to from the beginning of the crisis:

(i)   the unacceptability of the use of force;

(ii) the unacceptability of any change of borders by force, which the Community and its Member States were determined not to recognize;

(iii) respect for the rights of all who live in Yugoslavia, including minorities;

(iv) the need to take account of all legitimate concerns and aspirations.

The Community and its Member States regretted that the EC monitoring mission was no longer able to perform its task in full and therefore welcomed the WEU exploring ways in which the activities of the monitors could be supported.[6]

---

[1]   Bull. EC 7/8-1991, point 1.4.9.
[2]   Bull. EC 7/8-1991, point 1.4.15.
[3]   Bull. EC 7/8-1991, point 1.4.17.
[4]   Bull. EC 7/8-1991, point 1.4.25.
[5]   Bull. EC 9-1991, point 1.4.2.
[6]   Bull. EC 9-1991, point 1.4.7.

The Community and its Member States said in a joint statement of 5 October that they were not prepared to acknowledge decisions taken by only four members of the Yugoslav collective Federal Presidency, which could therefore no longer claim to speak for the whole of Yugoslavia. [1] In a further statement of 6 October, they expressed their dismay at the continued heavy fighting despite the agreements reached at The Hague on 4 October. [2] In a joint statement published on 18 October, the Community and its Member States, the United States and the Soviet Union expressed their deep concern at the continuing violence and bloodshed and rejected any outcome which violated the principles of the CSCE with regard to borders, minority rights and political pluralism. The United States and the Soviet Union reiterated their full support for the efforts of the European Community and its Member States to mediate a peaceful solution to the crisis. [3]

In a joint statement of 27 October on Dubrovnik the Community and its Member States strongly condemned the Federal Army's continuous attacks on Croatian towns. [4] Assessing the results of the seventh plenary session of the Yugoslav Conference, they concluded on 28 October that five republics had reiterated their readiness to cooperate on the basis of the draft arrangements submitted by Lord Carrington and the Presidency and that one republic continued to reserve its position. [5] They announced their decision in a joint statement of 8 November to take restrictive measures against Yugoslavia. They also called on those Member States which are also members of the UN Security Council to invite the Security Council to reach agreement on additional measures to enhance the effectiveness of the arms embargo. [6] On 11 November the Community and its Member States condemned the further escalation of attacks upon Vukovar, Dubrovnik and other towns in Croatia and noted that for the first time both the rump Presidency, made up of representatives of Serbia and Montenegro, and the government of Croatia, had called for the deployment of international peacekeeping forces in the crisis areas. Lord Carrington was also asked to explain to the parties concerned that any deployment of such forces would be contingent on the prior establishment of an effective cease-fire. [7] On 13 November the Community and its Member States agreed to conduct joint operations with Unicef in order to establish humanitarian peace and security corridors to allow for assistance and possible evacuation of Yugoslav children. [8]

---

[1]   Bull. EC 10-1991, point 1.4.6.
[2]   Bull. EC 10-1991, point 1.4.7.
[3]   Bull. EC 10-1991, point 1.4.10.
[4]   Bull. EC 10-1991, point 1.4.15.
[5]   Bull. EC 10-1991, point 1.4.16.
[6]   Bull. EC 11-1991, point 1.4.4.
[7]   Bull. EC 11-1991, point 1.4.8.
[8]   Bull. EC 11-1991, point 1.4.9.

1094.   In the light of guidelines adopted on the recognition of the new States in Central and Eastern Europe and the Soviet Union, on 16 December[1] the Community and its Member States adopted a common position on recognition of the Yugoslav republics.[2]

1095.   In a statement of 19 August on the Soviet Union the Community and its Member States indicated that they had learned with grave concern that President Mikhail Gorbachev had been removed from office.[3] On 20 August, another statement was published, strongly condemning the seizure of all power by a 'State Committee for the State of Emergency'.[4] On 22 August the Community and its Member States stated that they had learnt of the collapse of the coup with profound relief and satisfaction. And that they had decided to revoke their decision of 20 August to suspend the Community's economic assistance in the form of food aid and technical assistance.[5]

1096.   On 2 December the Community and its Member States took note of the referendum in Ukraine, in which a clear majority came out in favour of independence. They expected Ukraine to honour all commitments of the Soviet Union under the Helsinki Final Act, the Charter of Paris and other relevant CSCE documents and to honour all international obligations of the Soviet Union in respect of arms control and nuclear non-proliferation. They expected Ukraine to join the other republics in accepting joint and several liability for the Soviet Union's foreign debts.[2]

1097.   On 23 December the Community and its Member States adopted a statement on the future status of Russia and the other republics. They took cognizance of the decision of the participants at the Alma Ata meeting on 21 December to create a Commonwealth of Independent States and transfer the international rights and obligations of the former Soviet Union to Russia.[2] Furthermore, on 25 December they took note of Mr Gorbachev's decision to resign from his post as President of the Soviet Union.[2] In a further joint statement on 31 December the Community and its Member States welcomed the fact that Armenia, Azerbaijan, Belarus (formerly Belorussia), Kazakhstan, Moldova, Turkmenistan, Ukraine and Uzbekistan have declared their readiness to fulfil the conditions for the recognition of new States in Central Europe and the Soviet Union. In so doing, they indicated that they were prepared to recognize those republics and reaffirmed their determination also to recognize Kyrgyzstan (formerly Kirghizia) and Tadjikistan once they had given the same assurances and provided that all members of the Commonwealth of Independent States with nuclear weapons on their

---

[1]   Point 1102 of this Report.
[2]   Bull. EC 12-1991.
[3]   Bull. EC 7/8-1991, point 1.4.16.
[4]   Bull. EC 7/8-1991, point 1.4.19.
[5]   Bull. EC 10-1991, point 1.4.21.

territory acceded in the near future to the Non-Proliferation Treaty as States that would not have recourse to such weapons. [1]

1098.   In a joint statement of 4 February the Community and its Member States welcomed the decision to hold a referendum in each of the Baltic republics, considering such a decision to be in conformity with the spirit of the Paris Charter for a New Europe. [2]

On 11 January they expressed the hope that the Soviet Union would enter as soon as possible into negotiations with the elected representatives of the Baltic republics and that, in conformity with its commitments under the Helsinki Final Act and the Charter of Paris, [3] it would refrain from any act of intimidation. On 14 January a statement was made describing the use of force as unacceptable and containing an urgent appeal to the Soviet authorities to resume the path of dialogue and end the military intervention. [4] The Community and its Member States issued a statement on 4 March underlining the significance of the referendums held in Lithuania, Latvia and Estonia and urged an early opening of a dialogue between the central government of the USSR and the elected Baltic authorities. [5] In a statement of 28 August the Community and its Member States warmly welcomed the restoration of the sovereignty and independence of the Baltic States. [6] A further statement was published on 6 September on the occasion of a meeting with the Foreign Ministers of Estonia, Latvia and Lithuania and the Foreign Ministers of the Member States of the Community and the representatives of the Commission reiterated their willingness to explore together with the three Baltic States all avenues to assist them in their democratic and economic development. [7]

1099.   A statement was published on 26 February in which the Community and its Member States recalled their interest in the development of the process of democratization in Albania and gave their encouragement to any progress towards democracy in accordance with the principles of the rule of law. [8]

1100.   In their joint statement of 3 October on Romania the Community and its Member States called for all social claims to be negotiated and solved in a peaceful and democratic way. [9]

1101.   On 9 November the Community and its Member States and the United States expressed their support for the citizens of the new democracies of Central and Eastern

---

[1]   Bull. EC 12-1991.
[2]   Bull. EC 1/2-1991, point 1.4.21.
[3]   Bull. EC 1/2-1991, point 1.4.9.
[4]   Bull. EC 1/2-1991, point 1.4.12.
[5]   Bull. EC 3-1991, point 1.4.2.
[6]   Bull. EC 7/8-1991, point 1.4.23.
[7]   Bull. EC 9-1991, point 1.4.3.
[8]   Bull. EC 1/2-1991, point 1.4.27.
[9]   Bull. EC 10-1991, point 1.4.3.

Europe and for those of the Soviet Union and its republics in their struggle to rebuild their economies and their societies on a democratic basis. They underlined that respect for the principles and commitments of the CSCE and for minorities were essential to the development of good relations in the new Europe.[1]

1102.   A further statement was adopted on 16 December with regard to guidelines on the recognition of the new States in Central Europe and the Soviet Union and on the process of recognizing such States.[2]

1103.   In a joint statement of 4 February the Community and its Member States warmly welcomed the announcement of further important changes to come in South Africa, including the repeal of the Group Areas Act, the two Land Acts and the Population Registration Act, thus opening the path towards the abolition of apartheid. Such repeals would enable the Community and its Member States to proceed to ease the set of measures adopted in 1986. A joint statement on the 10th synthesis report on the code of conduct for Community companies with subsidiaries in South Africa was published on 14 May.[3] On 18 June the repeal of the acts referred to above was welcomed.[4] In a statement on 2 August the Community and its Member States noted with interest the statement made by President De Klerk on 30 July in answer to the revelations of secret funding by the South African Government of political and related organizations in South Africa and the alleged involvement of elements of the SADF and security forces in the violence.[5] On 22 August the Community and its Member States made a joint statement welcoming the agreement reached between the South African Government and the Office of the United Nations High Commissioner for Refugees on the process of the return of refugees and political exiles to South Africa.[6] On 16 September the Community and its Member States published a joint statement welcoming the signing of the National Peace Agreement on 14 September.[7] On 3 October the Community and its Member States expressed their concern at the detention of political prisoners in the so-called independent homelands.[8] In a joint statement on 29 November they warmly welcomed the announcement of a date for the start of negotiations in the framework of the Multi-party Conference on a new constitution establishing a united, non-racial and democratic South Africa.[9] In their statement of 17 December the Community and

---

[1]   Bull. EC 11-1991, point 1.4.6.
[2]   Bull. EC 12-1991.
[3]   Bull. EC 5-1991, point 1.4.5.
[4]   Bull. EC 6-1991, point 1.4.6.
[5]   Bull. EC 7/8-1991, point 1.4.13.
[6]   Bull. EC 7/8-1991, point 1.4.20.
[7]   Bull. EC 9-1991, point 1.4.6.
[8]   Bull. EC 10-1991, point 1.4.4.
[9]   Bull. EC 11-1991, point 1.4.18.

its Member States welcomed the start of the work of this conference and accepted the invitation to participate with observer status.[1]

1104.   On 31 May the Community and its Member States published a joint statement welcoming the signature by the Government of Angola and Unita of the peace agreements in Estoril.[2] On 27 May they indicated that they were following closely the course of the peace negotiations taking place between the Government of Mozambique and Renamo[3] and on 11 October they welcomed the resumption of these negotiations in Rome.[4]

1105.   On 15 February the Community and its Member States welcomed the opening of the port of Massawa and the successful start of the northern relief corridor in Ethiopia.[5] On 18 April they published a further joint statement expressing their worry about the recent escalation of the civil war and they urged all parties to the conflict to work urgently for the establishment of a cease-fire and the resumption of negotiations. They also urgently called upon them to ensure that emergency food aid and humanitarian aid be effectively distributed to those for whom they were intended.[6] Following the resignation of President Mengistu an urgent appeal was made on 23 May to all parties to the conflict to endeavour to achieve a cease-fire and to participate in a constructive manner in the peace talks which were due to open on 27 May in London.[7] The joint communiqué issued in London on 28 May and the commitments subscribed to on that occasion were warmly welcomed on 31 May.[8] In a statement on 12 July the Community and its Member States welcomed the successful conclusion of the Conference for Peaceful and Democratic Transition in Ethiopia, held in Addis Ababa from 1 to 5 July.[9] On 2 August a statement was published conveying the congratulations of the Community and its Member States to President Meles Zenawi on the occasion of his election as Head of the State of Ethiopia.[10]

1106.   On 2 January, following the deterioration of the situation in Mogadishu, Somalia, where violent military action had caused numerous victims, the Community and its Member States launched an urgent appeal to all the parties to the conflict for a cease-fire[11] and reiterated the appeal on 15 January.[12] In a further joint statement of

---

1   Bull. EC 12-1991.
2   Bull. EC 5-1991, point 1.4.13.
3   Bull. EC 5-1991, point 1.4.12.
4   Bull. EC 10-1991, point 1.4.9.
5   Bull. EC 1/2-1991, point 1.4.23.
6   Bull. EC 4-1991, point 1.4.5.
7   Bull. EC 5-1991, point 1.4.8.
8   Bull. EC 5-1991, point 1.4.14.
9   Bull. EC 7/8-1991, point 1.4.5.
10   Bull. EC 7/8-1991, point 1.4.14.
11   Bull. EC 1/2-1991, point 1.4.2.
12   Bull. EC 1/2-1991, point 1.4.13.

24 May all the parties concerned were urged to participate in talks dealing in particular with political reconciliation, institutional reorganization and the reconstruction of the country. The Community and its Member States also reaffirmed their commitment to pursue efforts to provide humanitarian relief for the famine victims.[1] On 2 August they welcomed the outcome of the Djibouti Conference.[2] On 28 November they expressed their concern at the situation in Mogadishu and strongly condemned the breaking into and looting of the Italian Embassy.[3]

1107.   In the prevailing situation of drought and famine in the country, the Community and its Member States issued a statement on 7 February expressing their shock and dismay at the Government of Sudan's continued failure to make any response to efforts by the donor community to engage in discussion on emergency assistance to ensure that supplies reached the needy population.[4]

1108.   In their statement of 14 June the Community and its Member States welcomed the appeal by the authorities of Burundi for Burundian refugees to return to their country on a voluntary basis.[5] On 22 March a statement was published in which the Community and its Member States conveyed their congratulations to the President-elect of Cape Verde, Mr António Mascarenhas Monteiro, and welcomed the fact that the elections had allowed for an exemplary democratic change-over.[6] With regard to Liberia they issued a joint statement on 27 September which welcomed the final communiqué of the second meeting of the Ecowas Committee of Five in Yamoussoukro on 16 and 17 September.[7] On 21 August the Community and its Member States expressed their deep concern about the recent tragic events in Madagascar and they urged both the authorities of Madagascar and the political forces to do their utmost in order to find a peaceful solution to the crisis respecting democracy and human rights.[8] On 4 April the Community and its Member States published a statement deploring the repression of demonstrations in Mali since 22 March as this had led to victims among the civilian population. The will of the new leaders to set up a stable framework of freedom and democracy was noted with hope.[9]

1109.   On 19 December the Community and its Member States adopted a statement in which they expressed their concern at the situation in the southern and eastern provinces of Sierra Leone as a result of renewed fighting on the border between Liberia

---

[1]   Bull. EC 5-1991, point 1.4.9.
[2]   Bull. EC 7/8-1991, point 1.4.12.
[3]   Bull. EC 11-1991, point 1.4.17.
[4]   Bull. EC 1/2-1991, point 1.4.22.
[5]   Bull. EC 6-1991, point 1.4.5.
[6]   Bull. EC 3-1991, point 1.4.4.
[7]   Bull. EC 9-1991, point 1.4.8.
[8]   Bull. EC 7/8-1991, point 1.4.18.
[9]   Bull. EC 4-1991, point 1.4.4.

and Sierra Leone.[1] On 23 December they deplored the loss of life caused by clashes in Togo.[1]

1110.   In their joint statement of 3 April the Community and its Member States conveyed to the President-elect of São Tomé and Príncipe their congratulations on his election and warmly welcomed the exemplary process of democratization which had led to the presidential elections.[2]

1111.   The Community and its Member States issued a statement on 27 September in which they expressed deep concern about the critical situation in Zaire and they urged both the government and all political and social forces to do their utmost to reach an agreement on the political future of Zaire, in which the rule of law, the organization of free elections and respect for human rights were guaranteed.[3] On 21 October they noted with satisfaction the formation of a government of consensus.[4] In a joint statement on 6 November they welcomed the fact that the elections in Zambia had been conducted in an exemplary democratic way.[5]

1112.   On 21 November, however, the Community and its Member States expressed their concern at the restraints on freedom of expression and assembly in Kenya.[6]

1113.   On 10 June the Community and its Member States issued a statement welcoming the sustained efforts of the United Nations to achieve an overall political solution to the problem of Afghanistan.[7]

1114.   In a joint statement on 2 December the Community and its Member States endorsed the issuing of warrants for the arrest of two Libyan nationals by France, the United Kingdom and the United States, in connection with the bombing of flights Pan Am 103 and UTA 772. They also repeated their condemnation of terrorism.[1]

1115.   The Community and its Member States welcomed the steps being taken by the interim government in Bangladesh to prepare for free and fair parliamentary elections on 27 February, and on 15 January they also welcomed the invitations extended to parliamentarians from the Member States and MEPs to attend the elections as observers.[8] A statement on the death of Mr Rajiv Gandhi, leader of the Congress party in India, was published on 22 May. The Community and its Member States expressed deep

---

[1]   Bull. EC 12-1991.
[2]   Bull. EC 4-1991, point 1.4.3.
[3]   Bull. EC 9-1991, point 1.4.9.
[4]   Bull. EC 10-1991, point 1.4.11.
[5]   Bull. EC 11-1991, point 1.4.3.
[6]   Bull. EC 11-1991, point 1.4.13.
[7]   Bull. EC 6-1991, point 1.4.3.
[8]   Bull. EC 1/2-1991, point 1.4.14.

dismay at the news of the assassination of Mr Gandhi and condemned this as a cowardly act of terrorism.[1] They reiterated their condemnation of terrorism on 25 October, with regard to the kidnapping of the Romanian chargé d'affaires in Kashmir.[2]

1116.   On 4 January the Community and its Member States issued a statement expressing their growing concern at the continuing failure of the Burmese military authorities to initiate a democratic process following free elections in May 1990.[3] Two statements on 27 May and 29 July recalled the representations and statements made by the Community and its Member States[4] and deplored the lack of respect for human rights and the expenditure of large amounts of the country's meagre resources on arms.[5] On 22 November they announced that, on behalf of the Community and its Member States, the Heads of Mission of the Twelve in Rangoon, in association with the Heads of Mission of Australia, the Czech and Slovak Federal Republic and the United States of America, had addressed a message to the Chairman of the State Law and Order Restoration Council, expressing their deep concern about the continued restriction of Nobel prize winner, Daw Aung San Suu Kyi, to her own house and compound where she was held incommunicado.[6]

1117.   In joint statements on 24 October[7] and 8 November[8] the Community and its Member States welcomed the signing of comprehensive political settlement of the Cambodian conflict by all parties participating in the Paris Conference. In a statement on 28 August 1991 the Community and its Member States welcomed the announcement by the Chinese Prime Minister, Li Peng, that China had decided, in principle, to accede to the Treaty on the Non-Proliferation of Nuclear Weapons (NPT).[9] On 20 November the Community and its Member States issued a joint statement on nuclear non-proliferation in the Korean Peninsula. In this connection they welcomed the announcement by the President of the Republic of Korea on 8 November of initiatives to establish a denuclearized zone in the region and called on the Democratic People's Republic of Korea to respond positively to this proposal. They also urged it to sign and implement the Safeguards Agreement with the International Atomic Energy Agency without further delay and without preconditions.[10] On 4 November the Community and its Member States welcomed the agreement reached on 29 October between the Governments of the United Kingdom, Hong Kong and Viet Nam, on the return to Viet Nam,

---

[1]   Bull. EC 5-1991, point 1.4.7.
[2]   Bull. EC 10-1991, point 1.4.14.
[3]   Bull. EC 1/2-1991, point 1.4.3.
[4]   Bull. EC 5-1991, point 1.4.10.
[5]   Bull. EC 7/8-1991, point 1.4.10.
[6]   Bull. EC 11-1991, point 1.4.14.
[7]   Bull. EC 10-1991, point 1.4.13.
[8]   Bull. EC 11-1991, point 1.4.5.
[9]   Bull. EC 7/8-1991, point 1.4.24.
[10]   Bull. EC 11-1991, point 1.4.12.

under procedures agreed with UN High Commissioner for Refugees, of Vietnamese migrants in Hong Kong not considered to be political refugees. [1]

1118. The EC-Japan Declaration, agreed at the EC-Japan ministerial meeting on 18 July, was made public the same day. This joint Declaration on relations between the Community and its Member States and Japan covers general principles relating to dialogue and cooperation between the two parties and both sides undertook to review regularly its implementation. [2]

1119. On 21 June a statement was issued in which the Community and its Member States deplored the Sri Lankan Government's decision to declare the British High Commissioner to be *persona non grata.* [3] The military *coup d'état* on 23 February in Thailand gave rise to a statement on 26 February opposing all illegal use of force, condemning the suspension of the constitution, the dissolution of the parliament, the dismissal of the government and the establishment of martial law. [4]

1120. On 13 November the Community and its Member States issued a joint statement expressing their grave concern at events in Dili on 12 November when members of the Indonesian armed forces opened fire on a group of demonstrators, killing and wounding a considerable number. [5] On 3 December they reiterated their condemnation of the unjustifiable actions of the Indonesian army in East Timor, stating that they would review cooperation between the Community and Indonesia in the light of the response of Indonesian authorities. [6]

1121. A statement was issued on 26 March welcoming the signing of the Treaty on the establishment of a common market in the Southern Cone of South America by Argentina, Brazil, Paraguay and Uruguay. [7] On 11 March the Community and its Member States expressed satisfaction, on the first anniversary of the election of President Aylwin, at the peaceful and constructive atmosphere in which the first year of Chile's return to democracy had passed. [8] The military coup of 24 December 1990 in Suriname was condemned by the Community and its Member States in a statement of 10 January. [9] On 27 May a further joint statement was issued in which they noted with satisfaction that free and fair elections had taken place in Suriname on 25 May. [10] On 13 September

---

[1]   Bull. EC 11-1991, point 1.4.2.
[2]   Bull. EC 7/8-1991, point 1.4.8.
[3]   Bull. EC 6-1991, point 1.4.7.
[4]   Bull. EC 1/2-1991, point 1.4.28.
[5]   Bull. EC 11-1991, point 1.4.10.
[6]   Bull. EC 12-1991.
[7]   Bull. EC 3-1991, point 1.4.5.
[8]   Bull. EC 3-1991, point 1.4.3.
[9]   Bull. EC 1/2-1991, point 1.4.7.
[10] Bull. EC 5-1991, point 1.4.11.

the Community and its Member States addressed their warmest congratulations to the newly installed President, Mr Runaldo Ronald Venetiaan.[1] In a statement on 8 January the Community and its Member States condemned the violent seizure of power in Haiti during the night of 6 to 7 January.[2] In a joint declaration on 3 October they roundly condemned the military coup of 30 September and called for an immediate return to the rule of law and the reinstatement of the legitimate authorities. They also decided to suspend economic assistance.[3] On 23 December the Community and its Member States deplored the fact that the legitimate authorities of Haiti had not been restored to office.[4]

1122.   In a statement on 15 January the Community and its Member States paid tribute to the UN Secretary-General for the significant progress made in his efforts to reach a negotiated settlement of the conflict in El Salvador.[5] On 13 May a further statement was issued in which the Community and its Member States said that they were most encouraged by the agreement signed in Mexico City on 27 April between the Salvadorean Government and the Farabundo Marti National Liberation Front (FMLN).[6] A statement on 17 July expressed grave concern at the escalating violence. In particular the brutal torture and murder of Martin Ayala, member of the Consejo de Comunidades Marginales (CCM), was strongly condemned.[7] On 1 October they stated that they were most encouraged by the agreement signed in New York on 25 September between the Government and the FMLN.[8] In a statement issued on 26 November, they warmly welcomed the announcement made by the FMLN on 14 November that it would cease all offensive operations in El Salvador at midnight on 16 November and called on both sides to respect the truce.[9]

1123.   On the occasion of the investiture of the President of Guatemala a joint statement was issued on 14 January congratulating the President-elect, Mr Jorge Serrano. The Community and its Member States hoped that peace could be restored through internal conciliation and in full respect of human rights.[10] Furthermore, in a joint statement on 10 June, they welcomed the agreements reached in Mexico on 26 April at the conclusion of the meeting held by the Government of Guatemala and the Guatemalan National Revolutionary Union (URNG) but expressed their concern at the

---

[1]   Bull. EC 9-1991, point 1.4.5.
[2]   Bull. EC 1/2-1991, point 1.4.6.
[3]   Bull. EC 10-1991, point 1.4.5.
[4]   Bull. EC 12-1991.
[5]   Bull. EC 1/2-1991, point 1.4.15.
[6]   Bull. EC 5-1991, point 1.4.4.
[7]   Bull. EC 7/8-1991, point 1.4.7.
[8]   Bull. EC 10-1991, point 1.4.2.
[9]   Bull. EC 11-1991, point 1.4.15.
[10]   Bull. EC 1/2-1991, point 1.4.10.

increase of violence just as efforts to seek a lasting peace were entering a crucial phase.[1] In a joint statement on 23 August the Community and its Member States reiterated their concern and strongly condemned the murder of José Miguel Merida Escobar, a police officer investigating the murder of a human rights activist.[2] In a joint statement on 9 September the Community and its Member States warmly welcomed the statement of 5 September concerning the recognition by the Government of Guatemala of the independence of Belize.[3] A joint statement on 22 October welcomed the resumption of negotiations between the Government and the URNG.[4]

1124.   On the occasion of the first anniversary of the elections which made possible a democratic change of government in Nicaragua, the European Community and its Member States issued a statement on 26 February reiterating their support for pluralist democracy.[5]

1125.   At the meeting on 9 November between Mr Delors, Mr Lubbers and President Bush a joint statement was adopted on the United Nations register for conventional arms transfers.[6]

1126.   In a joint statement on 28 November, the Community and its Member States expressed their regret that the 26th International Conference of the Red Cross and Red Crescent, scheduled to take place in Budapest, had been postponed. The decision had been influenced by concerns that political issues would dominate the Conference, which was contrary to the fundamental principles of those two bodies.[7]

[1] Bull. EC 6-1991, point 1.4.4.
[2] Bull. EC 7/8-1991, point 1.4.22.
[3] Bull. EC 9-1991, point 1.4.4.
[4] Bull. EC 10-1991, point 1.4.12.
[5] Bull. EC 1/2-1991, point 1.4.26.
[6] Bull. EC 11-1991, point 1.4.6.
[7] Bull. EC 11-1991, point 1.4.16.

Section 2

Other intergovernmental cooperation

1127.   The ministers with responsibility for immigration, together with Mr Bangemann representing the Commission, met for the 10th time in Luxembourg on 13 and 14 June.[1] At this meeting, the ministers accepted the principle of setting up a quick-reaction consultation centre under the troïka arrangements to deal with large and sudden migratory flows and they took note of the substantial progress made on the proposed Convention on the crossing of the Community's external borders. They also welcomed Denmark's signing of the Dublin Convention of 15 June 1990, determining the Member State responsible for examining an application for asylum, which meant that all 12 Member States had now signed this instrument of international law. The ministers with responsibility for internal security matters (Trevi Group) met on the same day[2] to deal with the work being carried out by the Trevi 1992 Group. For the first time a representative of the Commission was present at the meeting.

Despite two additional ministerial-level meetings on 26 June and 1 July, it was not possible to sign the draft Convention on the crossing of the Community's external borders. The issue of Gibraltar continues to be the outstanding obstacle and this can only be resolved bilaterally between the United Kingdom and Spain.

1128.   At their 11th meeting[3] on 2 and 3 December, attended by Mr Bangemann, the ministers with responsibility for immigration adopted a draft report on immigration and asylum to be submitted to the European Council at Maastricht on 9 and 10 December.[3] This report was drawn up in response to the mandate given by the European Council in Luxembourg on 28 and 29 June.[4] It is based partly on the Commission's communications on immigration and asylum.[5] The ministers adopted the Commission's conclusion that only a common approach can meet the challenges of immigration and asylum. The remainder of the report consists of a work programme for each of these areas which should be implemented before the Treaty on political union comes into

---

[1]   Bull. EC 6-1991, point 1.4.9.
[2]   Bull. EC 6-1991, point 1.4.10.
[3]   Bull. EC 12-1991.
[4]   Bull. EC 6-1991, point I.39.
[5]   Points 205 and 218 of this Report.

force. At Maastricht the European Council examined the reports on immigration and asylum drawn up at its request by the ministers with responsibility for immigration. It approved the work programme and timetables laid down and called on the ministers concerned to implement them. Finally, the ministers appealed to the Spanish and United Kingdom delegations to find a solution to the only remaining bilateral impediment to the signature of the draft Convention on the crossing of the Community's external borders. The Trevi Group met on the same day, with the Commission attending.[1] In particular, the ministers adopted the draft report for submission to the Maastricht European Council on the setting up of 'Europol'.[2] This report was drawn up in answer to the mandate received at the Luxembourg European Council.[3] It supports a phased approach to setting up Europol, under which the first phase would be the establishment of the EDU (European Drugs Unit). The European Council approved the report presented by the ministers responsible for internal security matters (Trevi Group) and assigned them the task of working with the Commission to take the measures required to set up Europol as swiftly as possible.

1129. On 15 June the agreements for the accession of Spain and Portugal to the Schengen Agreement were signed in Bonn by Mr C. Westendorp, Spain's State Secretary for European Affairs, and Mr V. C. Martins, Portugal's State Secretary for European Affairs, as well as by representatives of the other signatory States. Greece was given observer status on this occasion.

---

[1] Bull. EC 12-1991.
[2] Point 1016 of this Report.
[3] Bull. EC 6-1991, point I.40.

Section 3

Human rights and fundamental freedoms

Inside the Community

1130.   By agreeing on the Treaty on European union at the European Council meeting in Maastricht on 9 and 10 December the Heads of State or Government of the Member States established the concept of union citizenship, to complement nationality, as an element which will enhance the Community's democratic legitimacy. [1] In so doing they gave concrete expression to a coherent set of duties as well as rights such as participation in European and local elections in the country of residence, freedom of movement and the right of abode for Community nationals, joint protection outside the Community frontiers and the right to appeal to an arbitrator.

1131.   In its resolution of 9 July, [2] Parliament considered it necessary for the Community to ensure respect for human rights in the Member States and urged that it become party to the European Convention for the Protection of Human Rights and Fundamental Freedoms. [3]

1132.   Concerned at the steadily growing manifestations of racism and xenophobia in Europe, both in the Member States of the Community and elsewhere, the European Council in Maastricht issued a statement to encourage the governments and parliaments of the Member States to step up their efforts to counter the growth of such sentiments and manifestations. It also called on ministers and the Commission to strengthen the legal protection of non-Community nationals in the territories of the Member States.

1133.   At the Luxembourg meeting in June the European Council welcomed the signature of the Convention on asylum by all the Member States and noted with satisfaction that a very important step towards the establishment of an area without frontiers, where freedom of movement for persons was a reality, in accordance with the Treaty, would be taken shortly when full agreement was reached on the Convention between the Member States on the crossing of their external borders. [4]

---

[1]   Point 38 of this Report.
[2]   OJ C 240, 16.9.1991; Bull. EC 7/8-1991, point 1.3.92.
[3]   Twenty-fourth General Report, point 899.
[4]   Point 213 of this Report.

1134.   On 9 October the Commission adopted communications on immigration[1] and the right of asylum.[2]

1135.   Anxious to give ear to the misgivings voiced by the general public and policy-makers on the ethical aspects of biotechnology and to respond to them in a positive way, the Commission, as announced in its communication on biotechnology of 17 April,[3] set up an advisory body on the ethics of biotechnology.[3]

Outside the Community

1136.   The Community and its Member States pursued their policy throughout the year of promoting and safeguarding human rights and fundamental freedoms in the world at large, in the conviction that to do so is the legitimate and abiding duty of the international community and of all countries, acting individually or collectively. Their commitment was reaffirmed in the Declaration on Human Rights adopted by the European Council at its meeting in Luxembourg on 28 and 29 June, in which it stressed its commitment to the principles of parliamentary democracy and the rule of law.[4] The persistence of flagrant violations of human rights in numerous countries led the Community and its Member States to issue some 120 statements and make confidential representations on 150 occasions.[5]

1137.   Through its cooperation policy and by including clauses on human rights in economic and cooperation agreements with non-member countries, the Community actively promoted human rights and the participation, without discrimination, of all individuals or groups in the life of society. The topicality of this issue, due to the significant developments taking place both at international level and within numerous developing countries, and increased public awareness of these matters led Community institutions and political cooperation bodies to consider what links should be established between development cooperation policies and the fostering and defence of human rights and support for democratization in all developing countries. With a view to contributing to the debate, in March the Commission put before the Council and Parliament a communication on 'Human rights, democracy and development'. On 28 November the Council and the Member States meeting within the Council adopted a resolution providing the Community with a set of principles on the issue of good governance and military expenditure.[6]

---

[1]   Bull. EC 10-1991, point 1.2.2.1.
[2]   Bull. EC 10-1991, point 1.2.2.2.
[3]   Point 276 of this Report.
[4]   Bull. EC 6-1991, point I.45.
[5]   Bull. EC 12-1991.
[6]   Point 1023 of this Report.

1138.   To assist the countries of Central and Eastern Europe on the way to the economic and political changes they have embarked upon, the Community has entered into negotiations with them to arrive at European agreements intended to support them in the difficult task of transforming their economies and anchor them irreversibly to a pluralistic and democratic Europe.[1] The aim of the European Bank for Reconstruction and Development (EBRD), which became operational this year, is to promote the development of democracy, the safeguarding of human rights and the freedom of the press, in addition to economic reforms.[2]

1139.   The Community and its Member States followed with concern the developments in Yugoslavia and from the beginning subscribed to four fundamental principles: the unacceptability of the use of force; the unacceptability of any boundary changes effected by force and determination not to recognize any such changes; respect for the rights of all who live in Yugoslavia, including the minorities; and the need to take account of all legitimate concerns and aspirations.[3]

1140.   At ministerial meetings with groups of countries such as the Association of South-East Asian Nations (Asean)[4] or the countries of Central America,[5] the issue of human rights was systematically raised and the Community ministers agreed to launch multiannual programmes to promote human rights in Central America in close cooperation with existing bodies.

1141.   Faced with serious violations of human rights and fundamental freedoms, the Community and its Member States showed their concern and ability to react firmly on numerous occasions.

1142.   Within the framework of the United Nations — General Assembly, Commission on Human Rights and other bodies — and the Conference on Security and Cooperation in Europe (CSCE), the Community and its Member States played an active role in the promotion of human rights and democratic values.[6] Their contribution was significant both at the meeting of experts on ethnic minorities, at which specific initiatives to protect the rights of such minorities were advocated, and at the third meeting of the Conference on the Human Dimension of the CSCE,[7] whose concluding document stated that human rights are the collective responsibility of CSCE participating countries and established rules aimed at ensuring respect for human rights even where a state of emergency is declared.

---

[1]   Point 823 of this Report.
[2]   Point 72 of this Report.
[3]   Point 888 *et seq.* of this Report.
[4]   Point 917 of this Report.
[5]   Point 933 of this Report.
[6]   Point 1063 of this Report.
[7]   Point 1079 of this Report.

1143.   Among the numerous resolutions adopted by Parliament in the field of human rights, that of 12 September on human rights in the world for the years 1989 and 1990 and Community human rights policy deserves particular mention.[1]

1144.   On 10 July the Sakharov Prize for freedom of thought was presented by Mr E. Barón Crespo, President of the European Parliament, to the son of Mrs Aung San Suu Kyi, a prisoner of conscience in Myanmar (formerly Burma).[2]

---

[1]   OJ C 267, 14.10.1991; Bull. EC 9-1991, point 1.3.71.
[2]   Bull. EC 7/8-1991, point 1.3.93.

Chapter V

Community institutions and financing

Institutions and other bodies

Relations between the institutions

Commission programme

1145. On 13 March, after the Commission had presented its annual programme, Parliament, represented by its enlarged Bureau, and the Commission agreed the legislative programme for 1991. For the first time since this new interinstitutional practice was started in 1988, the programme was adopted by the two institutions with a representative of the Council Presidency in attendance. Parliament and the Commission reiterated their conviction that legislative programming is indispensable if the Community's decision-making procedure is to operate effectively.

Voting in the Council

1146. The improvement in the Council's decision-making procedure which began with the signing of the Single European Act continued in 1991.

1147. Wherever necessary, decisions were taken by qualified majority, either by means of a formal vote or by establishing that a majority existed without resorting to a formal vote. The possibility of majority voting has introduced an element of flexibility in the position of the Member States, which are forced to reach a consensus.

Inclusion of Parliament in the decision-making process

1148. Parliament's enlarged Bureau and the Commission met on 5 September to assess the implementation over the year of the code of conduct for improving interinstitutional relations.[1] The two institutions concluded that implementation had in general been successful and agreed to intensify contacts between them so as to streamline decision-making procedures.

1149. The cooperation procedure in general worked satisfactorily. Since the Single Act entered into force, 216 proposals have been adopted. More than 60% of the amendments requested by Parliament at first reading were accepted by the Commission and more than 46% by the Council. On second reading, 46.49% of the amendments requested were accepted by the Commission and 27.37% by the Council. The inclusion of Parliament in the decision-making process has certainly improved the texts.

Implementing powers conferred on the Commission

1150. The Council was still reluctant to grant the Commission implementing powers.[2]

Despite the request made by the intergovernmental conference[3] during the drafting of the Single European Act that the Council give priority to the advisory committee procedure for the exercise of implementing powers conferred on the Commission under Article 100a of the Treaty, the Council accepted that procedure only once (while the Commission proposed it 6 times). In all the internal market proposals, the Council has used this procedure only 13 times out of the 57 proposed by the Commission. And in some cases the Council again kept certain implementing powers for itself. In a report sent to the Council and Parliament in accordance with the 1987 decision laying down the procedures for the exercise of its implementing powers,[4] the Commission voiced its concern that developments in this area run contrary to the spirit of the Single Act and are likely to compromise the effectiveness of Community measures.

Composition and functioning of the institutions

Parliament

1151. The 518 seats in Parliament are distributed as follows:

---

[1]   Bull. EC 6-1991, point 1.7.16.
[2]   Twenty-fourth General Report, point 914.
[3]   Twentieth General Report, point 4.
[4]   OJ L 197, 18.7.1987; Twenty-first General Report, point 4.

Socialists	180
European People's Party	128
Liberal, Democratic and Reformist Group	45
European Democratic Group	34
European Unitarian Left	29
Greens	27
European Democratic Alliance	21
Rainbow Group	15
Technical Group of the European Right	14
Left Unity Group	13
Non-affiliated	12

1152. The proceedings at the two Intergovernmental Conferences on Political Union and on Economic and Monetary Union were very much on Members' minds during 1991. A resolution passed in January clearly expressed Parliament's desire to take an active part in the conferences and the importance it attached to a common foreign and security policy.[1] An initial interinstitutional conference was held, while the March part-session was in progress, at which this issue was considered along with the question of democratic legitimacy.[2] In April, after a joint debate with Mr Delors and the President of the Council, Mr Poos, Parliament passed two resolutions: one on the nature of Community acts[3] and the other on democratic legitimacy,[4] the latter registering Members' concern at the possibility that the intergovernmental approach might proliferate. The rejection of this approach was repeated on several occasions, particularly in June,[5] July[6] and October.[7] In May the House explicitly made implementation of any enlargement process dependent upon a strengthening of the Community institutions.[8] In the run-up to the Luxembourg European Council, Parliament restated its positions on the progress of the debates on political union and economic and monetary union, proposing its own definition of union and of the interinstitutional balance that must emerge from it.[5] In July,[9] appraising the results of the European Council,[10] Parliament reiterated the need for the six objectives defined by the Single European Act to be attained jointly and regretted the meagre results achieved on issues like social cohesion, common European security policy or revision of the Euratom Treaty. In October the House reaffirmed its

---

[1]   OJ C 48, 25.2.1991; Bull. EC 1/2-1991, point 1.7.1.
[2]   Bull. EC 3-1991, point 1.1.3.
[3]   OJ C 129, 20.5.1991; Bull EC 4-1991, point 1.1.4.
[4]   OJ C 129, 20.5.1991; Bull EC 4-1991, point 1.1.5.
[5]   OJ C 183, 15.7.1991; Bull. EC 6-1991, points 1.1.4 and 1.1.7.
[6]   OJ C 240, 16.9.1991; Bull. EC 7/8-1991, point 1.1.1.
[7]   OJ C 280, 28.10.1991; Bull. EC 10-1991, point 1.1.6.
[8]   OJ C 158, 17.6.1991; Bull. EC 5-1991, point 1.1.4.
[9]   OJ C 240, 16.9.1991; Bull. EC 7/8-1991, point 1.1.1.
[10] Bull. EC 6-1991, point I.1 *et seq.*

support for a federal-type union[1] and, after a debate on economic and monetary union, pointed out that Parliament and the Commission were working along parallel lines.[2] The House also several times reaffirmed its wish to see the Community equip itself with the means to achieve a common foreign and security policy[3] and reiterated its demands in regard to European citizenship and democracy.[4] The House also passed resolutions on the role of the Consultative Council of the Regions[5] and its relations with the national parliaments.[6] The interinstitutional conferences, held at the same monthly intervals as the meetings at ministerial level, enabled Parliament to restate all its views on the work in hand. The House was also concerned with the sequels to German unification; in June it called on the Federal Government to pursue an active industrial and employment policy in the former German Democratic Republic,[7] and in October it insisted that the number of German MEPs be augmented to ensure that the new *Länder* were represented.[6]

1153. Parliament also debated various vital issues for the Community, such as the completion of the internal market,[8] the free movement of persons,[9] social Europe,[10] transport policy[11] and the future of the European automobile industry.[12]

1154. Within the scope of its budgetary powers, Parliament gave a discharge to the Commission in respect of implementation of the 1989 budget[13] and examined draft supplementary and amending budget No 1/91[14] and the implementation of the 1991 budget.[15] It also passed resolutions and gave opinions at several stages of the 1992 budget adoption procedure.[16]

1155. There was intense parliamentary activity on the external relations front, reflecting the scale of events on the international scene. The Gulf War and its consequences

---

[1] OJ C 280, 28.10.1991; Bull. EC 10-1991, point 1.1.5.
[2] OJ C 280, 28.10.1991; Bull. EC 10-1991, point 1.1.2.
[3] OJ C 183, 15.7.1991; Bull. EC 6-1991, point 1.1.9; OJ C 305, 25.11.1991; Bull. EC 10-1991, point 1.1.6.
[4] OJ C 183, 15.7.1991; Bull. EC 6-1991, point 1.1.8; OJ C 280, 28.10.1991; Bull. EC 10-1991, point 1.1.5;
     OJ C 305, 25.11.1991; Bull. EC 10-1991, point 1.1.11; OJ C 326, 16.12.1991; Bull. EC 11-1991, point 1.1.9.
[5] OJ C 280, 28.10.1991; Bull. EC 10-1991, point 1.1.8.
[6] OJ C 280, 28.10.1991; Bull. EC 10-1991, point 1.7.1.
[7] OJ C 183, 15.7.1991; Bull. EC 6-1991, point 1.2.109.
[8] OJ C 267, 14.10.1991; Bull. EC 9-1991, point 1.2.56.
[9] OJ C 267, 14.10.1991; Bull. EC 9-1991, point 1.2.4.
[10] OJ C 158, 17.6.1991; Bull. EC 5-1991, point 1.1.5; OJ C 326, 16.12.1991; Bull. EC 11-1991, point 1.1.8.
[11] OJ C 240, 16.9.1991; Bull. EC 7/8-1991, points 1.2.104, 1.2.113 and 1.2.116.
[12] OJ C 183, 15.7.1991; Bull. EC 6-1991, point 1.2.66.
[13] OJ C 129, 20.5.1991; Bull. EC 4-1991, points 1.5.9, 1.5.10, 1.5.12, 1.5.13 and 1.5.14.
[14] OJ C 129, 20.5.1991; Bull. EC 4-1991, point 1.5.5; OJ C 158, 17.6.1991; Bull. EC 5-1991, point 1.5.1.
[15] OJ C 280, 28.10.1991; Bull. EC 10-1991, point 1.5.2.
[16] OJ C 129, 20.5.1991; Bull. EC 4-1991, point 1.5.6; OJ C 158, 17.6.1991; Bull. EC 5-1991, point 1.5.1;
     OJ C 183, 15.7.1991; Bull. EC 6-1991, point 1.5.1; OJ C 267, 14.10.1991; Bull. EC 9-1991, point 1.5.3;
     OJ C 305, 25.11.1991; Bull. EC 10-1991, point 1.5.4; OJ C 326, 16.12.1991; Bull. EC 11-1991, points 1.5.1
     and 1.5.2; Bull. EC 12-1991.

were the subject of many debates at the two special part-sessions on 30 January and 8 February, after the informal European Council on 8 April[1] and again during ensuing part-sessions.[2] The House also threw its support behind the Middle East Peace Conference, opened in Madrid in October.[3] Special attention was again devoted to the countries of Central and Eastern Europe,[4] and especially to the situation in the Baltic States,[5] the Soviet Union[6] and Albania.[7] Parliament also followed the development of unrest in Yugoslavia and supported the Community's efforts to restore peace.[8] Several other debates were held on topics that covered the conclusion of the agreement on the European Economic Area,[9] the food situation in Africa[10] and the ACP countries and implementing Lomé IV.[11]

1156. The parliamentary year was also distinguished by the official visits of Mr Pérez de Cuéllar, the UN Secretary-General, and of Mr Aylwin, President of Chile, in April. During the year the House welcomed many political personalities, including King Hussein of Jordan, Mr Antall, the Hungarian Prime Minister, the Presidents of the Federal and Republican Parliaments of Yugoslavia and Mr Mubarak, the President of Egypt.

1157. Parliament held 12 part-sessions, during which it adopted 620 resolutions and decisions, including 308 embodying its opinion, of which 62 were under the cooperation procedure (first reading). On second reading, Parliament approved the Council's common position without amendment in 16 cases and after amendment in 21 cases.

1158. The assent procedure (Articles 237 and 238 of the EEC Treaty as amended by the Single European Act) was applied in 3 cases.

---

[1]   Bull. EC 4-1991, point 1.3.13.
[2]   OJ C 48, 25.2.1991; Bull. EC 1/2-1991, points 1.3.27 and 1.3.28; OJ C 72, 18.3.1991; Bull. EC 1/2-1991, point 1.3.29; OJ C 106, 22.4.1991; Bull. EC 3-1991, point 1.3.18, OJ C 129, 20.5.1991; Bull. EC 4-1991, point 1.3.17; OJ C 158, 17.6.1991; Bull. EC 5-1991, point 1.3.99.
[3]   OJ C 305, 25.11.1991; Bull. EC 10-1991, point 1.7.2.
[4]   OJ C 129, 20.5.1991; Bull. EC 4-1991, point 1.3.5; OJ C 267, 14.10.1991; Bull. EC 9-1991, points 1.2.136, 1.3.15 and 1.3.23; OJ C 280, 28.10.1991, points 1.3.5 and 1.3.8.
[5]   OJ C 48, 25.2.1991; Bull. EC 1/2-1991, point 1.3.117; OJ C 72, 18.3.1991; Bull. EC 1/2-1991, point 1.3.118; OJ C 183, 15.7.1991; Bull. EC 6-1991, point 1.3.21.
[6]   OJ C 158, 17.6.1991; Bull. EC 5-1991, point 1.3.97; OJ C 267, 14.10.1991; Bull. EC 9-1991, point 1.3.7; OJ C 326, 16.12.1991; Bull. EC 11-1991, point 1.3.3.
[7]   OJ C 106, 22.4.1991; Bull. EC 3-1991, point 1.3.9; OJ C 183, 15.7.1991; Bull. EC 6-1991, point 1.3.13; OJ C 267, 14.10.1991; Bull. EC 9-1991, point 1.3.20.
[8]   OJ C 106, 22.4.1991; Bull. EC 3-1991, point 1.3.82; OJ C 158, 17.6.1991; Bull. EC 5-1991, point 1.3.96; OJ C 240, 16.9.1991; Bull. EC 7/8-1991, point 1.3.20; OJ C 267, 14.10.1991; Bull. EC 9-1991, point 1.3.25; OJ C 280, 28.10.1991; Bull. EC 10-1991, point 1.3.16; OJ C 326, 16.12.1991; Bull. EC 11-1991, points 1.3.21 and 1.3.24.
[9]   OJ C 106, 22.4.1991; Bull. EC 3-1991, point 1.3.1.
[10]   OJ C 129, 20.5.1991; Bull. EC 4-1991, point 1.3.53; OJ C 158, 17.6.1991; Bull. EC 5-1991, point 1.3.69.
[11]   OJ C 240, 16.9.1991; Bull. EC 7/8-1991, point 1.3.49.

1159.   Parliament adopted 271 own-initiative resolutions — 93 on the basis of reports, 117 by urgent procedure and 61 following an early vote to conclude debates on Commission or Council statements or on oral questions. The House adopted 26 resolutions and decisions on budgetary matters. It took 12 miscellaneous decisions concerning changes in the Rules of Procedure, requests to waive Members' immunity, etc.

1160.   A breakdown of Parliament's work in 1991 is shown in Table 16. A total of 3 281 written questions were tabled — 2 905 to the Commission, 257 to the Council and 119 to the Conference of Ministers for Foreign Affairs (political cooperation). Oral questions (Question Time) numbered 1 303 — 838 to the Commission, 238 to the Council and 227 to the Conference of Ministers for Foreign Affairs. There were also 367 oral questions with or without debate — 231 to the Commission, 93 to the Council and 43 to the Conference of Ministers for Foreign Affairs.

1161.   At 31 December the establishment plan of the Secretariat comprised 3 062 permanent posts and 503 temporary posts.

Council

1162.   Luxembourg was in the chair for the first half of the year and the Netherlands for the second half.

1163.   The European Council met three times during the year — two ordinary meetings in Luxembourg in June[1] and in Maastricht[2] in December, and an informal meeting in Luxembourg in April.[3]

1164.   At the informal meeting in April the Heads of State or Government considered the steps to be taken following the Gulf War and decided to grant ECU 150 million of humanitarian aid to help the Kurds and other refugees in the region, ECU 100 million of which would be charged to the Community budget. At the ordinary meeting in June the Heads of State or Government devoted most of their proceedings to the state of play at the intergovernmental conferences and confirmed that the conferences should proceed in parallel, on the basis of the draft Treaty prepared by the Luxembourg Presidency. They confirmed the areas of agreement already secured on the key components of economic and monetary union but pointed to the need to make progress on economic convergence. They also held a searching exchange of views on specific aspects of political union, particularly common foreign and security policy, democratic legitima-

---

[1]   Bull. EC 6-1991, points I.1 to I.47.
[2]   Bull. EC 12-1991.
[3]   Bull. EC 4-1991, point 1.3.13.

TABLE 16

The year in Parliament

Part-session	Normal consultations (single reading)	Cooperation procedures (Article 149(2) of the EEC Treaty)		Assents (Articles 237 and 238 of the EEC Treaty)	EP Rules 63 and 121 (own-initiative reports)	EP Rules 56 and 58 (resolutions following statements and oral questions)	EP Rule 64 (resolutions on urgent subjects)	Budget questions	Miscellaneous decisions and resolutions
		I[1]	II[1]						
January	7	6	3	—	7	4	—	—	2
February	14	4	5	—	9	6	15	1	2
March	8	3	2	—	2	3	11	1	1
April	7	2	8	1	3	3	10	8	3
May	70	8	2	—	4	2	11	2	1
June	23	7	5	—	12	7	11	1	—
July	15	5	5	—	12	9	16	—	—
September	8	1	—	—	14	6	17	1	—
October I	17	4	1	—	7	7	13	—	2
October II	7	4	1	—	5	4	—	7	—
November	12	10	4	1	12	8	13	2	1
December	21	8	1	1	6	2	—	3	—
Total	209[2]	62[3]	37[4]	3	93	61	117	26[5]	12

[1] I: first reading; II: second reading.
[2] Including 152 where Parliament proposed amendments to Commission proposals.
[3] Including 52 where Parliament proposed amendments to Commission proposals.
[4] Including 21 where Parliament proposed amendments to common positions by the Council.
[5] Including 7 own-initiative resolutions.
NB: Parliament applied Article 40(1) or (2) in 11 cases; it adopted resolutions complying with Article 41(4) (following Parliament's opinion) in 4 cases; and contested the legal basis of the Commission proposal in 3 cases. The House rejected the Commission proposal in 4 cases and a legislative resolution in 1 case.

cy and the co-decision procedure. The Heads of State or Government urged that the whole legislative programme essential to the single market be adopted by 31 December and that the implementation of the measures needed for the Social Charter be stepped up. On the external relations front, they appraised the situation in Yugoslavia, the Soviet Union and the countries of Central and Eastern Europe, as well as the progress made towards the establishment of the European Economic Area. In December, they reached agreement on a draft Treaty on European union providing for economic and monetary union and inserting provisions on a common foreign and security policy into the EEC Treaty.[1]

---

[1]   Points 15 and 43 of this Report.

1165.   Continuing the practice introduced in 1981, Mr Santer[1] and Mr van den Broek,[2] accompanied by Mr Delors, reported to Parliament on the conclusions of the European Council meetings.

1166.   At its 83 meetings in 1991 the Council adopted 72 directives, 335 regulations and 174 decisions.

1167.   There were 2 097 permanent posts and 1 temporary post on the Council's establishment plan at the end of the year.

Commission

1168.   The Commission held 47 meetings in the course of the year. It adopted 6 130 instruments (regulations, decisions, directives, recommendations, opinions) and sent the Council 652 proposals, recommendations or drafts and 208 communications, memorandums and reports.

1169.   In March the Commission received Mr Vaclav Havel, President of Czechoslovakia,[3] and in April Mr Lech Walesa, President of Poland.[4] In October it received Mr J. K. Bielecki, the Polish Prime Minister.[5]

1170.   The Commission's establishment plan for 1991 comprised 12 599 permanent posts (including 1 616 LA posts for the Language Service) and 558 temporary posts (including 30 LA) paid out of administrative appropriations; 3 271 permanent and 191 temporary posts paid out of research appropriations; 428 permanent posts in the Office for Official Publications; 69 at the European Centre for the Development of Vocational Training and 59 at the European Foundation for the Improvement of Living and Working Conditions.

1171.   Under the secondment and exchange arrangements between the Commission and Member States' government departments, 44 Commission officials were seconded to national civil services and some 600 national experts came to work for Commission departments.

Court of Justice and Court of First Instance

1172.   The composition of the Chambers of the Court of Justice was determined as follows for a period of one year from 7 October:

[1]   Bull. EC 7/8-1991, point 1.7.1.
[2]   Bull. EC 12-1991.
[3]   Bull. EC 3-1991, point 1.3.6.
[4]   Bull. EC 4-1991, point 1.3.3.
[5]   Bull. EC 10-1991, point 1.3.4.

First Chamber: President: Sir Gordon Slynn; Judges: Mr R. Joliet and Mr G. C. Rodríguez Iglesias;

Second Chamber: President: Mr F. A. Schockweiler; Judges: Mr G. F. Mancini and Mr M. Murray;

Third Chamber: President: Mr F. Grévisse; Judges: Mr J. C. Moitinho de Almeida and Mr M. Zuleeg;

Fourth Chamber: President: Mr P. J. G. Kapteyn; Judges: Mr C. N. Kakouris and Mr M. Díez de Velasco;

Fifth Chamber: President: Mr R. Joliet; Judges: Mr F. Grévisse, Mr J. C. Moitinho de Almeida, Mr G. C. Rodríguez Iglesias and Mr M. Zuleeg;

Sixth Chamber: President: Mr F. A. Schockweiler; Judges: Mr P. J. G. Kapteyn, Mr G. F. Mancini, Mr C. N. Kakouris, Mr M. Díez de Velasco and Mr M. Murray.

1173.   The composition of the Chambers of the Court of First Instance was determined as follows for a period of one year from 1 September:

First Chamber: President: Mr D. A. O. Edward; Judges: Mr B. Vesterdorf, Mr R. García-Valdecasas y Fernandez,   Mr K. Lenaerts,   Mr H. Kirschner   and Mr R. Schintgen;

Second Chamber: President: Mr J. L. da Cruz Vilaça; Judges: Mr D. P. M. Barrington, Mr A. Saggio, Mr C. G. Yeraris, Mr C. P. Briët and Mr J. Biancarelli;

Third   Chamber: President: Mr B. Vesterdorf;   Judges: Mr A. Saggio, Mr C. G. Yeraris and Mr J. Biancarelli;

Fourth   Chamber: President: Mr R. García-Valdecasas y Fernandez;   Judges: Mr D. A. O. Edward, Mr R. Schintgen and Mr C. P. Briët;

Fifth Chamber: President: Mr K. Lenaerts; Judges: Mr D. P. M. Barrington and Mr H. Kirschner.

1174.   In 1991, 340 cases were brought (182 references for preliminary rulings, 10 staff cases and 148 others). Of the 227 judgments given by the Court, 116 were preliminary rulings, 7 were in staff cases and 104 were in other cases. The Court of First Instance dealt with 92 cases and delivered 52 judgments.[1]

1175.   There were 672 permanent and 81 temporary posts on the Court's establishment plan at 31 December. The corresponding figures for the Court of First Instance were 35 and 12.

---

[1]   The Court's judgments are discussed in Chapter VI: Community law.

Court of Auditors

1176.   In July the Court published a report on the financial statements of the European Coal and Steel and Community at 31 December 1990.[1] On 7 November it adopted its annual report for 1990.[2]

1177.   The Court delivered opinions on the draft Financial Regulation applicable to cooperation under the Fourth Lomé Convention[3] and on a proposal for a Decision concerning the refund to Portugal of revenue from the accession compensatory amounts applied to supplies of common wheat.[4] It also gave opinions on the management of the Joint European Torus,[5] on the proposals for amending the Regulations relating to the European Centre for the Development of Vocational Training and the European Foundation for the Improvment of Living and Working Conditions,[6] and on the detailed rules for the implementation of certain provisions of the 1977 Financial Regulation.[7] The Court also adopted a series of special reports on the European Development Fund,[8] on the utilization of the results of Community research,[9] on financial and technical cooperation with the Mediterranean countries[10] and on the common organization of the sugar and isoglucose market.[11]

1178.   There were 320 permanent and 64 temporary posts on the Court's establishment plan at 31 December.

Economic and Social Committee

1179.   At its plenary session on 27 and 28 February the Economic and Social Committee welcomed Mr Delors, President of the Commission, who presented the programme for 1991.[12] At the same meeting, the priorities for the Luxembourg Presidency were set out by Mr Juncker, President of the Council.

1180.   During its plenary sessions the Committee adopted a host of opinions on Commission proposals and communications concerning the completion of the internal

---

[1]   Bull. EC 7/8-1991, point 1.7.13.
[2]   OJ C 324, 13.12.1991; Bull. EC 11-1991, point 1.7.19.
[3]   OJ C 113, 29.4.1991; Bull. EC 1/2-1991, point 1.7.21.
[4]   OJ C 113, 29.4.1991; Bull. EC 1/2-1991, point 1.7.22.
[5]   OJ C 324, 13.12.1991; Bull. EC 11-1991, point 1.7.21.
[6]   OJ C 152, 10.6.1991; Bull. EC 4-1991, points 1.7.28 and 1.7.29.
[7]   Bull. EC 4-1991, point 1.7.30.
[8]   OJ C 83, 27.3.1991; Bull. EC 1/2-1991, point 1.7.20.
[9]   OJ C 133, 23.5.1991, Bull. EC 3-1991, point 1.7.18.
[10]   Bull. EC 7/8-1991, point 1.7.14.
[11]   OJ C 290, 7.11.1991; Bull. EC 9-1991, point 1.7.21.
[12]   Bull. EC 1/2-1991, point 1.7.26.

market and on the implementation of other policies largely to do with the environment,[1] transport,[2] the health and safety of workers[3] and energy.[4]

1181. The Committee also delivered own-initiative opinions on Community relations with the United States and Japan,[5] the new Mediterranean policy,[6] immigration policy,[7] the status of migrant workers from non-member countries,[8] social developments in the Community,[9] employment in Europe in 1990,[10] the economic situation of the Community at mid-1991[11] and the completion of the internal market and protection of consumers.[12]

1182. There were 451 permanent posts on the Committee's establishment plan at 31 December.

ECSC Consultative Committee

1183. The Committee held three ordinary and two extraordinary meetings in 1991.

1184. Having been formally consulted by the Commission, the Committee expressed its opinion on the draft Commission Decision to conclude protocols on trade and commercial and economic cooperation with Hungary and Poland[13] and on the draft Commission Decision extending the earlier Decision to Czechoslovakia, Bulgaria, Yugoslavia and Romania.[14] It was also consulted on the report on the market for solid fuels in the Community in 1990 and the outlook for 1991,[15] on the revised forecasts for

---

[1] OJ C 102, 18.4.1991; Bull. EC 1/2-1991, point 1.2.226; OJ C 120, 6.5.1991; Bull. EC 3-1991, point 1.2.161; OJ C 159, 17.6.1991; Bull. EC 4-1991, point 1.2.76; OJ C 191, 22.7.1991; Bull. EC 5-1991, points 1.2.154, 1.2.158, 1.2.162 and 1.2.163; OJ C 269, 14.10.1991; Bull. EC 7/8-1991, points 1.2.122, 1.2.269 and 1.2.274; OJ C 290, 7.11.1991; Bull. EC 9-1991, point 1.2.125.

[2] Bull. EC 1/2-1991, point 1.2.43; OJ C 159, 17.6.1991; Bull. EC 4-1991, points 1.2.57 and 1.2.58; OJ C 191, 22.7.1991; Bull. EC 5-1991, points 1.2.67 and 1.2.68; OJ C 269, 14.10.1991; Bull. EC 7/8-1991, point 1.2.106; OJ C 290, 7.11.1991; Bull. EC 9-1991, points 1.2.48, 1.2.50 and 1.2.119.

[3] OJ C 120, 6.5.1991; Bull. EC 3-1991, point 1.2.80; OJ C 159, 17.6.1991; Bull. EC 4-1991, point 1.2.68; OJ C 191, 22.7.1991; Bull. EC 5-1991, points 1.2.86 and 1.2.88; OJ C 269, 14.10.1991; Bull. EC 7/8-1991, point 1.2.141.

[4] OJ C 102, 18.4.1991; Bull. EC 1/2-1991, point 1.2.107; OJ C 120, 6.5.1991; Bull. EC 3-1991, point 1.2.74; OJ C 269, 14.10.1991; Bull. EC 7/8-1991, points 1.2.118 and 1.2.122.

[5] OJ C 159, 17.6.1991; Bull. EC 4-1991, point 1.3.31.

[6] Bull. EC 12-1991.

[7] Bull. EC 11-1991, point 1.2.10.

[8] OJ C 159, 17.6.1991; Bull. EC 4-1991, point 1.2.73.

[9] OJ C 191, 22.7.1991; Bull. EC 5-1991, point 1.2.77.

[10] OJ C 269, 14.10.1991, Bull. EC 7/8-1991, point 1.2.132.

[11] OJ C 290, 7.11.1991; Bull. EC 9-1991, point 1.2.1.

[12] OJ C 290, 7.11.1991; Bull. EC 9-1991, point 1.2.127.

[13] Bull. EC 1/2-1991, point 1.3.11.

[14] Bull. EC 6-1991, point 1.3.12.

[15] Bull. EC 3-1991, point 1.2.75.

the outlook for the solid fuels market in 1991,[1] on the forward programmes for steel for the second quarter of 1991[2] and for the second half of 1991[3] and on the granting of financial aid from the ECSC levy for the 1991 steel and coal research programmes.[4]

1185.   The Committee was formally consulted on ECSC industrial loans for environmental protection[4] and on the advisability of granting ECSC financial assistance to fund studies on requirements and strategies with regard to workers' housing[5] and on specific action relating to the environment.[6] It also gave opinions on the draft Commission Decision laying down Community rules for aid to the steel industry from 1 January 1992[7] and on an application from the Italian Government for an extension of the time allowed for completing the restructuring of the State-owned steel industry.[8]

1186.   The Committee examined two Commission reports on the application of Community rules for State aid to the coal industry in 1988[9] and 1989[7] and on the Commission communication on the future of the ECSC Treaty.[10]

1187.   The Committee adopted resolutions on the negotiation of arrangements for steel imports from certain non-member countries in 1991,[11] on negotiations for the establishment of a European Economic Area[12] and on the association agreements with Central and East European countries.[13]

1188.   The Committee also discussed the Commission communication on a European Energy Charter and the ECSC operating budget.[7]

1189.   Lastly, the Committee formally approved the coal and steel research programmes for 1991.[7]

---

[1]   Bull. EC 10-1991, point 1.2.66.
[2]   Bull. EC 3-1991, point 1.2.56.
[3]   Bull. EC 6-1991, point 1.2.65.
[4]   Bull. EC 6-1991, point 1.7.26.
[5]   Bull. EC 10-1991, point 1.2.86.
[6]   Bull. EC 10-1991, point 1.2.190.
[7]   Bull. EC 10-1991, point 1.7.23.
[8]   Bull. EC 6-1991, point 1.2.50.
[9]   Bull. EC 1/2-1991, point 1.7.29.
[10]   Bull. EC 6-1991, point 1.2.64.
[11]   Bull. EC 1/2-1991, point 1.3.101.
[12]   Bull. EC 6-1991, point 1.7.25.
[13]   Bull. EC 6-1991, point 1.3.10.

Administration and management of the institutions

Screening exercise

1190.   The Commission had decided to carry out a screening exercise to assess how well the human resources available to it were matched in quantitative and qualitative terms to the tasks facing them. A task force was set up which in the first few months of the year analysed the situation in all Commission departments except the Joint Research Centre and the Publications Office to enable the Commission to identify its genuine indispensable staff requirements on the basis of optimum allocation of resources. The exercise was basically organized along the same broad lines as the Commission's programme so as to focus as far as possible on the priorities set by the Commission, highlighting in particular the new tasks emerging and the development of existing ones. This meant that it covered the following seven areas of activity: the frontier-free internal market, the social area, flanking policies, economic development and structural operations, common policies, external relations and horizontal departments (coordination, finance, financial control and administration, language services).

In the interviews and their evaluation, particular consideration was given to the following aspects: identification and development of tasks (subsidiarity, new tasks, priorities); changes in the nature of tasks (formulating policy, negotiation, implementation, evaluation and follow-up, monitoring, etc.); functional links and duplication; relationship between regular and outside staff; possibility of 'farming out' tasks; budgetary and financial control; administrative support and computer services; in-house procedures. Special attention was paid to the opportunities for administrative decentralization and the organization of computer services.

1191.   The follow-up programme adopted by the Commission in May envisaged, internally, an improvement in administration, departmental organization and the use of human resources through redeployment and reorganization. It also served as a basis for the allocation of new human resources made available under the 1991 budget and for requests for new resources in the 1992 budget. The programme covers the two years 1991 and 1992, and on 31 July the Commission approved a first series of measures and guidelines calling for certain structural changes in departments and for a degree of rationalization in their operation.

Commission Inspectorate-General

1192.   The Commission set up the Inspectorate-General on 6 February. Its remit is not to make routine, systematic inspections in each of the Directorates-General but to carry out inspections that reflect the Commission's concerns as regards the economic, efficient and effective utilization of resources, with due regard for the relevant legislation and the Commission's priorities.

1193.   The Inspectorate-General has a staff of 20, and is required to produce a programme for each year starting on 1 July. The results of each inspection will be strictly confidential and will be set out in a report analysing the situation and making recommendations and suggestions.

Reorganization of the Directorate-General for Personnel and Administration

1194.   On 24 January the Commission adopted a series of guidelines to simplify and streamline personnel and administration policy. These guidelines entail the gradual reorganization of the Directorate-General for Personnel and Administration (DG IX) with the aim of redeploying its resources towards programming, coordination, guidance and logistical support for the management of the institution's human and material resources, which will be handled on a more decentralized basis by the other Directorates-General. The various mechanisms and supporting arrangements for decentralized management of all the Commission's human resources are now regrouped within DG IX's Personnel Directorate. The Rights and Obligations Directorate, which implements and enforces the Staff Regulations, will see its staff service and assistance functions strengthened and expanded. Finally, the traditional logistic support and asset management functions, within the Administration Directorate, will be given a fresh boost with the establishment of a medium and long-term strategy for accommodation, infrastructure and supplies.

1195.   An appraisal was made of the allocation of staff management functions and responsibilities between DG IX and the other Directorates-General, from the dual angle of decentralization and the simplification of procedures. Administrative decentralization will be brought about in stages and pragmatically: description and simplification of procedures, adjustment and expansion of general computer services — the emphasis being on Sysper and the input, updating and checking of the data it is to hold and its functional objectives. To provide the essential support from the staff, meetings have been held and are still going on with the trade unions and staff associations, and seminars will be organized with the staff.

Operation Berlaymont

1196.   On 29 May the Commission irrevocably decided to move out of the Berlaymont building by 31 December, on the grounds that health and safety conditions had become altogether unsatisfactory. The Belgian Government, which owns the building, has undertaken to provide alternative accommodation up to the Commission's standards and representing an office space of 125 000 m^2, which is the area occupied in the Berlaymont. According to a relocation plan worked out jointly by Commission staff and the Belgian Régie des Bâtiments, the Commission will rent a total of 10 buildings that are under construction or being renovated in accordance with a precise schedule. Work immediately began on the refittings to enable some 4 000 people to move by the end of the year.

On the strength of its capacity and geographical location, the Breydel building, owned by the Commission, was chosen to house the Members of the Commission.

Salary adjustments and payment in ecus

1197. In October 1990 the Commission sent the Council a two-part proposal for remuneration policy in the Community civil service; the first part was concerned with the renewal of the salary adjustment method utilized hitherto, based on the principle of parallel development designed to ensure that salaries in the Community civil service move in line with salaries in the national civil services; the second part provided for the payment of Community officials and other staff in ecus. Parliament gave its opinion supporting the first part in April.

1198. The Council then began negotiations with the staff which culminated in a compromise proposal made at the 11 October meeting of the Concertation Committee. On that basis the Commission produced amended proposals introducing a new pay measure ('temporary contribution') and increasing the staff contribution to the pension scheme. Parliament delivered its opinion on these proposals in December.

1199. Parliament decided to refer the second part, concerning payment in ecus, for more detailed study to its Committee on Legal Affairs and Citizens' Rights.

Staff Regulations

Joint Sickness Insurance Scheme

1200. In some Community countries, members of the Joint Sickness Insurance Scheme have been less well off than officials in Belgium or Luxembourg owing to the difference between the high cost of medical treatment in their countries of employment or, in the case of pensioners, of residence, and the maximum rates of reimbursement set on the basis of statistics gathered mostly in Belgium and Luxembourg. To remedy this distortion, some slight adjustments to the rules are currently being considered and should allow weightings for each currency and benefit to be systematically applied with retroactive effect from 1 January 1991.

1201.   An amendment to the Regulations determining the emoluments of members and former members designed to clarify points relating to affiliation of former members and those entitled under them to the Scheme has been published.[1]

Transfer of pension rights

1202.   On 14 May the Commission sent the Council a proposal to amend Article 11 of Annex VIII to the Staff Regulations to take account of the judgment of the Court of Justice in Case C-37/89, which authorizes the transfer of pension rights by officials who were self-employed before they entered the service of a Community institution.

1203.   On 21 May Belgium enacted legislation on the transfer of pension rights acquired under the Belgian scheme to the Community scheme. The work of processing the files of the 3 500 officials concerned has since begun. Negotiations with France, Germany, the Netherlands and Denmark on the transfer of pension rights have made substantial headway.

Administration of Commission delegations ouside the Community and delegations and offices in the Community

1204.   The Commission has had to deal with a number of priorities in this area. The first task was to simplify and/or decentralize procedures. Using the possibilities offered by the revision of the Financial Regulation, the Commission launched a series of projects in areas such as the awarding of contracts, stock management, bookkeeping and accounting, imprest accounts, mission administration, the purchase of data-processing equipment, delegation training, and so on.

1205.   The development of relations between the Community and Eastern Europe has confronted the Commission with the challenge of swiftly opening delegations there. Those in Poland and Hungary have been operational since 1990; the Moscow Delegation opened in January 1991; preparations for two more (in Prague and Sofia) are under way. Establishing this external representation serves two immediate purposes: to foster economic and commercial cooperation between the Community and each of those countries and to provide local back-up for programmes in support of their newly initiated economic reforms.

---

[1]   OJ L 222, 10.8.1991.

1206. Last but not least, the year's many crises, most of them occurring in Africa and the Gulf region, placed heavier demands on staff; safety and security arrangements were made with great efficiency.

Implementing the social contract for progress

1207. Strict compliance with the letter and spirit of the social contract was a key factor in renewing an ongoing constructive dialogue between the Commission and staff representatives. This approach was also taken to clarifying the distribution of powers and responsibilities between the trade unions and staff associations and the formal staff representation bodies. Technical and policy consultations provided opportunities for fruitful dialogue on various matters directly affecting staff (welfare, training, careers, promotions, etc.) and yielded a consensus on matters of such crucial importance as the proposal to the Council on the salaries adjustment method. The shared aim was to streamline and simplify relations between the Commission and the staff representatives.

Positive action programme

1208. A new five-year programme, 1991-95, now being adopted, calls for more forceful action on the part of the administration and an active commitment on the part of the operational departments in implementing the Commission's equal opportunities policy.

Data processing

1209. The growth in data-processing resources available to users continued. At the end of the year, the level of computerization — the ratio of work stations to the total number of staff — was approaching 70%. The development and use of information and infrastructure systems, as well as training and assistance for users, followed the same trend.

1210. In 1991 there was a top-level review of the organization of the data-processing departments. Its conclusions generated a decision to proceed with more decentralization and redefine basic functions so that the Directorates-General and other departments will bear more responsibility themselves.

Language services

1211.   On account of the shortage of conference interpreters, the Joint Interpreting and Conference Service (JICS) continued its training efforts, maintaining the same standard for all languages. Following a wide advertising campaign in all the Member States, the Service organized 30 aptitude tests for young graduates (law, economics, science, etc.) with training provided, in particular in Athens, Florence, Hamburg, Lisbon and Madrid. The Commission made a financial contribution to postgraduate training courses in Athens, Copenhagen, Florence, Hamburg and Lisbon. Twenty staff interpreters were given study grants in order to learn another working language. Cooperation with non-member countries in the field of interpreter training continued, in particular with China and Turkey. Under the Tempus programme, the JICS was invited to Czechoslovakia to explore the possibilities for cooperation in vocational training with the authorities there. Two Hungarian lecturers came to learn about JICS interpreter training techniques and took part in courses and seminars of the Europa Kolleg in Hamburg.

Section 2

Information for the general public

Information activities

1212.   Information and communication activities focused mainly on completion of the internal market, promotion of a people's Europe and the role of the Community in the world, particularly in the wake of events in the Soviet Union, Yugoslavia, and Central and Eastern Europe, as well as on progress made in the two Intergovernmental Conferences. The Commission's drive to coordinate campaigns targeting a wide range of audiences, to improve communication and to make efficient use of information techniques continued under the priority information programmes adopted for 1990 and 1991.[1] These programmes are designed to ensure that the Commission's information priorities are consistent with the policy priorities set out in its annual programme. On 20 November the Commission adopted its priority information programme and priority publications programme for 1992.[2] Drawing on the experience gained since these programmes were introduced, the Commission laid down guidelines for future information campaigns and selected the following priority topics for its publications programme: 1992 Europe, economic and social cohesion, current operations, external relations, the new challenges (economic and monetary union, and political union) and general information. On 13 November[3] the Council adopted a resolution in which it stressed that the computerized documentation system for Community law (Celex) had a key role to play in increasing public awareness of Community law and the relevant national legislation. Information activities relating to completion of the internal market were aimed at a variety of target groups, but particular emphasis was again placed on the social dimension in anticipation of close cooperation with the trade unions on this front. The strategy of developing relay organizations providing information for the general public continued to bear fruit and, judging by the large number of enquiries received, the Commission's Team 92 was much in demand. The Commission's Offices in the capitals and some regions of the Community had to cope with an increased volume of enquiries from citizens wanting to be brought up to date with progress in Community affairs. A significant feature of 1991 was the development of special 'Europe Weeks' as a forum for expressing and promoting a feeling of belonging to the Community.

---

[1]   Twenty-fourth General Report, point 960.
[2]   Bull. EC 11-1991, point 1.2.203.
[3]   Bull. EC 11-1991, point 1.2.204.

1213.   The Commission's proposals for reforming the common agricultural policy have been accompanied by a large-scale PR initiative designed to convince public opinion in the Community — and consumer organizations in particular — of the need for such reform. Looking beyond 1992 towards 2000, a major information strategy is currently being devised to accompany implementation of the decisions taken by the Intergovernmental Conferences.

Information activities in non-member countries were developed further with special emphasis on providing information on progress in the Uruguay Round of the GATT talks. In view of the sweeping changes which have taken place on the international political scene and the increasing role now played by the Commmunity, greater priority is to be given to providing information not only for the Community's traditional partners both in the developing and in the industrialized countries, but also for Central and Eastern Europe. Hence the task force sent to the newly independent Baltic States to assess their requirements in the field of information and the special activities organized in the wake of German unification.

1214.   A considerable effort was also made to encourage initiatives promoting awareness of a people's Europe, including a campaign to make more information available to young people, implementation of the 'Symbiosis' relay project, which involves European and national associations and local communities in the European process,[1] the distribution of people's Europe factsheets and the organization of a contest for schools entitled 'For Europe: 40 questions for 1 000 schools'; the contest was a resounding success, and the winning schools each received a prize of ECU 1 000.

1215.   The determination of the Commission to give fresh impetus to its youth information activities was also reflected in the communication entitled 'Keeping young Europeans informed' adopted on 3 June,[2] in which it proposes using a specialized network to launch an information drive geared to encouraging information professionals to exchange experiences and keep up to date, diversifying information and spreading awareness of the concept of European citizenship. The communication was favourably received by the Council and will be followed up by a series of practical measures in the form of a programme due to be submitted to it shortly.

On 14 June Parliament passed a resolution on Community policies and their impact on youth, in which it called for the development of information programmes geared specifically to young people.[3]

1216.   The Commission also laid down guidelines for the Community's dealings with the world of sport. In the communication adopted on 31 July it declared its intention

---

[1]   Twenty-fourth General Report, point 960.
[2]   Bull. EC 6-1991, point 1.2.107.
[3]   OJ C 183, 15.7.1991; Bull. EC 6-1991, point 1.2.108.

of implementing an information campaign designed to enable the bodies concerned to take advantage of the opportunities offered by the single market and to help them bring the rules governing sport into line with Community law, with due regard for the principle of subsidiarity. [1]

Still on the sports front the Commission granted its patronage to the European Youth Olympic Games, [2] the European Swimming Championships, the European Yacht Race, the Constitution Race (Europe/United States) and the European Community Women's Cycle Race.

1217. The Commission took part in several public events and continued to prepare the ground for the Community's participation in the Seville Universal Exposition [3] and the Genoa International Exhibition [4] in 1992 and in the 1992 Olympics in Albertville and Barcelona; [5] it decided to conduct a massive publicity campaign on the occasion of the Olympics to enhance the Community's image, increase public awareness of the European ideal and celebrate the importance of 1992 for the Community.

1218. In the field of cooperation between the Commission and institutions of higher education, 1991 saw the launching of the next phase of the Jean Monnet Project, [6] which enabled the Commission to lend its support to the creation of a further 44 chairs of European integration.

Press, radio and television

1219. As in previous years the number of journalists accredited to the Commission in Brussels remained high, at over 650 journalists from 51 countries, of whom around 475 were from the press and 185 from radio and television. This total includes 62 national and international press agencies.

The Spokesman's Service held 240 meetings with the press on Commission decisions, proposals and reactions, and 50 press conferences following Commission meetings. The President and Members of the Commission gave 60 press conferences on key issues, several of which were given jointly with visitors to the Commission.

The Spokesman's Service also conveyed to the press the Commission position on the occasion of Council and European Council meetings and part-sessions of Parliament.

[1]   Bull. EC 7/8-1991, point 1.2.292.
[2]   Bull. EC 4-1991, point 1.2.146.
[3]   Twenty-third General Report, point 57; Twenty-fourth General Report, point 962.
[4]   Twenty-fourth General Report, point 962.
[5]   Twenty-fourth General Report, point 961.
[6]   Twenty-fourth General Report, point 963.

Special arrangements were made to cover international events involving the Community, such as the G7 Summit in London.

More than 3 000 information memos and papers were released to the accredited press, while the Offices in the Member States and the Delegations in non-member countries received over 900 telexed memos and commentaries drafted specifically to enable them to brief local press contacts on a daily basis.

Office for Official Publications

1220.   Publication of a training manual and the organization of an interinstitutional course were the first fruits of the assignment given to the Publications Office in 1990 to coordinate and advise the institutions on desktop publishing.[1] The Office also continued work begun in 1990 on a study on the consolidation of amended Community legislation with a view to providing the institutions with an effective work tool by 1992.

The Office was also instructed by its Management Committee to compile an interinstitutional administrative directory in database form accessible by computer and to carry out a study with a view to producing an interinstitutional guide to European information sources.

The Office continued to expand its computerized optical archive system (Arcdon) and extended the links between it and the electronic ordering systems ABEL (contents pages of 'L' series Official Journals) and Catel (electronic catalogue). These improvements, coupled with refinements to the indexing system, meant that the Office was able to comply with Parliament's request for direct electronic access to institutional documents from Brussels and Strasbourg.

Aware of the importance of information in motivating the general public and promoting its publications, the Office played an active part in setting up the Community's first 'Info-Point Europe', located in a Euro-bookshop in Luxembourg.

In accordance with the publications strategy defined by the Commission in 1989 and with due regard for the principle of subsidiarity the Office systematically looks into the possibilities of joint ventures with publishers in the public and private sectors whenever the subject matter is suitable. General guidelines have been laid down for the administrative and financial management of such ventures and a number of substantial publications have been successfully produced in this way.

---

[1]   Twenty-fourth General Report, point 968.

Historical archives

1221.   The Commission released the historical archives of the ECSC High Authority, the EEC Commission and the Euratom Commission for 1960 for consultation,[1] thus adding some 2 000 files to the 15 500 already accessible to the public.[2]

1222.   Work on the central archives was stepped up to cope with the exceptional number of files transferred from Members' Offices and departments in connection with the move out of the Berlaymont building and routine activities on the Commission's historical archives. Between 10 000 and 15 000 metres of shelving had to be installed to accommodate the files and other material released early into the public domain.

1223.   The guide to the archives of the Foreign Ministries of the Member States, the European Communities and the European political cooperation machinery, originally published by the Commission in English and French,[3] is now also available in the other Community languages, with updates from Ireland, Italy and Germany (following unification).

1224.   In a resolution adopted on 14 November the Council and the Ministers for Culture called on the Commission to look into the possibility of increasing the coordination of archives policy and practice within the Community.[4]

---

[1]   The historical archives are deposited at the European University Institute in Florence.
[2]   Twenty-fourth General Report, point 969.
[3]   Twenty-third General Report, point 64.
[4]   Bull. EC 11-1991, point 1.2.207.

Section 3

Statistics

1225. The Statistical Office continued its work this year to implement the five-year priority action plan adopted in 1989 to meet the Community's increased need for high-quality, detailed and reliable statistics, especially for purposes of the internal market.[1] A second progress report was submitted and discussed with the Commission and the national statistical institutes.

1226. The adoption by the Council on 25 February of decisions setting up a Committee on Monetary, Financial and Balance of Payments Statistics[2] and a European Advisory Committee on Statistical Information in the Economic and Social Spheres[3] led to important organizational changes. These two committees, the first of which has met twice so far, will help improve coordination with national statistical institutes by creating efficient lines of communication.

1227. Statistical cooperation was extended to include the EFTA countries, and the development of an integrated statistical system for the European Economic Area gathered momentum, with particular emphasis on environment, tourism, migration and transport statistics and electronic data exchange.[4]

1228. The Community was also concerned to develop statistical coordination and cooperation more particularly with the countries of Central and Eastern Europe, which are trying to establish a statistical system geared towards a market economy. A number of statistical projects were identified for Poland (ECU 1.5 million), Hungary (ECU 0.25 million) and Czechoslovakia under the Phare programme[5] and were already well under way. Statistical projects in the Soviet Union were also being prepared.

---

[1]   OJ C 161, 28.6.1989; Twenty-third General Report, point 65.
[2]   OJ L 59, 6.3.1991; Bull. EC 1/2-1991, point 1.6.3; Commission proposal: OJ C 212, 25.8.1990; Twenty-fourth General Report, point 970.
[3]   OJ L 59, 6.3.1991; Bull. EC 1/2-1991, point 1.6.4; Commission proposal: OJ C 212, 25.8.1990; Twenty-fourth General Report, point 970.
[4]   Point 846 of this Report.
[5]   Point 818 of this Report.

1229.   An administrative arrangement aimed at improving coordination was signed with the United States and Canada.

Statistical work associated with the Single Act

1230.   Methodological work has started on a review of the European system of integrated economic accounts (ESA) and classification for balance-of-payments purposes.

1231.   Following the adoption in 1990 of the Council Regulation on the transmission of data subject to statistical confidentiality to the Statistical Office,[1] the Committee on Statistical Confidentiality took up its duties and began taking stock of all data of a confidential nature and the protection measures in operation. The first draft of a manual on the protection of confidential data at Eurostat was sent to the Committee.

1232.   On 7 November the Council adopted a Regulation on the statistics relating to the trading of goods between Member States,[2] which introduces a new system for collecting data on intra-Community trade to replace the present system (based on customs formalities, documents and inspections) when the Community's internal frontiers are abolished.

1233.   As provided for in the Directive on the harmonization of the compilation of gross national product at market prices (GNPmp),[3] the GNP Committee continued its work on improving the comparability and reliability of GNP data for the determination of national contributions to the Community's own resources and the coordination of national economic policies.

1234.   The review of business statistics, needed to increase the transparency of the internal market and improve the competitiveness of firms, continued with work on the standardization of business registers throughout the Community; and the adaptation of statistics to the requirements of the single market made great progress this year. On 25 February the Commission adopted a proposal for a Regulation on the establishment of a Community survey of industrial production (Prodcom);[4] intensive discussions were held with national statistical institutes to determine the legal instruments to be intro-

---

[1]   OJ L 151, 15.6.1990; Twenty-fourth General Report, point 972.
[2]   OJ L 316, 16.11.1991; Bull. EC 11-1991, point 1.6.1; Commission proposals: OJ C 41, 18.2.1989; Twenty-second General Report, point 69; OJ C 177, 18.7.1990; Twenty-fourth General Report, point 973; OJ C 254, 9.10.1990; OJ C 47, 23.2.1991; Bull. EC 1/2-1991, point 1.6.2; Bull. EC 11-1991, point 1.6.1.
[3]   OJ L 49, 21.2.1989; Twenty-third General Report, point 68.
[4]   Bull. EC 1/2-1991, point 1.6.5.

duced in the next few years. A supplement to the *Panorama of EC industry*, capitalizing on close links with trade associations, was published to meet the needs of users within the single market.

1235.   On 19 April Parliament endorsed[1] the proposal for a Council Decision establishing a multiannual programme for the development of European statistics on services.[2]

Statistical support for common policies

1236.   The Commission continued its support for measures to improve statistical systems in some Member States. The second stage of the programme for restructuring Greece's system of agricultural surveys was launched;[3] the support programmes for Italy and Ireland came to an end this year.[4]

1237.   On 15 November the Commission extended by two years the Preder statistical programme for regional development in Portugal.[5] ECU 5.4 million was granted under the Phare programme[6] for restructuring the statistical system of the former German Democratic Republic, with particular emphasis on staff training and computerization, projects and programmes especially concerned with national and regional accounts, registers and agricultural statistics. On 26 April the Commission adopted Regulation (EEC) No 1057/91,[7] which gives the German authorities until 31 December 1992 to implement legislation on agricultural statistics in what was the GDR.

1238.   In December the Council adopted Regulation (EEC) No 3711/91 on the organization of an annual labour force survey.[8] These new and more efficient arrangements should replace the present system, on which this year's survey is based, from spring 1992. On 14 October the Council also adopted Directive 91/534/EEC to reduce the frequency of surveys on the earnings of agricultural workers to once every three years.[9]

1239.   Steps were taken to speed up the provision of harmonized and more reliable data by Member States in an enlarged Community; a review of the statistical legislation relating to livestock production was in progress. The medium-term module of the

---

[1]   OJ C 129, 20.5.1991; Bull. EC 4-1991, point 1.6.2.
[2]   Bull. EC 12-1990, point 1.7.1.
[3]   OJ L 190, 21.7.1990; Twenty-fourth General Report, point 977.
[4]   OJ L 359, 8.12.1989; Twenty-third General Report, point 72.
[5]   Twenty-fourth General Report, point 977.
[6]   Point 818 of this Report.
[7]   OJ L 107, 27.4.1991; Bull. EC 4-1991, point 1.6.3.
[8]   OJ L 351, 20.12.1991; Bull. EC 12-1991; Commission proposal: Bull. EC 4-1991, point 1.6.1.
[9]   OJ L 288, 18.10.1991; Bull. EC 10-1991, point 1.6.3; Commission proposal: Bull. EC 6-1991, point 1.6.2.

Eurostat agricultural sector model (SPEL/EC-MFSS) was used this year to analyse the impact of new measures to reform the CAP on production and income in the Community's farming sector. [1]

1240.   In view of the need to monitor the supply of fish to the Community and enhance market transparency, on 21 May the Council adopted a Regulation on the submission of data on the landings of fishery products in Member States; [2] on 17 December, [3] for stock monitoring purposes, it also adopted two Regulations on the submission of nominal catch statistics by Member States fishing in the north-east Atlantic [4] and the north-west Atlantic. [5]

1241.   To take account of the major changes in the industry and in anticipation of the single market, Commission Decision No 1566/86/ECSC on iron and steel statistics [6] was amended on 18 October. [7]

1242.   Directive 90/377/EEC concerning gas and electricity prices charged to industrial end-users was implemented to improve the transparency of the market. [8] Commission Decision No 612/91/ECSC and Commission recommendation 91/141/ECSC concerning coal statistics were adopted with the same purpose in view. [9]

[1]   Points 530 and 531 of this Report.
[2]   OJ L 133, 28.5.1991; Bull. EC 5-1991, point 1.6.1; Commission proposal: OJ C 214, 21.8.1989; Twenty-third General Report, point 72.
[3]   OJ L 365, 31.12.1991; Bull. EC 12-1991; Commission proposals: OJ C 230, 4.9.1991; Bull. EC 10-1991, points 1.6.4 and 1.6.5.
[4]   OJ C 230, 4.9.1991; Bull. EC 6-1991, point 1.6.3.
[5]   OJ C 230, 4.9.1991; Bull. EC 6-1991, point 1.6.4.
[6]   OJ L 141, 28.5.1986; Twentieth General Report, point 65.
[7]   OJ L 359, 30.12.1991; Bull. EC 10-1991, point 1.6.2.
[8]   Twenty-fourth General Report, point 601.
[9]   OJ L 74, 20.3.1991; Bull. EC 1/2-1991, point 1.6.6.

Section 4

Financing Community activities

Priority activities and objectives

1243.   In 1991 the Community had to assume the financial consequences of the pledges it made in connection with the year's important international events.

The 1991 budget thus contained large allocations for the countries most directly affected by the Gulf crisis and for the countries of Central and Eastern Europe. The financial perspective was also revised to provide cover in 1991 for technical assistance to the Soviet Union, financial assistance to Israel and the Occupied Territories, emergency aid to the Iraqi population of Kurdish origin and a special programme of food aid for Africa. The funds for these operations were made available when the first supplementary and amending budget was adopted on 15 May.

The 1992 budget is special in that it is the last budget to be drawn up under the financial perspective for 1988-92 contained in the Interinstitutional Agreement of June 1988 and is thus the reference base for the new framework for 1993-97: budgetary practice in the last three years will be the yardstick for measuring the usefulness of this mechanism, and for this reason the 1992 budget will be examined with particular attention. The preliminary draft budget for 1992 was therefore drawn up with the aim of imposing tighter budgetary discipline and past priorities were reviewed objectively on the basis of cost-effectiveness analyses.

The Community's external operations in Europe and in other regions of the world — support for the process of building a democratic base and rebuilding the economy in Central and Eastern Europe, Asia and Latin America and assistance for the countries of the Mediterranean — are now at the fore of the political and budgetary debate. However, although the appropriations proposed for these operations have been increased, the Community budget still revolves around internal policies, as shown by the substantial increase in the appropriations for the structural Funds. The Community is also concentrating on agricultural policy, research policy and a number of policies contributing to completion of the internal market. The allocations for all these sectors have been increased.

The Community's growing external policy responsibilities are thus not being allowed to obstruct stronger economic and social cohesion.

Budgets

General budget

Financial perspective

1244. On 7 March the Commission made the technical adjustment to the financial perspective in line with GNP growth and price movements for 1992[1] (point 9 of the Interinstitutional Agreement on budgetary discipline and improvement of the budgetary procedure)[2] and at the same time submitted to the budgetary authority a proposal to adjust the financial perspective in the light of the conditions of implementation (points 10 and 11 of the Agreement).[3] As a result, the budgetary authority decided to transfer to 1992 commitment appropriations of ECU 465 million which were not used in 1990; ECU 350 million concerned the structural Funds (heading 2) and ECU 115 million the IMPs (heading 3).[4] It was also agreed that ECU 193 million in commitment appropriations, corresponding to the appropriations not used in 1990, would be included in the allocation for the structural Funds in 1993.

1245. The Commission presented two proposals for the revision of the financial perspective as a result of international developments affecting the Community.[5] The decision of 15 May raised the ceiling for heading 4 (Other policies) by ECU 728 million in 1991 (non-compulsory expenditure) in order to finance technical assistance to the USSR of up to ECU 400 million, financial aid to Israel and the Occupied Territories amounting to ECU 87.5 million, emergency aid for the Iraqi population of Kurdish origin amounting to ECU 100 million and a special food aid programme for Africa amounting to ECU 140 million.[6] As a result, the total payment appropriations needed for non-compulsory expenditure were increased by ECU 423 million in 1991 and by ECU 180 million in 1992. Since this increase leads to a rise in the amounts to be earmarked for refunds to Spain and Portugal under heading 5, the amount for stock disposal in this heading, which will not be used in full, was reduced by ECU 3 million.

1246. The Commission presented a proposal on 27 September for the decision concerning 1992, which had been deferred until the autumn:

(i) an increase of ECU 720 million in the ceiling of heading 4 (Other policies), of which ECU 420 million is intended to raise to ECU 500 million the allocation to be

[1]   Bull. EC 3-1991, point 1.5.2; Bull. EC 4-1991, point 1.5.3.
[2]   OJ L 185, 15.7.1988; Twenty-second General Report, point 84.
[3]   Bull. EC 3-1991, point 1.5.1.; Bull. EC 4-1991, point 1.5.2.
[4]   Bull. EC 4-1991, point 1.5.3.
[5]   Bull. EC 1/2-1991, point 1.5.1.; Bull. EC 4-1991, point 1.5.1.
[6]   OJ C 158, 17.6.1991; Bull. EC 5-1991, point 1.5.1.

entered in the 1992 budget to continue technical assistance to the Soviet Union and ECU 300 million is to be drawn on as necessary for the implementation of any further humanitarian aid operations which might be needed in non-Community countries;

(ii) an increase of ECU 80 million in the margin available under the ceiling of heading 5 for administrative expenditure. This amount is intended to cover staff and administration requirements resulting in particular from the Commission's screening exercise at the start of the year, the new external priorities and the refunds to be made to Spain and Portugal. It is proposed that this additional margin should be provided by making an equivalent cut in the stock disposal entry.[1]

The 1992 budget was approved on 12 December without the budgetary authority adopting the revision proposed.[2]

Table 17 shows the financial perspective following these decisions.

Budget procedure

1991 financial year

Supplementary and amending budgets

1247. The budget for 1991 was finally adopted on 13 December 1990[3] with ECU 58 535.3 million in commitment appropriations and ECU 55 556 million in payment appropriations after the financial perspective had been revised to take account of the financial effects of German unification and the Gulf crisis.[4] There were three supplementary and amending budgets to the 1991 budget:

(i) Supplementary and amending budget No 1[5] was altered by three letters of amendment before being finally adopted by the budgetary authority on 15 May.[6] In the end, this supplementary and amending budget covered various items of revenue and expenditure in 1991. First, it made provision in the budget for technical assistance to the Soviet Union, financial aid to Israel and the Occupied Territories, humanitarian aid to the Iraqi population of Kurdish origin and the special food aid

---

[1]   Bull. EC 9-1991, point 1.5.1.
[2]   Bull. EC 12-1991.
[3]   OJ L 19, 28.1.1991; Twenty-fourth General Report, point 996.
[4]   Twenty-fourth General Report, point 992.
[5]   OJ C 158, 17.6.1991; Bull. EC 5-1991, point 1.5.2; Commission proposal: Bull. EC 1/2-1991, point 1.5.2.
[6]   Bull. EC 3-1991, point 1.5.11; Bull. EC 4-1991, point 1.5.5; Bull. EC 5-1991, point 1.5.2.

TABLE 17

Financial perspective 1988-92
(Appropriations for commitments — current prices)

(million ECU)

	1988	1989	1990	1991	1992
1. EAGGF Guarantee[1]	27 500	28 613	30 700	33 000	35 039
2. Structural operations	7 790	9 522	11 555	14 804	18 009
3. Policies with multiannual allocations[2]	1 210	1 708	2 071	2 466	3 115
4. Other policies[1]	2 103	2 468	3 229	5 648	5 224
of which: non-compulsory	1 646	1 864	2 523	4 738	4 204
5. Repayments and administration	5 700	5 153	4 930	4 559	4 205
of which: stock disposal	1 240	1 449	1 523	1 375	1 191
6. Monetary reserve[3]	1 000	1 000	1 000	1 000	1 000
Total	45 303	48 464	53 485	61 477	66 592
of which: compulsory[4]	33 698	33 764	35 454	37 199	38 729
non-compulsory[4]	11 605	14 700	18 031	24 278	27 863
Appropriations for payments required	43 779	46 885	51 291	58 458	63 241
of which: compulsory[4]	33 640	33 745	35 372	37 195	38 669
non-compulsory[4]	10 139	13 140	15 919	21 263	24 572
Appropriations for payments required as % of GNP	1.09	1.07	1.09	1.13	1.14

[1] In accordance with the joint declaration by the three institutions on the adoption of the revision of the Financial Regulation and to ensure the proper financing of food aid without having to revise the financial perspective, compliance with the ceilings for headings 1 and 4 will not prevent a transfer between the headings in Article 292 of the budget (Refunds in connection with Community food aid) and Chapter 92 (Food aid). This means that these transfers will not be included with the total appropriations to be taken into consideration for complying with the ceilings of the financial perspective. The criteria for examining these transfers are those agreed by the Council, Parliament and the Commission in their declaration of 12 February 1990.
[2] Chapter F on budget estimates of the European Council indicates a figure of ECU 2 400 million (1988 prices) for policies with multiannual allocations in 1992. The policies in question are research and development and integrated Mediterranean programmes. Only expenditure for which a legal basis exists may be financed under this heading. The present framework programme provides a legal basis for research expenditure of ECU 853 million (current prices) for 1992. The regulation on integrated Mediterranean programmes provides a legal basis for an estimated amount of ECU 300 million in 1992 (current prices).
[3] At current prices.
[4] Based on the classification in the budget for 1991. The amendments resulting from decisions by the budgetary authority to change classification will be implemented as a technical adjustment under point 9 of the Agreement.

programme for Africa following the revision of the financial perspective on 15 May.[1]

(ii) Additional headings were also entered on both the revenue and the expenditure sides to cover the Community guarantee to the EIB in respect of EIB loans to Czechoslovakia, Bulgaria and Romania,[2] exports of agricultural products and

---

[1]   Point 1245 of this Report.
[2]   Points 830, 839 and 841 of this Report.

foodstuffs from the Community to the Soviet Union[1] and the borrowing contracted to grant medium-term financial assistance to Czechoslovakia, Hungary and Bulgaria.[2] The balance from 1990 was revalued at ECU 2 000 million instead of ECU 1 370 million and the amount of the correction for budgetary imbalances in 1990 was increased from ECU 3 344 million to ECU 3 528 million. Finally, administrative expenditure was increased by ECU 29 million and repayments to Spain and Portugal were increased to take account of the fact that the refunds and the financial compensation in respect of the depreciation of agricultural stocks were higher than the amounts initially entered in the budget.

(iii) On 31 July the Commission adopted preliminary draft supplementary and amending budget No 2 to cover the probable increase in agricultural expenditure and a further change in the 1990 balance (ECU 2 250 million).[3] On 26 October a letter of amendment restored agricultural expenditure to the level initially provided for in the budget, as the expected overruns had not materialized by the end of the financial year (15 October for EAGGF-Guarantee), included ECU 40 million in the 1991 budget for the move out of the Berlaymont building and increased the budget of the Court of Justice by ECU 900 000. The amended preliminary draft was finally adopted on 20 November in the form of two separate supplementary and amending budgets.[4] Supplementary and amending budget No 2 contained two additional headings to extend the Community guarantee to loans to be granted to Romania[5] and Algeria[6] and inserted remarks on the Energy Charter.[7]

(iv) Supplementary and amending budget No 3 related to the other items contained in preliminary draft supplementary and amending budget No 2 — the Berlaymont operation, the balance of the Court of Justice, correction of budgetary imbalances, repayments to Spain and Portugal.

The three supplementary and amending budgets brought the total appropriations entered for 1991 to ECU 59 369.5 million in commitment appropriations and ECU 56 085.4 million in payment appropriations.

Implementation of the 1991 budget

1248.   The rates of utilization of appropriations in 1991 are shown in Tables 18 and 19. Overall, they come to 95% in commitments and 94% in payments.

---

[1]   Point 844 of this Report.
[2]   Point 74 of this Report.
[3]   Bull. EC 7/8-1991, point 1.5.2.
[4]   OJ L 353, 23.12.1991; Bull. EC 11-1991, point 1.5.1.
[5]   Point 814 of this Report.
[6]   Point 900 of this Report.
[7]   Point 761 of this Report.

The utilization rate for agricultural guarantee expenditure (heading 1) exceeded 98%, leaving ECU 559 million unused (as against ECU 1 436.7 million in 1990). This high level of utilization amounts to 94% of the ceiling for the heading in 1991; expenditure came to only 85% of the ceiling in 1989 and 82% in 1990.

The utilization rates for headings 2, 3 and 4, for which the appropriations available were considerably higher than in 1990, came to 97% in commitments and 92% in payments.

Virtually all the appropriations were used in heading 5 for the administrative expenditure of the institutions, repayments to the Member States in connection with stock disposal and the refunds and financial compensation for Spain and Portugal.

1992 financial year

Budget procedure for 1992

1249. On 30 April the Commission adopted its preliminary draft budget for 1992.[1] Three letters of amendment were adopted on 26 June, 24 September and 6 November to take account of the impact of the Council's decisions on agricultural prices in 1992, the new requirements in connection with administrative expenditure and the new breakdown of research expenditure under the third framework programme, and the entry of an estimated balance for 1991 and headings to guarantee borrowing and lending operations for Romania and Algeria. The amended preliminary draft contained a total of ECU 65 589.7 million in commitment appropriations (10.4% more than the 1991 budget) and ECU 62 632.2 million in payment appropriations (11.6% higher). This preliminary draft was drawn up with the dual aim of pursuing the objectives adopted in 1988 in connection with the Interinstitutional Agreement and the financial perspective and complying with the principles of budgetary discipline. This dual aim is reflected in:

(i) the amount of funds for both internal policies (an increase in the allocation for the structural Funds so that they can be doubled by 1992-93, additional outlay on operations considered particularly promising such as research and operations connected with the completion of the internal market) and external policies (assistance to the countries of Central and Eastern Europe, increased cooperation with developing countries in Asia, Latin America and the Mediterranean area);

(ii) the budgetary constraints on all headings, in particular in heading 1 to keep agricultural expenditure at the level set by the guideline, in heading 4 to continue some of the operations not provided for by the financial perspective (Gulf, Soviet Union, emergency aid) and leave the budgetary authority a margin of

---

[1]   Bull. EC 4-1991, point 1.5.7.

ECU 100 million by means of an internal redeployment of ECU 100 million, in heading 5 to guarantee a minimum level of operation for the institutions and, more generally, in headings 2, 3 and 4 to keep an overall margin of ECU 634.9 million within the ceilings of the financial perspective.

1250. The Commission sent this preliminary draft to the budgetary authority, stressing that it would have to be supplemented in the course of the budgetary procedure after a revision of headings 4 and 5 of the financial perspective. The positions of the Council[1] and Parliament[2] on this preliminary draft emerged clearly on first reading. The differing opinions of the two arms of the budgetary authority on the need for a revision were confirmed during the budgetary procedure for 1992.

The Council drastically changed the balance of the Commission's preliminary draft. By making major cuts in headings 4 and 5 to the detriment of the Commission's priorities, the Council was able to carry out large-scale redeployment: in the Council draft virtually all the assistance to the Soviet Union (ECU 400 million, the same as for 1991, instead of the ECU 40 million proposed in the preliminary draft) and the funds needed for the move out of the Berlaymont and for the creation of new posts were financed by means of heavy cuts in administrative expenditure, which was already considered the minimum possible in a preliminary draft based on a constant number of staff. In the Council's opinion, this showed that it was possible to avoid a revision of the financial perspective to boost external policies and increase administrative expenditure. Apart from a number of changes, the Council upheld its position during the second reading. The amounts adopted on 12 November thus totalled ECU 65 634 million in commitment appropriations and ECU 62 418 million in payment appropriations.

The Council draft was a reply to the Commission's proposal for a revision of the financial perspective; similarly, the draft amended on first reading and the budget voted in December[3] reflected Parliament's position concerning this revision: subject to a revision of the financial perspective, Parliament decided to set up a reserve to be financed by national contributions in the same way as the monetary reserve. A total of ECU 1 660 million in commitment appropriations is entered in this reserve: ECU 300 million for the structural Funds (to offset inflation), ECU 300 million for emergency aid, ECU 860 million for the countries of Central and Eastern Europe, ECU 100 million for tropical rain forests and ECU 100 million for administrative expenditure.

Disregarding this reserve, the budget voted on 12 December totalled ECU 66 119 million in commitment appropriations (11.37 % higher than in 1991 and an increase of ECU 528 million over the preliminary draft) and ECU 62 827 million in

---

[1]   Bull. EC 7/8-1991, point 1.5.3.
[2]   Bull. EC 10-1991, point 1.5.4.
[3]   Bull. EC 12-1991.

payment appropriations (12.02% higher than in 1991 and an increase of ECU 195 million over the preliminary draft) and in most cases reached the ceiling for the various headings of the financial perspective.

Detailed analysis by heading shows that agricultural expenditure (heading 1) comes to ECU 35 039 million, which is the amount proposed by the Commission and corresponds to the agricultural guideline. Structural operations (heading 2) are allocated ECU 18 009 million, the maximum authorized in the current financial perspective; the ECU 200 million contained in the preliminary draft to offset differences between inflation rates and actual rates has been increased by ECU 45 million for regions covered by Objectives 1 and 2 in order to rebalance the rate of increase in the allocations for these Objectives compared with the increases for Objectives 3 to 5b. The ceiling of ECU 3 115 million has also been reached in heading 3 (Policies with multiannual allocations); the IMPs have been allocated ECU 467 million; expenditure on research comes to ECU 2 648 million, which is higher than the amount in the Commission's proposals and the Council's draft, exceeding the amounts deemed necessary in the second and third framework programmes and virtually doubling the amount for operations outside the framework programmes compared with the preliminary draft. In heading 4 (Other policies), a distinction has to be made between compulsory and non-compulsory expenditure. The Council adopted compulsory expenditure of ECU 932 million for this heading, ECU 12 million less than in the preliminary draft and ECU 88 million below the ceiling for compulsory expenditure in the heading. With the exception of the mini-budgets, most of the Commission's proposals for non-compulsory expenditure in the preliminary draft were accepted in the budget. It was also decided to increase a number of allocations (see Table 20), in particular those for Perifra II (ECU 50 million), transport, fisheries, social operations and training, energy, consumer protection, the environment, cooperation with Asian and Latin American developing countries and other cooperation measures.

The total allocations (ECU 4 204 million) reach the ceiling for non-compulsory expenditure in this heading. At this stage, the 1992 budget does not contain any appropriations which can be used for technical assistance to the Soviet Union. These appropriations will not be available until after revision of the financial perspective. As regards administrative expenditure (heading 5), the budget increases the Commission's administrative expenditure (non-compulsory expenditure) by a total of 7.9%. All but ECU 17 million of what was proposed in the preliminary draft has thus been accepted; the cuts mainly affect infrastructure, computers and the DAD. The 1992 budget provides for 327 new posts, as set out in letter of amendment No 2/92. In the case of the other institutions, the 1992 budget contains an increase of 8.6% over 1991. Building policy is allocated ECU 66 million in the Council budget and ECU 20 million in Parliament's budget.

Overall, as in heading 4, the failure to revise the financial perspective — and the truncated budget which results — means that appropriations are still needed for repayments and administrative expenditure; provision for these requirements will have to be made in the course of the year.

Table 20 sets out the various stages of the budgetary procedure.

Own resources

1251.   The budget is financed in accordance with Council Decision 88/376/EEC, Euratom on the system of the Communities' own resources.[1]

1991 financial year

1252.   In 1991 the budget resources totalled ECU 56 089.8 million, i.e. 1.09% of Community GNP. The revenue for the year is shown in Table 21.

1992 financial year

1253.   Foreseeable revenue for 1992 is shown in Table 21.

Discharge procedure

1989 financial year

1254.   On 16 April Parliament adopted a package of decisions and resolutions completing the procedure for giving discharge to the Community institutions and other bodies (general budget, ECSC management, EDF, the Centre for the Development of Vocational Training and the Foundation for the Improvement of Living and Working Conditions) for 1989.[2]

---

[1]   OJ L 185, 15.7.1988; Twenty-second General Report, point 102.
[2]   OJ C 129, 20.5.1991; Bull. EC 4-1991, points 1.5.9 to 1.5.13; Council recommendations: OJ L 75, 21.3.1991; Bull. EC 3-1991, points 1.5.5 to 1.5.8.

TABLE 21

Budget revenue

(million ECU)

	1991 outturn	1992 estimates
Agricultural levies	1 621.1	1 351.3
Sugar and isoglucose levies	1 141.8	1 236.0
Customs duties	12 751.7	12 888.8
Own resources collection costs	−1 552.2	−1 547.6
VAT own resources	30 269.0	34 232.4
Financial contributions	—	—
GNP-based own resources	7 415.2	14 280.8
Balance of VAT and GNP-based own resources from previous years	1 160.6	token entry
Budget balance from previous year	2 841.6	token entry
Other revenue	441.0	385.9
Total	56 089.8	62 827.6

	% GNP	
Maximum own resources which may be assigned to the budget	1.19	1.20
Own resources actually assigned to the budget	1.09	1.14

1990 financial year

1255. On 30 April the Commission sent the budgetary authority and the Court of Auditors the revenue and expenditure account and balance sheet for 1990 together with the report[1] on action taken in response to the observations contained in Parliament's resolution accompanying the decision on the discharge in respect of the implementation of the 1988 budget.[2]

On 13 September Parliament adopted a resolution in which it reiterated the importance of bringing the greatest possible transparency to decisions to carry forward unused appropriations or reinstate cancelled commitment appropriations.[3]

---

[1] Bull. EC 3-1991, point 1.5.4.
[2] OJ C 113, 3.4.1990; Twenty-fourth General Report, point 1001.
[3] OJ C 267, 14.10.1991; Bull. EC 9-1991, point 1.5.4.

ECSC budget

1256. After taking note of Parliament's opinion[1] and after informing the ECSC Consultative Committee, the Commission decided on 18 December to reduce the ECSC levy rate for 1992 from 0.29 to 0.27% and adopted the ECSC operating budget for 1992 on this basis.[2] The foreseeable resources (levy, net balance from previous year, fines, cancellations and budgetary resources not used the previous year), estimated at ECU 484 million, should cover the ECSC's requirements, which break down as follows (million ECU):

Administrative expenditure	5
Redeployment aid	170
Aid for research	123
Interest subsidies on ECSC loans (Articles 54 and 56)	131
Social measures (steel)	5
Social measures (coal) (Rechar)	50

Changes to Financial Regulations

1257. Following the adoption by the Council of Regulation (Euratom, ECSC, EEC) No 610/90 amending the Financial Regulation of 21 December 1977 applicable to the general budget of the Communities on 13 March 1990,[3] the Commission, on 1 February 1991,[4] proposed an updating of Regulation (EEC) No 610/86 of 11 December 1986 laying down detailed rules for the implementation of certain provisions of the Financial Regulation[5] in order to take account of the new references in the amended Financial Regulation and make a number of additions required for the purposes of budget implementation. Opinions on the Commission proposal were given by the Court of Auditors on 25 April,[6] by the Court of Justice in its letter of 5 June, by the Economic and Social Committee on 29 May[7] and by Parliament on 13 December.[1]

1258. On 13 December[1] Parliament gave its opinion on the Commission's proposals to amend the rules on the Centre for the Development of Vocational Training and the Foundation for the Improvement of Living and Working Conditions.[8]

---

[1]   OJ C 13, 20.1.1992; Bull. EC 12-1991.
[2]   Bull. EC 12-1991.
[3]   OJ L 70, 16.3.1990; Twenty-fourth General Report, point 1003.
[4]   Bull. EC 1/2-1991, point 1.5.5.
[5]   OJ L 360, 19.12.1986.
[6]   OJ C 152, 10.6.1991; Bull. EC 4-1991, point 1.7.30.
[7]   OJ C 191, 22.7.1991; Bull. EC 5-1991, point 1.5.3.
[8]   Twenty-fourth General Report, point 1003.

Financial Control

1259.   Following the reform of the structural Funds, Financial Control stepped up its audit of the management and control systems operated by each Member State and the organization of on-the-spot inspections during and after operations. In 1991 it again organized seminars on the management, financing and control of the Funds in a number of Member States (Spain, Greece and Germany) with the collaboration of the national authorities. All the Member States were visited or contacted so that their financial systems could be analysed in common.

1260.   As part of increased Community aid to the countries of Central and Eastern Europe under the Phare programme and, in particular, as a result of Parliament's debates, the Financial Controller made high-level exploratory contacts with the appropriate authorities in Poland, Hungary and Czechoslovakia to step up the measures planned or put into practice for the management and control of Community aid and to draw the authorities' attention to the need for effective control of this aid and provide them with appropriate training.

1261.   In accordance with the Commission Decision of 7 June 1990 on the Financial Controller's role as an internal auditor, [1] Financial Control made a financial audit of two Directorates-General. The purpose of this internal audit is to assure the Commission that the systems and methods of financial management available within its departments function properly.

1262.   Following the latest revision of the Financial Regulation, [2] Financial Control's role as the Commission's financial adviser for the purposes of sound financial management has been strengthened through the development of the methods and concepts of cost-benefit and cost-effectiveness.

1263.   Financial Control began a systematic analysis of the financial monitoring of sanctions against fraud affecting the Community budget and, in cooperation with the national associations of lawyers for the protection of the Community's financial interests, increased its support for greater awareness of this subject by organizing conferences, round tables and seminars in a number of countries (Spain, Belgium, Italy).

---

[1]   Twenty-fourth General Report, point 1007.
[2]   Point 1257 of this Report.

Action to combat fraud

1264. Two Regulations were adopted in this sector in 1991 — Regulation (EEC) No 595/91 concerning the recovery of sums wrongly paid in connection with the financing of the common agricultural policy and the organization of an information system in this field[1] and Regulation (EEC) No 307/91 which provides financial support to Member States for reinforcement of monitoring and detection of fraud in connection with exports of agricultural products and intervention to stabilize certain markets.[2]

1265. On 20 March the Commission adopted the second report on the work done and progress achieved in the fight against fraud in 1990.[3] The report has two objectives: to keep all parties concerned fully mobilized on the question of financial crime affecting the Community's finances and to promote the action taken.

This report was favourably received by Parliament and discussed in detail with the Member States. The Member States were also informed of the progress made by the Community Committee for the Coordination of Fraud Prevention, which met in April and October.

1266. During its discussion of this report,[4] the Council welcomed the progress achieved, in particular as regards simplification of agricultural legislation, the increased number of cases of fraud reported by the Member States and the increased number of controls of Community expenditure in the agricultural sector. It also set priorities for 1991: continuation of efforts to simplify agricultural legislation, adoption of the European Customs Code, inclusion of any information regarding fraud prevention in the financial statements annexed to legislative proposals, further cooperation between the Commission and Member States to improve the cost-effectiveness of the fight against fraud and adequate funding for missions in non-member countries.

1267. The multiannual work programme drawn up by the Commission ensures that progress can be measured and continues to serve as a reference for the Community's fraud prevention policy. The year's developments will be set out in the third annual report. However, it may already be noted that considerable attention was paid to the legal protection of the Community's financial interests through a number of measures carried out in collaboration with the Member States (relationship between Community law and criminal law, establishment of a common approach to penalties, Community-wide introduction of national associations of specialist lawyers) and confirmed by the resolution of the Ministers for Justice meeting within the Council on 13 November.

---

[1]   OJ L 67, 14.3.1991; Bull. EC 3-1991, point 1.2.140.
[2]   OJ L 37, 9.2.1991; Bull. EC 1/2-1991, point 1.2.195.
[3]   Bull. EC 3-1991, point 1.5.17.
[4]   Bull. EC 7/8-1991, point 1.5.11.

Borrowing and lending operations

1268.   Table 22 shows the loans granted each year from 1988 to 1991.

Borrowing operations during the year totalled ECU 3 189.4 million, of which ECU 130.6 million was to refinance earlier operations.

TABLE 22

Loans granted

(million ECU)

Instrument	1989	1990	1991
New Community Instrument[1]	78.3	23.6	39.2
EEC balance-of-payments loans[1]	—	—	1 000
ECSC[1]	700.1	993.8	1 382.2
Euratom[1]	—	—	—
Financial assistance to countries of Central and Eastern Europe	—	350.0	695.0
EIB (from the Bank's own resources)	12 041.8	13 325.9	15 165.1
of which: loans to Community countries[2]	11 555.9	12 656.9	14 383.6
loans to ACP countries and overseas territories	155.1	117.5	269.5
loans to Mediterranean countries[1]	330.8	336.5	227.0
loans to Eastern Europe[1]	—	215	285.0
Total	12 820.2	14 693.3	18 281.5

[1]   With partial or total guarantee from the general budget.
[2]   With no guarantee from the general budget.

Operations concerning the New Community Instrument

New Community Instrument

1269.   In 1991 the EIB, acting on behalf of the Community, granted one global loan of ECU 39.2 million under the New Community Instrument.[1] The loan was concluded with an intermediary financial institution to promote investment by small and medium-sized firms. Since 1979 loans totalling ECU 6 386.4 million have been made under the NCI.

---

[1]   OJ L 71, 14.3.1987; Twenty-first General Report, point 141.

1270. During the year there were no NCI borrowing operations (as against ECU 76.3 million in 1990 for refinancing).

EEC — Balance of payments

1271. A loan of ECU 2.2 billion was granted to Greece[1] under Regulation (EEC) No 1969/88 providing medium-term financial assistance for Member States' balances of payments.[2] The first tranche of ECU 1 billion was contracted and paid to Greece in March; the other two tranches should be paid in 1992 and 1993 provided that the economic conditions are met.

1272. Following the Council's decision to grant Hungary medium-term financial assistance up to a maximum of ECU 870 million in a number of tranches,[3] the Commission raised ECU 350 million for the first tranche. An interest-rate swap arrangement was concluded so that the loan carried a variable rate of interest. The second tranche of ECU 260 million was contracted and paid to Hungary in February. In order not to undermine the reforms, a further loan of ECU 180 million was granted and the first tranche of ECU 100 million was contracted and paid in August. The Council also decided to grant medium-term financial assistance in two tranches to Czechoslovakia (a maximum of ECU 375 million), Bulgaria (ECU 290 million), Romania (ECU 375 million), and Algeria (ECU 400 million) of which the first tranche of ECU 250 million was paid in December.[4] The Commission paid the first tranches for Czechoslovakia (ECU 185 million) and Bulgaria (ECU 150 million) in August.

The Council also decided to grant financial assistance to Israel and the Occupied Territories.[5] The ECU 160 million agreed will be paid in one tranche and will carry an interest subsidy of ECU 27.5 million.

Financing ECSC activities

1273. Eligibility for ECSC loans of ECU 200 million was extended to Poland and Hungary, mainly to finance projects to promote the use of Community steel and industrial projects which could be undertaken in the form of joint ventures.[6]

---

[1]   OJ L 66, 13.3.1991; Bull. EC 3-1991, point 1.2.1.
[2]   OJ L 178, 8.7.1988; Twenty-second General Report, point 256.
[3]   Point 74 of this Report.
[4]   Points 74 to 77 of this Report.
[5]   Point 897 of this Report.
[6]   Twenty-fourth General Report, point 1015.

1274.   During 1991 the Commission continued to support coal and steel industry investment through ECSC financial loans totalling ECU 438.7 million.

ECSC loans paid out in 1991 totalled ECU 1 382.2 million, compared with ECU 993.8 million in 1990.

Loans for the steel industry rose from ECU 213 million in 1990 to ECU 362.9 million in 1991. Loans for the coal industry totalled ECU 75.8 million, while loans for investments to promote the consumption of Community steel under the second paragraph of Article 54 of the ECSC Treaty amounted to ECU 66.4 million.

1275.   The ECSC continued to look to the capital market for funds, raising a total of ECU 1 445.7 million, including ECU 81.9 million to refinance earlier operations (compared with ECU 1 058.9 million in 1990, including ECU 31.3 million to refinance earlier operations).

Financing Euratom activities

1276.   In view of the continuing unfavourable situation in the industry, there were again no loan operations in 1991 despite the fact that the Council raised the authorized ceiling by ECU 1 billion in 1990. [1]

The grand total of loans since such operations began in 1977 is now ECU 2 876 million (at the exchange rates obtaining when contracts were signed).

European Investment Bank

1277.   Since the activities of the European Investment Bank — an autonomous Community institution — in 1991 are described in its annual report, only the main figures are set out here. [2]

Financing operations by the Bank in 1991 both inside and outside the Community amounted to ECU 15 165 million from its own resources and ECU 174 million from resources supplied by the Community, a total of ECU 15 339 million compared with ECU 13 325.9 million in 1990.

---

[1]   Twenty-fourth General Report, point 48.
[2]   Copies of the report and of other publications relating to the Bank's work and its operations can be obtained from the main office (100 boulevard Konrad Adenauer, L-2950 Luxembourg, tel. 43791) or from its offices in Belgium (rue de la Loi 227, B-1040 Brussels, tel. 230 98 90), Italy (Via Sardegna 38, I-00187 Rome, tel. 47191), the United Kingdom (68 Pall Mall, London SW1Y 5ES, tel. 839 3351), Greece (Amalias 12, GR-10557 Athens, tel. 32 20 773, 32 20 774 or 32 20 775), Spain (Calle J. Ortega y Gasset 29, E-28006 Madrid, tel. 431 1340) and Portugal (144-156 Avenida de Liberdade, 8°, P-1200 Lisbon, tel. 342 89 89).

The Board of Governors' decision to increase the Bank's subscribed capital from ECU 28.8 billion to ECU 57.6 billion[1] became effective on 1 January 1991, enabling the EIB to continue to develop its activities to promote Community policies and at the same time keep its top-class credit rating.

1278.   The EIB's contribution to Community operations in favour of the countries of Central and Eastern Europe, which had already taken shape in 1990 with the first loans to Poland and Hungary, was extended to Czechoslovakia, Bulgaria and Romania.

1279.   Loans granted for projects in the Community totalled ECU 14 384 million from the Bank's own resources and ECU 39 million from NCI resources, a total of ECU 14 423 million compared with ECU 12 680.5 million in 1990 and 11 634.2 million in 1989. This increase, coming as it does at a time of economic difficulty, bears witness to the EIB's commitment to the completion of the single market. The breakdown by country is shown in Table 23.

TABLE 23

EIB loans in the Community in 1991

	From own resources (million ECU)	From NCI resources (million ECU)	Total million ECU	Total %
Belgium	115.6	—	115.6	0.8
Denmark	538.6	—	538.6	3.7
Germany	1 300.1	—	1 300.1	9.0
Greece	366.9	—	366.9	2.5
Spain	2 303.3	39.2	2 342.5	16.2
France	1 924.4	—	1 924.4	13.4
Ireland	237.0	—	237.0	1.7
Italy	4 000.7	—	4 000.7	27.7
Luxembourg	28.6	—	28.6	0.2
Netherlands	175.4	—	175.4	1.2
Portugal	1 002.1	—	1 002.1	7.0
United Kingdom	2 090.5	—	2 090.5	14.5
Miscellaneous (Article 18)	300.4	—	300.4	2.1
Total	14 383.6	39.2	14 422.8	100.0

---

[1]   Twenty-fourth General Report, point 1020.

1280. Loans for regional development projects account for almost 63 % of loans in the Community, most of them in regions covered by activities under the structural Funds.

1281. Loans for transport infrastructures and telecommunications remained stable at ECU 4 500 million. Loans for environmental protection remain high at ECU 1 888 million. Assistance for the energy sector has picked up considerably (ECU 3 102 million).

1282. Individual loans for industry and services totalled ECU 2 082 million. ECU 3 758 million was granted in the form of global loans to intermediaries, including ECU 39 million from NCI resources; more than 9 500. credits totalling around ECU 2 350 million were on-lent to small and medium-sized businesses from global loans.

Operations outside the Community totalled ECU 916 million, as against ECU 713 million in 1990, of which ECU 782 million was from the Bank's own resources. In the ACP countries loans totalled ECU 390 million, of which ECU 270 million was from the Bank's own resources and ECU 120 million from risk capital for private-sector projects. Mediterranean countries received ECU 242 million, mostly from the Bank's own resources. Loans totalling ECU 285 million were granted in Poland, Romania and Hungary for priority projects. Operations in Yugoslavia were suspended.

The Bank raised a total of ECU 13 672 million on the capital markets to provide itself with the funds it requires to grant loans from its own resources. Most of this amount was raised in Community currencies and in ecus in the form of public issues and private placings.

General budget guarantee for borrowing and lending operations

1283. The guarantee by the Community budget can cover both borrowing and lending operations. For borrowing operations the Community provides the budget guarantee to its own lenders when floating an issue under one of its financial instruments — balance-of-payments facility, Euratom loans, New Community Instrument, medium-term financial assistance for Hungary, Czechoslovakia, Bulgaria, Romania, Algeria and Israel. For loans granted, the guarantee is given to the European Investment Bank for the loans it makes from its own resources under the Mediterranean protocols. In May the Council extended to Czechoslovakia, Bulgaria and Romania its guarantee for loans which the Bank was to grant from its own resources to Hungary and Poland.[1] In March

---

[1]   Points 830 and 839 to 841 of this Report.

the Council approved a Regulation introducing a credit guarantee of up to ECU 500 million in respect of exports of agricultural products and foodstuffs from the Community to the Soviet Union.[1] In December the Council decided to grant a medium-term loan of up to ECU 1 250 million to allow the Soviet Union and its republics to import agricultural products, foodstuffs and medical supplies from the Community, Bulgaria, Czechoslovakia, Hungary, Poland, Romania, Lithuania, Latvia, Estonia (and Yugoslavia).[1]

In 1991 the ceiling for authorized borrowing and lending operations guaranteed by the general budget was ECU 36 059 million; at 31 December the guarantee was in operation for ECU 9 092.6 million of Community borrowings and for loans of ECU 2 097.3 million granted out of the EIB's own resources.

In 1991 the budget guarantee was again activated for loans granted by the EIB to Lebanon.[2] When Lebanon failed to make certain repayments, the Community paid the EIB ECU 2.098 million at the beginning of February, ECU 2.155 million at the end of August and ECU 2.051 million at the end of December. These were the eighth, ninth and tenth occasions on which the guarantee was activated in respect of Lebanon. At the end of 1991 Lebanon had still not repaid ECU 3.640 million of the amount guaranteed. The guarantee was also activated in respect of EIB loans to Syria, for which the Community paid the Bank ECU 1.782 million. On 31 December Syria had repaid the total amount guaranteed.

---

[1]   Point 844 of this Report.
[2]   Twenty-second General Report, point 134; Twenty-third General Report, point 120.

Chapter VI

Community law

General matters

General principles of Community law

1284. At the Commission's request the Court of Justice, acting under Article 228 of the Treaty, considered the draft agreement between the Community and the EFTA countries for the establishment of a European Economic Area. On 14 December, it issued Opinion 1/91 declaring that the judicial review arrangements envisaged by the agreement were incompatible with the EEC Treaty. The agreement was to establish a homogeneous European Economic Area based on common rules and fair competition. It was drafted in the same terms as the corresponding provisions of Community law. But the Court held that the context and objectives of the EEA agreement and of the Community legal order were different. The EEA aims solely to establish free trade and competition in economic and trade relations between the contracting parties, with no transfer of sovereign powers. The rules governing free trade and competition within the Community, by contrast, fall within the Community legal order, which has objectives going far beyond those of the agreement. The Community legal order is distinguished from the EEA by its essential characteristics (a Community based on law in which the Member States have limited their own sovereign powers, their citizens being also Community nationals; the primacy of Community law; and the direct effect of a whole series of provisions). The Court concludes that the objective of achieving uniform interpretation and application of the law in the EEA is counteracted by the divergent aims and context of the agreement and of the body of Community law. The planned judicial system constitutes a threat to the autonomy of the Community legal order in the pursuit of its own objectives.

1285. In Case C-63/89 [1] the Court rejected the applicants' claim for compensation for the damage which they had suffered as a result of the fact that export credit insurance operations for the account of or guaranteed by the State were excluded from the scope of the non-life insurance Directive of 22 June 1987. [2] The Court made the point that the drafting of common rules on harmonization, which were based on diverse and complex national rules and had to be approved unanimously or by a qualified majority in the Council, was a 'difficult' exercise which justified the Community institutions having some margin of discretion as regards the appropriate stages for the harmonization process. It also rejected the argument that the Directive was unlawful in that it infringed the principle of equality of treatment. It found that the institutions could legitimately exclude export credit insurance operations from the harmonization process, given the specific guarantees required for such operations. The applicants had claimed that, in its original version adopted in 1973, the Directive had provided for coordination of the insurance operations in question within four years and that this had not been done. The Court held that the four-year period was not mandatory or legally binding on the Community authorities and that failure to comply with it did not therefore constitute a wrongful omission of such a kind as to establish the Community's liability. Similar provisions were frequently included in Council legislation and should be regarded in the same light. Lastly, the Court pointed out that it had no jurisdiction to instruct the Community institutions to adopt additional legislative measures, as requested by the applicants.

1286. In *Francovich*, [3] the Court held that individuals are entitled to demand that a Member State make good damage which they sustain as a result of the Member State's failure to transpose a Directive within the prescribed period. Directive 80/987 [4] provides for specific forms of protection of workers in the event of the employer's insolvency, notably the establishment of a guarantee institution to cover their remuneration within certain limits. The Court held that the Directive had no direct effect. But then, recalling the very basis of the Community legal order and the fact that the courts were obliged to ensure that Community law was fully effective and that rights conferred on individuals were respected, it went on to hold that Community rules would not be fully effective and the protection of rights conferred by them would be weakened if individuals had no possibility of seeking reparation where their rights were invaded by an infringement of Community law by a Member State. Invoking Article 5 of the EEC Treaty, the Court came to the general conclusion that Community law imposes a principle to the effect that Member States must make good damage sustained by individuals as a result of their infringements of Community law. In the final part of the judgment, the Court establishes the circumstances in which a Member State will thus be liable where it has failed to

---

[1]   *Les Assurances du crédit and Compagnie belge d'assurance crédit* v *Council and Commission.*
[2]   OJ L 172, 4.7.1987.
[3]   Joined Cases C-6/90 and C-9/90 *Francovich and Bonifaci* v *Italy.*
[4]   OJ L 283, 20.10.1980.

transpose a directive. The results to be achieved by the directive must include the conferment of rights on individuals, these rights must be identifiable on the basis of the directive and there must be a causal link between the infringement of the Member State's obligation and the damage sustained. The procedure for obtaining redress will be that laid down by national law.

1287.   In Case 338/89 the Court supplemented its existing case-law on the Community definition of *force majeure* by ruling that a strike of which the employer had received advance notice did not constitute a case of *force majeure*.[1]

1288.   The Court gave judgment in an important case concerning the interpretation of Articles 2, 3, 34 and 85 of the EEC Treaty.[2] It held that the case-law of the French Court of Cassation on provisions of the Civil Code relating to the protection of buyers, which applied without distinction to all commercial relations governed by French law, did not tend to diminish the effectiveness of the Community rules in question — those designed to ensure fair competition in the common market and equal treatment for the internal and external trade of Member States. The interest of this judgment resides essentially in the Court's affirmation that the objectives set out in Article 2 of the Treaty cannot have the effect of creating obligations for the Member States or rights for individuals and cannot therefore be relied on by an individual before a national court.

1289.   The Court's judgment in *Kziber*[3] is mainly concerned with the interpretation of Article 41(1) of the EEC-Morocco Cooperation Agreement, which provides for equal treatment in matters of social security between Moroccan workers and their families, on the one hand, and nationals of the Member States, on the other. The Court held that the Article was directly applicable despite the fact that the Cooperation Council had not adopted provisions to ensure the implementation of the principles set out in Article 41, as provided for in Article 42(1). According to the Court, the fact that Article 42(1) provided for the implementation by the Cooperation Council of the principles set out in Article 41 could not be interpreted as calling in question the direct applicability of a provision which was not subject, in its implementation or effects, to the adoption of any subsequent measure. The role which Article 42(1) assigned to the Cooperation Council was to facilitate observance of the prohibition on discrimination, but this could not be considered to deprive that prohibition of its unconditional nature. The Court further held that the concept of social security in the Agreement was to be interpreted by analogy with the same concept in Regulation No 1408/71;[4] consequently, the interpretation given by the Court with regard to unemployment benefits would also apply, for example, to disability allowances or guaranteed incomes for elderly persons

---

[1]   *Organisationen Danske Slagterier* v *Danish Ministry of Agriculture.*
[2]   Case 339/89 *Alsthom Atlantique* v *Sulzer.*
[3]   Case C-18/90 *Office national de l'emploi* v *Kziber* [1991] ECR I-199.
[4]   OJ L 149, 5.7.1971.

since, according to earlier rulings of the Court, these were also social security benefits within the meaning of Regulation No 1408/71. On the other hand, the judgment has no bearing on conditions governing access to employment outside the scope of the Agreement.

Judicial review and fulfilment by the Member States of their obligations

1290.   The Court declared that Commission decisions finding ineligible the expenditure declared in certain applications for assistance from the European Social Fund were void for infringement of essential procedural requirements.[1] The Commission had failed to give the Member State concerned the opportunity to comment in advance on the contested decisions as required by Article 6(1) of Regulation No 2950/83.[2] The Court held that the Commission's practice (which gave a Member State the opportunity to object once a decision had been notified to it) was incompatible with the Regulation and constituted an infringement of formal requirements, non-compliance with which meant that the contested decisions had to be declared void, bearing in mind the Member State's central role and the extent of its responsibilities regarding the presentation and supervision of training courses.

1291.   Three judgments given in October in virtually identical terms gave valuable clarification of the Member States' obligations regarding the transposal of directives.[3] First, circulars are not a proper way of implementing directives where they are not legally binding on government departments or directly applicable to persons whose activities are such as to generate environmental nuisances. Such persons are not given precise information as to their obligations. Likewise, those for whose benefit the directive is issued are not in a position to ascertain the full range of their rights and to plead them, if the case arises, in the national courts. Moreover, the Court does not regard the fact that there are no known practical cases of failure to comply with the directive as removing the obligation to transpose it into the national legal order by means of provisions laying the law down clearly and precisely enough for citizens to be acquainted with their rights and obligations.

1292.   The judgment in Case C-367/89 was the first to consider the compatibility of Cocom with Community law.[4] The Court pointed out that the Community transit scheme under Regulation No 222/77[5] covers all goods, whether or not strategic, moving

---

[1]   Cases C-291/89 *Interhotel* v *Commission* and C-304/89 *Oliveira* v Commission.
[2]   OJ L 289, 22.10.1983.
[3]   Cases C-13/90, C-14/90 and C-64/90 *Commission* v *France*.
[4]   *Criminal proceedings against Richardt*.
[5]   OJ L 38, 9.2.1977.

within the Community: no specific areas were 'reserved' for the Member States, even in security-related areas. But this did not preclude the Member States from checking goods in transit by virtue of Treaty provisions such as Article 36. Imports, exports and transit of goods capable of being used for strategic purposes can affect the public security of a Member State, an interest which it is entitled to protect under Article 36 of the Treaty (special authorization, subject to the principle of proportionality).

1293. In Case C-303/90[1] the Court annulled the code of conduct specifying the information which the Member States are required to notify to the Commission under the Regulation organizing an information system on irregularities affecting the structural Funds. It held that the code of conduct, informally established by the Commission, regulated the type of information to be provided and the frequency and procedures for notification in detail. Accordingly the code went beyond what was provided for in the Regulation and imposed new obligations on the Member States; the Commission had no power to do this.

---

[1]   *France v Commission.*

Section 2

Interpretation and application of the substantive rules of Community law

Free movement of goods and customs union

1294.   In Case C-312/89 the Court, while confirming its earlier judgment in *Torfaen Borough Council*, where it held that rules governing opening times for retail sales reflected political and economic options which were a matter for the Member States, assessed itself whether the measures at issue were in proportion to the legitimate objective in view and found that the restrictive effects which a prohibition on employment in retail shops on Sunday could have on trade did not seem disproportionate to the aim in view. [1] The Court has thereby ensured uniform interpretation of Community law.

Competition

1295.   Having received an application from the French Government for annulment of Commission Directive 88/301/EEC on competition in the markets in telecommunications terminal equipment, [2] the Court held that Article 90 of the EEC Treaty gave the Commission a general power to lay down, in directives, provisions concerning the Member States' obligations under the Article. [3] The power was distinct from the power which the Commission had under Article 169 to require a particular Member State to put a stop to a specific infringement and could not be regarded as equivalent to the Council's powers under Article 100a (adoption of measures to approximate legislation).

The Court appeared to set certain limits on the Commission's powers in that it held that Article 90(3) could not be used to establish a specific infringement by a particular Member State and declared Article 2 of the Directive void in that it did not provide

---

[1]   *Union départementale des syndicats CGT de l'Aisne* v *Sidef Conforama, société Arts et meubles and société Jima.*
[2]   OJ L 131, 27.5.1988.
[3]   Case C-202/88 *France* v *Commission.*

details of the precise rights referred to, as also Article 7, which required the cancellation of long-term leasing and maintenance contracts entered into by undertakings, in that it did not show that national rules had brought about the conduct on the part of undertakings to which the charge related. The Court ruled, however, that exclusive rights for the importation, marketing, connection, bringing into service and maintenance of terminal equipment were such as to restrict trade within the Community, while at the same time confirming the fact that assessment under Article 30 involved taking the point of Article 3(f), which was to promote competition, into account. Following the same line of argument, the Court held that to permit an undertaking which markets terminal equipment to draw up specifications for such equipment, supervise their implementation and approve the equipment would be to give it an obvious advantage over its competitors. In other words, it confirmed the Commission's decision on this point.

1296.   In response to a request from a Munich court for a preliminary ruling on the interpretation of Article 90 the Court held that the Bundesanstalt für Arbeit (Federal Employment Office), which has the exclusive right to put job-seekers in touch with prospective employers and to administer unemployment benefits, was an 'undertaking' for the purposes of Articles 85 and 86 of the Treaty when it engaged in placement activities.[1] A public agency of this kind is therefore subject to the Community rules on competition until such time as it is shown that their application would obstruct the performance of its duties, in accordance with Article 90(2). This was not in fact the case, since the Bundesanstalt was manifestly unable to satisfy the demand existing on the market and allowed private companies to exercise the placement activities of which it had a monopoly. The Court concluded that the creation of a dominant position by the grant of an exclusive right was not in itself incompatible with Article 86 of the Treaty; but the grant of an exclusive right to a particular State agency was contrary to Article 90 in conjunction with Article 86 if it led to a situation where the provision of such services by private-sector companies was rendered illegal to the detriment of those seeking such services since the agency holding the exclusive right was unable to satisfy the market demand, provided it could be shown that the agency's abuse of its position was likely to affect intra-Community trade.

1297.   A request for a preliminary ruling gave the Court the opportunity to rule on the compatibility of a television monopoly as such with Community law, DEP having broadcast programmes in breach of ERT's monopoly.[2] The Court reaffirmed that the Treaty provisions did not prevent the Member States, on non-economic grounds affecting the public interest, from awarding to one or more undertakings the exclusive right to transmit radio and TV broadcasts and that a television monopoly as such was not

---

[1]   Case C-41/90 *Höfner and Elser* v *Macrotron.*
[2]   Case C-260/89 *Elliniki Radiophonia Tileorassi* v *Dimotiki Etairia Pliroforissis and Kouvelas.*

contrary to the principle of free movement of goods. Where the free movement of goods and services was concerned, however, the arrangements would have to be changed if the exclusive rights thus conferred led to any discrimination between national and imported products. Where a company was granted a monopoly for both the transmission and the retransmission of broadcasts, the company was in a position to favour its own programmes by limiting the retransmission of programmes from other Member States, thus jeopardizing the freedom to provide services. Discriminatory rules could be justified only on grounds of public policy, public security or public health, as provided in Article 56, which was to be strictly construed. Any disturbances arising from the restricted number of channels available could not serve as a justification, where the company not holding the monopoly used only a restricted number of the channels available.

1298.   In a case concerning the situation of Italian docks companies enjoying a legal monopoly for the loading, unloading and storage of goods in ports, whose workers, also being members of the companies, are required to be of Italian nationality, the Court spelled out and applied principles already laid down in judgments in monopoly cases given in the course of the year (see foregoing paragraphs).[1] The Court declared that, although the mere fact of creating a dominant position through the grant of exclusive rights was not as such incompatible with Article 86 of the EEC Treaty, a Member State would infringe the prohibition in Article 90 if, merely by exercising its exclusive rights, the firm concerned abused its dominance or where those rights were of such a nature as to create a situation in which the firm could so act. This was precisely the situation of the Italian docks companies, which were imposing unfair prices and terms.

1299.   In *AKZO Chemie* v *Commission* the Court for the first time ruled on the compatibility of predatory pricing practices of a dominant firm with Article 86.[2] It upheld the Commission's conclusion that AKZO had abused its dominant position by using massive, prolonged price cuts as a means of driving a competing company, ECS, off the market. Prices less than the average variable cost and prices less than the average total cost must be regarded as an abuse where they are set as part of a plan to eliminate a competitor. The Court accepted a 50% market share as adequate evidence of dominance and agreed that dominance could be defined by reference to a market other than that on which the abuse occurred. The Commission decision was accordingly set aside on minor technicalities alone. The fine imposed by the Commission was reduced, partly because, as the Court saw it, the offending firm's failure to comply with the decision laying down interim measures could not constitute an aggravating circumstance.

1300.   A long line of cases, beginning with *Alfa-Romeo* and *Lanerossi*, has established that a State holding in a firm's capital does not of itself constitute a form of State aid

---

[1]   Case C-179/90 *Merci convenzionali porto di Genova* v *Siderurgica Gabrielli*.
[2]   Case C-62/86.

within the meaning of Article 92 of the Treaty if, in comparable circumstances, a private-sector investor large enough to be compared with the State agency would have injected similar amounts of capital. The Court considers a favourable long-term profitability outlook to be sufficient evidence here. In Case C-261/89 the Court confirmed this approach but added that the fact that a financial injection is to cover productive investment does not of itself disqualify the injection as State aid if, given the general state of the firm, it would seem unlikely that a private-sector firm would have made the same investment. [1]

1301.   Article 93(3) of the EEC Treaty requires Member States to notify the Commission of their plans to grant aid. By the last sentence of that paragraph, the Member State may not put its proposed measures into effect until the Commission has given a final decision on their compatibility with the Treaty. Past cases establish that the Commission may not declare unnotified aid schemes unlawful simply because they have not been notified; it must in all cases consider the question of compatibility. In Case C-354/90 [2] the Court held that individuals may apply to the national courts for a declaration that an aid scheme is unlawful where it has not been notified or violates the procedural rules of Article 93, even if the Commission subsequently declares that the planned aid is compatible with the Treaty.

Free movement of persons and social provisions

1302.   In Case C-292/89 the Court held that a statement entered in the Council minutes at the time a regulation was adopted had no legal force unless the content of the statement was reflected in the text of the regulation itself. [3] In deciding the case at issue, therefore, the Court did not rely on a statement in the minutes which set at three months the maximum period during which Community nationals could stay in a Member State while seeking employment. But it put a broad construction on Article 48(3), taking the view that, since no maximum period had been prescribed by Community law, the period of six months prescribed by national law did not appear to be insufficient; even after the expiry of the six-month period, persons seeking employment could not be required to leave the host country if they provided evidence that they had a real chance of finding work, notwithstanding that their entitlement to unemployment benefits in the Member State of origin would expire after three months under Community law.

1303.   In Case C-376/89 the Court clarified its earlier rulings to the effect that the right of nationals of one Member State to enter another and reside there for purposes

---

[1]   *Italy* v *Commission.*
[2]   *Fédération nationale du commerce extérieur des produits alimentaires* v *France.*
[3]   *The Queen* v *Immigration Appeal Tribunal, ex parte Antonissen.*

provided for by the EEC Treaty derives directly from the Treaty or, as the case may be, the legislation to give effect to it.[1] The Court held that Member States were obliged to recognize the right of residence in their territory of workers referred to in Directive 68/360/EEC[2] if they could produce either an identity card or a valid passport, irrespective of the type of document on the basis of which they had entered the Member State concerned and irrespective of the fact that the identity card had been issued before the issuing Member State's accession to the Communities.

1304.   In line with its earlier rulings on freedom of movement for persons, the Court held that nationals of one Member State were not required to answer questions put by border officials regarding the purpose and duration of their journey and the financial means at their disposal for it before they were permitted to enter another Member State.[3]

1305.   In Case C-179/90[4] the Court further held that the prohibition in Article 90 of the EEC Treaty has the effect that a Member State may not reserve jobs in a firm that has been given exclusive rights for its nationals, since this would be contrary to the general prohibition on nationality discrimination against workers under Article 48. In the present case the Court observed that the concept of 'worker' for the purposes of Article 48 was not affected by the fact that the worker, although in a subordinate status within the firm concerned, also had a partnership relation with other workers.

1306.   The Court's judgment in Case C-227/89[5] implies that Article 6 of Regulation No 1408/71[6] is incompatible with the objectives of Article 51 of the EEC Treaty and therefore invalid in cases where it has the effect of reducing workers' rights as compared with those held under conventions in force between two or more Member States which are embodied in their national law. The importance of this judgment is obvious, in view of the negotiations for agreements with EFTA countries. The judgment amounts to a reversal of a ruling of 1973,[7] whereby Regulation No 1408/71 had to take the place of existing conventions even if this proved less advantageous to the workers concerned.

1307.   The Association de soutien aux travailleurs immigrés, Luxembourg, was ordered to pay contributions to the Chambre des employés privés under Luxembourg law on behalf of employed persons who, being nationals of other Member States, were not entitled to take part in elections to it. In response to a question from the Luxembourg

---

[1]   *Giagounidis* v *City of Reutlingen.*
[2]   OJ L 257, 19.10.1968.
[3]   Case C-68/91 *Commission* v *Netherlands.*
[4]   See point 1298 of this Report.
[5]   *Rönfeldt* v *Bundesversicherungsanstalt für Angestellte.*
[6]   OJ L 149, 5.7.1971.
[7]   Case 32/72 *Walder* v *Sociale Verzekeringsbank* [1973] ECR 599.

Court of Cassation, the Court of Justice held that this was contrary to Community law. [1] It added that the exercise of the right of association goes beyond the framework of strictly trade union organizations and extends to participation in bodies which defend the interests of affiliated workers even if they also exercise a consultative function in the law-making process.

Freedom of establishment and freedom to provide services

1308.   In Case C-340/89[2] the Court added to the body of case-law on freedom of establishment.[3] It defined the scope and content of the obligation which the host Member State has to assess the professional qualifications of nationals of another Member State who wish to carry on their profession in its territory. The Court noted that national conditions governing qualifications, even if applied without discrimination based on nationality, could have the effect of impeding the exercise by nationals of other Member States of the right of establishment guaranteed to them by Article 52 of the Treaty. This could be the case if the national rules in question disregarded knowledge and qualifications which had already been acquired by the person concerned in another Member State. It followed that, where qualifications were not mutually recognized at Community level, Member States were under an obligation to establish a procedure for the examination of qualifications acquired in another Member State, although they were authorized to take into consideration any objective differences in the legal framework of the profession concerned and in the field of activities covered. If comparative examination revealed only partial equivalence, the person concerned could be required to prove that he had acquired the knowledge and qualifications lacking. Stressing the concept of equivalence of knowledge and qualifications, and upholding its earlier rulings to the effect that compliance with national rules was a legitimate requirement, the Court thus narrowed the scope for concealed discrimination in the application of Article 52.

1309.   In *Factortame* the Court held that the nationality and domicile requirements of British legislation governing the registration of fishing vessels were contrary to the principle of freedom of establishment.[4] While it was for the Member States to lay down those requirements in accordance with international law, they had to do so in a manner consistent with Community law. The principle of freedom of establishment guaranteed by Article 52 of the EEC Treaty was infringed by, notably, the requirement that legal and beneficial owners, charterers and operators of a vessel be UK nationals or com-

---

[1]   Case C-213/90 *ASTI* v *Chambre des employés privés.*
[2]   *Vlassopoulou* v *Ministerium für Justiz, Bundes- und Europaangelegenheiten Baden-Württemberg.*
[3]   See Case 222/86 *Unectef* v *Heylens* [1987] ECR 4097.
[4]   Case C-221/89 *The Queen* v *Secretary of State for Transport, ex parte Factortame.*

panies registered in the UK, and that, in the latter case, at least 75% of the company's shares be owned by UK nationals or by companies fulfilling the same requirements, and that 75% of the company's directors be UK nationals, and that legal owners, beneficial owners, charterers, managers, operators, shareholders and directors be resident and domiciled in the UK. But there was no infringement in the requirement that a vessel be operated and its use controlled or directed from UK territory as a condition of registration. As a result of this judgment it will be possible for vessels with capital and crews from other Member States to be registered in the UK and fly its flag, provided there is a link with British territory.

1310. In three similar judgments the Court held that, since the optimum use of historical treasures and the optimum dissemination of knowledge concerning a country's artistic and cultural heritage were in the public interest, this could constitute an imperative reason justifying a restriction on freedom to provide services.[1] In this particular case, however, the Court declared that the imperative reason did not justify the requirement that employed or self-employed guides accompanying groups of tourists over a fixed itinerary must hold a licence issued only to those who have obtained a specific qualification.

1311. In two broadly identical judgments, one giving a preliminary ruling and one in infringement proceedings against the Netherlands, the Court held that the conditions imposed by Dutch law on the retransmission of television programmes containing advertisements (duration, scheduling) placed a dual restriction on freedom to provide services.[2] For one thing, they prevented the managers of cable-distribution operators established in other Member States from retransmitting radio or TV programmes not meeting the conditions. For another, they restricted the possibility for broadcasting stations in other Member States to schedule advertisements for the public in the Member State of reception ordered by advertisers there. The Court did not accept the Dutch Government's argument based on the need to preserve pluralism in broadcasting. While conceding that cultural policy might afford an imperative reason of public interest justifying a restriction on the freedom to provide services, the Court none the less held that it was by no means essential for Dutch law to require broadcasters in other Member States to conform to the Dutch model when transmitting advertising material addressed to the Dutch public. To preserve pluralism as it wished, the Dutch Government could be content with establishing appropriate rules governing its own broadcasting organizations. This implicitly but necessarily meant that protecting the revenues of

---

[1]   Cases C-154/89 *Commission* v *France*, C-180/89 *Commission* v *Italy* and C-198/89 *Commission* v *Greece*.
[2]   Cases C-288/89 *Stichting Collectieve Antennevoorziening Gouda* v *Commissariaat voor de Media* and C-353/89 *Commission* v *Netherlands*.

STER (a body which finances TV production from advertising charges) was not the only way in which the cultural policy objective could be attained. The Court also declared that the Netherlands had infringed Community law by requiring Dutch TV stations to use the services of a Dutch company for their production activities.

1312. Abortion is illegal in Ireland. The question consequently arose whether it was permissible under Community law for Ireland to ban student associations from distributing information about clinics in another Member State where abortions are performed lawfully. After acknowledging that the medical termination of pregnancy, performed in accordance with the law of the Member State in which it takes place, is a service for the purposes of Article 60 of the EEC Treaty, the Court held that the distribution of the information in question was not a trade restriction within the meaning of Article 59 of the Treaty since the information was not distributed on behalf of a firm in another Member State.[1] It belonged to the general freedom of information and expression, independent of the business activity of the clinics concerned. The Court declined to verify the conformity of the rules with the fundamental rights conferred by, for instance, the European Convention on Human Rights so long as the rules were not a matter of direct Community concern. There was extensive comment on this ruling in Ireland, and it was presumably behind Ireland's proposal for a Protocol relating to the right to life, made at the Intergovernmental Conference.

Equal treatment for men and women

1313. In Case C-377/89[2] the Court clarified the consequences of its 1987 judgment[3] in which it had ruled that where no measures implementing Directive 79/7/EEC prohibiting all forms of discrimination based on sex in matters of social security[4] had been adopted, women were entitled to the same treatment as men in the same circumstances. The Court now held that the Directive must be fully effective from the date on which the Member States were required to comply with it, even if in some circumstances that would result in double payment of increases in social security benefits and even if it thereby infringed the prohibition on unjust enrichment laid down by national law.

---

[1]   Case C-159/90 *Society for the Protection of Unborn Children Ireland* v *Grogan*.
[2]   *Cotter and McDermott* v *Minister for Social Welfare*.
[3]   Case 286/85 [1987] ECR 1463.
[4]   OJ L 6, 10.1.1979.

Company law

1314. The importance of the judgment given in Joined Cases C-19/90 and C-20/90[1] lies in the fact that the Court ruled for the first time on the direct effect of the second company law directive (77/91/EEC[2]). It held that, in the absence of a derogation under Community law, the Directive applied as long as matters had not been taken out of the hands of the shareholders or usual management bodies of the company; this would certainly be the case with straightforward restructuring operations involving public authorities or private-sector companies where the members' right to company capital or decision-making powers within the company was at stake. The Court further declared as a matter of principle that a general derogation for exceptional situations which were not covered by the specific terms of the Treaty or the second Directive was liable to detract from the binding nature and uniform application of Community law.

Taxation

1315. In February the Court gave judgment clarifying its two *Gaston Schul* judgments by pointing out that, notwithstanding the direct effect of Article 95, the Member States were obliged by that Article to make clear to their citizens and administrations, by means of circulars, the ways in which deduction of VAT could be claimed if VAT had already been paid in another Member State.[3]

Common commercial policy

1316. In Case C-69/89 the Court for the first time had to consider whether the Community's basic anti-dumping Regulation was compatible with the GATT Anti-dumping Code.[4] It recalled an earlier judgment[5] to the effect that the provisions of the General Agreement were binding on the Community and that this was also true of the Anti-dumping Code, and found that the Community's new Regulation was compatible with the Code. The wide powers of discretion available to the Community authorities in applying the anti-dumping rules to complex factual situations were not restricted by the general principles of legal certainty and legitimate expectations.

---

[1]   *M. Karella and N. Karellas* v *Minister for Industry, Energy and Technology (intervener: Organismos Anasinkrotiseos Epikhiriseon).*
[2]   OJ L 26, 30.1.1977.
[3]   Cases C-120/88 *Commission* v *Italy,* C-119/89 *Commission* v *Spain* and C-159/89 *Commission* v *Greece.*
[4]   *Nakajima All Precision Co.* v *Council.*
[5]   Joined Cases 21 to 24/72 *International Fruit Company* v *Produktschap voor Groenten en Fruit* [1972] ECR 1219.

Institutional and budgetary questions

1317.   In Case C-300/89 the Court, ruling in favour of the Commission and Parliament, held that the Council should have based its titanium dioxide waste Directive on Article 100a and not on Article 130s.[1] The Directive was therefore void. The Court found, in the first place, that this Directive, which establishes harmonized levels for the treatment of various types of waste from the titanium dioxide industry, was concerned, by virtue of its aim and content, with both the protection of the environment and the elimination of disparities affecting the conditions of competition. Its reasoning was based on the following considerations: the Court confirmed that the market envisaged in Article 8a presupposed fair conditions of competition. It followed that, to implement the fundamental freedoms referred to in Article 8a, Article 100a empowered the Community to adopt harmonization measures, not only to remove barriers to trade but also where there was a risk that disparities in national legislation would create or maintain distortions of competition. Although the Commission had held this view from the outset, this was the first time that it had been confirmed by the Court. The Court also stressed that Parliament's involvement in the legislative process was the reflection at Community level of a fundamental democratic principle whereby the people participate in the exercise of power through a representative assembly. It was an essential part of the cooperation procedure that the Council should act by a qualified majority when accepting Parliamentary amendments which the Commission had incorporated into its re-examined proposal but should, on the other hand, act unanimously if it was amending a re-examined proposal or if Parliament had rejected the common position. The Court consequently ruled out recourse to a dual legal basis where the one Article referred to the cooperation procedure and the other required unanimity, since this would call in question the very purpose of the cooperation procedure and render it devoid of any substance. Lastly, the Court referred to the wording of Article 130r(2) itself, which states that 'environmental protection requirements shall be a component of the Community's other policies'. It followed that a measure could not be covered by Article 130s simply because it also pursued environmental objectives. On the other hand, Article 100a(3), which required the Commission to base its proposals on a high level of protection, indicated that such objectives could be effectively pursued by means of harmonization measures introduced under Article 100a, on which the Directive at issue should therefore have been based.

1318.   The judgment in Case C-70/88 is important in terms both of admissibility and of substance.[2] The Court had already declared that Parliament had the standing to apply for annulment of a Council or Commission instrument provided the action sought only

---

[1]   *Commission* v *Council.*
[2]   *Parliament* v *Council.*

to safeguard Parliament's prerogatives and was founded only on submissions alleging their infringement.[1] It therefore dismissed without consideration arguments based on the allegedly incorrect form of the act and on the failure to delegate implementing powers to the Commission: Parliament had adduced no evidence of infringement of its prerogatives. On the substance, Parliament argued that Regulation (Euratom) No 3954/87[2] was incorrectly based on Article 31 of the Euratom Treaty, which provided only for consultation of Parliament, whereas the proper base would have been Article 100a of the EEC Treaty, which involves the cooperation procedure.

The Court confirmed its constant doctrine that the legal basis for an act must be selected on objective criteria capable of being reviewed, including the act's purpose and content. Having found that the Regulation in issue had the purpose of protecting the population against the hazards of foodstuffs and feedingstuffs that had been contaminated by radiation, the Court concluded that Article 31 Euratom was the right legal base, the harmonization of conditions for the free movement of goods within the Community being only of secondary importance in this case.

1319. In Joined Cases C-51/89, C-90/89 and C-94/89[3] the Court dismissed applications from the United Kingdom, France and Germany for annulment of Decision 89/27/EEC concerning the Comett II programme[4] on the ground that it was based solely on Article 128 of the EEC Treaty. The Court, noting that neither the operational nature of a programme nor its budgetary implications prevented the use of Article 128 as a legal basis,[5] ruled that Comett did not extend beyond the field of vocational training; the programme in question, which provided for intra-Community cooperation between universities and industry regarding basic training and ongoing technological training, merely ensured that the training was consistent with and complementary to the forms of research receiving assistance from other Community policies. The Court distinguished between Comett II and the Erasmus programme, which specifically provided for cooperation between universities on scientific research programmes. Lastly, the Court took the view that, although Article 128 was directed at a common vocational training policy, it made no distinction between initial training and continuing training.

1320. In Joined Cases C-213/88 and C-39/89[6] the Court dismissed the application brought by Luxembourg for annulment of various decisions and resolutions of Parliament concerning its places of work and procedures. The Court held that, although the Member States had not yet fully discharged their duty to determine the definitive headquarters of the institutions, Parliament was required to abide by governmental

---

[1] See interim order of 22 May 1990 in Case C-70/88 *Parliament* v *Council* [1990] ECR I-2041.
[2] OJ L 371, 30.12.1987.
[3] *United Kingdom* v *Council.*
[4] OJ L 13, 17.1.1989.
[5] Case 242/87 *Commission* v *Council* [1989] ECR 1425.
[6] *Luxembourg* v *Parliament.*

decisions establishing provisional places of work. But, having considered each of the objectives pursued by Parliament in increasing its facilities in Brussels (press service, staff attached to members, staff responsible for serving committees and delegations), the Court concluded that these staff transfers did not go beyond the room for manoeuvre available to Parliament in internal management matters and were not on such a scale as to violate the decisions taken by the Member States.

Section 3

Computerization of Community law

1321.   At the end of the year the interinstitutional computerized documentation system for Community law (Celex) contained approximately 124 000 documents. Work on the Greek, Spanish and Portuguese bases continued.

1322.   There were approximately 4 600 users of the system, including 1 600 external subscribers and 20 commercial hosts. Demand remained high. Most subscribers are private or public bodies in Member States, though a number of users are from outside the Community.

1323.   Celex's resources and operational structures have been found in need of boosting in line with its expanded objectives and the growth in demand. Since it is an interinstitutional base, talks began this year on attaching it to the Publications Office, which is already accustomed to handling material for all the institutions. The resultant synergies should be a useful stimulus to the modernization process.

1324.   The Council also supported the modernization process by a resolution passed on 13 November, stressing the vital need for easily accessible computerized documentation facilities in all Community languages. It also asked the Commission to speed up its work on completion of the Celex system and on structural changes to enhance its efficiency. [1]

---

[1]   OJ C 308, 28.11.1991; Bull EC 11-1991, point 1.2.204.

The year in brief[1]

1991

Dublin, European City of Culture

January

16 January

Commission adopts communication on relief of ACP debt.   Point 963 of
                                                                          this Report

23 January

Mr Delors, President of the Commission, presents Parliament   Bull. EC 1/2-1991,
with Commission's programme for 1991.   point 1.7.10;
                                                               Supplement 1/91 —
                                                               Bull. EC

New Council President, Mr Poos, presents Parliament with pro- Bull. EC 1/2-1991,
gramme for Luxembourg's six-month term in Council chair.   point 1.7.1.

31 January

Commission adopts communication on future of common agricul- Point 530 of
tural policy.   this Report

Commission adopts proposal for Regulation establishing a finan- Point 632 of
cial instrument for the environment (LIFE).   this Report

---

[1] This chronological summary does not claim to be exhaustive. For further details, see the passages of this
     Report and the Bulletin cited in the margin.

February

13 February

Commission adopts communication on European Energy Charter.   Point 761 of this Report

Commission adopts proposal for Directive fixing certain rates of excise duty on mineral oils.   Point 199 of this Report

March

4 March

Council lifts embargo on trade with Kuwait.   Point 908 of this Report

6 March

Commission adopts communication on internal trade in Community setting out a programme designed to create conditions for single market in distribution.   Point 303 of this Report

13 March

Commission adopts Community support framework for structural assistance in the five new German *Länder* and eastern Berlin.   Point 408 of this Report

Commission adopts communication on future of ECSC Treaty.   Point 264 of this Report

18 March

Council adopts conclusions in respect of VAT.   Point 194 of this Report

Conference on political dialogue and economic cooperation (San José VII) opens in Managua.   Point 933 of this Report

19 March

Commission adopts communication on human rights, democracy and development cooperation policy.   Point 1137 of this Report

20 March

Commission adopts proposal for Directive on monitoring and controlling large exposures of credit institutions.	Point 160 of this Report

26 March

Commission adopts communication on European electronics and information technology industry.	Point 278 of this Report; Supplement 3/91 — Bull. EC

April

8 April

European Council, meeting informally, discusses problems in Middle East created by Gulf War and decides to provide emergency humanitarian aid for Kurdish and other refugees in the region.	Point 909 of this Report

14 April

Inauguration of European Bank for Reconstruction and Development.	Point 72 of this Report

17 April

Commission adopts communication on biotechnology industry.	Point 276 of this Report; Supplement 3/91 — Bull. EC
Commission adopts proposal for Directive on landfill of waste.	Point 645 of this Report
Commission adopts proposal for special food aid programme for Africa.	Point 1016 of this Report

26 April

Opening of EC-Rio Group Ministerial Conference.	Point 932 of this Report

May

8 May

Commission adopts communication on regional energy planning in Community.

Point 744 of this Report

14 May

Council adopts Directive on legal protection of computer programs.

Point 187 of this Report

15 May

Commission adopts amended proposal for a Directive on tobacco advertising.

Point 225 of this Report

17 May

Commission welcomes decision of Swedish authorities to base their exchange-rate policy on the ecu.

Point 64 of this Report

21 May

Council adopts resolution on third action programme on equal opportunities for women and men.

Point 442 of this Report

22 May

Commission adopts revised Annual Economic Report 1990-91.

Point 51 of this Report

Commission adopts proposal for Directive on comparative advertising.

Point 686 of this Report

31 May

Council adopts Directive on transit of natural gas through grids.

Point 766 of this Report

June

4 June

Council and Health Ministers adopt 'Europe against AIDS' programme.

Point 223 of
this Report

Commission welcomes Finnish Government's proposal to Finnish Parliament to link markka to the ecu.

Point 64 of
this Report

5 June

Commission adopts draft of new aid code for steel.

Point 254 of
this Report

Commission adopts communication on framework for Community/G24 balance of payments assistance to Central and East European countries.

Point 811 of
this Report

10 June

Council adopts Directive on preventing use of the financial system for the purpose of money laundering.

Point 159 of
this Report

16 June

Council adopts Directive on measures to combat air pollution by motor-vehicle emissions.

Point 662 of
this Report

18 June

Council adopts Directive on control of the acquisition and possession of weapons.

Point 208 of
this Report

Council fixes cereal prices for 1991-92 marketing year.

Point 532 of
this Report

19 June

Commission adopts proposal for Directive on posting of workers in the framework of the provision of services.

Point 452 of
this Report

Opening of first meeting of Council of CSCE Foreign Ministers.

Point 1081 of
this Report

24 June

Council reaches agreement on VAT and excise duties.

Points 194 and 201 of
this Report

25 June

Council adopts Directive on safety and health at work of workers
with fixed-duration or temporary employment relationship.

Point 413 of
this Report

26 June

Council adopts Regulation and two Decisions on most remote
regions.

Point 526 and 528 of
this Report

28 and 29 June

Luxembourg European Council confirms need to conduct
proceedings of the two Intergovernmental Conferences in parallel
on basis of draft Treaty prepared by Presidency.

Bull. EC 6-1991,
point I.1 *et seq.*

July

1 July

Sweden applies for membership of European Community.

Point 849 of
this Report

9 July

New Council President, Mr Van Den Broek, presents Parliament
with programme for Netherlands six-month term in Council chair.

Bull. EC 7/8-1991,
point 1.7.1

Commission adopts second communication on development and
future of common agricultural policy.

Point 530 of
this Report;
Supplement 5/91 —
Bull. EC

Commission adopts proposal for Directive on standards for satellite broadcasting of television signals.

Point 231 of
this Report

Commission adopts proposal for recommendation concerning employee participation in profits and enterprise results.

Point 453 of
this Report

15 July

Council adopts Regulation concerning provision of technical assistance to Soviet Union.

Point 820 of this Report

15 to 17 July

17th Western Economic Summit is held in London.

Point 853 of this Report

17 July

Commission adopts three proposals for Regulations relating to third stage in liberalization of air transport.

Point 724 of this Report

Commission adopts proposal for Directive on coordination of certain rules concerning copyright and neighbouring rights applicable to satellite broadcasting and cable retransmission.

Point 186 of this Report

22 July

Council provides financial aid for Israel and Palestinian population of Occupied Territories.

Point 897 of this Report

24 July

Commission adopts proposal for Regulation on access to market for carriage of goods by road in European Community.

Point 699 of this Report

Commission adopts communication on encouraging audiovisual production in context of strategy for high-definition television.

Point 231 of this Report

29 July

Council adopts Directive on development of Community's railways.

Point 696 of this Report

31 July

Commission adopts opinion on Austria's application for accession.

Point 848 of this Report

Community and Japan conclude transitional arrangement for imports of Japanese motor cars into Community.

Point 863 of this Report

August

22 August

Unsuccessful *coup d'état* in Soviet Union.

Point 1095 of
this Report

September

1 September

Fourth Lomé Convention enters into force.

Point 955 of
this Report

7 September

Peace Conference on Yugoslavia opens in The Hague.

Point 1093 of
this Report

18 September

Commission adopts communication on maritime industries.

Point 270 of
this Report

Commission proposes changes to rules governing collective redundancies to take account of accelerated corporate restructuring at transnational level.

Point 454 of
this Report

23 September

Council authorizes Commission to negotiate trade and cooperation agreement with Albania.

Point 825 of
this Report

Council decides to grant medium-term loan to Algeria.

Point 900 of
this Report

25 September

Commission adopts proposal for Directive on public service contracts (excluded sectors).

Point 152 of
this Report

October

1 October

Council adopts Regulation providing emergency food aid for Albania.

Point 826 of this Report

Council adopts negotiating Directives for free trade agreement with Gulf Cooperation Council.

Point 907 of this Report

9 October

Commission adopts two communications on immigration and right of asylum.

Point 205 of this Report

9, 16 and 23 October

Commission adopts proposals for regulations implementing the reform of agricultural policy.

Point 531 of this Report

14 October

Commission adopts communication on Community strategy for limiting carbon dioxide emissions.

Point 622 of this Report

16 October

Commission adopts proposal for Regulation on road haulage cabotage.

Point 698 of this Report

Commission approves 'Europe 2000' report on future of regional development.

Point 497 of this Report

21 October

Council reaches agreement on establishment of European Economic Area, on fishery agreements with EFTA countries and on transit agreements with Austria and Switzerland.

Point 846 of this Report.

23 October

First session of EEC-China Joint Committee since 1987 opens.

Point 923 of this Report

Commission adopts two communications on Community textile and clothing industry.

Point 275 of this Report

29 October

Council adopts SAVE programme for energy efficiency.

Point 781 of
this Report

30 October

Middle East Peace Conference opens.

Point 905 of
this Report

November

6 November

Commission decides to set up a European Humanitarian Aid Office.

Point 1017 of
this Report

7 November

Council reaches agreement on debt relief for ACP countries.

Point 963 of
this Report

Council adopts Regulation on statistics relating to trade in goods.

Point 1232 of
this Report

9 November

JET fusion reactor, under Community fusion and plasma physics programme, is first in the world to generate a substantial quantity of energy.

Point 343 of
this Report

11 November

Council adopts restrictive measures against Yugoslavia.

Point 889 of
this Report

18 November

Council adopts resolution on electronics, information and communications technologies.

Point 366 of
this Report

26 November

Community accedes to FAO, thus becoming first organization for economic integration to enjoy full membership of a UN specialized agency.

Point 994 of
this Report

27 November

Commission proposes creation of a European Drugs Monitoring Centre

Point 1006 of
this Report

December

2 December

Council adopts positive measures for Republics of Bosnia-Hercegovina, Croatia, Macedonia and Slovenia.

Point 890 of
this Report

4 December

Commission adopts report on situation and future of common fisheries policy establishing main guidelines for next decade.

Point 578 of
this Report

9 and 10 December

Maastricht European Council reaches agreement on draft Treaty on European Union.

Point 14 of
this Report

12 December

Council reaches agreement on several key proposals concerning Community eco-label, Community exports and imports of certain dangerous chemicals, conservation of natural and semi-natural habitats and establishment of financial instrument for environment (LIFE).

Points 637, 635, 659
and 632 of this Report

16 December

'Europe Agreements' signed with Poland, Hungary and Czechoslovakia.

Point 823 of
this Report

Council adopts Decision granting ECU 1 250 million loan to Soviet Union and its republics and Regulation granting ECU 95 million of emergency food aid for Moscow and St Petersburg.

Point 844 of
this Report

Council adopts Directive concerning transitional VAT regime and supplementing common VAT system, and reaches agreement on movement and holding of products subject to excise duties.

Points 195 and 201 of
this Report

Council adopts Regulation on inland waterway cabotage.   Point 712 of
                                                                         this Report

17 December

European Energy Charter is signed.   Point 738 of
                                                                         this Report

21 December

Presidents of Soviet republics, except Georgia, sign Agreement at   Point 1097 of
Alma Ata, creating Commonwealth of Independent States (CIS).   this Report

25 December

Mikhail Gorbachev resigns as President of the Soviet Union.   Point 1097 of
                                                                         this Report

Annexes

Annex to Chapter II, Section 2

Directives and proposals on the removal of technical barriers to trade in industrial products

I — Directives adopted by the Council

Reference	Subject	Date adopted	OJ No and page ref.	OJ date
91/60/EEC	Maximum authorized dimensions for road trains (amendment of Directive 85/3/EEC)	4.2.1991	L 37/37	9.2.1991
91/173/EEC	Restrictions on marketing and use of certain dangerous substances and preparations (ninth amendment of Directive 76/769/EEC)	21.3.1991	L 85/34	5.4.1991
91/225/EEC	Roadworthiness tests for motor vehicles and their trailers (amendment of Directive 77/143/EEC)	27.3.1991	L 103/3	23.4.1991
91/226/EEC	Spray-suppression systems of certain categories of motor vehicles and their trailers	27.3.1991	L 103/5	23.4.1991
91/238/EEC	Indications or marks identifying the lot to which a foodstuff belongs (amendment of Directive 89/396/EEC)	22.4.1991	L 107/50	27.4.1991
91/338/EEC	Restrictions on marketing and use of certain dangerous substances and preparations (10th amendment of Directive 76/769/EEC)	18.6.1991	L 186/59	12.7.1991
91/339/EEC	Restrictions on marketing and use of certain dangerous substances and preparations (11th amendment of Directive 76/769/EEC)	18.6.1991	L 186/84	12.7.1991
91/368/EEC	Machinery (amendment of Directive 89/392/EEC)	20.6.1991	L 198/16	22.7.1991

| 91/441/EEC | Measures against air pollution by emissions from motor vehicles (amendment of Directive 70/220/EEC) | 26.6.1991 | L 242/1 | 30.8.1991 |
| 91/542/EEC | Measures against emission of gaseous pollutants from diesel engines for use in vehicles (amendment of Directive 88/77/EEC) | 1.10.1991 | L 295/1 | 25.10.1991 |

II — Directives adopted by the Commission

Reference	Subject	Date adopted	OJ No and page ref.	OJ date
91/325/EEC	Classification, packaging and labelling of dangerous substances (12th adaptation to technical progress of Directive 67/548/EEC)	1.3.1991	L 180/1	8.7.1991
91/155/EEC	Detailed arrangements for system of specific information relating to dangerous preparations (implementing Article 10 of Directive 88/379/EEC)	5.3.1991	L 76/35	22.3.1991
91/326/EEC	Classification, packaging and labelling of dangerous substances (13th adaptation to technical progress of Directive 67/548/EEC)	5.3.1991	L 180/79	8.7.1991
91/184/EEC	Cosmetic products (adaptation to technical progress of Annexes II, III, IV, V, VI and VII to Directive 76/768/EEC)	12.3.1991	L 91/59	12.4.1991
91/269/EEC	Electrical equipment for use in potentially explosive atmospheres in mines susceptible to firedamp (adaptation to technical progress of Directive 82/130/EEC)	30.4.1991	L 134/51	29.5.1991
91/321/EEC	Infant formulae and follow-on formulae	14.5.1991	L 175/35	4.7.1991
91/356/EEC	Principles and guidelines of good manufacturing practice for medicinal products for human use	13.6.1991	L 193/30	17.7.1991
91/422/EEC	Braking devices of certain categories of motor vehicles and their trailers (adaptation to technical progress of Directive 71/320/EEC)	15.7.1991	L 233/21	22.8.1991
91/507/EEC	Analytical, pharmacotoxicological and clinical standards and protocols in respect of the testing of medicinal products (amendment of the Annex to Directive 75/318/EEC)	19.7.1991	L 270/32	26.9.1991

91/410/EEC	Classification, packaging and labelling of dangerous substances (14th adaptation to technical progress of Directive 67/548/EEC)	22.7.1991	L 228/67	17.8.1991
91/412/EEC	Principles and guidelines of good manufacturing practice for veterinary products	23.7.1991	L 228/70	17.8.1991
91/442/EEC	Dangerous preparations, the packaging of which must be fitted with child-resistant fastenings	23.7.1991	L 238/25	27.8.1991
91/632/EEC	Classification, packaging and labelling of dangerous substances (15th adaptation to technical progress of Directive 67/548/EEC)	28.10.1991	L 338/23	10.12.1991
	Restrictions on marketing and use of certain dangerous substances and preparations (asbestos) (adaptation to technical progress of Annex 1 to Directive 76/769/EEC)	3.12.1991		
91/662/EEC	Interior fittings of motor vehicles (adaptation to technical progress of Directive 74/297/EEC)	6.12.1991	L 366/1	31.12.1991
91/663/EEC	Installation of lighting and light-signalling devices on motor vehicles and their trailers (adaptation to technical progress of Directive 76/756/EEC)	10.12.1991	L 366/17	31.12.1991

III — Proposals sent to the Council but not yet adopted

Reference	Subject	Date sent	OJ No and page ref.	OJ date
COM(90) 488 final	Cosmetic products (sixth amendment of Directive 76/768/EEC)	12.2.1991	C 52/6	28.2.1991
COM(91) 7 final	Restrictions on marketing and use of certain dangerous substances and preparations (amendment of Directive 76/769/EEC)	8.2.1991	C 46/8	22.2.1991
COM(91) 16 final	Assistance to the Commission and cooperation by the Member States in the scientific examination of questions relating to food	27.3.1991	C 108/7	23.4.1991
COM(91) 51 final	Permissible sound level and exhaust system of motor vehicles (amendment of Directive 70/157/EEC)	28.6.1991	C 193/3	24.7.1991
COM(91) 126 final	Electromagnetic compatibility (amendment of Directive 89/336/EEC)	7.6.1991	C 162/7	21.6.1991
COM(91) 154 final	Sulphur content of gasoil	22.5.1991	C 174/18	5.7.1991
COM(91) 238 final	External projections forward of the cab's rear panel of motor vehicles of category N	16.7.1991	C 230/32	4.9.1991
COM(91) 239 final	Masses and dimensions of certain categories of motor vehicles and their trailers	17.7.1991	C 230/46	4.9.1991
COM(91) 240 final	Speed limitation devices of certain categories of motor vehicles	24.7.1991	C 229/5	4.9.1991
COM(91) 279 final	Type-approval of motor vehicles and their trailers (amendment of Directive 70/156/EEC)	2.8.1991	C 301/1	21.11.1991
COM(91) 287	Medical devices	30.8.1991	C 237/3	12.9.1991

COM(91) 291	Installation and use of speed limitation devices for certain categories of motor vehicles in the Community	31.7.1991	C 225/11	30.8.1991
COM(91) 297	Indications or marks identifying the lot to which a foodstuff belongs (amendment of Directive 89/396/EEC)	31.7.1991	L 219/11	22.8.1991
COM(91) 441 final	Infant formulae and follow-up formulae intended for export to third countries	20.11.1991		
COM(91) 444 final	Colours for use in foodstuffs	10.12.1991	C 12/7	18.1.1992
COM(91) 502 final	Extraction solvents used in the production of foodstuffs and food ingredients (amendment of Directive 88/344/EEC)	11.12.1991	C 11/5	17.1.1992
COM(91) 516	Equipment and protective systems intended for use in potentially explosive atmospheres	16.12.1991		

Annexes to Chapter VI

Activities of the Court of Justice

TABLE 1

Cases analysed by subject-matter
1991

	ECSC		Euratom	EEC														Privileges and immunities Article 220 Conventions	Appeals in staff cases	Total
	Direct actions	Appeals		Free movement of goods	Customs	Agriculture	Fisheries	Right of establishment and freedom to supply services	Free movement of workers and social security	Transport	Competition Direct actions	Competition Appeals	State aid	Taxation	Commercial policy and dumping	Environment	Other			
Actions brought	1		1	20	16	88	9	10	77	7	19	5	11	24	7	5	26	6	6	340
Cases not resulting in a judgment				13	2	11	1	7	6	2	1	3		1	1	4	2		1	55
Cases decided				19	13	41	7	21	44	8	7	–	6	17	5	16	14	3	6	227

TABLE 2

Cases analysed by type (EEC Treaty)[1]
1991

	Proceedings brought under											Total
	Art. 169	Art. 173				Art. 175	Art. 177	Arts 178 and 215	Art. 181	Art. 220 Conventions	Appeals (competition)	
		By governments	By Community institutions	By individuals	Total							
Actions brought	59	18	4	36	58	5	182	18	2	3	3	330
Cases not resulting in a judgment	33	1	–	6	7	–	11	–	–	–	3	54
Cases decided	62	16	2	19	37	—	116	1	1	3	–	220
In favour of applicant	58	3	1	5	9	–	–	–	1	–	–	67
Dismissed on the merits	4	13	1	5	19	–	–	1	1	–	–	25
Rejected as inadmissible	–	–	–	9	9	–	–	–	–	–	–	9

[1] ECSC cases: 1 (Articles 31 and 40), 1 (Article 33 and Article 173 of the EEC Treaty).
[2] Euratom cases: 1 (Article 148).
[2] Excluding cases brought under Article 179.

Activities of the Court of First Instance

TABLE 1

Cases analysed by subject-matter
1991

	ECSC	EEC (competition)	Staff cases	Total
Actions brought	1	11	80	92
Cases not resulting in a judgment	1	1	13	15
Cases decided	1	15	36	52

Institutions and other bodies

European Parliament
Secretariat
Centre européen, Plateau du Kirchberg
L-2929 Luxembourg
Tel.: 43001

Council of the European Communities
General Secretariat
Rue de la Loi 170
B-1048 Brussels
Tel.: 234 61 11

Commission of the European Communities
Rue de la Loi 200
B-1049 Brussels
Tel.: 235 11 11

Court of Justice
Plateau du Kirchberg
L-2925 Luxembourg
Tel.: 43031

Court of Auditors
12 rue Alcide de Gasperi
L-1615 Luxembourg
Tel.: 43981

Economic and Social Committee
Rue Ravenstein 2
B-1000 Brussels
Tel.: 512 39 20

List of abbreviations

ACE	Action by the Community on the environment
Acnat	Action by the Community relating to nature conservation
ACP	African, Caribbean and Pacific countries party to the Lomé Convention
Asean	Association of South-East Asian Nations
Asset	Assessment of Safety-Significant Event Team
ATA	Admission temporaire — Temporary admission
BAP	Biotechnology action programme
BCC	Business Cooperation Centre
BC-Net	Business Cooperation Network
BCR	Community Bureau of Reference
Bridge	Biotechnology research for innovation, development and growth in Europe
Brite/Euram	Basic research in industrial technologies for Europe/raw materials and advanced materials
Caddia	Cooperation in automation of data and documentation for imports/exports and agriculture
CAP	Common agricultural policy
CCAMLR	Commission for the Conservation of Antarctic Marine Living Resources
CCC	Consumers' Consultative Committee
CCT	Common Customs Tariff
Cecaf	Fishery Committee for the Eastern Central Atlantic
CEN	European Committee for Standardization
Cenelec	European Committee for Electrotechnical Standardization
CERM	Coordinated emergency response measures
Cites	Convention on International Trade in Endangered Species of Wild Fauna and Flora
CN	Combined Nomenclature
Comett	Community programme in education and training for technology
Cordis	Community research and development information service
Corine	Coordination of information on the environment in Europe
COST	European cooperation on scientific and technical research

Craft	European cooperative research action for technology
Crest	Scientific and Technical Research Committee
CSCE	Conference on Security and Cooperation in Europe
CSF	Community support framework
CTS	Conformance testing services
DECT	Digital European cordless telecommunications
Delta	Development of European learning through technological advance
DSRR	Digital short-range radio
EAGGF	European Agricultural Guidance and Guarantee Fund
EBRD	European Bank for Reconstruction and Development
ECB	European Central Bank
ECCD	European Committee to Combat Drugs
ECE	Economic Commission for Europe (UN)
ECIP	EC International Investment Partners
Eclair	European collaborative linkage of agriculture and industry through research
Ecu	European currency unit
EDF	European Development Fund
EDMC	European Drugs Monitoring Centre
EEA	European Economic Area
EEIG	European economic interest grouping
EFTA	European Free Trade Association
Ehlass	European home and leisure accident surveillance system
EIB	European Investment Bank
EIC	Euro-Info-Centres
EMI	European Monetary Institute
EMS	European Monetary System
EMU	Economic and monetary union
Envireg	Community initiative concerning the environment in the regions
Epoch	European programme on climatology and natural hazards
Erasmus	European Community action scheme for the mobility of university students
ERDF	European Regional Development Fund
ESA	European system of integrated economic accounts
ESCB	European System of Central Banks
Esprit	European strategic programme for research and development in information technology
ETSI	European Telecommunications Standards Institute

Euret	European research for transport
Euroform	Community initiative for the development of new qualifications, new skills and new employment opportunities
FADN	EEC farm accountancy data network
FAO	Food and Agriculture Organization of the United Nations
FAST	Forecasting and assessment in the field of science and technology
Flair	Food-linked agro-industrial research
Force	Action programme for the development of continuing vocational training
GATT	General Agreement on Tariffs and Trade (UN)
GCC	Gulf Cooperation Council
GFCM	General Fisheries Council for the Mediterranean
GSP	Generalized system of preferences
HDTV	High-definition television
Helios	Action programme to promote social and economic integration and an independent way of life for disabled people
Horizon	Community initiative on handicapped persons and certain other disadvantaged groups
IACTT	Inter-American Commission for Tropical Tuna
IAEA	International Atomic Energy Agency (UN)
IATA	International Air Transport Association
IBC	Integrated broadband communications
IBRD	International Bank for Reconstruction and Development (World Bank) (UN)
ICES	International Council for the Exploration of the Sea
ICRC	International Committee of the Red Cross
ICRP	International Commission on Radiological Protection
IEA	International Energy Agency (OECD)
IEC	International Electrotechnical Commission
IEFR	International Emergency Food Reserve
ILCA	Instituto Latinoamericano de la Cooperación para la Agricultura
IMF	International Monetary Fund (UN)
IMP	Integrated Mediterranean programme
Impact	Information market policy actions
Insis	Interinstitutional system of integrated services
Interreg	Community initiative concerning border areas
IRCC	International Radio Consultative Committee
ISDN	Integrated services digital network
ISIS	Integrated standards information system

ISO	International Organization for Standardization
ITER	International thermonuclear experimental reactor
ITTO	International Tropical Timber Organization
JET	Joint European Torus
JOPP	Joint venture Phare programme
Joule	Joint opportunities for unconventional or long-term energy supply
JRC	Joint Research Centre
LAIA	Latin American Integration Association
Leader	Links between actions for the development of the rural economy
LIFE	Financial instrument for the environment
Lingua	Action programme to promote foreign language competence in the Community
MAST	Marine science and technology
MCA	Monetary compensatory amount
Media	Measures to encourage the development of the audiovisual industry
Medspa	Strategy and plan of action for the protection of the environment in the Mediterranean
Metap	Mediterranean environmental technical assistance programme
MFA	Multifibre Arrangement (Arrangement regarding International Trade in Textiles)
MGS	Mutual guarantee schemes
Nasco	North Atlantic Salmon Conservation Organization
NCI	New Community Instrument
NET	Next European Torus
NGO	Non-governmental organization
Norspa	Action to protect the environment in the coastal areas and coastal waters of the Irish Sea, North Sea, Baltic Sea and North-East Atlantic Ocean
NOW	Community initiative for the promotion of equal opportunities for women in the field of employment and vocational training
OAS	Organization of American States
OCTs	Overseas countries and territories
OECD	Organization for Economic Cooperation and Development
ONP	Open network provision
OPET	Organization for the promotion of energy technologies
PACE	Community action programme for improving the efficiency of electricity use
Pedip	Programme to modernize Portuguese industry
Petra	Action programme for the vocational training of young people and their preparation for adult and working life

Phare	Poland and Hungary — Aid for economic restructuring
PINC	Community's illustrative nuclear programme
PIP	Priority information programme
Poseican	Programme of options specific to the remote and insular nature of the Canary Islands
Poseidom	Programme of options specific to the remote and insular nature of the overseas departments
Poseima	Programme of options specific to the remote and insular nature of Madeira and the Azores
Prisma	Preparation of industries situated in the regions for the single market
RACE	Research and development in advanced communications technologies for Europe
R&TD	Research and technological development
Rapat	Radiation Protection Advisory Team
Rechar	Programme to assist the conversion of coalmining areas
Regen	Community initiative on energy networks
Regis	Community initiative concerning the most remote regions
Renaval	Programme to assist the conversion of shipbuilding areas
Resider	Programme to assist the conversion of steel areas
Retex	Community initiative for regions heavily dependent on the textiles and clothing sector
SAST	Strategic analysis in the field of science and technology
SAVE	Specific actions for vigorous energy efficiency
Scent	System for a customs enforcement network
Science	Plan to stimulate the international cooperation and interchange necessary for European researchers
Sedoc	European system for the international clearing of vacancies and applications for employment
SELA	Latin American Economic System
SPA	Special programme of assistance for sub-Saharan Africa
Spear	Support programme for a European assessment of research
SPES	Stimulation plan for economic science
Sprint	Strategic programme for innovation and technology transfer
Stabex	System for the stabilization of ACP and OCT export earnings
STEP	Science and technology for environmental protection
Sysmin	Special financing facility for ACP and OCT mining products
TAC	Total allowable catch
Taric	Integrated Community tariff
Tedis	Trade electronic data interchange system

Teleman	Research and training programme on remote handling in hazardous or disordered nuclear environments
Tempus	Trans-European mobility scheme for university studies
Thermie	Programme for the promotion of energy technology
TIR	International carriage of goods by road
UN	United Nations
Unctad	United Nations Conference on Trade and Development
UNDP	United Nations Development Programme
UNEP	United Nations Environment Programme
Unesco	United Nations Educational, Scientific and Cultural Organization
UNHCR	United Nations High Commissioner for Refugees
UNIDCP	United Nations International Drug Control Programme
Unido	United Nations Industrial Development Organization
UNRWA	United Nations Relief and Works Agency for Palestine Refugees in the Near East
WFC	World Food Council (UN)
WFP	World Food Programme (UN)
WHO	World Health Organization (UN)
WIPO	World Intellectual Property Organization (UN)

Publications cited in this Report

General Report on the Activities of the European Communities
(abbr.: General Report), published annually by the Commission

Works published in conjunction with the General Report:

— *The Agricultural Situation in the Community*
(abbr.: Agricultural Report), published annually

— *Report on Social Developments*
(abbr.: Social Report), published annually

— *Report on Competition Policy*
(abbr.: Competition Report), published annually

Bulletin of the European Communities
(abbr.: Bull. EC), published monthly by the Commission

Supplement to the Bulletin of the European Communities
(abbr.: Supplement ... — Bull. EC), published at irregular intervals by the Commission

10/72   Proposal for fifth Directive on the structure of sociétés anonymes
2/86   Single European Act
3/89   Takeover and other general bids
2/90   Community merger control law
1/91   The Commission's programme for 1991
2/91   Intergovernmental Conferences: Contributions by the Commission
3/91   European industrial policy for the 1990s
5/91   The development and future of the common agricultural policy

Official Journal of the European Communities
Legislation series (abbr.: OJ L)
Information and notices series (abbr.: OJ C)
Supplement on public works and supply contracts (abbr.: OJ S)

Reports of Cases before the Court
(abbr.: ECR), published by the Court of Justice in annual series, parts appearing at irregular intervals throughout the year

**All the above publications are printed and distributed through
the Office for Official Publications of the European Communities,
L-2985 Luxembourg**

Annual Report of the European Investment Bank
    published and distributed by the EIB,
    100, boulevard Konrad Adenauer
    L-2950 Luxembourg

European Communities — Commission

Twenty-fifth General Report on the Activities of the European Communities — 1991

Luxembourg: Office for Official Publications of the European Communities

1992 — xxiv, 464 pp. — 16.2 × 22.9 cm

ISBN 92-826-3777-8

Price (excluding VAT) in Luxembourg: ECU 15

The General Report on the Activities of the European Communities is published annually by the Commission as required by Article 18 of the Treaty of 8 April 1965 establishing a Single Council and a Single Commission of the European Communities.

The Report is presented to the European Parliament and provides a general picture of Community activities over the past year.